BUILDING ON FIRM FOUNDATIONS

EVANGELISM: GENESIS TO THE ASCENSION

Trevor McIlwain

Building on Firm Foundations - Volume 2: Evangelism: Genesis to the Ascension

Copyright © 2018 Trevor McIlwain

ISBN: 978-0-9944270-8-3

All Rights Reserved. Except as may be permitted by the Copyright Act, no part of this publication may be reproduced in any form or by any means without prior permission from the publisher. Requests for permission should be made to info@accesstruth.com

Unless otherwise indicated, all Scripture quotations are taken from the New King James Version®. Copyright © 1982 by Thomas Nelson. Used by permission. All rights reserved.

Scripture quotations marked (NIV) are taken from the Holy Bible, New International Version®, NIV®. Copyright © 1973, 1978, 1984, 2011 by Biblica, Inc.™ Used by permission of Zondervan. All rights reserved worldwide. www.zondervan.com The "NIV" and "New International Version" are trademarks registered in the United States Patent and Trademark Office by Biblica, Inc.™

Published by AccessTruth
PO Box 8087
Baulkham Hills NSW 2153
Australia

Email: info@accesstruth.com
Web: accesstruth.com

Cover and interior design by Lokal Workshop

This book was previously published under New Tribes Mission (ISBN: 1-890040-65-7)

CONTENTS

Overview VII

Lesson 1: The Bible is God's message to all people 1

Lesson 2: The Bible tells us what God is like and that He alone existed before everything and everyone else 11

Lesson 3: God created the spirits. God created the heavens and the earth 21

Lesson 4: God revealed His nature and attributes through His creative acts (Days 1-3) 29

Lesson 5: God revealed His nature and attributes through His creative acts (Days 4-6) 37

Lesson 6: God created Adam 45

Lesson 7: God placed Adam in Eden 57

Lesson 8: God told Adam not to eat fruit from the tree of knowledge of good and evil 65

Lesson 9: God created a wife for Adam 73

Lesson 10: Lucifer rebelled against God 79

Lesson 11: Let's review what we have learned about God, man and Satan 85

Lesson 12: Adam and Eve disobeyed God 93

Lesson 13: Adam and Eve's sin separated them from God 101

Lesson 14: God judged Adam and placed a curse on the earth, and He promised to send the Deliverer 109

Lesson 15: God provided clothing for Adam and Eve, and He put them out of the garden 119

Lesson 16: God rejected Cain and his offering, but He accepted Abel and his offering 125

Lesson 17: The Bible tells about Cain's descendants and Seth's descendants 139

Lesson 18: God said He would punish the world, but He promised to save Noah and all who entered the boat. 145

Lesson 19: God destroyed everyone in the world except Noah and his family who were in the boat 155

Lesson 20: God scattered the rebels at the tower of Babel ____ 163

Lesson 21: God chose Abram and guided him to Canaan ____ 169

Lesson 22: God renewed His promises to Abram ____ 175

Lesson 23: God destroyed Sodom and Gomorrah ____ 181

Lesson 24: God gave Isaac and delivered Isaac from death ___ 187

Lesson 25: God chose Jacob and rejected Esau ____ 195

Lesson 26: God guided and protected Joseph ____ 203

Lesson 27: God promoted Joseph.
God took Jacob's family into Egypt ____ 207

Lesson 28: God preserved the Israelites and protected Moses _ 211

Lesson 29: God chose Moses to lead the Israelites out of slavery _ 217

Lesson 30: The Lord sent plagues on the Egyptians ____ 225

Lesson 31: God killed the firstborn of the Egyptians,
but He saved the firstborn of the Israelites ____ 233

Lesson 32: God delivered the Israelites at the Red Sea ____ 241

Lesson 33: God gave food and water to the Israelites ____ 249

Lesson 34: God made an agreement to bless
the Israelites if they obeyed Him ____ 255

Lesson 35: God gave the Ten Commandments. (Part 1) ____ 263

Lesson 36: God gave the Ten Commandments. (Part 2) ____ 273

Lesson 37: God told the Israelites to build the Tabernacle ____ 281

Lesson 38: The Israelites worshiped a golden calf ____ 291

Lesson 39: The Israelites did not believe that God
would give them the land of Canaan ____ 297

Lesson 40: The Lord gave the Israelites water from the rock.
He healed those who looked at the bronze snake _ 303

Lesson 41: God took the Israelites into Canaan.
God chose their leaders and their king ____ 309

Lesson 42: God chose David to be king. God chose Solomon to
build the temple ____ 317

Lesson 43: God chose Jonah and other men to be
His messengers ____ 323

Lesson 44: God told the prophets to write many things
about the coming Deliverer ____ 331

Lesson 45: God punished Israel and Judah, but He brought
some of His people back from Assyria and Babylon _ 339

Lesson 46: God foretold the births of John and of Jesus ____ 347

Lesson 47: God fulfilled His promise in the birth of John ____ 355

Lesson 48: God's angel explained to Joseph how Jesus would be born _____ 361

Lesson 49: God fulfilled His promises by sending Jesus, the Deliverer. Jesus grew into manhood _____ 367

Lesson 50: God sent John to teach and to baptize. John baptized Jesus _____ 375

Lesson 51: Jesus resisted Satan's temptations _____ 385

Lesson 52: Jesus began His ministry _____ 391

Lesson 53: Jesus taught that people must be born again _____ 399

Lesson 54: Jesus had power to heal sickness and to forgive sins _ 407

Lesson 55: Jesus foretold His death, burial and resurrection __ 413

Lesson 56: The Jewish leaders plotted to kill Jesus because He healed a man on the Sabbath _____ 417

Lesson 57: Jesus told the parable of the sower _____ 423

Lesson 58: Jesus calmed a storm and released a man from the control of demons _____ 429

Lesson 59: Jesus fed five thousand people _____ 437

Lesson 60: The way of the Pharisees is not God's way _____ 445

Lesson 61: Jesus is the Christ, the Son of God _____ 449

Lesson 62: Jesus is the only doorway to eternal life _____ 457

Lesson 63: Jesus raised Lazarus from the dead _____ 463

Lesson 64: Jesus taught that we need to be humble and admit our guilt _____ 469

Lesson 65: It is foolish to trust in riches _____ 475

Lesson 66: Jesus healed blind Bartimaeus and rode into Jerusalem _____ 483

Lesson 67: Jesus and His disciples celebrated the Passover ___ 489

Lesson 68: Jesus was arrested by His enemies _____ 495

Lesson 69: Jesus was crucified, buried, and raised from the dead _ 503

Lesson 70: Jesus appeared to His disciples and returned to Heaven _____ 517

Additional Lessons to Present the Gospel _____ 523

Appendix: Scripture Portions to be Used with Phase 1 Lessons _ 547

OVERVIEW

Proper use of the lessons will depend on a thorough knowledge of *Volume 1, Guidelines for Evangelism and Teaching Believers*. Be sure to read that volume prior to teaching these lessons.

The lessons in this book cover Phase 1 of the chronological teaching program. These lessons are designed for evangelism.

The lessons are to be a resource for the teacher. They were written primarily for missionaries to guide them step by step as they write Bible lessons, but the lessons can be easily adapted for use in other situations.

The lessons have been written as though I were actually addressing a group of tribal people. However, I have not included all the reiteration and expansion of each point which I would normally give when teaching. The teacher is responsible to emphasize, illustrate, and expand each point until he is satisfied that his hearers have clearly grasped it.

The primary goals of each lesson are to tell clearly the Bible story and, while doing so, to emphasize the doctrinal themes important for evangelism. These doctrinal themes are exemplified through the actions of the characters and the historical events in the Bible.

Interspaced throughout the lesson are directives to the teacher, such as outline points, lesson developer's notes, and teacher's notes. The directives to the teacher are not intended to be spoken as part of the lesson. These directives are on a gray background, a visual cue that they are not meant to be spoken or read to the tribal people.

Proper use of the lessons will depend on a thorough knowledge of *Volume 1, Guidelines for Evangelism and Teaching Believers*. Be sure to read that volume prior to teaching these lessons.

LESSON 1: THE BIBLE IS GOD'S MESSAGE TO ALL PEOPLE.

Lesson Outline

(1) Think carefully about how we can know the truth.

(2) We are going to begin telling you God's message.

(3) We believe all that God says in His Book.

(4) God's message is the most important message in the whole world.

(5) God gave His message to chosen men.

(6) The Bible has been translated into many languages.

(7) We will teach you from the Bible a little at a time.

Lesson Outline Developed

Teacher: As you begin evangelism, you will build on the foundations that you laid down in pre-evangelism. (Refer to Part 2 of Volume 1 for more information on pre-evangelism.)

During your pre-evangelism ministry, you did not give your thoughts, or even what the Bible says, when you raised discussion topics which caused them to think about the basis for their beliefs. Now, however, you are going to introduce the Bible which will be the final authority for all the subjects you previously talked about.

Nevertheless, in this lesson you should not try to prove that the Bible is the Word of God. Some teachers have prepared lessons in which they immediately tried to prove that the Bible is the Word of God. In their very first lesson, they presented Old Testament prophecies with the New Testament fulfillment as proof that God is the author of the Bible. But until the students are taught, they would not have a frame of reference to understand these prophecies. For example, they would not have a clear concept for the time span between the Old and New Testaments, nor would they know about the Bible characters mentioned in the prophecies. This type of approach is contrary to the basic teaching principle of moving from the known to the unknown.

It is far better to leave the proof of the divine authorship of the Scriptures right where it is – in the Word of God itself. The great Bible teacher, Charles Spurgeon, when asked to defend the Bible, said, "What! Defend a lion? Let it loose!"

We, too, must let the Word of God "loose" in total dependence upon the Spirit of God and His promise to use His Word. The power of God is inherent in the Word of God. The proof that the Bible is the Word of God is in the Word itself. As we slowly but clearly teach the story of the Old and New Testaments, it will become evident that the Bible is truly God's Word.

Building on Firm Foundations
- Volume 2: Evangelism:
Genesis to The Ascension

1) Think carefully about how we can know the truth.

We want you to think carefully about the questions we are going to ask you. We are not asking for you to answer these first few questions. Just listen and think about them.

- **How can we know the truth about the beginnings of all things?**
    - Where did this world come from? Has it always been here, or was there a time when it began? Did someone make this world?
    - Where did all the people come from? Were they always here, or was there a time when they began to exist? How did they begin to exist? Did someone make them?
    - Where did all the different kind of animals come from? Were they always here, or was there a time when they began to exist? How did they begin to exist? Did someone make them?
    - Did the sky always exist? Was there a time when the sky began to exist? Did someone make the sky?

Teacher: Apply similar questions to the clouds, the rain, the wind, the sun, the moon and the stars. Be sure to raise the same topics which you did during pre-evangelism which caused the people to question the validity of their beliefs. If they ask questions, assure them that they will be answered as you continue to teach them. Do not become involved in trying to answer their questions on individual topics at this stage in the teaching program.

- **How can we know the truth about the Creator?**
    - Who made all the things we see around us?
    - Where is the Creator who made all things?
    - Is the Creator like us? Does He need to eat? Does He need to sleep? Does He need to drink?
    - Is the Creator powerful or weak?
    - Is He good or is He bad?
    - Does He have any enemies? Are they stronger than He is?
    - Does the Creator love us? Does He know when we get sick or when we die?
    - Can a person hide from the Creator?

- **How can we know the truth about death?**
  - Why do people die?
  - Where do people go when they die? Is the place of the dead a good place or is it a bad place?
  - Will those who have already died ever come back to life again?
  - How can we know that what we believe about those who have died is correct?
  - Do you know someone who has died and then come back to explain what happens after death?
- **How can we know the truth about the spirits?**
  - Are there spirits that we cannot see who have power over people and the things that happen to them?
  - Where did the spirits come from?
  - Did the same Creator who made us also make the spirits?
  - Are the spirits stronger than the Creator who made the world and everything else?
- **How can we know the correct answers to any of these questions?**

  All over the world, people give different answers to these questions. How do we know which answers are correct? Is there anyone who can definitely tell us?

② We are going to begin telling you God's message.

We are here to tell you God's answer to these questions and His message to you. We know that God's message is true, and we want you to also know the truth.

- **Previously we did not tell you God's message.**

  We have discussed many things with you about God, people and the spirits. Previously, we did not tell you what we believed about these things because we were not yet ready to begin teaching you God's message. We did not come here to tell you what we think or what other people say. We came to tell you what God says.

- **Only God can tell us the truth.**

  No one can know or understand who God is, where He is or what He is like unless He tells us. As you listen to God's message, you will learn about God, and you will learn what God says about all the subjects we discussed with you previously.

  God's thoughts about all these different topics are written in this book called the Bible.

Building on Firm Foundations
- Volume 2: Evangelism:
Genesis to The Ascension

> **Teacher:** As you teach this lesson, hold or touch the Bible as you refer to it. If you do not have a Bible in the tribal language, take Bibles in other languages, such as your own and one in the national language, to the meeting.
>
> It is good to show more than one copy of the Bible so that the people will realize there is more than just one copy of the Bible in the world. Having different translations will help when you explain that God's words have been translated into different languages.
>
> Even though the people may not be able to read, pass the Bibles to them. Let them open and look at the Bibles. They need to see that the Bible is a real book and is made of paper like other books. You do not want them to be superstitious about the actual book.

- **Many people in this world do not know God's message.**

  Our ancestors did not understand many of the things we talked to you about until they heard God's words which are written in this book.

  Many people all over the world do not know the truth about God. Some of them do not know the truth about God because they have not heard God's message that is written in this book. Others do not know the truth because they refuse to listen to and believe what God says in the Bible.

  You have chosen to listen to God's message. If you listen and believe what God says in the Bible, you will learn the truth about God.

③ We believe all that God says in His Book.

- **We have read God's Book, and we believe all God says.**

  In the Bible, God has taught us the truth about God, people and the spirits.

> **Teacher:** Give a testimony about believing God's message. Your testimony at this stage should be limited to these points:
>
> - How you actually came to know God's message and His thoughts about the topics you have discussed with the people.
> - That you believe God's message.
> - That God taught you that His message is for all people.
> - That you have come to them so that they, too, can hear, understand and believe God's words.
>
> Include the testimonies of other team members, your wife and your children who are believers. You may wish to ask other Christians present, "Do you believe God's words which are written in this book?" Call on them by name, and give them the opportunity to answer. If they wish, they may also give a short testimony, but be sure that you have instructed them prior to the meeting that they need to limit what they say to the points above.
>
> In your testimonies, do not talk about sin, hell, salvation or the Savior. The people would not understand what you are talking about because you have not yet taught them about God, and they probably do not realize that they need to be saved.

LESSON 1: THE BIBLE IS GOD'S MESSAGE TO ALL PEOPLE.

④ God's message is the most important message in the whole world.

- **God's message is the most important message you will ever hear.**

Lesson Developer: Give an illustration about important messages. In choosing the illustration, consider what type of message would be very important to them and who would bring them that important message. For example:

> 💡 *If the chief called all of you together because he had an important message, all of you would want to listen and understand what he had to tell you, wouldn't you?*
>
> *Or if you knew your enemies were preparing their weapons to attack you, your village scouts would check to see what the enemy was doing. When the scouts came running back to the village, you would quickly gather around and listen carefully to their report. The scouts' message would be important because it might save you from being killed by your enemies.*

God's message in His Book is the most important message in the world. God is the only One who can tell us the truth about everything.

You do not understand yet who God is or why His message is so very important, but the more you listen to what we will teach you, the more you will understand that God is greater than all and that His message is the most important message you will ever hear.

- **The Bible is God's message to every person.**

God's message is to every person in every part of the world. God gave His message for adults and children, for men and women. God's message is to each one of you.

Teacher: Make sure they understand that the Bible is God's message to every person - young and old, men and women. Address the different classes of people individually and directly, assuring them that the Bible is God's message to them.

- **It is important that you take the time to hear God's message to you.**

Lesson Developer: To help show the importance of listening to God's message, give an illustration using activities that are important in the people's daily lives. For example:

> 💡 *You women have children to take care of, and you have lots of work to do in your homes and in the gardens. You men have hunting and fishing to do. You young people like to play and swim.*
>
> *If you are somewhere else working, fishing or swimming while we are meeting here, will you be able to hear God's message? No! You must be here to listen carefully if you want to understand God's message.*

Listening to God's message is the most important thing you can do. This is your opportunity to hear what God wants to tell you. If you don't take the time now to understand God's message, some day you will be sorry that you did not listen, and you will regret forever that you did not take the opportunity to hear God's message.

⑤ God gave His message to chosen men.

- **A long time ago, God chose men to write down His exact message.**

    God could have written His own words in a book and then given it to all people in the world to read, but He didn't choose to do it that way. Instead, God chose approximately 40 men to write different parts of the Bible. These men were called God's prophets. God guided the thoughts of these men so they wrote exactly what He wanted them to write. The prophets also spoke God's message to the people.

    ☞ **Teacher:** Show a picture of a Jewish prophet writing on a scroll.

    Lesson Developer: Use an illustration about receiving an important message through a representative. For example:

    > *If the President had something to say to you, what would he do? Would he come to your village to speak to you? No! He would give his message to other men, his representatives, and they would come to tell you what the President had said.*

    In the same way God chose men to be His spokesmen. They spoke and wrote the message of God as His representatives.

- **The men who wrote God's message didn't all live at the same time.**

    Many years passed from the time the first prophet lived until the time the last prophet lived. About 1600 years passed from the time when God began to give His words to people until all of God's words were completely written down.

    Most of the men who wrote down God's message didn't know one another because they lived at different times.

    Teacher: Open a Bible and show the people some of the books which different men wrote. Prior to the teaching session, place markers between the different books so you can find the books quickly as you teach.

LESSON 1: THE BIBLE IS GOD'S MESSAGE TO ALL PEOPLE.

- **God chose the Jews to write His words.**

  All but one of the men whom God chose to write for Him were Jews. The Jews' land is Israel.

  ☞ **Teacher:** Point to the country of Israel on the world map that you used during pre-evangelism. If the people read maps, ask one of them to point to the country of Israel. You may also show some pictures of Israel.

  You are going to learn many things about the Jews and how God chose and used them to bring His message to the world. All of these things are written in the Bible.

  None of the writers of the Bible spoke English, and they did not write God's message in English.

⑥ The Bible has been translated into many languages.

- **The prophets wrote God's message in the languages spoken in the land of Israel.**

  At different times, the Jewish people used different languages. The Bible was written in the languages that the Jewish people understood.

  Later, other men from countries near Israel read the words of the Bible and then translated them into their languages.

- **The words of God have been translated into many different languages of the world.**

  The Bible has been translated into English and also into the main languages of many of the people here in this country.

Lesson Developer: Some missionaries have found it helpful to use a world map while giving a brief historical account of how God's Word has spread around the world. If you choose to do this, be sure to avoid giving unnecessary details.

Begin by telling them that God's Word originated in Israel. Then explain that God's Word went into Europe and was then taken by missionaries to many different countries to be translated into their languages. Finally, explain that God's message has come to them.

Teacher: If you or someone else is or will be translating the Bible into their language, tell them that. You may wish to illustrate the process of translation. On a chalkboard, write Psalm 119:130 in the national language and then in the language of the people you are speaking to. Explain simply and briefly that this is the process of translation.

⑦ We will teach you from the Bible a little at a time.

- It will take a long time for us to teach you God's message. God wants you to know many things, and we want to teach you all of them. That will take a long time. We will teach you God's message, little by little.

Lesson Developer: Give an illustration to show the methodical way you are going to teach and to show that the teaching program will take time. One possible illustration is gardening. For example:

> 💡 *We will teach in a methodical way, just as you follow a methodical way when you plant, weed and harvest your gardens. Teaching the message of the Bible takes a long time just like gardening. Think how long it takes from the time you begin to clear your fields to the time you harvest your crops.*
>
> *Teaching can also be likened to how you build a house. Think about how you build a house. Can you put the roof on before you put the big posts in the ground? No, of course not! The roof would have no support. Instead, you first put the large main posts into the ground and then you add to these, piece by piece, until the house is finished.*

That is the way that we will teach you God's words. We will begin in the beginning, that is, we will begin with the first things that God says in the Bible. If you don't understand these things first, then you will not be able to understand all of the other things God wants to teach you.

- **It is important that you come to hear God's message each time we meet.**

If you do, you will learn the things that God wants you to know. It will be easier for you to understand if you come each time we study the Bible.

Think about this: Do you eat food every day? Why do you do that? Yes! You eat food every day because you get hungry.

Your babies need food every day so they will be strong and healthy. In the same way that eating food every day makes babies strong, listening to the Bible will help you to grow strong in your understanding about God and what He wants you to know. As you listen frequently to God's words, you will soon learn many wonderful things that will be a great help to you in this life and even after your death.

Teacher: If there is a literacy program, you may wish to encourage the people to learn to read so that they can read the Bible themselves.

LESSON 1: THE BIBLE IS GOD'S MESSAGE TO ALL PEOPLE.

❓ Questions

1. Whose message are we going to teach you?
   You are going to teach us God's message.

2. Whose message is the most important message in the world?
   God's message is the most important message in the world.

3. Why is God's message the most important message in the world?
   God's message is the most important message because only God knows the truth about everything.

4. In what book is God's message written?
   God's message is written in the Bible.

5. What did God do so His message would be correctly written down for all people?
   God chose men and guided their thoughts so they wrote down His exact message.

6. What were the men whom God chose to write down His words called?
   The men who wrote down God's words were called prophets.

7. Did God's prophets all live at the same time?
   No. Many of the prophets lived at different times.

8. How many years passed before God's message was completely written down?
   About 1600 years passed before God's message was completely written down.

9. What nationality were the men who wrote down God's words?
   The men were all Jews, except for one man.

10. When the prophets wrote God's words, what peoples' languages did they use?
    The prophets wrote God's words in the languages of the Jewish people.

11. Has the Bible been translated into other languages?
    Yes. The Bible has been translated into many different languages of the world.

12. For whom did God give His message?
    God gave His message for every person in every part of the world.

LESSON 2: THE BIBLE TELLS US WHAT GOD IS LIKE AND THAT HE ALONE EXISTED BEFORE EVERYTHING AND EVERYONE ELSE.

Scripture

Genesis 1:1

Lesson Outline

(1) God begins His story with these words, "In the beginning." (Genesis 1:1)

(2) God is the only One who has always existed.

(3) God is Spirit.

(4) God is in all places at the same time.

(5) God is a Trinity.

(?) Review Questions from Lesson 1.

Lesson Outline Developed

Teacher: Genesis is the foundation for all the Scriptures, and Genesis 1 is the foundation for Genesis. Do not rush through Genesis 1 because the basic revelations of the nature and character of God are presented in this chapter.

In this lesson, we will begin to lay the foundations for the doctrine of God. We will develop the doctrine of God on the basis of both Scripture and logical deductions. After we introduce the basic attributes of God, we will emphasize these attributes continually as we teach through the Scriptures.

(1) God begins His story with these words, "In the beginning."

📖 Read this portion of Genesis 1:1, *"In the beginning."*

God began His story with these words so that we would know there was a beginning to all things. Everything that we can see and everything that we know about but cannot see had a beginning.

- **None of the things we see around us have always existed.**

   Before the beginning, the earth did not exist.

   Before the beginning, things on the earth did not exist. The mountains, oceans, rivers, rocks and trees did not exist.

   Lesson Developer: As you go through this section, use illustrations about the created things the people use or see every day. For example:

    The river where you bathe and where you get your drinking water did not exist.

   Before the beginning, the sky, sun, moon and stars did not exist. None of the things we see on the earth or in the sky existed before the beginning.

   Teacher: Ask questions to make sure that the people really understand that nothing that they see around them existed before the beginning.

- **No human beings existed before the beginning.**

   Knowing that the earth, sun, moon and stars did not exist before the beginning, do you think it is possible that there were any people? Think about it. Could your ancestors or my ancestors have been living then?

   Teacher: Do not be concerned if the people answer questions such as these incorrectly. They can only answer according to what they have been taught in the past. This may be their first time to hear God's truth.

   We human beings cannot live without the sun, the earth, water and food. None of these things were here before the beginning; therefore, we know that human beings were not here either.

   None of my ancestors were alive before the beginning. None of your ancestors were alive before the beginning.

   Teacher: Name different groups of people that they are aware of and reiterate that none of these groups were alive before the beginning. Talk about this with them, and let them discuss it. You want them to know for certain that no people existed before the beginning.

LESSON 2: THE BIBLE TELLS US WHAT GOD IS LIKE AND THAT HE ALONE EXISTED BEFORE EVERYTHING AND EVERYONE ELSE.

- **The spirits did not always exist.**

    Lesson Developer: The following point is written as if it were being taught to animists. If the culture in which you are teaching is not animistic, you will need to change how you express these truths.

    > The spirits that you believe in did not always exist. You have told us how you seek help from the spirits to make your gardens grow and how you are fearful of the spirits in the jungle. Many people have different ideas about the spirits. God's Word will explain more about them as we continue to study, but for now we want you to think about a time when none of the things you see or know about existed. None of the spirits that you have told us you believe in have always existed. Think about that. All people and all spirits had a beginning.

    Teacher: It is important that the people do not think that you agree with their beliefs about the spirits, so be careful how you refer to those spirits. For example, if you call their spirits by name, the people may think that you agree with what they believe about those spirits. You do not want the people to think that you are agreeing with their beliefs. If possible, use terminology such as, "The spirits that you believe in."

    The spirits in which the people believe do not exist – as they know them. These spirits are actually demonic powers who have disguised themselves and have presented themselves to the people as spirits of the trees, the rocks, the dead, etc. (As you prepare to teach, read 1 Corinthians 10:19-20, but do not read these verses to the people when you teach the lesson.)

    The people will continue to express their own cultural understanding of the spirit world. Do not correct them at this point in the teaching program. Furthermore, wait until Lesson 3 to talk about the spirits mentioned in the Scriptures (e.g., angels and Lucifer) and wait until Lesson 10 to talk about Satan and his demons. Speak of the people's spirit world in general terms.

    Ask questions to make sure that the people understand that there was a time when no part of creation, including human beings, spirit beings and animals, were in existence. Take whatever time is necessary to make this truth clear so that, as you go on to teach that God alone is eternal, He will be magnified and exalted before the people as the supreme and sovereign source of all life.

② God is the only One who has always existed.

> Before the earth was here and before there were any people or spirits or anything else, God was already living.
>
> God is the only One who existed before all things began. Although there was no earth, ocean, sun, moon, stars, animals, people or spirits, God was already living.

> ☞ **Teacher:** Point to the word, "God," on the chronological chart. Do not reveal the words, "Father, Son, Spirit," on the chart because you should not explain the Trinity at this stage in the lesson. You will teach that three Persons are the one God in the last point of this lesson.

- **Because God was the only One who existed before everything else, we know that**

  God is greater than all. God is greater than the earth, the ocean, the moon, the sun and stars. God is greater than all animals, all people and all spirits. God existed before all other things; therefore, we know that He is greater than all.

- **God alone can tell us about the beginning of all things.**

  God is the only One who was here before all things began. Therefore, God is the only One who can really tell us what happened in the beginning.

Lesson Developer: To illustrate this point, use an incident that occurred before the majority of your hearers were living but which an older person experienced. For example:

> 🕯 *You have told us about a time long ago when you were fighting with the people who live over the mountains. [Name] was there. He is an old man now, but he was a young man then. He took part in the fighting. If I wanted to know what really happened during that fight, would I ask one of these children or one of these young women? Who do you think would be the best person to ask? It would be best to ask the man who was there.*

Lesson Developer: Another appropriate illustration would be to remind the people of something that happened recently but was experienced by only one or two people. For example,

> 🕯 *Most of you haven't been to Manila, but [Name] has been to Manila. If you wanted to know what Manila is like, who would be the best person to ask? It would be best to ask [Name.] Because he has visited Manila, he knows what it is really like.*

Just as we depend on people who were there and experienced something to tell us what happened or to describe what a place is like, so we can depend on God to tell us how all things had their beginning. He was there before all things began, and so He knows what really happened.

LESSON 2: THE BIBLE TELLS US WHAT GOD IS LIKE AND THAT HE ALONE EXISTED BEFORE EVERYTHING AND EVERYONE ELSE.

- **God alone is eternal.**

    God has always lived. God had no beginning. He was not created. He was not born. He did not make Himself. He has always been alive, and He will never die.

Teacher: The Palawanos agreed when we said that God was neither born nor made by someone else, but they thought that He suddenly began to exist. A good question to ask is, "Was there ever a time when God was not living?"

- **God is completely independent of everything and everyone.**

    God does not need anyone or anything. God lived before the beginning. He lived before the earth, sun, moon, stars or anything else was here.

    You and I were born into this world. We needed someone to take care of us when we were babies. But God was not born. He did not need anyone to take care of Him.

    God does not need the earth or anything on it. He can see without any light, so He doesn't need the sun, moon or stars in order to see. He does not get tired, so He does not need the darkness of night to sleep.

    God lives by His own power. He does not need anything to keep Him alive, so He does not need air to breathe. God never gets hungry or thirsty, so He does not need food to eat or water to drink.

    We are dependent on many things. Think about this: Could you live without the sun, the rain or the ground? Could you live without food? What do you need when you get hungry or thirsty?

Teacher: Mention the kinds of food that make up the people's main diet. Ask them if they could live without those foods.

    We need food to eat and water to drink. We need the earth to walk on. We need the air to breathe.

    God, however, is not like man. And God is not like the animals, the birds or reptiles. These creatures all have needs, but God doesn't need anything. Because God lived before the beginning of all things, we know that He doesn't depend on anything or anyone.

- **God is supreme and sovereign — He is greater than all.**

Lesson Developer: The following points (that is, things, people, spirits and animals) are listed in order of importance according to the way the Palawano people would think. You should arrange these points according to the way your hearers would think.

God is greater than the sun, the moon, the stars and everything on the earth. He existed before the sun, the moon, the stars and the earth.

God is greater than all people. He existed before all people, and He doesn't need any of the things that people need.

God is greater than the spirits. He was alive before any of the spirits.

Teacher: Make it clear that God is totally independent of the things on which the tribal people think the spirit world is dependent. As they learn that God is independent of all things, the people themselves will begin to make comparisons between the spirits and God. When they openly do this, you will have greater liberty to speak the truth about the spirits.

Be careful to avoid saying anything that will make the people think that you agree with their beliefs about the spirits.

For example, the people will probably believe that the spirits live in the trees, rocks and rivers. Do not teach in such a way that the people will think that you believe that the spirits really do live where the people say they do. The Scriptures seem to indicate that Satan and his demons inhabit the lower atmosphere above the earth (Ephesians 2:2).

Likewise, do not teach as if the spirits actually do eat or need food as the people believe they do. The spirits in which the people believe are demonic powers and do not need material things, even though they have made the people believe that they do.

Do not make comparisons between the spirits and God. For example, do not say, "Your spirits need trees and rocks to live in and food and clothes, but God doesn't need any of these things." If you make comparisons like this, the people will think that their beliefs about the spirits are correct. In addition, they will think that you, too, believe that the spirits really do need these things. Instead of comparing, simply state, for example, "God does not need the trees to live in."

Be careful not to speak in a way that would make the people feel that their beliefs are under direct attack or are being ridiculed. At this point in the teaching program, simply make it very clear that God doesn't need any of the things which they claim the spirits need.

If one of them should begin talking about the spirits' need of these things, do not argue. Instead, tell the person that we will soon be learning what God's Book says about the spirits.

God is greater than the animals. He existed before the animals did, and He doesn't need any of the things that the animals need.

Teacher: Mention those birds and animals that are significant in the lives of the people. Ask the people what the birds, animals and reptiles need in order to live. Then ask the people if the birds, animals and reptiles could exist without those things.

But God is not like the animals. He doesn't need or use any of the things they do. God is greater than everyone and everything.

LESSON 2: THE BIBLE TELLS US WHAT GOD IS LIKE AND THAT HE ALONE EXISTED BEFORE EVERYTHING AND EVERYONE ELSE.

③ God is Spirit.

Human beings, animals, birds and reptiles each have bodies of flesh and bones. We need many things. But God does not need the earth to live on or the many things that people need because God does not have a body as we do. God does not have a body of flesh and bones. God is Spirit.

As you learn more and more about God from His Book, you will understand that God is Spirit.

We have already learned that, before the beginning, there was no earth, no sun, no moon and no stars. Where do you think God lived before the beginning? Where do you think God is now?

④ God is in all places at the same time.

- **The Bible tells us where God is.**

    We cannot see God, and we cannot know where He is unless He tells us. Through God's Book, we learn that God is everywhere.

    God is where the sun, the moon and the stars are. And God is in all places on the earth.

    God is here right now and can see us all.

Lesson Developer: Use illustrations of places where God is. Choose locations that will be familiar to the people. For example:

> God is here right now, and God is also in your houses, out in your gardens, in the jungle, down at the river and far out in the ocean. He is up on the highest mountain near where you live, and He is also on the mountains near where your neighboring tribe lives.

- **God is greater than people.**

    Think about this: Can a person be in more than one place at a time?

Lesson Developer: Use illustrations to show that people cannot be in more than one place at a time. For example:

> Can you be up at the head of the river at the same time that you are down at the ocean? When you are in your house, can you also be out in the jungle? When you go hunting, can you still be at home with your family? No, of course not!

- **We humans can only be in one place at a time.**

Lesson Developer: Use an illustration about the fact that you left your homeland and came to where the people are. For example:

> When I am here with you, I live in my house near you. When I leave here and go to my country, then I live in my house there. I can't be here and there at the same time. But God is in every country of the world, in every place, all at the same time.

- **God is Spirit, and He is everywhere at the same time.**

    God does not say in His Book that He travels to every place or that He has a big body that is everywhere. God's Book simply says that God is everywhere.

    God is near each one of us all of the time, no matter where we go. He can see all of us all of the time.

Teacher: Expand this point by naming places where you know the people would go to hide from their enemies, or where they may think the spirits cannot find or see them. Be sure you make it clear that God is everywhere all the time, even in their hiding places.

Ask them, "Is there anywhere we can go where God is not already there? Can we hide from God?" If the people think they can hide from God, then perhaps you have not communicated clearly, or perhaps they do not yet believe what you are saying about God. Be sure you have communicated clearly, but do not be concerned if they do not believe what has been taught to them about God in this lesson. You will continue to teach the same truths in the following lessons. Trust the Holy Spirit to convince each person of the truth.

At this time, do not mention the fact that God can see them when they sin. You have not taught yet from the Scriptures that they are sinners, nor have you taught what sin is. After you have taught about Adam and Eve's sin, you will be able to warn the people that God sees them when they are sinning.

   As we continue to teach you the story from God's Book, you will understand more clearly that God is Spirit and is everywhere at the same time.

- **God is the only One who is everywhere at the same time.**

    There is no one and nothing like God. He is greater than everything and everyone.

(5) God is a Trinity.

- **As you listen to God's message, you will learn that there is only one God, yet there are three Persons who are equally God.**

    The three Persons who are God are absolutely equal in every way.

LESSON 2: THE BIBLE TELLS US WHAT GOD IS LIKE AND THAT HE ALONE EXISTED BEFORE EVERYTHING AND EVERYONE ELSE.

☞ **Teacher:** Point to the words, "God: Father, Son, Spirit," on the chronological chart.

These are the three Persons who are the One God: The Father who is God, the Son who is God, and the Spirit who is God.

Teacher: Do not try to explain the Trinity by using illustrations (such as water, an egg or a triangle). Illustrations fall far short of the truth and may even cause confusion because the people may understand the illustration in a literal sense. It is better to admit that we cannot understand the Trinity.

Listed below are reasons why we introduce the Trinity now. However, do not teach this to your students and do not read the verses to them. This is for your information only. The Trinity is introduced now because:

- The Trinity is eternal and therefore comes chronologically before the "beginning."
- The word "God" in Genesis 1:1 is the Hebrew word Elohim. Because of its ending, Elohim is a plural name with a singular meaning.
- Genesis 1:26 uses the plurals, "us" and "our."
- Since the Holy Spirit is mentioned in the Old Testament, the subject of the Trinity cannot be avoided (Genesis 1:2 and Genesis 6:3.) God the Son was there in the beginning with God the Father and God the Holy Spirit. They are the one God who, in
- Teaching on the Trinity in the beginning and throughout the Old Testament makes it much easier to teach the deity of Jesus when we come to the story of His birth. If we have taught from the beginning that the Son was forever co-equal with the Father, active in creation, and in the entire Old Testament story, the people will be better able to understand that Jesus is God. For example, in order for the people to be able to understand Jesus' statement, "…before Abraham was, I am" (John 8:58), they need to know that God the Son was there, even before the beginning.

Note: Do not use His name, Jesus, or His title, Christ, while teaching the Old Testament. Both are connected with His earthly ministry. Refer to Him only as God the Son during the Old Testament teaching.

Special note for those teaching Muslims: If you are teaching Muslims, it would be better not to mention the Trinity until much later in the teaching program. At the close of the Old Testament teaching, you will present a list of prophecies. Some of these prophecies clearly identify the coming Redeemer as God. As you present the prophecies on the list, then it should be obvious to the hearers that the One who is coming in fulfillment of the prophecies will be divine.

Even though the deity of the Holy Spirit comes out clearly in Genesis 1:2, you do not need to place great emphasis on this point to your Muslim listeners. For them, it would be better for you to point out that the Spirit is also God when you teach the Gospels.

Throughout the Old Testaments lessons, we have used the names, "God the Spirit" and "God the Son," but you may decide to use different titles until you decide to introduce the deity of Christ and the Holy Spirit.

**Building on Firm Foundations
- Volume 2: Evangelism:
Genesis to The Ascension**

? Questions

1. What exists on this earth that did not have a beginning?
   Nothing on this earth exists that didn't have a beginning.

2. Who is the only One who has always existed?
   God is the only One who has always existed.

3. Did someone make God?
   No. No one made God.

4. On a specific day, each of us was born. Was God also born?
   No. God was not born.

5. Did God make Himself?
   No. God did not make Himself.

6. Was there ever a time when God wasn't living?
   No. There was never a time when God was not living. God has always existed.

7. We need food, water, air, the earth and the sun in order to live. What does God need?
   God needs nothing.

8. Since God does not need food or water or air to live, by what power does He live?
   God lives by His own power.

9. Who is greater than the earth, the sun, the moon, the stars, all people and all spirits?
   God is greater than the earth, the sun, the moon, the stars, all people and all spirits.

10. Does God have a body of flesh and bones like we do?
    No. God is Spirit.

11. Where is God?
    God is everywhere at the same time.

12. How many true gods are there according to the Bible?
    There is only one true God.

13. Who are the three Persons who are the one God?
    The Father, the Son and the Spirit are the three Persons who are the one God.

LESSON 3: GOD CREATED THE SPIRITS. GOD CREATED THE HEAVENS AND THE EARTH.

Scripture

Genesis 1:1

Lesson Outline

(1) God created all of the spirits.

(2) God created the heavens and the earth. (Genesis 1:1)

(3) God created everything out of nothing.

(4) God is all-powerful.

(5) God knows everything.

(?) Review Questions from Lesson 2.

Lesson Outline Developed

Teacher: Remember these important teaching principles:

- Take adequate time to teach clearly. Be sure the people think through the logic of what you are teaching.

- Encourage the people to talk about the subject being discussed. Show them respect by listening to what they say.

- If they are wrong, don't always correct them immediately. If you immediately correct them, they may feel humiliated and may stop contributing to the discussion. Instead, keep in mind the point they didn't understand and be sure to cover it at another time.

- If they don't know the answer, then simply tell them what God says but don't argue with them. They will then realize that the difference of opinion is between them and God, not between them and you.

- Do not let them draw you into subjects or details that you should not teach yet. If they ask you a question relating to anything later in the chronological story, answer them, "That is a very good question. We will read the answer to that question later on in the story that is written in God's Book."

**Building on Firm Foundations
- Volume 2: Evangelism:
Genesis to The Ascension**

(1) God created all of the spirits.

Teacher: Before we teach that God created the material things which can be seen, we will first teach that God created the spirit world which generally cannot be seen. It is best to teach about the spirits and Lucifer now because the angels witnessed the creation of the earth (Job 38:4-7). It is easier for both teacher and learner if we introduce each character from God's story at the time it was created or born. Otherwise, the teacher has to return to an earlier point in the story to fill in the missing details.

- **No spirits existed until God gave them life.**

   God lived before the spirits were created. God is the One who planned what the spirits would be like, when He would give them life and what He planned for them to do. Therefore, God is greater than all of the spirits. God is greater than anyone or anything.

- **God did not give the spirits bodies when He created them.**

   The spirits do not have bodies of flesh and blood; therefore, they are not limited in the way they move around. Spirits do not have to use the door in order to enter into a house. Even if you close the door, the spirits can still come in.

   Even though the spirits do not have bodies like we do, they sometimes appear as human beings or in some other form that people can see.

Teacher: It is necessary to mention that angels can appear in human form so the people will be prepared when you speak of the appearances of angels in the Old and New Testaments. Furthermore, the evil spirits have probably revealed themselves in various forms to the people. If the people speak of these appearances, agree that the spirits can do this. Then tell the people that they will understand exactly who the spirits are as they continue to listen to God's Word.

   The spirits do not have bodies, just as God does not have a body. However, the spirits cannot be everywhere at the same time as God can. Each spirit can only be in one place at one time just like every person can only be in one place at one time. Only God can be everywhere at the same time.

- **God created the spirits to be His servants.**

   In His Book, God sometimes uses the name, "angels," for the spirits. Angels are God's messengers.

☞ **Teacher:** Point to the words, "God's angels," on the chronological chart.

   God wanted the spirits to love Him and to obey Him, doing whatever He wanted them to do.

LESSON 3: GOD CREATED THE SPIRITS. GOD CREATED THE HEAVENS AND THE EARTH.

- **Because God created the spirits, they belong to Him.**

Lesson Developer: Use an illustration about the fact that the person who makes an object owns that object. For example:

> *If you build a house, then to whom does that house belong? If you make a blow-gun or a bow and arrows, aren't you the rightful owner?*

Just as you are the owner of whatever you make, so God is the owner of all that He created.

God was the One who made all of the spirits. He gave them life. Therefore, all of the spirits rightfully belong to God.

- **God created the spirits to be perfect.**

All of the spirits were good and kind when God created them. They were perfect, because God created them to be perfect.

None of the spirits were evil or unkind when God created them. God cannot create anything evil because God is holy. Everything He thinks, says and does is perfect.

- **God created the spirits to have great wisdom and strength.**

The spirits know and understand many things, and they are able to do great things. However, even though the spirits are very wise and very strong, they do not know everything, and they cannot do everything. Only God knows everything and can do everything He wants to do. God is wiser and stronger than all of the spirits.

- **God created many, many spirits.**

How many spirits do you think God created to be His messengers? God created so many spirits that we are unable to count them.

How could God create so many spirits? God could create so many spirits because He is almighty. God can do everything He wants to do.

- **All the spirits lived with God in Heaven.**

Heaven is the special, wonderful place where God lives. Although God is everywhere, all the time, Heaven is the special place where God lives. We don't know where it is, but it isn't here on earth. It is far away, past the moon, the sun and stars. Heaven is the place where all the spirits lived with God.

> **Teacher:** The people's understanding of Heaven will grow with the developing story. Do not get sidetracked into spending too much time talking about Heaven.
>
> Be aware that the people may misunderstand when you speak of Heaven as "the special, wonderful place where God lives" because you taught previously that God is everywhere. If they misunderstand, assure them that while God is everywhere, nevertheless, Heaven is the special place where God lives.

- **God gave an important position to Lucifer, who was one of the created spirits.**

    God didn't create all of the angels exactly the same. Some were wiser, more beautiful and more intelligent than others.

    The greatest angel was named Lucifer. God gave Lucifer an important position in Heaven. Lucifer was given a place of great authority and power over the other angels.

    ☞ **Teacher:** Point to the word, "Lucifer," on the chronological chart.

② God created the heavens and the earth.

> **Teacher:** Do not teach in this present lesson the details about God creating the heavens and the earth. These details will be covered as we teach about the six days of creation, beginning with the next lesson.

📖 Read Genesis 1:1.

The beginning was the time when God the Father, God the Son and God the Spirit created the earth, the sun, the moon, the stars, and all other things that we see around us.

The spirits whom God had created watched Him create everything else. As they saw God creating all things, the spirits praised and worshipped God as the almighty and all-wise creator.

③ God created everything out of nothing.

We have already learned that no one and nothing has always existed except God. Since there was nothing here in the beginning, what did God use to make the earth, the sun, the moon, the stars and everything else? There were no materials for God to use. Therefore, we know that God created everything out of nothing.

- **None of us can make something out of nothing.**

    If people are going to make something, we must have material to use to make it.

LESSON 3: GOD CREATED THE SPIRITS. GOD CREATED THE HEAVENS AND THE EARTH.

Lesson Developer: Use illustrations to show that people cannot make something out of nothing. For example:

> 💡 *What do you men use to make canoes? If there were no trees or logs, could you make a canoe? Could you make a canoe out of nothing?*
>
> *You women use plants to make baskets and carrying bags. But what if there were no plants? Could you make your baskets and bags out of nothing?*
>
> And you children make spinning tops out of wood. Could you make spinning tops if there were no wood? Could you make spinning tops out of nothing?
>
> Look at your houses. You use lots of different materials from the jungle to make houses. Could you build houses if there were no jungle? Could you build houses out of nothing?

Teacher: Give the people time to think through these illustrations. If you feel the people need to consider this concept further, you can also use birds and animals as illustrations. Birds and animals must have materials in order to make their nests.

- **Only God can make something out of nothing!**

    What materials did God have in the beginning? Was there anything here before the beginning that God could use to make the heavens and the earth? No! There was nothing to use.

    God made everything from nothing. Only God could make something out of nothing.

Teacher: If the people dispute what you are telling them, do not be concerned. Answer, "God was the only One there in the beginning. We (missionaries) were not there. You were not there. Your ancestors and my ancestors were not there. Only God was there in the beginning; therefore, God is the only One who can tell us what happened."

④ God is all-powerful.

How was it possible for God to make everything out of nothing?

God could make everything out of nothing because God is able to do everything He wants. Nothing is too difficult for God to do.

Look at all the things God has made out of nothing. Is anyone stronger than God? Are you? Is Lucifer? Are any of the spirits? No! Only God has the power to make something out of nothing

Is anything too hard for God to do? No! God can do anything He wants to do. God is all-powerful.

⑤ God knows everything.

- **People need to be taught.**

    There are many things that people do not know until we are taught. Think about children. Babies can't walk or talk until they learn. Little children cannot hunt, fish, build houses, make gardens or cook until they are taught.

    Even adults have to be taught how to make things and do things.

    Lesson Developer: Use an illustration to show that people have to be taught how to make things. For example:

    > 💡 If I wanted to make a canoe, I would have to get you men to show me how to do it. If my wife wanted to make a carrying bag, you women would have to teach her how to make it. If you wanted to make an airplane or a radio, you would have to learn how.

    We people need to be taught before we can make things.

- **God has always known everything.**

    Think about this: Was anyone living in the beginning who could teach God? No! God existed before anyone else existed. No one was there to teach God.

    Did God need someone to teach Him how to make the heavens and the earth? No! God did not need anyone to teach Him. God is not like us. God doesn't need to be taught. God knows everything.

- **Only God knows and understands everything. He is greater than all.**

    God is greater than all that He created. The spirits whom God created do not know and understand everything like God does. People do not know and understand everything like God does. Only God knows and understands everything. God is greater than all.

❓ Questions

1. Who is the only One who has always existed?

    God is the only One who has always existed.

2. Where did all the spirits come from?

    God created all of the spirits.

LESSON 3: GOD CREATED THE SPIRITS. GOD CREATED THE HEAVENS AND THE EARTH.

3. Did God create the spirits with bodies?

   No. God did not create the spirits with bodies.

4. Did God create some good spirits and some bad spirits?

   No. God created them all good.

5. For what purpose did God create the spirits?

   God created the spirits to be His servants and His messengers, to love Him and obey Him.

6. How many spirits did God create?

   God created more spirits than we are able to count.

7. Where did all of the spirits live in the beginning when God created them?

   When God first created them, the spirits all lived with God in Heaven.

8. God is everywhere at the same time. Can any of the spirits be everywhere at the same time?

   No. None of the spirits can be everywhere at the same time.

9. What is another name for the spirits that serve God?

   Another name for the spirits that serve God is "angels."

10. Who was the most intelligent and beautiful angel created by God?

    Lucifer was the most intelligent and beautiful angel created by God.

11. What position did God give Lucifer?

    God gave Lucifer an important position of authority over the other angels.

12. Who created the heavens and the earth?

    God created the heavens and the earth.

13. Who watched as God created the heavens and the earth?

    The spirits watched as God created the heavens and the earth.

14. What did the spirits do as they watched God create the heavens and the earth?

    They praised Him as the almighty and all-wise creator.

15. What materials did God use to make the heavens and the earth?

    God didn't use any materials to make the heavens and the earth. He made everything out of nothing.

16. How was it possible for God to make the heavens and the earth out of nothing?
    God is all-powerful. Nothing is too difficult for God to do.

17. Who taught God how to make everything?
    No one taught God.

18. How did God know how to make the heavens and the earth?
    God knew how to make the heavens and the earth because God knows everything.

19. Is there any person or any spirit who knows everything like God does?
    No. Only God knows everything.

LESSON 4: GOD REVEALED HIS NATURE AND ATTRIBUTES THROUGH HIS CREATIVE ACTS (DAYS 1-3).

Scripture

Genesis 1:2-13

Lesson Outline

1. The earth was formless and covered with darkness. (Genesis 1:1-2)

2. God the Spirit was present, ready to begin creating everything. (Genesis 1:2)

3. On the first day, God created light. (Genesis 1:3-5)

4. On the second day, God created the air and the sky. (Genesis 1:6-8)

5. On the third day, God moved the waters from the land to make dry land and oceans. God created all plants. (Genesis 1:9-13)

(?) Review Questions from Lesson 3.

Lesson Outline Developed

1. The earth was formless and covered with darkness.

Teacher: As you teach the following point, be sure the people understand the dark and disordered state of the earth. Although there was nothing wrong with what God had made to this point, it wasn't yet arranged in the way God had planned. The condition of the earth in the beginning is the backdrop for teaching God's creative power.

📖 Read Genesis 1:1-2.

- **The earth was formless.**

    When God first created the earth, all the different parts that the earth is made of were mixed together and in complete disorder. God had not yet put the earth in the order He planned. It was impossible for anything to grow or for anyone to live on the earth.

- **Light did not exist.**

    Darkness covered the whole earth.

> **Lesson Developer:** Use an illustration to explain the type of darkness that covered the earth. For example:

> 💡 *Would you like it if there were no sunlight by day or moonlight by night? Wouldn't it be terrible if there were no firelight or flashlights or any light on the earth at all? You wouldn't be able to see where to go. You wouldn't be able to see one another. You wouldn't be able to see to fish, hunt or plant your crops.*

Light did not exist. Darkness covered the whole earth.

- **Dry land did not exist.**

    Water covered the whole earth.

② God the Spirit was present, ready to begin creating everything.

📖 Read Genesis 1:2.

- **God the Spirit was ready to create everything.**

    Although there was no life on the earth, God the Spirit was there. He was waiting to begin His great work of creating all things.

> **Lesson Developer:** Use an illustration about being ready to start building a house. For example:

> 💡 *When you are going to build a house, you get everything ready to begin. In a similar way, God was ready to begin the work of making everything.*

God the Spirit was ready to begin the work of making the earth the way God had planned. He was fully prepared to release the almighty power which would begin the great work of making everything.

We have learned that there is only one God, but there are three Persons who are the one God. God the Father, God the Son, and God the Spirit created everything.

③ On the first day, God created light.

> **Teacher:** God's nature and attributes are clearly displayed in His creative acts. Therefore, as you teach the six days of creation, point out the attributes of God through His creative acts.

LESSON 4: GOD REVEALED HIS NATURE AND ATTRIBUTES THROUGH HIS CREATIVE ACTS (DAYS 1-3).

📖 Read Genesis 1:3.

- **God commanded the light to shine.**

    Think about this: Do you know of anyone besides God who can make light just by speaking?

Lesson Developer: Use an illustration to show that people cannot make light by speaking. For example:

> Have you ever been out in the jungle without a light when it becomes dark? What did you do? Did you speak and cause the darkness to be changed into light? Of course not.

People cannot make light by speaking, but God could make light just by speaking. God commanded the light to shine in the darkness, and there was light.

- **How did God know how to make light?**

    God knew how to make light because God knows everything. There isn't anything that God doesn't know.

- **Was it difficult for God to make light?**

    No! It was not difficult for God to make light because God is all-powerful. He can do anything He wants to do.

    There was no light in the world until God made the light. He created the light just by speaking. Only God has the power to make light.

- **God created light because He is loving and kind.**

    God planned to create people. And God knew that people would need light to live. God created light for the people whom He planned to create.

    📖 Read Genesis 1:4.

- **Everything that God made is good because God is perfect.**

    The light God made was very good. Each time God created, He saw that it was good. It was really good. It was perfect.

Lesson Developer: Use an illustration to show that the things people make are not perfect. For example:

> People often make things that are not really perfect. Perhaps you men have made a canoe that you are not quite satisfied with. Even though the canoe is not useless, you know that it is not really right. You wish that you had done something differently so it would be better.

We don't always make things right, but everything that God made was exactly right. Why? Because God is holy. There is nothing wrong with God, and therefore there is nothing wrong with what God made. Everything God makes is perfect because He is perfect.

📖 Read Genesis 1:5.

- **God made the day and the night.**

  God separated the light from the darkness.

  God called the light, day; and God called the darkness, night. That was the first day in the beginning of the world.

Lesson Developer: If it would be significant to the group you are teaching, you may wish to mention that God created light at that time, not the sun.

④ On the second day, God created the air and the sky.

📖 Read Genesis 1:6-8.

- **God continued His work of creation on the second day.**

  The light that God had created the first day was there on the second day. Then God created the air and the sky.

Lesson Developer: Although the "firmament" can refer to all space in the universe, in this lesson, it is described as "the air and the sky." Describe this in a way that your audience will be able to understand.

- **God placed water above the sky.**

  We learned already that, in the beginning, the earth was covered with water. Now we learn that God took some of the water from the earth and placed it high above the sky.

Teacher: Although we are not told specifically in Scripture what God actually did, many dependable scientists believe that these waters were not the clouds like we see today, but water which God turned into mist or vapor and placed as a canopy surrounding the earth, above the atmosphere. (Reference: *The Genesis Record* by Henry M. Morris. Baker Book House, Grand Rapids, Michigan. Pages 58-59.)

It is important to establish clearly in the people's understanding what God did. Later, when you teach the story of the flood, it will be simple to explain how God reversed the process and sent back to the earth the water that He had placed above the firmament.

LESSON 4: GOD REVEALED HIS NATURE AND ATTRIBUTES THROUGH HIS CREATIVE ACTS (DAYS 1-3).

⑤ On the third day, God moved the waters from the land to make dry land and oceans. God created all plants.

Teacher: To prepare your heart to teach about the awesome power that God displayed when He established the boundaries of the ocean, read Psalm 104:5-9. Although you should not read these verses when you teach, read them before you teach so that your heart will be filled with praise because of God's great power.

📖 Read Genesis 1:9-10.

- **God moved the waters from the land.**

   When God first created the earth, it was covered with water. There was no dry ground.

   God told the water to move back to where He wanted it. When the water moved back, the dry land appeared, and so the oceans were formed.

Lesson Developer: Use an illustration to show that people cannot make water obey us by speaking. For example:

> 💡 Could a man stand by the edge of the river and say, "River, move back! I want to cross over to the other side"? Would the river move back? No, of course not.

   Only God can control the water and tell it what to do. God is powerful. God created the water, and He can tell it what to do.

Teacher: Establish clearly that only God can control the ocean and all bodies of water. Later, we will teach that Jesus walked on the water and rebuked the storm. If the people already know that only God can control the waters, they will logically conclude that Jesus is God, as evidenced by the fact that He was able to control the waters.

📖 Read Genesis 1:11-13.

- **God created all the plants and trees.**

   God created a great variety of plants, trees and fruit with many colors, shapes and sizes. What a wonderful God He is to be able to create so many different plants and trees.

   God put seeds into each plant and tree that He created so that more plants and trees would grow just like the first ones that He made. All the trees and plants that you can see came from the first ones that God created.

Teacher: Tribal people are very knowledgeable about the amazing variety of plants and trees that grow in their vicinity. As you teach that all the plants and trees were created by God, ask the people about the many types of trees and varieties of fruits that they have seen. Give them opportunity to talk about the great variety of trees and plants. As they discuss this, point out how awesome God is to be able to create these things.

- **God made all the trees and everything else in an orderly way.**

    God is a God of law and order. God is never confused in what He does. Everything that God created was done in the best way.

Lesson Developer: Use illustrations about the design of plants. For example:

> *Look at this flower. Notice how the petals are arranged. God created everything with a special design. God knows what He is doing, and He created everything perfect.*
>
> *Look at the pawpaw tree. God didn't place all the limbs on one side. When you stand underneath it, you can see that every branch is arranged so it looks just like a beautiful umbrella.*

God made things to be orderly because He is a God of law and order.

- **God created the trees and plants for a specific purpose.**

    Think about this: Why did God make trees? Why did He make the plants? Did God make them because He needed them? No! We have already learned from God's Book that God existed before everything existed. He doesn't need anything.

    God made the trees for the people whom He planned to create.

Lesson Developer: Use illustrations about what life might be like if there were no trees. For example:

> *What would life be like if there were no trees? What would you use to cook your food if there were no trees for firewood? What would you use to build your houses if there were no trees for posts? How would you escape from the heat of the sun if you didn't have the shade of the trees?*

God knew that life would be very difficult for people if there were no trees. God was planning to create man, so God made the trees for man. God made the trees for us because He is loving and kind.

God also created fruits and vegetables for people.

LESSON 4: GOD REVEALED HIS NATURE AND ATTRIBUTES THROUGH HIS CREATIVE ACTS (DAYS 1-3).

Lesson Developer: To help the people realize that God did not need the fruits and vegetables that He created, ask questions about specific foods that are important to the people. For example:

> *Why did God make fruit? Was God hungry? Do you think God said, "I have been making many things, and I am really hungry. I will make a banana tree and eat a banana"? Of course not. God does not need to eat.*

God doesn't have a body like ours. God doesn't get hungry. God doesn't need food.

God made fruit and vegetables for us because He is loving and kind. God was preparing the world for people to live in it. He planned to give us bodies that would need food in order to grow and live.

Lesson Developer: Use an illustration about preparing something for someone special. For example:

> *When a young man is going to get married, he builds a house. He prepares the house so that it is ready for his bride. The young man wants everything to be ready.*

God was preparing the earth as a place for people to live. God prepared everything that is good and beautiful in this world for us to enjoy.

- **Everything that God made in the beginning was good.**

  Nothing bad existed. The thorns and weeds did not grow as they do now. No fruit was poisonous. The vegetables and fruit had no defects.

  Everything was perfect in the beginning because God is perfect. He cannot do anything wrong. Everything He does is perfect.

Teacher: If the people ask you why things are no longer perfect as they were when God created them, talk with them about the differences they see. Explain that they will learn later from God's Book what caused things to change. Encourage them to be inquisitive because this will make them listen more intently.

**Building on Firm Foundations
- Volume 2: Evangelism:
Genesis to The Ascension**

? Questions

1. What was the condition of the earth before God began to prepare it as a place where people could live?

   The earth was formless. It was covered with darkness and water.

2. How did God create everything?

   God created everything by speaking. He spoke, causing each thing to appear.

3. Where did light come from in the beginning?

   The light came from God. God said, "Let there be light!" and the light appeared.

4. In the beginning, the earth was covered with water. Where did God place some of the water from the earth?

   God placed some of the water high above the sky.

5. When water covered the whole earth, who moved the water back so that dry land appeared?

   God moved the water back and caused the dry land to appear.

6. People cannot control water or move it simply by speaking, but when God told the water to move back from the dry ground, it did. Why was God able to command the water to do what He wanted it to do?

   God could command the water because He is all-powerful. He had created the water, and He could tell it what to do.

7. How did God know how to make everything?

   God knows everything.

8. God didn't need the things that He created. He didn't need light, or trees, or plants or anything else. So why did God create these things?

   God was preparing the earth for the people He planned to make. God is loving and kind. He prepared everything on the earth for us.

9. Everything that God created was good; it was perfect. Why was God able to create everything to be perfect?

   God could create everything to be perfect because He is perfect.

LESSON 5: GOD REVEALED HIS NATURE AND ATTRIBUTES THROUGH HIS CREATIVE ACTS (DAYS 4-6).

Scripture

Genesis 1:14-25

Lesson Outline

(1) On the fourth day, God created the sun, moon and stars. (Genesis 1:14-19)

(2) On the fifth day, God created all sea life and birds. (Genesis 1:20-23)

(3) On the sixth day, God created the animals. (Genesis 1:24-25)

(4) God created everything by His great power and wisdom.

(?) Review Questions from Lesson 4.

Lesson Outline Developed

(1) On the fourth day, God created the sun, moon and stars.

Teacher: To prepare your heart to teach these points, read Psalm 104. Do not read these verses to the people as you teach, but read them as you prepare to teach so that your heart will be filled with praise because of God's wisdom, power and goodness.

📖 Read Genesis 1:14-19.

- **God created the sun, the moon and the stars just by speaking.**

    Could anyone other than God just speak so that something comes into existence? No! Only God could do this.

Lesson Developer: Use an illustration to show that people cannot make anything by just speaking. For example:

If you want to make a canoe, can you make it by just speaking? Can people make airplanes and other machines by simply saying what they want? No! They cannot.

Only God can make something just by speaking. It was not difficult for God to create the sun, moon and stars simply by speaking. God can do anything He wants to do.

- **God placed the sun, moon and stars high in the sky.**

  When God created the sun, the moon and the stars, He put them high in the sky. They may not look very far away to you, but they are very, very far from the earth. How do you think God was able to put them so high in the sky?

Lesson Developer: Use an illustration to show that in order for people to reach up high, they need to climb up on something. For example:

> When you want the eggs from a bird's nest that is high in a tall tree, how do you get them down?
>
> When you want a fresh coconut, how do you get it down from the tree?
>
> When you want to put a roof on your house, how do you get on top of your house?

In order for people to reach up high, we need to climb up something. Do you think God needed to climb up something when He put the stars, the sun and the moon in the sky? Do you think God said, "I want to put the sun really high in the sky, so I have to make something so I can climb up to where I want to place the sun"? Is that what God said and did? How did He reach so high? Did He climb? Did He fly?

No. God isn't like people. God is everywhere, all of the time. Because God is everywhere, He doesn't need to climb to reach high places. He doesn't need to walk or fly to reach some distant place.

God is where the sun, moon and stars are, and God is also here on earth. God doesn't need to move from one place to another when He wants to do something. He is already there. God is everywhere, all of the time.

So God was able to place the sun, moon and stars high in the sky. But what keeps the sun, the moon and the stars in the sky? Why don't they fall down?

- **God keeps the sun, moon and stars in the sky by His power.**

Lesson Developer: Use an illustration about how things that people put in the sky fall down. For example:

> If you threw a coconut in the air, it would fall down immediately, wouldn't it?

The sun, moon and stars do not fall. Why not? They do not fall because God keeps the sun, moon and stars in the sky by His great power. He made them by speaking. He put

LESSON 5: GOD REVEALED HIS NATURE AND ATTRIBUTES THROUGH HIS CREATIVE ACTS (DAYS 4-6).

them where He wanted them, and He keeps them in place by His great power.

God knows how to do everything, and He has the power to do everything He wants to do.

Teacher: The people probably have their own theories about how the sun, moon and stars are held in position. Do not spend much time on this point, trying to convince the people to agree with the scientific facts relating to creation. The important thing is for them to learn the nature and character of God.

- **God made the sun, moon and stars to follow an orderly pattern.**

    When God created the sun, He made it to rise and set every day. The sun has risen and set every day, year after year, because that is how God created it. God also made the moon and the stars to follow the same course year after year.

    God is a God of law and order. He is not careless about anything. Everything God does is done according to His perfect laws.

    God made everything orderly so that our lives would be guided and organized the way He wanted them to be.

Lesson Developer: Use an illustration to show how people depend on the sun to rise every day. For example:

> Think about how very difficult it would be if you did not know if the sun would rise in the morning. How could you plan to go fishing or to work in your fields in the morning if you didn't know when the sun would rise? How would you know when to gather your food if you didn't know when the sun would rise?

The sun rises every day because God made it to rise every day. Whenever you see the sun rise, remember that God made the sun and that He causes it to rise and set. He does this so we can work, eat, and sleep, and so the crops will grow.

God also made the moon and stars to follow a set course. He placed the sun, moon and stars in the sky to show us the days, the months, the seasons and the years.

Lesson Developer: Use an illustration to remind them of how they watch the position of the moon and stars to decide when is the best time to do something. For example:

> Think about how you watch the moon and the stars. You know that the moon and stars will follow a set course every year. You watch the stars and the moon to know when to begin clearing the forest for your rice fields. You watch the stars and moon to know when to plant and when to harvest your fields.

God arranged for the moon and stars to follow a set course. When you see the moon and the stars, remember who made them and remember who controls them so that they always follow the same course.

Because God is a God of law and order, He made the sun, moon and stars to follow a very orderly pattern. He is not a careless God. Everything must be done in the right way for God to be satisfied.

- **The sun, the moon and the stars that God created were all very good.**

    God is perfect, and so everything that He does is perfect.

Lesson Developer: Use an illustration to show that people cannot do all things perfectly. For example:

> We all know people who try to do everything right. They take time and make the effort to build a good strong house. They make straight borders for their rice fields, and they plant their gardens in straight, neat rows. They build strong and straight fences to keep out the pigs. But no one can do everything perfectly.

No one is perfect like God so no one except God can do everything perfectly.

God was very pleased with the sun, moon and stars that He had made because they were perfect.

② On the fifth day, God created all sea life and birds.

Read Genesis 1:20-23.

- **God spoke and filled the waters with living creatures and the sky with birds.**

    God said that the waters were to be full of living creatures. As soon as God spoke, the oceans, the lakes and the rivers filled up with fish and all the other creatures that live in the water. God also made all of the birds, just by speaking. When God gave the command, all the fish and the birds were immediately made.

    God made the fish to live in the water and the birds to fly in the sky. God always does things in the right way.

    God created a great variety of fish and birds. God made fish and birds in many different shapes, sizes and colors.

- **Only God could make fish and birds that have life.**

    God is all-powerful. Only God could make fish and birds which have life.

LESSON 5: GOD REVEALED HIS NATURE AND ATTRIBUTES THROUGH HIS CREATIVE ACTS (DAYS 4-6).

Lesson Developer: Use an illustration about the fact that people cannot make living birds or fish. For example:

> 💡 *Think about this: Can a person make a bird or a fish? Some people can carve a fish or a bird out of wood. But people cannot put life into the bird or fish after they carve it. The things people make can't breathe. The things people make can't fly or swim. The things people make can't lay eggs or have young ones. People cannot make birds or fish that have life.*

Only God can make living things. When you hear the birds singing, remember that God made all the birds. When you go fishing, remember that God made all the fish. God made all the fish and birds by His great power and wisdom.

- **Only God can make creatures that can reproduce young ones like themselves.**

When you carve the shape of an animal out of wood it might be very lifelike, but it has no life and it cannot reproduce itself. No one except God has the power to create creatures with the ability to have young ones like themselves.

③ On the sixth day, God created the animals.

📖 Read Genesis 1:24-25.

- **God created all animals.**

God gave the command, and the animals were all made out of the earth.

Teacher: As you prepare to teach, read Genesis 2:19, but do not read these verses to the people when you teach the lesson.

Think about the many different animals that God made. Do you know how many different kinds of animals there are in the world?

God made the animals that live in this part of the world. Also God made many other types of animals that live in other parts of the world.

Teacher: Encourage the people to name some of the animals that live in their part of the world. In addition, show them pictures of animals that they may have never seen.

God made many, many types of animals.

- **God made the animals by His great power.**

The animals could not make themselves. People could not make animals. Only God could make the animals. What a great God He is!

- **God knows everything so He was able to make all the animals just the way He wanted.**

    God made each kind of animal to be just what He wanted each to be. God made them to be able to live in different places. He made them to eat different kinds of food. He made them to have different shapes, sizes and colors.

    Teacher: Encourage the people to talk about the uniqueness of the animals. As the people mention different kinds of animals, ask questions such as: Where does *[that animal]* live? What does *[that animal]* eat?

    God knows everything so He was able to make a great variety of animals.

    All the animals that God made were just the way God wanted them. Everything that God makes is perfect.

④ God created everything by His great power and wisdom.

- **God knew how to make everything because God is almighty and knows everything.**

    God did not need to be taught how to make anything. But people need to be taught how to make things.

    Lesson Developer: Use an illustration to show that people need to be taught how to make things. For example:

    > *You make baskets and many other things. I don't know how to make baskets. If I wanted to make one, I would need you to teach me how to make it. There are many things I don't know. I'm sure if I made a canoe, it wouldn't float. It would tip over. I don't know how to make canoes, but you do. If I wanted to make a canoe, I would need one of you men to show me how to make it.*

    People need to be taught how to make things, but God did not need to be taught how to make anything.

    God knows how to do everything. People may know how to do many things, but there is no one who knows how to do everything.

    Lesson Developer: Use an illustration to show that no one knows how to do everything. For example:

LESSON 5: GOD REVEALED HIS NATURE AND ATTRIBUTES THROUGH HIS CREATIVE ACTS (DAYS 4-6).

> *Who in this village knows how to make the best blowguns? If I wanted a blowgun, I would get one from the person who makes the best blowguns. But although that man knows how to make good blowguns, he may not know how to make a basket. If I wanted a basket, I would get one from the person who makes good baskets. But that person who makes good baskets may not know how to make other things.*

No person knows how to make everything, but God knew how to make everything! God created everything by His great power and wisdom.

- **Look around you at the many things that God created.**

☞ **Teacher:** Show a picture of the beautiful earth that God created for mankind.

God created the light, the dry land, the oceans and rivers, all the trees and plants, the stars, moon and sun, the birds, the fish and all the animals. God knew how to make all of these because God knows everything. He can do anything He wants to do.

Teacher: Carefully lay these foundations regarding the nature and character of God. For example, you have been teaching them that God knows everything. With these foundations, later, you will be able to teach that God knows everything about every person. God knows about our sin. God even knows our thoughts. God knows everything. "…all things are naked and open to the eyes of Him to whom we must give account" (Hebrews 4:13). If you don't lay these foundations of truth deeply in the understanding of the people, you are not going to be able to use these truths to build upon later. But if you build these foundations firmly, the Holy Spirit will be able to use these truths to bring conviction of sin.

⟨?⟩ Questions

1. God placed the sun, moon and stars high in the sky. Did God need to climb up something in order to place the sun, moon and stars in the sky?

    No. God didn't need to climb up something to put the sun, moon and stars high in the sky.

2. God created the sun to rise and set each day, and God causes the moon and the stars to follow the same path every year. What does that show us about God?

    This shows us that He is a God of law and order.

3. Why did God place the sun, moon and stars in the sky?

He placed the sun, moon and stars in the sky to show us the days, the months, the seasons and the years.

4. Who created all the different kinds of fish, birds and animals?
   God created the fish, birds and animals.

5. How did God create all fish, birds and animals?
   God created them just by speaking.

6. God created the fish, birds and animals just by speaking. What does that show us about God?
   God is all-powerful.

7. God created many kinds of animals. What does that show us about God?
   God knows everything so He was able to make a great variety of animals.

8. Who taught God how to make everything?
   No one taught God. God knows everything.

9. People are able to do many things, but none of us can do everything. Who is the only One who can do anything He wants to do?
   God is the only One who can do anything He wants to do.

LESSON 6: GOD CREATED ADAM.

Scripture

Genesis 1:26-31, Genesis 2:7

Lesson Outline

① God finished preparing the earth for man.

② God planned to create man in the image of God.(Genesis 1:26)

③ God created Adam. (Genesis 1:27; 2:7)

④ Adam was the first and only man God created from the ground. (Genesis 1:27-28; 2:7)

⑤ God placed the first man and woman as managers over the earth. (Genesis 1:28- 30)

⑥ Everything God made was good. (Genesis 1:31)

⑦ God's angels, along with their leader, Lucifer, all witnessed man's creation.

(?) Review Questions from Lesson 5.

Lesson Outline Developed

① God finished preparing the earth for man.

- **God prepared the earth for man.**

Before God created the first man, He prepared everything that people would ever need. God prepared all that people would need because God is loving and kind.

Lesson Developer: Use an illustration about getting ready to move to a new property. For example:

> 💡 *There have been times when you have chosen one of the men of your village to go to the capital town to represent your district and to speak to the government officials for you. You chose that person and sent him off as your representative to tell the officials your message to them.*

In a similar way, God prepared the earth. God prepared every part of the earth, but it was not for Himself. He prepared the earth for man.

- **God finished preparing the earth for man.**

   On the sixth day, after God had finished creating all of the animals, the earth was completely prepared for man.

② God planned to create man in the image of God.

📖 Read Genesis 1:26.

- **God said, "Let us make man in our image."**

   To whom do you think God was speaking? God the Father, God the Son and God the Spirit were talking together. They were discussing their plan to make man.

- **God planned what He wanted man to be like.**

   Previously, God had decided what the spirits would be like. He had decided what the sun, the moon and the stars would be like. God had decided the design of all things on the earth. Likewise, God also decided what He wanted man to be like.

Lesson Developer: Use an illustration about planning the design of something. For example:

> 💡 *When you are going to make something that is very important, such as a house or a garden, you first think about it. You plan the design carefully.*

God Himself decided to design man. God didn't ask for anyone's advice. He didn't ask the spirits what He should do. He didn't ask the animals what He should do. God does not need to ask anyone for advice. God is supreme. He is greater than all. God is greater than all things, people and spirits. God alone designed and made all of His creation.

- **Man was to be created greater than any of the animals.**

   Of all God created on the earth, man would be the most important. God decided to make man in the "image of God." None of the animals were created in this way to be like God.

LESSON 6: GOD CREATED ADAM.

- **God tells us in His Book that man would be made in God's image.**

   What does it mean that man would be made in God's image?

   We know God is not talking about our bodies because God is Spirit. God doesn't have a body of flesh and bones like we do. So we know that God did not make our bodies in God's image.

   The part of us that was made in God's image is the part that cannot be seen. The Bible calls this part of us which cannot be seen our soul and our spirit. Man's body was created to be the house for the part that was created in the image of God. God planned that the unseen part of man would have a mind, emotions and a will.

- **God planned to give man a mind.**

   God has a mind. God thinks, makes plans and communicates His thoughts.

   God wanted man to be able to think, make plans and communicate. So God planned to give man a mind. With a mind, man would have the ability to know God and communicate with God. God wanted to talk to man, and He wanted man to talk to Him. God wanted man to be able to think and reason so that man could do God's work here on earth.

- **Animals cannot think and communicate like people.**

   Animals do not have minds like we do.

Lesson Developer: Use an illustration to show that people cannot communicate fully with animals. For example:

> *Would you like to live out in the jungle with just animals to talk to? None of us would enjoy talking to animals all of the time. We can't enjoy their company like we can enjoy the company of people. We can't have a conversation with animals like we can with people. Animals don't have the ability to communicate with people because animals do not have minds like people do.*
>
> *When you are very happy, do you want to tell your pig why you are happy? No! A pig can't understand why you are happy. Pigs can't think like people can because pigs do not have minds like people do.*
>
> *If you wanted to build a house, could you explain to your dog or your pig how you want the house to be built? Can you sit down and talk to an animal so it will understand and help you with your work? No! You can't explain things to an animal because animals can't think and reason like we can.*

God did not make animals in His image. Animals don't have minds like people.

- **God planned to give man a mind that could think and reason.**

    God can think and reason, and He wanted man to be able to think and reason.

    God wanted to be able to communicate with man, therefore, God planned to make man with the ability to think and reason. Of course, people could never think and reason to the same degree that God can. God knows everything. Even the wisest man in this world is like a little child compared to God. God's wisdom is greater than the wisdom of all people.

Lesson Developer: Use an illustration comparing the minds of children and adults. For example:

> It is just like your children. Do your little children know all the things that you do? No, they don't. But because they have a mind like you, they are able to be taught to think and reason like you do.

Because God planned to make man with a mind, man would be able to listen to God's message, understand it and then do what God said. That is what God intended for man. God planned to give man a mind so God could talk with man, enjoy man's friendship and teach man to do God's work.

- **God planned to give man emotions.**

    God has a mind, and He also has emotions. God loves, hates, feels sadness and also feels joy and happiness.

    Because God has emotions, He wanted man to have emotions as well. He wanted man to be able to feel joy and happiness. He wanted man to be able to love God.

Lesson Developer: Use an illustration to show how parents want their children to love them. For example:

> You love your children, don't you? Do you want your children to love you too? Of course, you do! Every parent wants his children to love him.

God wanted man to be able to love Him. God planned to love man, but God also wanted man to be able to love Him, so God planned to create man with emotions.

- **God planned to give man a will.**

    God has a mind and emotions. God also has a will. God is able to make choices. He can decide that He will do something or that He will not do it.

    God wanted man to also be able to make decisions. God wanted man to be able to choose to love and obey God.

LESSON 6: GOD CREATED ADAM.

Lesson Developer: Use an illustration about an object that has no choice in how it is used. For example:

> *When you fit an arrow into your bow, you point the arrow where you want it to go. Does your arrow have any choice where it goes? Does your arrow have the ability to choose whether it should shoot a bird or a monkey? No. Your arrow cannot make a choice. You make the decision where to shoot the arrow. The arrow doesn't have a mind or a will to enable it to make decisions.*
>
> *When you go fishing, you step into your canoe, and you paddle it in the direction where you think the fish will be. Do you ask your canoe where it wants to go? No. You paddle the canoe to wherever you choose to go. You make the decision. The canoe doesn't have a mind or will so it cannot decide what to do.*

God could have made man so that man could not decide what to do or where to go. If man couldn't make choices, then man would have had to do everything that God made him do, just as objects we control have to do what we make them do.

Think about the sun, moon and stars. God made the sun, the moon and the stars to do the same thing every day, every month and every year. The sun, moon and stars do not have the ability to make choices. But God planned to make man with the ability to make choices.

God has a will. God decides what to do, and God wanted man to be able to make choices just like God makes choices. God wanted man to be able to choose to love and obey God. This is the reason God planned to create man with a will.

God wanted man to have a mind so he could understand that God is wise and loving. God also planned for man to have a will so he could choose to love and obey his wonderful Creator.

Lesson Developer: Use an illustration to show that children find it easier to obey if their parents display love and wisdom. For example:

> *If children know and are convinced that their parents are wise and kind, then it is much easier for them to obey their parents.*

God's plan was to make man so he could understand with his mind what God is like; and because he would have a will, he would be able to choose to love and obey Him.

- **God planned for the first man and woman to be managers of the things God created on the earth.**

  Read Genesis 1:26 again.

God planned for man to be made in God's image so man could do a special job for God. Man was to be manager of the things God created on the earth. Man was to take care of the things God created here on the earth, and man was to be the leader over the animals, the birds and the fish.

Teacher: The creation of mankind was unique. Just as it is important to give God His rightful position, so also we should establish the original, unique position that God gave mankind as manager of the things God created on the earth. Our true value and self-worth is best seen in the light of how much God values us. As the tribal person understands how much God values him, he can better understand the necessity of having a right relationship with God. Therefore, it is important for us to teach mankind's unique creation and place of authority on the earth. (You will teach more extensively about this issue later in this lesson.)

Man was created a rational, moral and spiritual being, for he was created in the image of God. In other words, man was created so that he could respond to God. He was created with intellect, so he could know God. He was created with emotions, so he could love God. He was created with a will, so he could obey God. Make it clear that, when the Bible says that man was created in God's image, this does not mean that man was created in the physical image of God.

③ God created Adam.

Read Genesis 1:27; 2:7.

- **God created the first man and woman.**

    God created a man first. On this same day, after God had made the first man, God also made the first woman.

    At a later time, we will read from God's Book how God made the woman. Today, we are reading in God's Book about how God made the first man.

    God named the first man Adam. This name means "man." Later, we will read that Adam named his wife, Eve.

☞ **Teacher:** Point to the names, "Adam and Eve," on the chronological chart.

- **God made Adam's body from the dust of the ground.**

    When God made everything else, God just spoke the words and they were made. But when God made man, God took the dust of the earth and He formed the first man's body the way He wanted it from the dust.

LESSON 6: GOD CREATED ADAM.

Teacher: Avoid literal terminology or explanations that may give an incorrect picture of God. I once heard a teacher say that God put out His hand and picked up the dust to make Adam. This teacher even asked the people if they thought God may have gotten dirt under His fingernails. Avoid this type of literalism that presents God as a superhuman. Teach just what His Word says, and give it neither a literal nor spiritual meaning beyond what is written. God did not take the dust in His hands to form Adam. God does not have physical hands as we do. God is Spirit.

After God had made man's body, the man still didn't have life. Every part of man's body was there, but he was like a dead person. His body was not breathing. The part of man that was to be in God's image and to live in man's body was not yet made.

- **God breathed life into Adam's body.**

When God breathed into Adam's body, he became a living person who could know, love and obey God.

Think about this: Who had the power to give life to Adam's body?

- Could the angels of God give the man life? No! The angels were all created by God, and they do not have the same power as their Creator.
- Could Lucifer, the leader of the angels, give the man life? No! All the angels were created beings, and none of them, not even Lucifer, could give man life.
- Could the sun or the moon give the man life? No! The sun and moon were created by God, but they had no mind or will or power to give life to man.
- Could the earth give the man life? No! The earth was created by God, and He gave it no ability to give life to others.
- Could the birds or the animals give the man life? No! They received life from God, but they are only able to reproduce life according to their own kind.
- Could the man give himself life? No! Before God breathed into Adam, he was not living, so he could not give himself life.

All things received their life from God and are unable to give life to anything or anyone else.

Only God can give life. God is the source of all life. God gave life to the man.

Lesson Developer: Use illustrations to show that things come from a source. For example:

> 💡 *The water you drink from the river comes from the springs high in the mountains. If the springs dry up, so will your river.*
>
> *The sun shines on the earth and gives light. If the sun stopped shining, there wouldn't be any daylight.*
>
> *As the springs are the source of water and the sun the source of light, God is the source of all life.*

All living things received their life from God. Man received his life from God. Only God could give man life.

When God breathed into the first man's nostrils, the man became alive immediately. He was breathing, and he was strong and healthy.

Everything that God created was healthy and perfect in the beginning. There wasn't any sickness or death in the world.

(4) Adam was the first and only man God created from the ground.

📖 Read Genesis 2:7.

- **God created only one man from the ground.**

God did not make a white man and a black man and other races of people. Adam was the only man that God formed from the ground. Later we will read the story from the Bible which explains how God made Adam's wife.

📖 Read Genesis 1:27-28.

God only made one man and one woman. God told the man and the woman to have children so that the world would eventually be filled with people.

Adam is the ancestor of all people. Adam is your ancestor. Adam is also my ancestor. He is the ancestor of all people. We all came from this first man. He is the ancestor of the entire human race.

Teacher: All tribal people have their own beliefs concerning their origins. Satan does not want people to know that all people are descendants of one man. It is imperative that your hearers come to understand that they, too, had their beginnings "in Adam." They will never be able to accept their salvation "in Christ" unless they accept that they died "in Adam" (Romans 5:12-21; 1 Corinthians 15:22). Therefore, we must show them that they are descendants of Adam. They must come to understand that they are related to the rest of humanity and that all people share one original ancestor who was created by the one and only true God. They must realize that the history recorded in the first 10 chapters of Genesis is their history. We will apply this truth to them personally again and again as we teach the first 10 chapters of Genesis.

LESSON 6: GOD CREATED ADAM.

⑤ God placed the first man and woman as managers over all living things on the earth.

📖 Read Genesis 1:28-30.

- **God gave responsibility to man.**

    God put the first man and woman in charge of the earth and everything in it. God explained to the man and the woman what they were to do as God's representatives on earth.

Lesson Developer: Use an illustration about how a man is pleased with his adult son and gives him responsibility. For example:

> 🕯 *How do you men feel when you look at your strong, healthy adult son? How do you feel when he is able to hunt and kill a large wild pig? You are very pleased with him. You are proud to be his father. You are glad to be with him, and you want to assist him in anything he needs to learn or do. Because he is now grown and is wise, you can make him responsible for many things in the family. You can talk to him and explain to him what you want him to do.*

In the same way, God was very pleased with the first man that He had created. God spoke to the first man and woman and told them what they were to do. God put them in charge of the earth and everything in it.

- **God had the authority to put the man and woman in charge of all living things on the earth.**

    Why did God have the authority to give them control of the earth and everything in it? God created everything. Therefore, God could give the earth to whomever He pleased.

    God did not put His angels in charge of the earth. The spirits do not own the earth or anything in it. They did not create the earth, and God did not give it to them. Therefore, they do not have the right to control anything on the earth.

Teacher: Remember that you have not yet taught on the fall of Lucifer. You will teach the fall of Lucifer just before you teach about the fall of man. Therefore, at this stage, do not speak of Lucifer as Satan or of any of the spirits as followers of Satan. Refer to them as spirits or angels of God

Lesson Developer: Use an illustration about a man's rights over his possessions. For example:

Building on Firm Foundations
- Volume 2: Evangelism:
Genesis to The Ascension

> *Does anyone have the right to take your canoe without your permission? No! You have the right to give someone permission to use your canoe, but no one has the right to take it without your permission.*
>
> *Does anyone have permission to give your canoe to someone else? No! No one has the right to take your things and then give other people permission to use them. Only the owner of something has the right to use it or let other people use it.*

God is the creator of all things. This world and everything in it belongs to God. He decided to whom He would give the earth. He gave it to the first man and woman, the ancestors of all people. God had the authority to give the earth to people because God is supreme and sovereign.

Lesson Developer: You may be able to illustrate the position that God appointed man to act for God as manager over all living things on the earth. The people may be familiar with a governor who is under the president, or a mayor who is under some higher authority. Or perhaps there is someone in the tribe to whom the chief has delegated responsibility.

⑥ Everything God made was good.

Read Genesis 1:31.

Because God is perfect and good, everything He made was perfect and beautiful.

In the beginning, no animal would hurt or harm man. In the beginning, thorns, thistles and weeds didn't grow like they do now.

Teacher: Be sure the people understand this point so that, later, when you teach from Genesis 3:17-19 about God cursing the earth, they will understand the terrible consequences of sin. If the people ask why things are no longer perfect as they were when God created them, (for example, "Why do snakes bite? Why do thorns grow?"), tell them that the answer will be given later in the story.

⑦ God's angels, along with their leader, Lucifer, all witnessed man's creation.

God's angels were watching when God prepared the earth and then made man. The angels were pleased. They sang together with joy about how great and wonderful God was to have made everything. They praised and worshiped God.

Teacher: This point is based on Job 38:4-11. As you prepare to teach, read these verses, but do not read them to the people when you teach the lesson.

LESSON 6: GOD CREATED ADAM.

? Questions

1. For whom did God prepare the earth?

   God prepared the earth for man.

2. What does it mean that God created man in His image?

   God created man to have, like God, a mind, emotions and a will.

3. What great difference was there between the creation of man and the creation of the animals?

   God made man in the "image of God." None of the animals were created in this way to be like God.

4. Why did God give man a mind?

   God gave man a mind so that man would have the ability to know God and communicate with God.

5. Why did God give man emotions?

   God gave man emotions so that man would to be able to love God.

6. Why did God give man a will?

   God gave man a will so that man would be able to choose to love and obey God.

7. How many men and women did God make in the beginning?

   God created only one man and one woman.

8. Who is the ancestor of all people?

   Adam is the ancestor of all people.

9. God gave the first man and woman a very important responsibility. What was that responsibility?

   God gave them the responsibility to be managers of the earth and everything in it.

10. Why don't the spirits have the right to control the earth and everything on it?

    The spirits do not have the right to control the earth and everything on it because God did not give them that right.

11. In the beginning, everything in the world was created perfect. Why was God able to make everything perfect?

    God was able to make everything perfect because God is perfect.

12. Who was watching as God prepared the earth and then made man?

    God's angels, including their leader, Lucifer, watched as God prepared the earth and then made man.

LESSON 7: GOD PLACED ADAM IN EDEN.

Scripture

Genesis 2:1-8

Lesson Outline

(1) God finished His work of creation. (Genesis 2:1)

(2) God rested from His work of creation. (Genesis 2:2-3)

(3) The earth was not watered by rain. (Genesis 2:4-6)

(4) God planted a garden for Adam. (Genesis 2:7-8)

(?) Review Questions from Lesson 6.

Lesson Outline Developed

(1) God finished His work of creation.

📖 Read Genesis 2:1.

- **God finished creating all that He planned to create.**

Lesson Developer: Use an illustration about how people often do not finish what they begin. For example:

> 💡 *Some of you have started to make a canoe, but you stopped when it was only half finished. Why was that?*

Many times, people decide to make something, but then they change their minds. They may lose interest in what they are making. Or they may decide that it is too hard to finish making it.

God is not like people. God always finishes what He plans to do. God does not change His mind or lose interest in what He is making. God never decides that He is going to do something different from what He has planned. When God begins a work, He always finishes it.

- **Nothing can hinder God from finishing what He plans to do.**

Lesson Developer: Use an illustration to show that sometimes things prevent people from finishing what they set out to do. For example:

> *Sometimes, you have made a plan to go fishing the next morning. But when the morning comes, you couldn't go fishing because the river was flooding or because your child was sick.*

Many things can happen to prevent people from carrying out their plans. But nothing can prevent God from carrying out His plans. Nothing and no one can hinder God from doing all that He plans to do. No person can stop God. None of the spirits can stop God. No one can hinder God because He is the most powerful. God is almighty.

God always does what He has determined to do. Therefore, when God promises to do something, we can be confident that He will do it.

(2) God rested from His work of creation.

Read Genesis 2:2-3.

How many days did God take to create everything?

- **God created everything in six days.**

Lesson Developer: Use an illustration to show that it takes people a long time to make things. For example:

> *How many days does it take you to build a house? It takes a long time, doesn't it? First, you have to collect the building materials from the jungle, you have to prepare the building site, and then you need to construct the house. When people make things, it usually takes a long time.*

But look at all the things God created in just six days. No one is as great as God. He is almighty. He can do anything He wants. God finished creating in six days all He planned to create.

LESSON 7: GOD PLACED ADAM IN EDEN.

- **On the seventh day, God rested from His work of creating.**

    Think about this: Did God rest from His work because He became tired? He had created everything in the heavens and on the earth. Was God exhausted because of all the work He had done? Do you think God said, "I'm tired. I am going to rest today"?

Lesson Developer: Use an illustration to show that people get tired when they work hard and therefore need to rest. For example:

> 💡 When you have been away on a long hunting trip, what do you want to do when you get home? You want to rest, don't you?
>
> After working hard all day, do you want to begin to do more hard work such as pounding rice or cutting wood? No! Why not?
>
> When people have worked hard or walked a long way, they are tired and want to rest.

Was God tired? Think about the many things that God had created:

- God had created the light.
- He had made the water to move back so that the dry ground appeared.
- He had created all the plants and the trees.
- He had made the sun and the moon and millions of stars.
- God had filled the waters with living creatures and the sky with birds.
- God had created all the different kinds of animals.
- God had created the first man and the first woman.

Teacher: As you briefly describe all that God had created in only six days, do not just list the above facts. Draw the people into this review. Point to the things God created as you review. Mention particularly those aspects of creation which fascinated the people as you taught previously.

God had created so many things. Was God tired from creating all that He had created? No! God doesn't get weary or sleepy like we do. He doesn't have a physical body that needs rest or sleep. God is Spirit.

- **God rested from the job of creating because He was finished making all He planned to make.**

**Building on Firm Foundations
- Volume 2: Evangelism:
Genesis to The Ascension**

Lesson Developer: Use an illustration about finishing a project. As you give the illustration, ask the people questions to involve them in developing the illustration. Although the questions themselves add nothing to the subject being taught, involving them in the illustration helps to hold the people's interest. Use this teaching technique throughout these lessons to involve them in thinking with you. For example:

If you made a canoe, how would you go about it? What is the first thing you would do? Select a tree? Right! After having selected an appropriate one, what would you do then?

After you have finished the canoe and there is no more work to do on it, what would you say if I asked, "Are you going to work on your canoe today?" You would probably say, "No. I have finished my canoe. Now I am going to use it." You are not going to work more on your canoe because your work is finished.

God rested because His work of creating was finished.

Lesson Developer: Use an illustration about how people rest from work once the job is finished. For example:

To plant your rice fields, you first prepare the fields. You cut down the trees and burn them. You clear the ground. And then you plant the rice. What a relief when that field has been planted with rice! You can rest from planting.

Does that mean that you don't do any more work? No, of course not, but you can rest from planting your rice. You won't get up the next morning and say, "I must go out and plant my rice field." No. You have finished planting the rice so you can rest from planting rice.

God created everything in six days. On the seventh day, after God finished creating, He rested. God rested from creating because He saw all His work that He had planned to do was finished.

③ The earth was not watered by rain.

Read Genesis 2:4-6.

- **God uses another name for Himself.**

    In the first chapter of Genesis, God called Himself "God." The name "God" means that God is the great and mighty God who created the heavens and the earth and all things that are in them.

    Here in these verses, God called Himself "the LORD." The name "the LORD" means that God is the eternal One who is totally independent of all things and who will never change.

LESSON 7: GOD PLACED ADAM IN EDEN.

From this point onward, the Bible sometimes uses the name "God." At other times, it uses the name "the LORD God" or just "the LORD."

- **God did not water the earth by rain.**

  During the early years of the earth's history, God did not water the earth by giving rain. Instead, God watered the earth by mist that came up from the earth. There were also rivers and streams which were fed from great underground lakes. But, God did not give rain until much later in the history of the world.

Teacher: This explanation is necessary preparation for the story of the flood and the first rain seen by men. "By faith Noah, being divinely warned of things not yet seen…" (Hebrews 11:7).

This point also states the truth that God is the giver of rain. The people may believe that a spirit gives rain.

④ God planted a garden for Adam.

📖 Read Genesis 2:7-8.

- **God prepared a beautiful garden for Adam.**

  God loved Adam very much. So God planted a beautiful garden especially for Adam.

Lesson Developer: Use an illustration to show that God's action in preparing a garden for Adam shows His great love, a love that is far superior to love that people would have. The garden illustration shown in the example below fits the context best and should be used if appropriate for the people.

> 💡 Do you know anyone who has made a garden and then given it to someone else? No! It would be very unusual for a person to do all that is necessary to plant a complete garden and then give it all away. People would not do that, but God did.

God loved Adam, and so God planted a beautiful garden for him. God included in that garden all the vegetables and fruit trees that Adam would need to keep him happy, strong and healthy.

- **God put Adam in the garden.**

  📖 Read Genesis 2:8 again.

  This garden was planted in a place called Eden.

  When God had the garden ready, He took Adam and put him there. God didn't ask Adam if he wanted to live there. God didn't say, "Adam, I have planted a garden. It is a really beautiful place. Would you like to live there?" God didn't offer this garden to Adam as a place in which to live. Instead, God took the man whom He had formed, and He put him in the garden.

Why did God have the right to take Adam and put him in the garden?

- **God had the right to put Adam in the garden because God made Adam.**

    God had created man. Therefore, God had the right to put man where He wanted him and to tell him what to do.

Lesson Developer: Use illustrations about doing what you want with the things you own. Give appropriate illustrations for your audience, including both men and women. For example:

> 🕯 *You men, would I have the right to go into your house, pick up one of your spears, examine it and say, "That's a wellmade spear," and then take it with me out into the jungle? No! The spear is yours. You made it. You have the right to take it wherever you wish. I do not have the right to take your spear. It is not mine.*
>
> *People only have the right to take their own things and move them where they want them. No one has the right to take something that belongs to someone else and put it in a different place.*

What about Adam? Did God have the right to take Adam and put him in the garden? Who owned Adam? God did, because God made Adam.

God is the owner of all things. He has the right to do what He wishes with all the things that He has made.

God created Adam, so Adam belonged to God. God had the right to tell Adam what to do. God made all people; therefore God has the right to tell people what to do. Because God is good and loves us, He will never do the wrong thing to anyone or anything He has made.

God is the greatest authority. There is none who is higher than God.

- **God told Adam to take care of the garden.**

    Taking care of the garden was not hard work. Weeds did not grow. Snails, grubs and insects did not eat the fruit or vegetables. Everything was perfect. So Adam did not need to work hard.

LESSON 7: GOD PLACED ADAM IN EDEN.

❓ Questions

1. Many times, people begin something, but then they don't finish it. Does God ever begin something and then not finish it?

   No. God always finishes what He begins.

2. God always finishes what He begins. What does this tell us about God?

   Because God always finishes what He begins, we know that God never changes. We also know that God is all-powerful. Nothing and no one can hinder God from doing all that He plans to do.

3. Because God is almighty, He just spoke and all the work of creation was completed in only six days. On the seventh day, God rested. Did God rest from His work because He was tired?

   No! God does not get tired. He does not have a physical body that needs rest or sleep. God is Spirit.

4. Why did God rest on the seventh day?

   God rested because His work of creating was finished.

5. With what did God water the earth when it was first created?

   God watered the earth by a mist that rose up from the earth and by rivers and streams which were fed from great underground lakes.

6. God planted a beautiful garden in Eden. For whom did God plant this garden?

   God planted the garden for Adam.

7. Why did God have the right to put Adam in the garden even though God didn't ask Adam if he wanted to live there?

   God had created Adam, so Adam belonged to God. Therefore, God had the right to put Adam in the garden and tell Adam what to do.

8. To whom do all things, spirits and people belong?

   God is the owner of all things, all spirits and all people because He created everyone and everything.

LESSON 8: GOD TOLD ADAM NOT TO EAT FRUIT FROM THE TREE OF THE KNOWLEDGE OF GOOD AND EVIL.

Scripture

Genesis 2:9, 16-17

Lesson Outline

(1) God planted two special trees in the middle of the garden. (Genesis 2:9, 16-17)

(2) Death is the punishment for disobedience to God. (Genesis 2:17)

(3) God had authority over Adam.

(?) Review Questions from Lesson 7.

Lesson Outline Developed

(1) **God planted two special trees in the middle of the garden.**

📖 Read Genesis 2:9.

- **God caused many kinds of trees to grow in the garden.**

    Many kinds of trees grew in the garden. There were trees that were beautiful to look at. And there were trees that produced fruit for Adam to eat.

    In addition, God planted two special trees in the garden.

☞ **Teacher:** Show a picture of the two trees in the garden in Eden.

- **God planted the tree of life in the middle of the garden.**

    God was the source of Adam's life. God had breathed life into Adam when He created Adam.

    At this time, there was no sickness, disease or death in the world. But in order for Adam to live forever, he had to eat the fruit from the tree of life.

God didn't make Adam eat the fruit. It had to be Adam's choice. God wanted Adam to choose to eat the fruit from the tree of life which He had given to him.

- **Adam was to be totally dependent on God.**

  God wanted Adam to always remember that he was totally dependent upon God for everything. God wanted Adam to acknowledge, "I am totally dependent upon You, God. You are my life. You are my creator. I depend upon You for all things. I cannot live without this fruit from the tree of life that You have provided for me. Because You are my creator, You have the right to tell me what to do and what not to do. I will obey You because I cannot live independently of You, my creator."

  By eating from the tree of life, Adam would be acknowledging that he was dependent on God for his life.

- **God planted the tree of the knowledge of good and evil in the middle of the garden.**

  The tree of the knowledge of good and evil was to remind Adam that he must never choose to be independent of God. He must always depend on God to know what was right and what was wrong.

  From the time God created Adam, God had decided what was good for Adam. God had decided what Adam needed, and God put Adam in the garden in Eden. Adam didn't know anything that was bad because God had given him everything that was good.

  The fruit from the tree of the knowledge of good and evil that God created was not evil. It was good fruit.

  Neither was it bad to understand what was good and what was evil. God already had full knowledge of everything that was good and everything that was evil.

- **Adam was to depend on God to know good and evil.**

  The reason God did not want Adam to eat the fruit from the tree of the knowledge of good and evil is because He did not want Adam to decide what was good and what was bad, independently of Him. God already knew the best things for Adam. God planned that He would be the one to tell Adam the good things that he should do when he needed to know. Adam was to depend on God at all times to tell him what was the right thing. God is good and knows all that is good and all that is evil. God would always choose the best for Adam. Adam was to always let God be the boss.

  God is still the same today. He has not left it up to us to decide what is right and what is wrong. God has given the Bible so we can know what pleases and displeases God.

- **God told Adam that he must not eat fruit from the tree of the knowledge of good and evil.**

  📖 Read Genesis 2:16-17.

LESSON 8: GOD TOLD ADAM NOT TO EAT FRUIT FROM THE TREE OF THE KNOWLEDGE OF GOOD AND EVIL.

God told Adam that he could eat any of the fruit in the garden except for the fruit of one tree. Adam must not eat the fruit from the tree of the knowledge of good and evil.

If Adam decided to be independent of God and disobey Him by eating the forbidden fruit, he would immediately know what was good and what was evil. Once he ate, he would be separated from God and no longer dependent on God to tell him what was good and what was evil. Adam would have to make his own decisions about what was good and what was evil.

- **God told Adam that if he ate fruit from the tree of the knowledge of good and evil, he would die.**

God clearly told Adam that he must not eat fruit from the tree of knowledge of good and evil. And God clearly told Adam what would happen if he disobeyed. Adam would die if he disobeyed God.

2) Death is the punishment for disobedience to God.

Read Genesis 2:17 again.

God said to Adam that, if he ate fruit from this tree, he would die immediately.

Until this time, Adam had only experienced good things because God provided everything for him. However, at this time, God warned Adam that disobeying would result in death. If Adam wanted to be independent of God and disobey Him by eating the forbidden fruit, Adam would die.

What did God mean when He told Adam that he would die?

- **Adam would be separated from God.**

God warned Adam that, if he disobeyed God's command, he would die. He would be separated from God. He would no longer be God's friend. He would become God's enemy.

Lesson Developer: Use an illustration to show that when people have a serious disagreement with one another, they no longer continue to be friends. For example:

> What happens if two friends have a big dispute and argument that they refuse to forget? Do they continue fishing, hunting and spending time together? No!
>
> If a husband and wife are continually quarreling, do they still like to be together? No! People don't want to be with those with whom they disagree.
>
> Disagreement causes separation.

God warned Adam that, if Adam chose to disobey God, the relationship that they had enjoyed since God created Adam would be broken.

God had created Adam in God's image so that Adam could know, love and obey God. If Adam disobeyed God's command, that part of Adam that was made in God's image would be marred and separated from God.

- **Adam would eventually be separated from his body.**

When God told Adam that he would die if he ate the fruit from the tree of knowledge of good and evil, God did not mean that Adam would die physically on that same day. God meant that, if Adam ate the forbidden fruit, he would immediately be cut off from God who was the source of his life. Because of this, in the future, his body would also die.

Lesson Developer: Use an illustration to show that a tree or plant will die if it is cut off from its source of life. For example:

> When you cut down the jungle to make your rice field, the trees don't die immediately, do they? Think about what a tree looks like when you cut it down. The leaves are still green for a few days. The tree looks just like it did before you cut it down. However, because it has been separated from the root, it cannot receive what it needs to keep it alive. It has been cut off, and it can no longer receive water and strength from the earth. Very soon, the tree will wither and dry up. The moment it was separated from the source of its life, it began to die.

That's what God meant would happen to Adam if he ate this fruit. Adam would be immediately cut off from God, the source and sustainer of his life. The result would be that one day he would die physically.

When a person dies physically, he is separated from his body. A person's spirit and soul, the part of him that cannot be seen, leaves his body when he dies.

Do you remember what happened when God first created Adam's body? Adam didn't have any life. His body was like a dead person's body. Then God breathed life into Adam's nostrils. When God breathed into Adam's body, God gave Adam his soul and spirit. His body was the house for his soul and spirit.

Lesson Developer: Use an illustration to show what it means for the soul and spirit to reside in the body. For example:

> When you come to visit me, you come to my house. You call out to me, and I answer you from inside my house. However, if I go to visit my country, I will leave my house that is here among you. I will no longer be living in it. I will be separated from my house. If someone asks you where I am living, you will say, "He has gone to his own country. He is not living here in his house anymore."

LESSON 8: GOD TOLD ADAM NOT TO EAT FRUIT FROM THE TREE OF THE KNOWLEDGE OF GOOD AND EVIL.

A person's body is the house of his soul and spirit. When a person dies, the soul and spirit leave the body.

God told Adam that, if Adam disobeyed God and ate the fruit from the tree of the knowledge of good and evil, Adam would be separated from God who gave him his life. Adam's body would die eventually. Some time in the future, Adam's soul and spirit would leave his body and it would die.

- **Adam would continue forever in separation from God.**

    When God told Adam that he would die if he ate the fruit, God was also telling Adam that, when his body died physically, he would continue forever separated from God. He would never again have an opportunity to become God's friend.

    If Adam chose to disobey God, there would be no way of escape. No one can escape from God.

Teacher: To illustrate what death means, bring to the teaching session a branch that you have broken off from a tree. (For even greater impact, at the point when you are ready to teach this, walk outside of the meeting place, break off a limb and bring it back to show the people.) Use this branch which is broken off from its source of its life to illustrate that Adam would be separated from God, the source of his life, if he disobeyed God. Just as a branch cannot continue to live once it had been separated from its source of life; likewise, if Adam disobeyed God, he, too, would be separated from God, the source of his life.

Keep this branch to use as an illustration as you continue through the chronological teaching. The evidences of death will become more visible as time goes by. You will be able to use this broken-off branch as an illustration of Adam being separated from God after Adam ate the forbidden fruit. You will be able to use one of the smaller limbs as an illustration of Eve, the outer branches as illustrations of Cain and Abel, and the twigs on the very top as illustrations of all Adam's descendants.

Following is a short illustration of death and the way Adam would be separated from God, the source of his life. Adapt the illustration as needed according to your particular situation. For example:

> *Look at this branch that I broke off from a tree. Will this branch continue to live now that it has been separated from its source of life? No, of course not! This branch will die because it has been cut off from the tree. It can no longer receive the nourishment it needs in order to live. It has been cut off from its source of life. It started to die the moment I broke it off the tree.*
>
> *If Adam disobeyed God, he would be separated from God, the source of his life, in the same way that this branch has been cut off from its source of life.*

If Adam disobeyed God, he would no longer be in oneness or friendship with God.

Adam would also die physically when his soul and spirit were separated from his body. And after death, Adam would be separated from God forever.

Teacher: If the people need further explanation of the truth that death means separation from God, the source of life, you could describe what would happen if an arm were cut off from the body. Once the arm is separated from the body, the arm will die. The hand and the fingers will also die.

- **Death is the punishment for disobedience to God.**

    God said that Adam would die if he ate the fruit from the tree of knowledge of good and evil. Adam would be separated from God, the source of life and all that is good.

    Adam would no longer be able to enjoy God's love and friendship.

    Adam would die physically when his soul and spirit left his body.

    Adam would then be separated from God forever.

Teacher: Do not talk about hell or the Lake of Fire at this stage in the teaching program. You will introduce the Lake of Fire in Lesson 10 as the place created for the punishment of Satan. At this point, only stress that Adam would be separated from God.

③ God had authority over Adam.

- **God had the right to tell Adam what to do because God created Adam.**

    God made Adam. God gave Adam his life. Therefore, Adam belonged to God. God had created Adam; therefore, God had the right to tell Adam what to do.

- **God had the right to tell Adam what to do because God loved Adam.**

    God loved Adam and only wanted what was best for him. God wanted to enjoy Adam's love and friendship. God had the right to tell Adam what to do because God loved Adam.

- **God had the right to tell Adam what to do because God was wiser than Adam.**

    God knows everything. God knew what was best for Adam. God had the right to tell Adam what to do because God was wiser than Adam.

Lesson Developer: Use an illustration to show that older men are wiser than younger men and can tell the younger men what to do. For example:

> *Do you older men have the right to tell the younger men to do the correct things? Yes, you do. You are older. You have had many experiences. You know the ways of life. You are wiser than the younger men so it is your right to explain to them the correct things to do.*

LESSON 8: GOD TOLD ADAM NOT TO EAT FRUIT FROM THE TREE OF THE KNOWLEDGE OF GOOD AND EVIL.

No person is as wise as God. God knows everything. He knew what was best for Adam. God knew that, if Adam ate the fruit from the tree of the knowledge of good and evil, Adam would be separated from God.

God still knows what is best. He knows the truth. He has given us the Bible so that we, too, can know the truth. We should listen carefully to God's words because He made us, He loves us, and He is wiser than we are.

? Questions

1. Of how many trees in the garden was Adam allowed to eat the fruit?

   Adam was allowed to eat the fruit from all of the trees in the garden except one.

2. God planted two special trees in the middle of the garden. What were the names of those trees?

   The trees were named "the tree of life" and "the tree of the knowledge of good and evil".

3. By eating fruit from the tree of life, what would Adam be acknowledging?

   By eating fruit from the tree of life, Adam would be acknowledging that he was dependent on God for his life.

4. God had told Adam that he could eat any of the fruit in the garden except for the fruit of one tree. What was the name of that tree?

   The name of the tree was "the tree of the knowledge of good and evil."

5. What did God say would happen to Adam if he ate fruit from the tree of the knowledge of good and evil?

   God said that Adam would die.

6. What did God mean when He said that Adam would die?

   God meant that Adam would immediately be separated from God, the source of life. Adam would no longer be God's friend. Adam would eventually die physically when his soul and spirit left his body. And when his body died, he would be separated from God forever.

7. Why did God have the right to tell Adam not to eat fruit from the tree of knowledge of good and evil?

   God had the right to tell Adam what to do because God created Adam and knew what was best for Adam. God loved Adam and was wiser than Adam.

LESSON 9: GOD CREATED A WIFE FOR ADAM.

Scripture

Genesis 2:18-25

Lesson Outline

(1) God decided that Adam needed a wife as a helper. (Genesis 2:18)

(2) God brought all of the animals before Adam to be named by him. (Genesis 2:19-20)

(3) There was no suitable companion for Adam among the animals. (Genesis 2:20)

(4) God created a companion for Adam. (Genesis 2:21- 22)

(5) Marriage was ordained by God. (Genesis 2:23-24)

(6) Adam and his wife were unaware that they were naked, and they were totally unembarrassed. (Genesis 2:25)

(?) Review Questions from Lesson 8.

Lesson Outline Developed

(1) God decided that Adam needed a wife as a helper.

We have already learned from God's Book that on the day when God made Adam, He also made Eve, the first woman.

☞ **Teacher:** Point to the names, "Adam and Eve," on the chronological chart.

📖 Read Genesis 1:26-27.

We also learned that God made Adam's body from the ground.

📖 Read Genesis 2:7.

What we have not yet learned is how God made Eve's body. The part of God's Book that we are now going to read first explains why God made Eve and then how God made her body. All that we are going to read in this lesson happened on the same day. After God had made Adam's body and given him life, God decided to make a wife for Adam.

📖 Read Genesis 2:18.

- **God decided that Adam should not live alone.**

God didn't ask Adam what he wanted or thought best. God made the decision to make a companion for Adam.

God had created Adam, and God knew what was best for him. God loved Adam and wanted him to be happy. God knew that Adam wouldn't continue to be happy if he was alone. Because God loved Adam and wanted the best for him, He decided to make a wife for him.

② God brought all of the animals before Adam to be named by him.

📖 Read Genesis 2:19-20.

God had given man the responsibility to be manager of all the things that God created on the earth. God had placed Adam as the leader over all the animals, the birds and the fish. So God also gave Adam the responsibility of naming each living creature. God brought to Adam each animal and bird that He had created, and Adam named each of them.

③ There was no suitable companion for Adam among the animals.

📖 Read Genesis 2:20 again.

- **No animal could be a suitable companion for Adam.**

God created man to be very different from the animals. Man was made in God's image. God gave man a mind, emotions and a will so that man could know, love and obey God. The animals, however, were not made in God's image. Animals are not able to know, love and obey God like man can.

Adam needed someone who was interested in the same things as he was. He needed someone who could do the same things that he could do. He needed someone with whom he could communicate.

Animals are not interested in the same things that people are interested in. Animals cannot do the same things that people can do. Animals cannot communicate as people communicate. Animals are very different from people. Therefore, no animal could be a suitable companion for Adam.

LESSON 9: GOD CREATED A WIFE FOR ADAM.

- **Only God could provide a suitable companion for Adam.**

    Adam could not do anything to provide himself with a companion. The spirits could not make a companion for Adam. Only God could make a companion for Adam. God can do anything He wants to do.

④ God created a companion for Adam.

📖 Read Genesis 2:21-22.

Only God could make a woman from Adam's rib. He knows everything and can do anything He wants to do.

- **God made the first woman as a gift for man.**

    If someone who loves you gave you a good and expensive gift, would you take good care of it? Of course, you would!

Lesson Developer: Give an illustration to show how the people would take care of a precious gift. Help them to realize that Adam considered Eve to be a precious gift. For example:

> *Would you be very pleased if someone gave you a young, healthy water buffalo? I know you would. A buffalo would be a very precious gift and a tremendous help to you in many ways so I know you would take very good care of it. You would make sure your buffalo had plenty of the right food, and you would take it to the river two and three times a day to drink and to enjoy the cool water.*
>
> *Eve, Adam's new wife and helper, was very much more precious than a buffalo. Of course, we can't really compare an animal to Eve who, like Adam, was made in the image of God. She was a precious gift, given by God to Adam, and it was only right that he should love her and take very good care of her.*

Teacher: Although we will not begin to teach on husband and wife relationships at this point in the teaching program, we should take this opportunity to give women their rightful value according to the Scriptures. In societies where women are illtreated and looked upon as less important than the men, the Lord may use this to convict the men and cause them to consider God's estimation of women. It may also encourage the women to learn that, although they are not appreciated by the men, yet God knows all about them and loves them. This should encourage the women to listen to the Word of God.

God gave the woman to Adam, and God expected Adam to take good care of her and to love her.

Adam was very pleased with God's gift of a wife for him.

5. Marriage was ordained by God.

📖 Read Genesis 2:23-24.

God made Eve for Adam so they could be married, live together and have children. God commanded Adam and Eve to "Be fruitful and multiply; fill the earth."

Teacher: Do not teach on adultery, polygamy or sexual immorality at this point in the teaching program. We must teach about the root of sin before we teach about the fruit of sin. In Genesis 3, we will teach about the root of sin. Man, through disobedience, was separated from God and so became a sinner by nature. In Genesis 4, we will begin to teach about the fruit of man's sin nature as it is clearly evidenced in the life of Cain. If we emphasize the fruit of sin (such as adultery, stealing or lying) before people realize that what they do only shows what they are, they may turn to self-reformation in an effort to become acceptable to God. Do not teach ahead of the chronological story in either its historical or doctrinal development.

6. Adam and his wife were unaware that they were naked, and they were totally unembarrassed.

📖 Read Genesis 2:25.

Teacher: That Adam and Eve were naked and unembarrassed is preparation for teaching Genesis 3:7.

❓ Questions

1. Who decided that Adam needed a wife as a companion?
   God decided that Adam needed a companion.

2. Why did God decide to make a wife as a companion for Adam?
   God loved Adam and knew that it was not good for Adam to live alone.

3. Was it right for God to decide to create a companion for Adam without asking Adam?
   Yes. God had the right to decide to create a companion for Adam because God had created Adam and knew what was best for Adam.

4. Why was no animal suitable to be a companion for Adam?
   Animals were not made in God's image. Animals are not interested in the same things as man, animals cannot do the things man can do, and animals cannot communicate like man can.

LESSON 9: GOD CREATED A WIFE FOR ADAM.

5. How did God make the first woman?

    God put Adam to sleep and took out one of Adam's ribs. God then made the first woman from Adam's rib.

6. How was it possible for God to make the first woman from one of Adam's ribs?

    God can do anything He wants to do.

7. Who told Adam and Eve to marry and to have children?

    God told Adam and Eve to marry and have children.

LESSON 10: LUCIFER REBELLED AGAINST GOD.

Lesson Outline

(1) God created the spirits to be His servants.

(2) Lucifer rebelled against God, and other angels followed Lucifer in his rebellion.

(3) God knew what Lucifer and his spirit followers were thinking and planning.

(4) God removed Lucifer and his spirit followers from their positions as God's servants.

(5) God prepared a terrible place of punishment for Lucifer and his spirit followers.

(6) Lucifer and his spirit followers hate God.

(7) Satan and his spirit followers no longer live in Heaven.

(?) Review Questions from Lesson 9.

Lesson Outline Developed

(1) God created the spirits to be His servants.

- **God wanted the spirits to love Him and to obey Him.**

  We learned previously that God was the One who created the spirits. God gave the spirits life. God is greater than the spirits, and all the spirits rightfully belong to Him.

  God created the spirits to be His servants. In His Book, God sometimes uses the name "angels" for these spirits. Angels are God's messengers. God wanted them to love Him and to obey Him, doing whatever He wanted them to do.

- **All the spirits were good and kind when God created them.**

  They were perfect, because God created them perfect. None of the angels were evil or unkind when God created them. God cannot create anything evil because God is holy. Everything He thinks, says and does is perfect.

- **God created the spirits with great wisdom and strength.**

    Although God chose to give the spirits great wisdom and strength, none of them, not even Lucifer, their leader, were all-wise and all-powerful like God. God is far superior to them in everything.

- **All the spirits lived in Heaven with God when they were created.**

    God created the spirits to be His servants so originally they all lived with God in Heaven. Not all the spirits still live with God in Heaven, and later we will learn why they don't live there.

(2) Lucifer rebelled against God, and other angels followed Lucifer in his rebellion.

Teacher: As you prepare to teach, read Isaiah 14:12-15 and Ezekiel 28:12-16, but do not read these verses to the people when you teach the lesson.

- **God gave an important position to Lucifer, who was one of the created spirits.**

    God didn't create all the spirits exactly the same. Some were wiser, more beautiful and more intelligent than others.

    The greatest angel was named Lucifer. God gave Lucifer an important position in Heaven. Lucifer was given a place of great authority and power over the other angels.

- **Lucifer rebelled against God.**

    Because Lucifer was created by God and given the highest position over all the other angels, he should have loved, obeyed and served God.

    But Lucifer became very proud of his beauty, intelligence and position. Lucifer decided that he wanted to take God's place as ruler over all things. Lucifer rebelled against God.

- **Lucifer was the first one to do evil.**

    What is evil? Evil is anything that is against what God wants or agrees with.

    Think about this. What did God want the angels to do? He wanted them to love Him and to obey Him, doing whatever He wanted them to do. Did Lucifer do what God, his creator, wanted? No! By rebelling against God and what God wanted him to do, Lucifer became the first one to do evil.

- **Other angels followed Lucifer in his rebellion.**

    Many of God's angels followed Lucifer in his revolt. They, too, rebelled against God. These angels chose to do evil. They chose to follow Lucifer, rather than to continue to obey and serve the only true God.

3) God knew what Lucifer and his spirit followers were thinking and planning.

- **God knew that Lucifer had become proud and wanted to take the place of his Maker.**

   God created all the spirits, and He knew exactly what they were thinking and planning. God knew Lucifer's thoughts and the thoughts of each of the rebellious spirits.

- **Nothing can be kept secret from God.**

   Nothing can surprise God. He knows everything before it ever happens. He knows what we are going to think before the thought even comes into our minds. He is everywhere. He sees everything. He knows everything.

- **God knew what Lucifer and his spirit followers were** planning.

   Do you think God would allow Lucifer to take His position? What do you think God's reaction was to Lucifer's selfish ambition?

4) God removed Lucifer and his spirit followers from their positions as God's servants.

- **God would not allow Lucifer to take His position.**

Lesson Developer: Use an illustration about a leader's response to someone who tries to take over the leader's position. For example:

> *If a man were chief over a village, would he let an inexperienced young man take his position? Should a wise and strong man allow a simple and weak man to take his position? Should a wise man allow his "big-headed" son to rule the household? No! Of course not!*

Who is wiser than God? Who is stronger than God? No one! Only He is the true God. He existed before all things, and He doesn't need anything to live. He lives by His own power, and He gives life to everything. He also gave life to Lucifer and the other spirits, so he would not allow Lucifer to take His place. No one can take God's place.

- **God removed Lucifer and the other rebellious angels from Heaven.**

   God, in His great anger against evil, removed Lucifer from his important position of leadership over the angels. God also removed the other rebellious spirits from their places of service in Heaven.

God is perfect and right in everything He thinks and does. Anyone who doesn't think and act like God cannot be His friend. God would not allow Lucifer and his spirit followers to continue to live in Heaven.

⑤ God prepared a terrible place of punishment for Lucifer and his spirit followers.

God prepared a large fire which will never be extinguished as a place of everlasting punishment for Lucifer and his spirit followers. This terrible place of punishment is called the Lake of Fire. One day, God will send Lucifer and his spirit followers to this terrible place of punishment.

Lesson Developer: The "Lake of Fire" can be a difficult concept to translate. Although the Lake of Fire is a real place, the language is figurative because the "lake" is not a "body of water." At these early stages in the teaching program, terminology such as "a large place of fire" or "a large fire" would be adequate. Be sure you communicate that this is a place of terrible and everlasting punishment.

Teacher: At this point, teach about the Lake of Fire in relationship to Satan and his spirit followers only. Do not teach that people are going to the Lake of Fire at this stage in the teaching program.

God will not tolerate disobedience. God always punishes those who fight against Him.

⑥ Lucifer and his spirit followers hate God.

- **Lucifer and his spirit followers hate God and every good thing that God loves.**

    Ever since God removed them from His service, Lucifer and these other spirits have been fighting against God and everything God does. Even today, they continue to fight against God.

- **Lucifer is now named Satan, and his spirit followers are named demons.**

    The name, Satan, means "enemy." Satan is God's great enemy. Satan fights against God day and night to try to stop the things God does. Satan's demons help Satan in opposing God.

☞ **Teacher:** Point to the names, "Lucifer (Satan) and the angels who followed Lucifer (demons)" on the chronological chart.

⑦ Satan and his spirit followers no longer live in Heaven.

- **Satan and his demons live all over the earth.**

    After Satan and his spirit followers were removed by God from their positions in Heaven, they began their evil work on the earth.

Satan and his demons now live all over the earth, but they are not like God. God is everywhere at the same time, but Satan and his demons are not able to be everywhere at the same time. Satan has many, many evil spirits who are under his command. They are doing whatever Satan tells them all over the world. Wherever there are people, Satan has some of his spirits doing his evil work.

Teacher: This point may prompt the people to begin asking questions about the spirits in which they believe. We must be careful not to appear to be attacking their beliefs in the early stages of teaching. However, if they ask, let the people know that all of the spirits in which they believe were originally the angels of God but are now under Satan's leadership.

Some have suggested that the seemingly good spirits in whom the people trust to help and heal them may be the angels of God. We have absolutely no scriptural basis for this idea. The unsaved are the children of Satan and are under his control. The angels of God take care of the children of God (Hebrews 1:14).

Although some demons present themselves as good and kind, they are deceivers. They may transform themselves, like Satan does, into angels of light, but they are still the servants of Satan and are deceiving the people (2 Corinthians 11:14).

It is very important that the people eventually realize that all the spirits in which they believe were created by God as good angels but are now followers of Satan. Understanding and accepting this truth, however, may take time.

Questions

1. Who was the most intelligent and beautiful angel created by God?

   Lucifer was the most intelligent and beautiful angel created by God.

2. What position did God give Lucifer?

   God gave Lucifer the position of leadership over all the other angels.

3. What evil thing did Lucifer want to do?

   Lucifer wanted to be like God and to take God's position.

4. Who followed Lucifer in his rebellion against God?

   Many of God's angels followed Lucifer in his rebellion against God.

5. Did God know what Lucifer and his followers were planning?

   Yes. God knew what Lucifer and his followers were planning.

6. What did God do in response to Lucifer's rebellion?

   God removed Lucifer and all the rebellious spirits from their positions as God's servants in Heaven.

7. Is there anything that God doesn't see, doesn't hear or doesn't know?

   No! God sees everything, hears everything and knows everything.

8. What did God prepare as a place of punishment for Lucifer and his demons?

   God prepared a large fire as a place of punishment for Lucifer and his demons.

9. What is Lucifer's name now?

   Lucifer's name is now Satan.

10. What does the name, "Satan," mean?

    Satan means "enemy."

11. Whom does Satan fight against?

    Satan fights against God.

LESSON 11: LET'S REVIEW WHAT WE HAVE LEARNED ABOUT GOD, MAN AND SATAN.

Scripture

Genesis 1, Genesis 2

Lesson Outline

(1) We are going to review what we have learned from God's Book.

(2) We have learned many things about God.

(3) We have learned many things about the spirits.

(4) We have learned many things about man.

> (?) **Do not ask Review Questions for Lesson 10** at the beginning of this session. The review questions from Lesson 10 are included as part of this lesson.

Lesson Outline Developed

Teacher: As we have taught through Genesis 1 and 2, we have introduced God, man and Satan, the three main characters in the whole historical drama recorded in the Scriptures. In the next lesson, we will begin to teach Genesis 3, one of the most important chapters in the whole Bible. The origins of man's sinfulness, death and all earth's miseries, along with the first promise of a Savior are revealed in Genesis 3. However, the historical and the doctrinal foundational truths of Genesis 3 cannot be grasped apart from a basic understanding of the character of God, man and Satan. So in order to ensure that our hearers really do comprehend these truths, this lesson will review the main points already taught.

We will review by asking questions. Many of the questions in this lesson were selected from the questions in the previous lessons, although some are new questions and some are worded a little differently.

Building on Firm Foundations
- Volume 2: Evangelism:
Genesis to The Ascension

① We are going to review what we have learned from God's Book.

Before we learn more about the story of Adam and Eve from God's Book, we are going to review what we have already learned about God, Satan and the first man and woman God created. We will begin by asking you some questions about God.

② We have learned many things about God.

- **Is there anything or anyone on this earth that did not have a beginning?**

  No. Nothing on this earth exists that didn't have a beginning.

- **Who is the only One who has always existed?**

  God is the only One who has always existed.

- **Did someone make God?**

  No one made God.

- **We were all born into this world. Was God also born?**

  No. God was not born.

- **Did God make Himself?**

  No. God did not make Himself.

- **Will God ever die?**

  No. God is eternal. He has always been alive, and He will never die.

- **Does God have a body of flesh and bones like we do?**

  No. God is Spirit.

- **We need food, water, air, the earth and the sun in order to live. What does God need?**

  God doesn't need anything.

- **Since God does not need food or water or air to live, by what power does He live?**

  He lives by His own power.

- **Where is God?**

  God is everywhere at the same time.

- **How many true gods are there according to the Bible?**

  There is only one true God.

- **Who are the three Persons who are the one God?**

LESSON 11: LET'S REVIEW WHAT WE HAVE LEARNED ABOUT GOD, MAN AND SATAN.

God the Father, God the Son, and God the Spirit are the three Persons who are the one God.

- **Who created the heavens and the earth and everything in them?**

  God created the heavens and the earth and everything in them.

- **What materials did God use to make the heavens and the earth?**

  God didn't use any materials to make the heavens and the earth. He created everything out of nothing.

- **How was it possible for God to make the heavens and the earth out of nothing?**

  God is all-powerful. Nothing is too difficult for God to do.

- **How did God create everything?**

  God created everything by just speaking.

- **How did God know how to make the heavens and the earth?**

  God knew how to make the heavens and the earth because God knows everything.

- **In the beginning, everything in the world was created perfect. Why was God able to make everything perfect?**

  God was able to make everything perfect because God is perfect.

- **God didn't need the things that He created. He didn't need light, or trees, or plants or anything else. For whom did God create these things?**

  God was preparing the earth for the people He planned to make. God is loving and kind. He prepared everything on the earth for us.

- **God created the sun to rise and set each day, and God made the moon and the stars to follow the same path every year. What does that show us about God?**

  This shows us that He is a God of law and order.

- **Why did God place the sun, moon and stars in the sky?**

  He placed the sun, moon and stars in the sky to show us the days, the months, the seasons and the years.

- **Who is greater than the earth, the sun, the moon, the stars, all people and all spirits?**

  God is greater than the earth, the sun, the moon, the stars, all people and all spirits.

- **Why is God the rightful owner of everything?**

  God is the owner of all things because He created everything.

③ We have learned many things about the spirits.

- **Where did all the spirits come from?**

  God created all the spirits.

- **Did God create the spirits with bodies?**

  No. God did not create the spirits with bodies.

- **Did God create some good spirits and some bad spirits?**

  No. God created them all good.

- **What was God's reason for creating the spirits?**

  God created the spirits to be His servants and His messengers, to love Him and obey Him.

- **Where did all the spirits live in the beginning when God created them?**

  When God first created them, the spirits all lived with God in Heaven.

- **God is everywhere at the same time. Can any of the spirits be everywhere at the same time?**

  No. None of the spirits can be everywhere at the same time.

- **Who watched as God created the heavens and the earth?**

  The spirits watched as God created the heavens and the earth.

- **What did the spirits do as they watched God create the heavens and the earth?**

  They praised Him for His great power and wisdom.

- **What name does God sometimes use in His book for the spirits who are His messengers?**

  God sometimes uses the name "angels" for the spirits who are His messengers.

- **Who was the most intelligent and beautiful angel created by God?**

  Lucifer was the most intelligent and beautiful angel created by God.

- **What position did God give Lucifer?**

  God gave Lucifer the position of leadership over all the other angels.

- **What evil thing did Lucifer want to do?**

  Lucifer wanted to be like God and to take God's position.

- **Who followed Lucifer in his rebellion against God?**

  Many of God's angels followed Lucifer in his rebellion against God.

LESSON 11: LET'S REVIEW WHAT WE HAVE LEARNED ABOUT GOD, MAN AND SATAN.

- What did God do in response to Lucifer's rebellion?

  God removed Lucifer and all the rebellious spirits from their positions as God's servants in Heaven.

- What did God prepare as a place of punishment for Lucifer and his demons?

  God prepared a large fire which will never be extinguished as a place of punishment for Lucifer and his demons.

- By what name is Lucifer now known?

  Lucifer is now known as Satan.

- What does the name "Satan" mean?

  Satan means "enemy."

- Whom does Satan fight against?

  Satan fights against God.

④ We have learned many things about man.

- After God had prepared the earth, whom did God create?

  God created Adam.

- What great difference was there between the creation of man and the creation of the animals?

  God made man in the "image of God." None of the animals were created in this way to be like God.

- What does it mean that God created man in His image?

  God created man to have, like God, a mind, emotions and a will.

- Why did God give man a mind?

  God gave man a mind so that man would have the ability to know God and communicate with God.

- Why did God give man emotions?

  God gave man emotions so that man would to be able to love God.

- Why did God give man a will?

  God gave man a will so that man would be able to choose to love and obey God.

- **Was man good or bad when God created him?**

  Man was good.

- **After God created Adam and Eve, He gave them a very important responsibility. What was that responsibility?**

  God gave them the responsibility to be managers of the earth and everything in it.

- **Where did God place Adam after He created him?**

  God placed Adam in a beautiful garden in Eden.

- **Why did God have the right to put Adam in the garden even though God didn't ask Adam if he wanted to live there?**

  God had created Adam, so Adam belonged to God. Therefore, God had the right to put Adam in the garden and tell Adam what to do.

- **God planted two special trees in the middle of the garden. What were the names of those trees?**

  The trees were named "the tree of life" and "the tree of the knowledge of good and evil."

- **God had told Adam that he could eat any of the fruit in the garden except for the fruit of one tree. What was the name of that tree?**

  The name of that tree was "the tree of the knowledge of good and evil."

- **Why did God have the right to tell Adam not to eat fruit from the tree of the knowledge of good and evil?**

  God had the right to tell Adam what to do because God created Adam and knew what was best for Adam. God loved Adam and was wiser than Adam.

- **What did God say would happen to Adam if he ate fruit from the tree of the knowledge of good and evil?**

  God said that Adam would die.

- **What did God mean when He said that Adam would die?**

  God meant that Adam would be separated from God, the source of his life. Adam would no longer be God's friend. Adam would die physically when his soul and spirit left his body. When his body died, he would be separated from God forever.

LESSON 11: LET'S REVIEW WHAT WE HAVE LEARNED ABOUT GOD, MAN AND SATAN.

- **Why did God have the right to demand obedience from Adam?**

  God had the right to demand obedience from Adam because He created him.

- **Who decided that Adam needed a wife as a companion?**

  God decided that Adam needed a wife as a companion.

- **Why was no animal suitable to be a companion for Adam?**

  Animals were not made in God's image. Animals are not interested in the same things as man, animals cannot do the things man can do, and animals cannot communicate like man can.

- **Why did God decide to make a wife for Adam?**

  God loved Adam and knew that it was not good for Adam to be alone.

- **How did God make the first woman?**

  God put Adam to sleep and took out one of Adam's ribs. God then made the first woman from Adam's rib.

- **Who told Adam and Eve to marry and to have children?**

  God told Adam and Eve to marry and have children.

- **How many men and women did God make in the beginning?**

  God created only one man and one woman.

- **Who are the ancestors of all peoplc?**

  Adam and Eve are the ancestors of all people.

LESSON 12: ADAM AND EVE DISOBEYED GOD.

Scripture

Genesis 3:1-6

Lesson Outline

(1) Satan entered into the snake to disguise himself. (Genesis 3:1)

(2) Satan tempted and deceived Eve. (Genesis 3:1-5)

(3) Eve ate the fruit and also gave some of the fruit to Adam. (Genesis 3:6)

> (?) **Review Questions from Lesson 10.** (Note that you should review with the students the questions from **Lesson 10, "Lucifer rebelled against God,"** at this time, and not the questions from Lesson 11.)

Lesson Outline Developed

(1) Satan entered into the snake to disguise himself.

- **Adam and Eve were living in the garden in Eden.**

  God had placed everything in the garden that Adam and Eve needed. They had a vast variety of fruits and vegetables to eat. Their surroundings were beautiful. God was their friend. He loved them, and they were very happy.

- **God's great enemy wanted to destroy Adam and Eve.**

  We talked before about God's great enemy, and we're going to talk about him again. Do you remember the name of God's enemy? Yes. God's enemy was named Satan.

  Before Satan had rebelled against God, he had seen God create man, and he knew that God loved Adam and Eve. Satan had seen God appoint Adam and Eve as managers over the earth and everything in it. Satan also knew about God's warning to Adam that they would die if they ate the fruit from the tree of the knowledge of good and evil.

Because Satan hates God, he wanted to destroy the man and woman that God had made.

- **Satan disguised himself so that he could deceive Eve.**

    📖 Read Genesis 3:1.

    This wasn't just a snake talking to Eve. Satan had entered into the snake to disguise himself so that he could deceive Eve. Satan chose to enter the snake because Eve would be more likely to listen to it than to any other animal. The snake was more clever than any other animal that God had made.

    Teacher: Don't get sidetracked into discussing whether animals could talk originally. We don't know, so we need to leave it at that.

    Satan deceived Eve when he didn't allow her to know that he was the one talking through the snake. And Satan still deceives people today. The more you learn from God's Book, the more you will realize how deceitful and wicked Satan is. Satan disguises himself so people will not realize that he is trying to trap them and destroy them.

    Lesson Developer: Use an illustration about someone who disguises a trap to catch an animal. For example,

    > *When you want to catch a wild pig in a trap, do you set the trap so the pig will see it? No! If the pig sees the trap, it will be frightened and run away. So what do you do? You disguise the trap. As you disguise your traps to deceive the pig, Satan disguises himself to deceive people.*

    Satan disguised himself so that Eve would not know that he was speaking to her. Eve thought the snake was talking to her. She did not know that God's enemy, Satan, was talking to her.

- **Satan still disguises himself so he can deceive people.**

    Satan does not speak today through snakes or other animals, but he still disguises himself so he can deceive people. Satan has continued to hide and disguise his activities so your forefathers would not know that he was speaking to them. Even today, Satan still hides and disguises himself so that he can trap and destroy people all over the world. He wants to deceive you and trap you too.

    Many times Satan deceives people by speaking lies directly into their minds. Satan doesn't let people know that he is the one who is speaking to them. They think that the thoughts in their minds are their own, but it is really Satan who is putting the thoughts into their minds. For example, Satan might speak to you even when you are listening to God's

LESSON 12: ADAM AND EVE DISOBEYED GOD.

Word. He may put a question into your mind, such as, "Why should I believe the Bible?" Satan is trying to trap you.

Sometimes, Satan uses other people to speak his lies to turn people away from the truth which God tells us in His book. For example, someone may ask you questions like these, "How do you know that the missionary is telling you the truth? Are you sure the Bible is true?" Others may say, "That Bible you are listening to is just the missionaries' beliefs. We don't need that. We have our own ways and beliefs." Beware! Satan uses people even though they do not realize it. He will put thoughts into their minds and words in their mouths to try to keep you from listening to the truth. Satan does not want anyone to believe the truth of God. He does not want you to believe the Bible.

Satan also speaks through the spirits in this world. Your ancestors thought that it was the spirits of the trees and the spirits of the jungle who spoke to them. You also think the same thing. Consider, however, what we have learned from God's Word. Who are the spirits of the trees and the spirits of the jungle? The spirits that you know are those spirits who followed Satan when he rebelled against God. Satan uses these spirits to tell you his lies. He wants to keep you from believing the words of God.

Satan traps people everywhere by causing them to believe lies. Satan doesn't want anyone to believe God and the truth. He doesn't want you to believe God's Word. Beware! He will try to deceive you just as he deceived Eve. Satan is clever, and he will disguise himself so you do not know that he is the one who is telling you lies.

Teacher: The people you are teaching need to understand that Satan is a deceiver. They need to realize that, throughout hundreds of years, Satan has lied to and deceived their ancestors, and he has also deceived them.

Be praying that the people will realize that truth is to be found in the Scriptures alone. Their own religious beliefs are the deceptions of Satan. Do not try to prove that their beliefs are false. Instead, clearly teach the truth and pray that God will show the people that the Bible is true. Trust God to work in their hearts. The time will come when God will expose to them Satan's destructive schemes. Do not hurry or jump ahead as you teach. Give the Holy Spirit time to work. Teaching this way is like planting seeds, watering them, and waiting for the plants to grow.

The people also need to come to realize that all people are either under God's control or under Satan's control. Man was created a physical and spiritual being; therefore, he belongs to the spiritual realm as well as the physical realm. Man is either being guided and directed by Satan, the "god of this world," or he is being guided and directed by the true God, the owner and creator of all things.

Lesson Developer: To illustrate Satan's evil intentions, tell a story about someone who has been deceived and destroyed by his enemy. For example:

Building on Firm Foundations
- Volume 2: Evangelism:
Genesis to The Ascension

> 💡 *I want to tell you a story. It is not about real people, but it has an important meaning for every one of you.*
>
> *There was a man who had everything that he needed. He had a good rice field, a strong house, a large coconut plantation and a water buffalo. He had everything that a person could want. But he also had an enemy who hated him and planned to destroy him.*
>
> *One night, this enemy hid and waited in the bushes on the side of the trail. When the man came along, his enemy attacked him and deliberately blinded him. As a result, the man could no longer enjoy the things that he possessed. He could no longer go out and tend his rice field or harvest his coconuts. Soon, he was in a terrible, poverty-stricken condition.*
>
> *One day, after having endured this condition for a long time, he was sitting in his house which was now dilapidated and falling down. While sitting there, he heard a voice calling him, "Friend." He was scared. He wondered who it could be. He didn't answer immediately, but when the person persistently called him, "Friend," he answered and invited the caller to come into his house.*
>
> *The visitor offered to help the blind man. He brought gifts and was very kind. He led the blind man by the hand down to the river so he could bathe. Gradually, he won the blind man's confidence and trust. The blind man became more and more dependent on this man whom he now believed was his friend and helper.*
>
> *But one day, this man said to the blind man, "Today, we are going for a long walk." He spoke to the blind man in such a soothing, friendly manner that the blind man trustingly stepped out of his house and gave his hand to the man to go ahead of him as his guide.*
>
> *That man who claimed to be his friend led the blind man through the jungle; but suddenly as the blind man put his foot forward, the man who was leading him pulled his hand away. There was nothing beneath the feet of the blind man. As he felt himself falling over a cliff, he heard laughter and jeering above him. As he fell to his death, he recognized the voice and the laughter of his enemy, the one who had blinded him.*

This is like what Satan did to your ancestors. Satan blinded their minds so they would not know and understand God. Satan tricked them and convinced them to trust him. Through the spirits who are his servants, Satan controlled your ancestors' whole lives. He promised your ancestors many things, and he still promises you many things. At times you think that the spirits help you when you have troubles and sickness. This is just what Satan wants you to believe. Satan's real purpose in having his spirits help you is to keep you in his power so that he can destroy you.

Teacher: Satan does powerful things, but Satan does these things for his own purpose. He desires to destroy all people. Make it clear to the people that what appear to be good things done by the spirits originated in the evil mind of Satan. He wants to trick the people to bring about their final destruction.

Satan is glad when people will not listen to God's Word because he wants all people to remain under his control and to be destroyed.

LESSON 12: ADAM AND EVE DISOBEYED GOD.

② Satan tempted and deceived Eve.

📖 Read Genesis 3:1 again.

Satan asked Eve this question even though he knew exactly what God had said. Satan deliberately changed what God had said to Adam because he was planning to deceive Eve.

📖 Read Genesis 3:2-3.

- **When Eve replied, she added words to God's command.**

God did not say that they could not touch the fruit from the tree of knowledge of good and evil. God had said that they must not eat the fruit.

Let's read what God had said.

📖 Read Genesis 2:16-17.

- **God's command was for both Adam and Eve.**

God spoke this command to Adam. Even though God did not speak the command directly to Eve, the command was for her to obey too. Whatever God said to Adam was also for Eve.

The Bible was given to people many years ago, but the Bible is still God's message to all of us today. God doesn't have a different message for different people. It is the same to everyone – no matter what color your skin is or how old you are or if you are a man or a woman. What He says to me in the Bible, He also says to you.

📖 Read Genesis 3:4-5.

- **Satan said the opposite from what God had told Adam.**

God had said that Adam would die if he ate the fruit from the tree of knowledge of good and evil. Satan said that Adam would not die. By saying the opposite from what God had said, Satan was calling God a liar.

God had told Adam that if he ate the fruit from the tree of the knowledge of good and evil, he would die that same day. God meant that Adam and Eve would be separated from God, the One who gave them life.

God said that they would die. Satan said that they would not die. Who do you think was telling the truth? Was God telling the truth, or was Satan telling the truth?

Teacher: Allow them to answer these questions. If they say that God was telling the truth, you can praise God that the people are understanding the truth of God's Word.

- **Satan was lying in order to trick Eve.**

    Satan wanted Eve and Adam to rebel against God just as he had done previously. Satan had wanted to take God's place. He didn't want to obey God any more. Instead, he wanted to be independent of God and rule his own life. Now he was trying to make Eve think that it would be to their advantage if she and Adam ate the fruit and were independent of God.

    When Satan told Eve that she could eat the fruit and would not die, he was lying so he could deceive her. He knew that disobedience to God would be punished by death. But Satan was trying to make her think that she could be equal with God. He wanted her to think that she wouldn't need God to tell her what was right and what was wrong. But God didn't make people to live by their own ideas and thoughts. God made us to be guided by the words of God. It doesn't matter what I think, what you think, what other people think, or what Satan and the spirits say. The important thing is what God says.

③ Eve ate the fruit and also gave some of the fruit to Adam.

📖 Read Genesis 3:6.

☞ **Teacher:** Show a picture of Adam and Eve eating the fruit from the tree of the knowledge of good and evil.

- **Satan deceived Eve, and she believed him.**

    Eve believed that Satan was telling the truth. Satan had tricked her and made her think that if she ate the fruit she would be wise like God. Satan tempted Eve to disobey God's command by eating the fruit from the tree of the knowledge of good and evil. Eve was deceived by Satan's lie, and she disobeyed God.

- **Adam deliberately disobeyed God's command.**

    Even though Adam knew that God had said not to eat the fruit from the tree of knowledge of good and evil, he ate it anyway. When he disobeyed God's command, Adam deliberately turned away from depending on God. He wanted to be independent of God. He wanted to decide for himself what was good and what was evil.

    Adam didn't want God to rule over him any more. Instead of allowing God to be first in his heart, Adam put himself first. He wanted to be his own boss and do whatever he wanted to do.

    Did God have the right to rule over Adam? Yes. God was his creator. Everything he had came from God so God had the right to rule over him.

    Does God have the right to tell us what to do? Yes. All that we have comes from God. He gave us our life so He has the right to tell us what to do.

? Questions

1. What did God's enemy, Satan, want to do to the man and woman that God had made?
   Satan wanted to destroy the man and woman that God had made.

2. Why did Satan want to destroy Adam and Eve?
   Satan wanted to destroy Adam and Eve because God had made them and he hates God.

3. Did Satan come and talk to Eve face to face so that she could see him and know who he was?
   No. Satan disguised himself so that Eve would not know who he was.

4. What did Satan enter into in order to disguise himself when he spoke to Eve?
   Satan entered into a snake to disguise himself.

5. Does Satan still deceive and trap people today?
   Yes. Satan still deceives and traps people.

6. What are ways that Satan deceives people today?
   Sometimes, Satan deceives people by speaking lies right into their minds. Sometimes, Satan uses other people to speak his lies. And sometimes, Satan uses the spirits to tell his lies.

7. Why does Satan deceive people today?
   Satan deceives people so he can destroy them.

8. God had told Adam that they would die if they ate the fruit from the tree of the knowledge of good and evil. Satan told Eve that they would not die if they ate the fruit. By saying the opposite from what God had said, what was Satan suggesting God to be?
   Satan was suggesting that God was a liar.

9. What did Satan tell Eve would happen if they ate the fruit from the tree of knowledge of good and evil?
   Satan said that they would become like God and be able to decide for themselves what is good and what is evil.

10. What did Eve do when Satan tricked her?
    Eve believed that Satan was telling the truth, and she ate the fruit.

11. What did Adam do when Eve gave him the fruit?

    Adam deliberately disobeyed God's command.

12. By eating the fruit, what was Adam deciding to do?

    When he ate the fruit, Adam was deciding to be independent of God.

13. Why did God have the right to rule over Adam?

    God was his creator. Everything he had came from God so God had the right to rule over him.

LESSON 13: ADAM AND EVE'S SIN SEPARATED THEM FROM GOD.

Scripture

Genesis 3:7-8

Lesson Outline

1. When Adam and Eve sinned, they were immediately separated from God. (Genesis 3:7-8)

2. Adam and Eve's attitudes and actions showed that they had become separated from God. (Genesis 3:7-8)

3. Satan led Adam and Eve to disobey God because Satan hates God and people.

4. This story teaches us many things.

> (?) Review Questions from Lesson 12.

Lesson Outline Developed

1. When Adam and Eve sinned, they were immediately separated from God.

📖 Read Genesis 3:7-8.

God had told Adam and Eve that they would die if they ate fruit from the tree of knowledge of good and evil. What did God mean by "die"? They didn't die physically at the moment when they ate the fruit. They were still alive. Does this mean that what God said would happen didn't come true? Had God lied to them? Was Satan right after all? No!

Teacher: In Lesson 8, you brought to the teaching session a branch that you had broken off from a tree as an illustration of what death means. You explained that the branch could not continue to live once it had been separated from its source of life. Likewise, if Adam disobeyed God, he, too, would be separated from God, the source of his life.

Show that same branch as you teach this lesson. By now, the evidences of death will be clearly visible. Seeing an actual object that has been broken off from its source of life will help make it clear that Adam and Eve were cut off from God, their source of life. Keep this branch to use as an illustration in Lesson 16.

Here is the branch that I previously broke off from a tree. When I broke the branch off, the leaves still looked fresh and alive. But as soon as the branch was no longer joined to the tree from which it had received life, the branch began to die. The branch didn't look dead right away, but it started to die the moment that it was separated from its source of life.

The same thing happened to Adam and Eve. Death wasn't evident in their bodies on the day they disobeyed God. They were still breathing. They were still walking around. But they had died to God. That part of them that was made in God's image so they could know, love and obey God was immediately separated from God when they disobeyed His command. Disobedience to God's commands is sin.

God always does what He says. God doesn't threaten to punish sin and then not do it. God faithfully carries out what He says He will do. God hates everything that is wrong and punishes all disobedience to His commands. The punishment for sin is death.

Because of Adam and Eve's sin, their relationship to God was now dead. Their bodies would also eventually die, and they would be separated from God forever. Because they had joined Satan in his rebellion against God, immediately when they died physically, they would go to the place of everlasting punishment that God prepared for Satan and the evil spirits.

- **Adam and Eve had become the enemies of God.**

Because God is holy and righteous, He will not continue in friendship with those who disobey His commands. Because Adam and Eve disobeyed God, they were cut off from their friendship with Him. They were no longer in oneness with God. They had taken sides with God's great enemy, Satan.

Lesson Developer: Use an illustration to help the people understand what happens when one's friend sides with one's enemy. For example:

LESSON 13: ADAM AND EVE'S SIN SEPARATED THEM FROM GOD.

> *If a friend of yours turned away from you and began to follow the thinking and the ways of an enemy who hated you and wanted to kill you, wouldn't your friend also have become your enemy?*

Satan is God's great enemy. Adam and Eve turned away from God and followed Satan, so they, too, became the enemies of God.

② Adam and Eve's attitudes and actions showed that they had become separated from God.

When Adam and Eve sinned, they were immediately separated from God. Their attitudes and actions showed that their relationship with God had died.

Teacher: Show a picture of Adam and Eve wearing fig leaf coverings and hiding from God.

- **First, their attitudes toward their bodies changed immediately.**

  Read Genesis 3:7 again.

Before Adam and Eve disobeyed God, they were naked but were not embarrassed. But, once they were separated from God because of their sin, their thoughts were no longer under God's control. Their thoughts had become evil, and their attitude toward their bodies changed. They were embarrassed by their naked bodies.

- **Secondly, they tried to provide for their own needs.**

Before they were separated from God, they looked to God to provide everything they needed. But once they were separated from God, they tried to do things for themselves. They clothed themselves with fig leaves. They no longer trusted God to give them whatever they needed. They were trying to live independently of God.

- **Thirdly, they tried to hide from God.**

  Read Genesis 3:8 again.

God loved Adam and Eve, and so He came to talk with them. Before they were separated from God, they loved Him and wanted to talk with Him. But when God came to visit with them after they had disobeyed Him, Adam and Eve hid. They no longer wanted to talk with Him.

Lesson Developer: Use an illustration about friends who have different opinions and no longer want to be together. For example:

> *If two friends quarrel, will they continue to fish and hunt together? Will they talk and laugh together like they did before they quarreled? No! People who are of different opinions and attitudes or who have had an argument don't want to be together.*

Adam and Eve's attitude toward God had changed. Because of their disobedience to God, they were no longer His friends. When God first made Adam and Eve, they were of one mind with God. But as soon as they disobeyed God, their thinking was different. They were of one mind with Satan. They could no longer know and understand God, and they didn't love God any more. They were under Satan's control. They were on Satan's side.

- **Because they had disobeyed God's command, Adam and Eve were afraid of God.**

Lesson Developer: Use an illustration about how children hide when they have disobeyed their parents. For example:

> *When your children deliberately disobey you, do they want to be near you? Can they look you in the eye? Are they happy to be in your presence? No! Children who have deliberately disobeyed want to avoid their parents.*

When God created Adam and Eve, they didn't fear anything. They were not afraid of God because He was their friend. Everything in the world was good and beautiful. No animals would hurt them. Sickness and death did not exist. But after Adam and Eve sinned, they were afraid.

Do you think that Adam and Eve were right to be afraid of God? Would God really punish them for their disobedience?

Lesson Developer: Use an illustration about how some people get angry, but fail to carry out their threats. For example:

> *When someone gets really angry, he might threaten to kill someone, but later, when his anger cools, he doesn't do anything. The things he said were only idle threats.*

Does God merely give idle threats? Think about what happened to Lucifer and the angels who rebelled against God. Did God merely threaten them when they rebelled? No! God removed them from their place of service in Heaven.

What about Adam and Eve? God had created them to depend upon Him for everything. He had given them the very breath in their bodies. All that they had came from Him. But Adam and Even had disobeyed their creator. They had separated themselves from their source of life.

- **It was right for Adam and Eve to be afraid of God.**

    Adam and Eve had disobeyed God, and He always punishes those who disobey His commands.

    Disobedience to God is the reason that we have fear in the world. Think about this. When God first created Adam and Eve, they had no fear. Fear came because of sin.

    Ever since Adam and Eve disobeyed God, there has been terrible fear in the hearts of men and women.

    Teacher: Ask them, "What things do you fear?" Give the people the opportunity to discuss some of their fears or the fears that their people generally have. During the discussion, remind them that fear came into the world because of sin.

- **Adam and Eve were afraid of God, so they tried to hide from Him.**

    Do you think that God saw them? Of course He did. God saw Adam and Eve when they were trying to hide among the trees.

    Can anyone hide from God? Is there anywhere we can go where God is not already there? No! God is everywhere. No one can hide from Him.

    When people do things that they know are wrong, they usually try to do them when other people cannot see them. People do evil things in the dark. But God can see in the darkness just as He can see in the light. People may try to hide their evil actions by going to the jungle where others cannot see them. But nothing can be hidden from God.

    God has heard everything that you have said and He has seen everything that you have done from the day that you were born.

③ Satan led Adam and Eve to disobey God because Satan hates God and people.

God created Lucifer, but he became proud and wanted God's position. Therefore, God removed Lucifer from his position of service in Heaven.

Satan still hates God, and he fights against God all the time. He does all he can to hinder God's plans for man.

Satan not only hates God, but he also hates people. Because God created people to know, love and obey God, Satan and his spirit followers hate all people.

Because Satan hates all people, he wants them to go to the place of everlasting punishment that God prepared for Satan and his spirit followers. Satan doesn't want anyone to listen to God's Word. He doesn't want you to hear, understand and believe the Bible.

Building on Firm Foundations
- Volume 2: Evangelism:
Genesis to The Ascension

④ This story teaches us many things.

We should learn many things from this story.

- **We should learn that God always tells the truth.**

    When Adam and Eve disobeyed God, they were separated from Him, just as He said they would be.

- **We should learn that Satan is a liar.**

    Satan said that Adam and Eve would not die if they disobeyed God, even though he knew that they would be separated from God and die. Satan lied.

- **We should learn that Satan is a murderer.**

    Satan wanted Adam and Eve to die, so he tempted them to sin by deceiving them. He deceived them by lying to them.

Teacher: As you prepare to teach, read John 8:44, but do not read this verse to the people when you teach the lesson.

Beware! Satan is still the same today. He doesn't want you to listen to God's Word because he wants all of you to be separated from God forever.

❓ Questions

1. God said that Adam and Eve would die if they ate the fruit from the tree of the knowledge of good and evil. Satan said they would not die. Who spoke the truth?

    God spoke the truth.

2. Adam and Eve didn't die physically at the moment when they ate the fruit from the tree of the knowledge of good and evil. In what way did they die?

    Adam and Eve were separated from God, the source of their life.

3. What did Adam and Eve do when they realized they were naked?

    They made clothes of leaves for themselves.

4. What did Adam and Eve do when they heard God in the garden in Eden, after they had disobeyed Him?

    Adam and Eve hid.

**LESSON 13: ADAM AND EVE'S SIN
SEPARATED THEM FROM GOD.**

5. Is it possible to hide from God?

   No! It is not possible to hide from God.

6. Adam and Eve hid from God because they were afraid of Him. Did they have a reason to be afraid of God?

   Yes. Adam and Even had disobeyed their creator, and God always punishes those who disobey His commands.

7. When Adam and Eve ate the fruit from the tree of the knowledge of good and evil, were they still friends of God?

   No. They became God's enemies.

8. Does Satan want you to listen to and believe God's words?

   No. Satan does not want us to listen to and believe God's words.

9. Why doesn't Satan want people to hear and believe God's words?

   Satan hates God, and Satan hates the people whom God created.

10. What is Satan's desire for all people?

    Satan wants all people to be separated from God forever.

LESSON 14: GOD JUDGED ADAM AND PLACED A CURSE ON THE EARTH, AND HE PROMISED TO SEND THE DELIVERER.

Scripture

Genesis 3:9-20

Lesson Outline

1. God called out to Adam. (Genesis 3:9)
2. Adam and Eve tried to hide from God. (Genesis 3:10)
3. God questioned Adam. (Genesis 3:11)
4. Adam blamed Eve, and Eve blamed the snake. (Genesis 3:12-13)
5. God cursed the snake. (Genesis 3:14)
6. God promised to send the Deliverer. (Genesis 3:15)
7. God said Eve would suffer because of her sin. (Genesis 3:16)
8. God said Adam would suffer because of his sin. (Genesis 3:17-19)
9. Adam and Eve are the ancestors of all people. (Genesis 3:20)

(?) Review Questions from Lesson 13.

Lesson Outline Developed

1) God called out to Adam.

God loved Adam and Eve and wanted to be with them. Before they were separated from God, they, too, enjoyed being with Him. But when they knew God was there to visit with them after they had disobeyed Him, Adam and Eve hid. Listen to what God did.

📖 Read Genesis 3:9.

- **Why did God call out to Adam?**

    Didn't God know where they were hiding? Isn't He everywhere? Wasn't He there beside them among the trees? Couldn't He see them all of the time? Yes! God knew where they were hiding. God knows everything, and God is everywhere. God could see Adam and Eve where they were hiding.

- **So why did He call out to Adam?**

    God called out to Adam because God still loved Adam and Eve. Even though Adam and Eve had disobeyed, God still loved them. And even though God intended to punish them for their sin, He still loved them. So God called out to them because He wanted Adam and Eve to come to Him voluntarily and admit their sin. He wanted them to agree with Him that they were wrong to believe Satan, and He wanted them to agree that all He had said to them was the truth.

- **God calls out to people today.**

    God has not changed. He still calls out to us today, even though we cannot hear His voice like Adam did.

- **How does God speak to people today?**
- **God speaks to us through all the things we can see around us.**

    We know that God exists and we know what His character is like because of the things He created and we enjoy. Every day, as we see all the things God has created, God is saying to us, "I am the true God, and I am the creator of all things. Look at all I have created for you. This shows you that I am almighty and that I love you. Listen to me and seek Me."

Teacher: As you prepare to teach, read Psalm 19:1-4, but do not read these verses to the people. When you are teaching, mention those specific parts of creation that the people naturally notice or that play an important part in their lives. These things show God's character to your hearers.

- **God is also speaking to us through the Bible.**

    The Bible is God's message to everyone in the world. It is God's message to you personally. God wants you to know, understand and believe His message.

② Adam and Eve tried to hide from God.

📖 Read Genesis 3:10.

Adam and Eve were afraid of God because they had disobeyed His command.

LESSON 14: GOD JUDGED ADAM AND PLACED A CURSE ON THE EARTH, AND HE PROMISED TO SEND THE DELIVERER.

Lesson Developer: Use an illustration about someone hiding because he has sinned. For example:

> *If a person is stealing vegetables from a garden and he hears the owner of the garden coming, what will the thief do? Yes. He will hide just as Adam and Eve did.*

Adam and Eve hid, but God could see Adam and Eve where they were hiding.

③ God questioned Adam.

📖 Read Genesis 3:11.

Did God already know the answer to these questions? Yes! God already knew the answers. So why did God question Adam? Because God was giving Adam the opportunity to repent, that is, to change his mind and agree with God that he had done the wrong thing.

- **Both Adam and Eve belonged to God.**

  God had created Adam, and then He made Eve from Adam's rib.

  Because God was their rightful owner, God had the authority to hold them accountable. Adam and Eve had to answer to God for what they did.

- **God is our rightful owner.**

  God has given life to all people. Each of us will have to answer to Him for everything we have thought and done during our lives. God wanted Adam and Eve to acknowledge that they had sinned, so God questioned them.

④ Adam blamed Eve, and Eve blamed the snake.

📖 Read Genesis 3:12-13.

- **Adam and Eve would not take personal responsibility for what they had done.**

  When a person gets caught for something he does wrong, he usually tries to blame someone else. Sometimes an innocent person is punished because the one who did wrong puts the blame on him.

- **No one can deceive God.**

  We may be able to deceive other people into punishing someone else for our sin, but can we deceive God so that He will punish someone else for our sins? No! God sees and knows the truth about each person. We cannot escape God's punishment by blaming someone else. Adam blamed Eve, and Eve blamed the serpent, but God already knew everything that had happened. Nothing is hidden from Him.

⑤ God cursed the snake.

📖 Read Genesis 3:14.

God cursed the snake because it had been used by Satan. God does not tell us how the snake moved around when God first created it, but we know it did not crawl on its belly. After Satan had used it to deceive Eve, God said it must crawl on its belly and eat dust.

⑥ God promised to send the Deliverer.

- **Adam and Eve were under Satan's control.**

When Adam and Eve disobeyed God and submitted to Satan's control, their relationship with God was broken. They were no longer God's children. They were Satan's children and were under Satan's control. As we learn more and more from the Bible, it will become clear that from the time Adam obeyed Satan, Satan began to lead most people to do the things Satan wanted them to do.

Satan probably thought that he had defeated God. He probably thought that he would have complete control of the world and all people. But no one can win against God. He is the Almighty Creator.

- God promised that He would send a Deliverer who would overcome Satan and deliver people from Satan's power.

📖 Read Genesis 3:15.

God planned that the promised Deliverer would be the child of a virgin woman.

God did not mean that the Deliverer would literally crush the serpent's head but that the Deliverer would fight against Satan and overcome him. Satan would not literally hurt the heel of the Deliverer. Satan would fight against the Deliverer, but Satan would not be able to defeat the Deliverer. The Deliverer would defeat Satan He would destroy Satan and deliver people from Satan's power. Through the promised Deliverer, people would no longer need to stay separated from God.

LESSON 14: GOD JUDGED ADAM AND PLACED A CURSE ON THE EARTH, AND HE PROMISED TO SEND THE DELIVERER.

Teacher: In the Bible, the head always refers to authority. Placing the foot on the neck or head indicated victory (Joshua 10:24). Genesis 3:15 tells us that the promised Deliverer would defeat Satan and crush the authority and power that Satan had gained over the world and over man.

The story of redemption begins here in Genesis 3:15. Starting with this lesson, you will point forward to the coming Deliverer. You will not yet reveal who fulfilled this prophecy and promise because the Old Testament does not reveal the specific identity of the Savior. Wait to reveal His identity when you teach on Jesus' birth from the New Testament. Do not jump ahead of the story, but continually point forward to the coming Deliverer.

- **We have already learned many things about God.**

    What have we learned about God as we have studied the Bible?

Teacher: Give the people opportunity to talk about what they have learned about God's character. Ask questions as necessary to bring out the following attributes:

- God is eternal. He never had a beginning. He will never have an end.
- God is all-powerful.
- God knows everything.
- God is everywhere all of the time.
- God is loving and kind.
- God is holy and righteous.
- God punishes those who rebel against Him and disobey His commands.

Today, we learn something new about God. By promising to send the Deliverer, God was showing us that He is merciful and gracious.

- **God is loving, merciful and gracious.**

    Adam and Eve deserved to die and go to everlasting punishment. Adam and Eve had disobeyed God, and as a result, they were immediately separated from God. God could have abandoned them. But instead, God promised the Deliverer who would make a way to deliver them and all people from Satan's control. This Deliverer would provide the way for man to come back to God. God promised to send the Deliverer because He is merciful and gracious.

Lesson Developer: Use a story to explain the concepts of mercy and grace. For example:

> 💡 Suppose that a man whom I had never met came to my house. This man had big tropical ulcers on his legs, and he desperately needed medical help. So I gave him medicine, and I dressed his ulcers. I also gave him a meal. I was very kind to him. But as the man left my house, he saw a pair of my shorts on the clothesline. He quickly stole them and put them in his bag. I saw him do it.
>
> Suppose that the next day, he came back again, asking for my help. I took the dirty bandages off his legs and cleaned up his ulcers. When lunchtime came, I fed him again. I was very kind to him even though he didn't deserve my kindness even though he actually deserved to be punished.
>
> When he first came to me, he had done nothing to deserve my love or my kindness, but the second time he came to me, he had done something to deserve punishment from me. Nevertheless, I still helped him and gave him food. By giving him what he did not deserve, I was being gracious. By not punishing him for stealing from me, I was being merciful.

God had given Adam and Eve everything they needed when He created them. God did not have to give so many good things to them, but He did because God is loving and kind. But when Adam and Eve rebelled against God, they deserved the wrath of God. Did God immediately send them to everlasting punishment? No! Because He is merciful and gracious, God promised to send the Deliverer to save them from the punishment they deserved.

Teacher: In the beginning, God, the Creator, showed His love and kindness by giving man everything that he needed. This was not grace. But when man turned against God and deliberately disobeyed His command, God reached out to save undeserving man. That is the grace of God!

⑦ God said Eve would suffer because of her sin.

📖 Read Genesis 3:16.

God spoke to Eve and told her that, because she had disobeyed the Lord, she would suffer in childbirth. God also said that her desire would be for her husband, and that her husband would have authority over her.

⑧ God said Adam would suffer because of his sin.

📖 Read Genesis 3:17-19.

- **Adam and Eve fell into Satan's trap because they listened to Satan.**

    Satan deceived Eve, and then Satan used Eve to tempt Adam to sin against God. Adam listened to Eve instead of remembering what God had said to him. Satan used

LESSON 14: GOD JUDGED ADAM AND PLACED A CURSE ON THE EARTH, AND HE PROMISED TO SEND THE DELIVERER.

Eve to lead Adam away from the truth.

Lesson Developer: Help the people realize that Satan sometimes uses other people to try to make us turn away from listening to the Word of God. For example:

> *Sometimes members of our own family try to stop us from listening to God's Word. Husbands might try to hinder wives from coming to hear God's message. Wives might encourage their husbands to cling to the old beliefs and refuse the truth from the Bible. Parents might tell their children not to listen to God's message. Children might even try to hinder parents from listening to God's talk. This is the way Satan works.*

You must be careful, because Satan will try to stop you from listening to God. Satan may even try to use you to lead others away from God's truth. If you listen to Satan and believe him instead of God, not only will you go to everlasting punishment but you also may cause others to do the same.

Lesson Developer: Use an illustration about a blind person leading another blind person. For example:

> *What will happen if a blind person leads another blind person down a path where pig traps have been set? Both of them will probably be killed.*

If you listen to Satan and believe him instead of God, you will be like a blind person. You won't be able to see the right path, and you won't be able to recognize Satan's traps. If you try to influence other people by turning them away from God's Word, you will be like a blind person leading another blind person. You will both fall into Satan's trap as Adam and Eve did. You will both go to everlasting punishment.

Because Adam and Eve listened to Satan, they fell into his trap and disobeyed God.

- **Because Adam sinned, God cursed the ground.**

  Before he sinned against God, Adam took care of the garden. Everything grew without Adam doing any hard work. But when Adam sinned, God cursed the earth so that many weeds began to grow. This made Adam's work hard.

- **Because Adam sinned, God told Adam that his body would die.**

  God had made Adam's body from the dust of the ground. Because Adam sinned, God told Adam that his body would die and go back to the dust of the earth. When God created Adam and Eve, He did not intend for them to die. But because of their disobedience to Him, Adam and Eve would die.

This is why your ancestors died, and it is also why people die today. You know that people die. People here in your village have died, and people all over the world have died. The punishment for sin is death – physical death and then separation from God forever in the place of everlasting punishment.

- **All the bad things in the world are here because Adam disobeyed God.**

    Think about the hard things that you face in your lives.

    - You have to work hard.
    - The ground produces thorns and weeds.
    - Your women suffer pain in childbirth.
    - You face devastating storms or droughts.
    - Many plants, snakes and spiders are poisonous.
    - Many animals are ferocious.
    - You have sickness and sorrow.
    - And you face death.

    The Bible teaches that all these things are in the world because Adam disobeyed God.

Teacher: The people know through experience the reality of the curse. They will have their own cultural beliefs about each aspect of the curse. You will need to teach clearly the true reason for the struggles that they face in this world.

⑨ Adam and Eve are the ancestors of all people.

📖 Read Genesis 3:20.

Eve was the first woman; therefore, she became the mother of all humanity. Adam was the first man; therefore, he became the father and original ancestor of every human being. Even though people have different colors of skin and different features, we all originally came from the same ancestors – Adam and Eve.

Adam was separated from God because he turned away from obeying Him. Because of his sin, Adam died. This meant that all his descendants would also die. All people everywhere die because all are descendants of Adam.

Teacher: The truth that all people die because they are descended from Adam (Romans 5:12; 1 Corinthians 15:21-22) is a very important part of our teaching. Do not brush over it. Establish it clearly in the understanding of your hearers.

LESSON 14: GOD JUDGED ADAM AND PLACED A CURSE ON THE EARTH, AND HE PROMISED TO SEND THE DELIVERER.

(?) Questions

1. Adam and Eve hid when they knew God had come to the garden to visit with them. Can anyone hide from God?

    No. God sees us, even if we try to hide.

2. Why did God call out to Adam?

    God called out to Adam because He wanted Adam and Eve to voluntarily come to him and admit their sin.

3. Why did God have the right to question Adam and to hold him accountable for his actions?

    God had the right because He had created Adam and therefore was his rightful owner.

4. Why are all people accountable to God for what they have done?

    All people are accountable to God because He gave life to all people.

5. What was God's curse on the snake?

    God cursed the snake so that it had to crawl on its belly and eat dust.

6. Whom did God promise to send?

    God promised to send a Deliverer who would be the son of a virgin.

7. What did God say that the virgin's son would do?

    He would overcome Satan and deliver people from death and Satan's power.

8. Did Adam and Eve deserve God's love and His promise of the Deliverer?

    No. Adam and Eve deserved to go to everlasting punishment.

9. Adam and Eve deserved to be punished for their sin, but God promised to send the Deliverer. What does this show us about God?

    It shows us that God is loving, merciful and gracious.

10. What did God say that Eve would suffer because of her sin?

    God said that Eve would suffer in childbirth.

11. What did God say that Adam would suffer because of his sin?

    God said that Adam's future work in growing food would be hard and that his body would die and go back to the dust of the earth.

12. What was God's curse on the earth?

    God cursed the earth so that many weeds began to grow.

13. What are some things we see today that are the result of Adam and Eve's sin and God's curse on the earth?

    Sickness, sorrow, pain in childbirth, death, hard work, thorns and weeds, droughts, devastating storms, poisonous plants, snakes and spiders, and ferocious animals are all results of Adam and Eve's sin and God's curse on the earth.

14. Who were the ancestors of all people?

    Adam and Eve were the ancestors of all people.

15. Why do all people die?

    All people everywhere die because all are descendants of Adam.

LESSON 15: GOD PROVIDED CLOTHING FOR ADAM AND EVE, AND HE PUT THEM OUT OF THE GARDEN.

Scripture

Genesis 3:21-24

Lesson Outline

(1) God provided clothing for Adam and Eve. (Genesis 3:21)

(2) God put Adam and Eve out of the garden, away from the tree of life. (Genesis 3:22-23)

(3) God put cherubim and a flaming sword to keep them away from the tree of life. (Genesis 3:24)

(?) Review Questions from Lesson 14.

Lesson Outline Developed

(1) **God provided clothing for Adam and Eve.**

Teacher: After reviewing Lesson 14, ask the question at the beginning of this lesson. After asking the question, give the people time to think and to answer. When someone answers correctly, repeat the answer and then read the Scripture.

> Do you remember what Adam and Eve did after they had eaten the forbidden fruit and realized that they were naked? Yes. They made coverings of leaves.
>
> Let's read about this from God's Word.
>
> 📖 Read Genesis 3:7.
>
> Because they had disobeyed God, they were embarrassed for God to see them naked. So Adam and Eve made coverings of leaves.

- **God refused to accept the clothing that Adam and Eve had made.**

📖 Read Genesis 3:21.

God refused to accept the coverings that Adam and Eve had made. Why? It was not because God doesn't like leaves or grass for clothing. The reason God refused to accept the clothes that Adam and Eve had made was because He wanted to teach them that they couldn't do anything to make themselves acceptable to God.

People often try to do things to make themselves acceptable to God, but no one can make himself acceptable to God by what he does.

Teacher: Consider the people you are teaching and give meaningful examples of the things that people do to try to please God.

God will not accept anything that is done according to man's ideas. God only accepts whatever is done according to His way.

- **Animals had to die so that Adam and Eve could be clothed.**

  Before Adam and Eve sinned, there had never been death in the world. Because they sinned, all people, animals and plants would die. The first death in the world was caused by God to provide clothing for Adam and Eve. When God killed the animals, He was showing Adam and Eve that disobedience to Him had brought death into the world.

- **God was the only One who could provide acceptable clothing for Adam and Eve.**

  Adam and Eve did not kill the animals to make clothing. God killed the animals. God shed the animals' blood. And then God took the skins off the animals and made clothing for Adam and Eve.

- **God provided clothing for Adam and Eve even though they had disobeyed Him.**

  Adam and Eve were guilty of disobeying God, but God is merciful and gracious. God provided clothing for them, even though they did not deserve it. He wanted to show them that He was the only One who could make them acceptable to Him.

- **God put clothing of skin on Adam and Eve.**

  God had killed the animals. God had made the clothing. And then God put the clothing on Adam and Eve. He didn't just give them clothing and tell them to put it on. God clothed them.

LESSON 15: GOD PROVIDED CLOTHING FOR ADAM AND EVE, AND HE PUT THEM OUT OF THE GARDEN.

Teacher: The fact that God put the clothing of skin on Adam and Eve is a redemptive analogy of the truth presented in Isaiah 61:10, "He has clothed me with the garments of salvation, He has covered me with the robe of righteousness." Later in the teaching program, you will use this analogy to explain the truth of substitution and the covering of the righteousness of Christ received through faith.

For now, however, you are laying foundations and establishing spiritual principles. Do not jump ahead to try to explain this analogy. Just make it clear that God would not accept what Adam and Eve had made and that God provided them with clothing. Make sure you teach clearly that there is nothing people can do to make themselves acceptable to God. Later, when you teach the Gospel, you can point back to this analogy.

(2) God put Adam and Eve out of the garden, away from the tree of life.

Read Genesis 3:22-23.

God the Father, God the Son and God the Spirit said this. They were talking to each other, and they were talking about Adam and Eve.

- **Because Adam and Eve had disobeyed God, they knew good and evil.**

When God first made Adam and Eve, they didn't know or experience anything bad. They only knew what was good. Everything God made and gave to them was good. Everything God told them to do was good. They didn't know about Satan or his deceptive ways. God knew that Satan wanted to destroy them, but they didn't. But after they disobeyed, they came to know things that God knew. They realized that not everything was good. Some things were evil.

Satan had deceived Eve so that she thought it would be good for her and Adam to eat the fruit from the tree of the knowledge of good and evil. As soon as Adam and Eve ate that fruit, they were filled with shame and fear. Then they knew that not everything was good but that some things were evil.

God knew what was good and what was evil. Adam and Eve should have trusted God to tell them what was good and what was evil instead of finding out for themselves.

- **Because Adam and Eve had disobeyed God, He would not allow them to eat from the tree of life.**

God had planted two important trees in the middle of the garden in Eden, the tree of life and the tree of the knowledge of good and evil. He planted the tree of life because he wanted Adam and Eve to eat the fruit of it so they would never die.

However, after they had disobeyed God and eaten the fruit from the tree of the knowledge of good and evil, He would not allow them to eat the fruit from the tree of life. Because they were separated from God, they would also have to die physically. Therefore, God put Adam and Eve, the father and mother of us all, out of the garden, away from the tree of life.

When Satan sinned, God put him out of his wonderful position in Heaven. After Adam and Eve sinned, God put them out of the garden. God doesn't ask anyone what He should do. He is supreme. God hates sin and always punishes those who rebel against Him.

③ God put cherubim and a flaming sword to keep Adam and Eve away from the tree of life.

📖 Read Genesis 3:24.

- **God put Adam and Eve out of the Garden of Eden.**

   Then at the east of the garden, God put some of His good angels, called cherubim, and a sword of fire which turned every way. The cherubim and the sword were to prevent anyone coming to the tree of life. God put them there to make sure that Adam and Eve could not return and eat the fruit from the tree of life.

☞ **Teacher:** Show a picture of Adam and Eve leaving the garden in Eden. Show a picture of an angel and the sword prohibiting Adam and Even from approaching the tree of life. These may be the same picture.

- **There was absolutely no way Adam and Eve could get back into the garden.**

   If they had tried to get back to the tree of life, the cherubim would have seen them, and they would have been killed by the sword of fire. Once God put Adam and Eve out of the garden, there was nothing they could do to get back and eat fruit from the tree of life. They would now grow old and die.

Teacher: That there was no way back for Adam and Eve into the garden is important because you are laying the foundations for the people to realize that, if God doesn't make a way back to Him, they are destined for eternal punishment.

Lesson Developer: Present possible scenarios so that the people realize that Adam and Eve had no hope of getting back to the tree of life. For example:

💡 *Suppose Adam had said to Eve, "You stand over there and distract the angels. Talk to them so they will not watch me, and I will sneak around the back way with this basket. I will get a basketful of fruit from the tree of life."*

Do you think it would be possible for them to get past God's cherubim? Could they sneak around the back way and trick God?

No! God could see them all the time. He would have known if they had tried to sneak around another way. They couldn't get past God's angels.

LESSON 15: GOD PROVIDED CLOTHING FOR ADAM AND EVE, AND HE PUT THEM OUT OF THE GARDEN.

- **Adam and Eve could not trick or deceive God.**

    He could see what they were doing all the time. And the same is true today. God has not changed. It is impossible to deceive or trick God. God sees and knows everything you do. There is no place where you can hide from Him.

    Teacher: Mention specific places where the people might try to hide from God.

    There is never a time when you are out of God's sight. He even knows your every thought.

    No one can fight against God and win. God hates disobedience to His commands and will not allow any disobedient person to live with Him.

? Questions

1. Why did God refuse to accept the clothing that Adam and Eve had made?

    God refused to accept the clothing that Adam and Eve had made because He wanted to teach them that they couldn't do anything to make themselves acceptable to God.

2. Can a person make himself acceptable to God by anything that he does?

    No. A person can never make himself acceptable to God by what he does.

3. Who is the only One who could make Adam and Eve acceptable to God?

    God was the only One who could make Adam and Eve acceptable to Him.

4. What was God showing Adam and Eve when He killed the animals to make clothing for them?

    When God killed the animals, He was showing Adam and Eve that the punishment for sin is death.

5. Did Adam and Eve deserve to have God provide clothing for them?

    No! Adam and Eve had sinned against God, and they did not deserve to have God provide clothing for them.

6. In what way did Adam and Eve become like God after they ate the fruit from the tree of the knowledge of good and evil?

    After they ate the fruit, Adam and Eve knew that there was evil as well as good.

7. Why did God put Adam and Eve out of the garden in Eden?

   God put Adam and Eve out of the garden so that they would not be able to eat the fruit from the tree of life and live forever.

8. What did God do to make sure Adam and Eve would not be able to return and eat the fruit from the tree of life?

   God placed cherubim and a sword of fire flashing every way so that Adam and Eve could not return and eat the fruit from the tree of life.

9. Can anyone trick or deceive God?

   No. No one can trick or deceive God.

LESSON 16: GOD REJECTED CAIN AND HIS OFFERING, BUT HE ACCEPTED ABEL AND HIS OFFERING.

Scripture

Genesis 4:1-16

Lesson Outline

1. God is the giver of life. (Genesis 4:1)
2. Cain and Abel were both born outside of the garden. (Genesis 4:2)
3. Cain and Abel both came to offer sacrifices to God. (Genesis 4:3-4)
4. God accepted Abel's offering. (Genesis 4:4)
5. God rejected Cain's offering. (Genesis 4:5)
6. Cain refused to listen to God. (Genesis 4:6-8)
7. God judged Cain for killing Abel. (Genesis 4:9-16)

(?) Review Questions from Lesson 15.

Lesson Outline Developed

1. God is the giver of life.

Read Genesis 4:1.

Eve knew that God is the giver of all life.

God had formed Adam from the dust of the ground and had breathed into him to give him life. God had made Eve from Adam's rib and given her life. And we know from this verse that God gave life to Adam and Eve's son.

Every person is given life by God. Your life was given to you by God.

Building on Firm Foundations
- Volume 2: Evangelism:
Genesis to The Ascension

(2) Cain and Abel were both born outside of the garden.

📖 Read Genesis 4:2.

☞ **Teacher:** Point to the names, **"Cain and Abel,"** on the chronological chart.

- **Cain and Abel were born sinners because their father, Adam, was a sinner.**

    Because Adam and Eve had sinned against God, they were put outside of the garden, away from the tree of life. As a result, Cain and Abel were born outside of the garden, away from the tree of life.

Lesson Developer: As you develop the following illustration, be sure to use appropriate group and country names to fit your teaching situation.

> 🕯 *How did you come to belong to this particular tribe and be born in this place? Why do you look, think, talk and act like Palawanos? It is because of your parents, isn't it? If your parents were Australian and lived in Australia, you, too, would have been born in Australia and you would have looked, thought, talked and acted like Australians.*

When God created Adam and Eve, they were perfect before God. If they had obeyed Him, they would have continued to live in the garden and eat of the tree of life. Their children would have been born perfect and would also have lived in the garden. But Adam sinned when he ate the forbidden fruit, so he was put out of the garden and away from the tree of life. Therefore, his children, Cain and Abel, were born sinners, separated from God, outside of the garden, and away from the tree of life. Cain and Abel were born sinners because their father, Adam, was a sinner.

- **All people have been born sinners because our ancestor, Adam, was a sinner.**

    Not only was Adam the father of Cain and Abel, but he was also the father of the whole human race. Adam was your ancestor, and Adam is also our ancestor. Because Adam disobeyed God and was separated from Him, all people in this world are born cut off from God.

- **Cain and Abel were born into Satan's family because their father, Adam, had chosen to listen to Satan.**

    When Adam decided to disobey God, he allied himself with Satan and entered his family. As a result, Adam's children were also born in Satan's family. That part in Cain and Abel that should have been in God's image so they could know, love and obey God was under Satan's control.

LESSON 16: GOD REJECTED CAIN AND HIS OFFERING, BUT HE ACCEPTED ABEL AND HIS OFFERING.

God gave life to Cain and Abel, but they were not born in friendship with God. When they were born, they were already separated from God because their father, Adam, was separated from God. They were born Satan's children, under Satan's control, and therefore, God's enemies.

- **All Adam's descendants have been born in Satan's family.**

Lesson Developer: Give an illustration to show that Adam and Adam's descendants became the enemies of God. For example:

> *Suppose another tribe over the mountains was fighting against your tribe. They hated you, and they wanted to do all they could to hurt you. Now suppose there was a young man in your tribe who was enticed by a young woman to go over to the enemy tribe. He married the girl and adopted their customs. Then he and his wife had children. Think about this: To what tribe would the children belong? They would belong to the tribe over the mountain. They would be your enemies because their father left his tribe and joined the enemies of his people.*

God is the One who gives life to all people, but we are not born in friendship or oneness with God. Satan has taken God's place as our spiritual father. The part in us that should have been in God's image so we could know, love and obey God was under Satan's control from the time of our birth. We were all born sinners. We were all born Satan's children, under Satan's control and God's enemies.

It is important that you realize you were born a sinner. You were born separated from God, with Satan as your father, just as all people are.

Teacher: Make sure that the people do not think that Satan actually fathered their human life and physical body.

- **Satan has told many lies to people about the beginning of the human race.**

People all over the world have many different stories about their beginnings, where they came from and who their first ancestors were. You have your own beliefs about the beginning. But the Bible gives the true story of how all people began and why all people were born under Satan's control. The Bible tells us that because Adam disobeyed God and allied himself with Satan, he and all his descendants became members of Satan's family.

Teacher: In this lesson, you are teaching the truth of John 8:44; Ephesians 2:1-2; 1 John 3:8, 10. Read these verses as you prepare to teach, but do not read these verses to the people when you teach the lesson.

You are also teaching the truth of Romans 5:12, "Therefore, just as through one man sin entered the world, and death through sin, and thus death spread to all men, because all sinned." Do not jump ahead in the teaching program. Do not read this verse when you teach the lesson. Nevertheless, clearly teach the truth that sin and death passed to all people because Adam sinned.

In Lessons 8 and 13, you used a branch as a visual aid to illustrate that Adam and Eve were separated from God, their source of life. Use that same branch as you teach this lesson to show that all people have been born separated from God.

Here is the branch that I broke off from a tree. The branch was dead from the moment it was separated from the tree because it was cut off from its source of life. In the same way, when Adam and Eve disobeyed God's command, they were immediately separated from God.

Look at these outer branches that grew from the main branch. Are these outer branches still alive? No! They died because they were also cut off from the source of life when the main branch was cut off. In the same way, Cain and Abel were born separated from God because of their father's disobedience. They were born sinners and were born dead to God because Adam had sinned against God.

Look at these twigs and leaves at the ends of the outer branches. These twigs and leaves are dead also, aren't they? They were cut off from their source of life when the main branch was separated from the tree. In the same way, all people in the world, including all of us, were cut off from God. Because of Adam's sin, all people have been born dead to God.

---

③ Cain and Abel both came to offer sacrifices to God.

Teacher: The verses you are about to read introduce sheep and the role of the shepherd. Sheep and shepherds are very prominent in Bible stories. Therefore, if the people you are teaching don't know about sheep, take time to talk about and show pictures of sheep and to explain the work of the shepherd.

📖 Read Genesis 4:3-4.

☞ **Teacher:** Show a picture of Cain bringing produce that he had grown to God and Abel bringing a lamb to offer to God.

LESSON 16: GOD REJECTED CAIN AND HIS OFFERING, BUT HE ACCEPTED ABEL AND HIS OFFERING.

- **Both Cain and Abel believed in the existence of God, and both came to offer sacrifices to Him.**

  Just believing that God exists will not make us acceptable to Him. The Bible says that even Satan believes in God and that Satan trembles through fear when he thinks of God. But believing in God does not make Satan acceptable to God.

  Even offering to God what we think is very good will not make us acceptable to Him. Man can come to God only according to God's will and plan.

- **God told them what they must do in order to worship Him.**

  Adam and Eve and Cain and Abel were all sinners and were separated from God. The punishment for sin is death. Adam and Eve could not give anything to God to pay for their sins. Neither could Cain and Abel. There was no way that they could come to God and be accepted by Him.

  But God planned a way so they could come to Him. It was not man's way. It was God who decided on this way. No one else could provide the way for them. God provided the way for them because He loved them.

  God must have told Adam and Eve what they must do if they wanted to come to Him. Adam and Eve probably told Cain and Abel what God said they must do if they wished to come to God.

  God told them that, when they came to Him, they had to bring a sheep as an offering to God. They had to kill the sheep so that its blood would flow out.

  The blood of the sheep could not pay for their sin. So why did God tell them to kill a sheep?

  God told them to kill a sheep because He wanted them to remember that the punishment for sin is death. He wanted them to remember that they would die and go to everlasting punishment unless He saved them. If they agreed with God that they were sinners and that only He could save them from everlasting punishment, then they were to bring a sheep and kill it as God instructed.

Teacher: It is important that you understand clearly why God rejected Cain and his offering but accepted Abel and his offering. Scripture emphasizes that it is impossible to please God without faith (Hebrews 11:6). Abel was a man of faith (Hebrews 11:4); Cain was not a man of faith (1 John 3:12). Faith was the great difference between Cain and Abel.

Genuine faith is always based on the Word of God (Romans 10:17). To approach God apart from a divine directive is presumption and will always be rejected by God. Everything that originates with man is unacceptable to God. On this basis, we can be sure that Abel's faith was dependent on a clear directive given by God. If it had not been, Abel's sacrifice would not have been acceptable to God. God told Cain that if he would do the right thing then he too would be accepted just like Abel was (Genesis 4:7). God didn't explain to Cain what the right thing was, for, like Abel, Cain already knew what God expected of him before he brought his unacceptable offering.

Another indication that Abel was following God's command is that Abel brought the fat of the lamb to God. Later in Scripture, God commands the Israelites to bring the fat to Him (Leviticus 3:16). To suggest that bringing the fat originated with Abel is contrary to the whole emphasis of Scripture. God doesn't accept anything that originates with man.

In addition, since there were acknowledged clean and unclean animals even in Noah's day, it is likely that God had already classified animals as clean and unclean in Cain and Abel's time. Surely it was no coincidence that Abel chose a lamb, a clean animal (Leviticus 11), and the most perfect type of the spotless Son of God (Isaiah 53:7; John 1:29; I Peter 1:19-20). The Lord Jesus and His sacrifice as a spotless lamb originated in the mind of the eternal God before the foundation of the earth, not in the mind of Abel (Revelation 13:8).

④ God accepted Abel's offering.

Read Genesis 4:4 again.

- **Abel brought sheep as an offering to God.**

    Abel brought sheep and the fat from the sheep just as God had instructed them.

    Abel killed sheep, allowing their blood to flow out. Then he offered the sheep, along with the fat, to God. By doing this, Abel showed that he agreed with God that he was a sinner and that only God could save him from everlasting punishment.

    The Bible tells us that Abel brought sheep, killed them, shed their blood and offered them to God because he believed God. Abel believed what God had told his parents. God had promised that He would send a great Deliverer to destroy Satan and save man from Satan's power.

    Was God pleased with Abel's offering? Yes, God was very pleased with his offering. Did God accept Abel? Yes, God accepted Abel.

- **The blood of animals could never pay for sin.**

    It is important for you to understand that God did not accept Abel's sheep as the payment for sin instead of Abel's death. Sin must be paid for by the sinner's death. The sinner must be separated from God forever.

    So why did God accept Abel? God forgave Abel's sin and accepted him because Abel trusted, not in himself, but in God who had promised to send the Deliverer.

LESSON 16: GOD REJECTED CAIN AND HIS OFFERING, BUT HE ACCEPTED ABEL AND HIS OFFERING.

Teacher: There is potential for the people to misunderstand this story of Abel's offering of sheep. For example, when a group of people in Africa was taught this story, they were willing to offer sheep to God because they raised sheep. In contrast, a group of people in the Philippines was frustrated and angry when they were taught the story because they felt it was unfair of God to demand sheep when they didn't have any way to get sheep. Both groups misunderstood, thinking that they needed to bring sheep to God.

Therefore, make certain that your hearers understand that the blood of animals could not and did not pay for sin and that God is not asking them to make offerings to Him. Sin must be paid for by human life. Animal blood or life is not equal to human life (Hebrews 10:4-5). Make it absolutely clear that God will not overlook sin. Sin must be paid for in full. *"The soul who sins shall die"* (Ezekiel 18:4). The payment for sin is eternal separation from God.

Your hearers must come to realize that man cannot contribute anything to his salvation. As you teach these stories, you are laying the foundation so that your hearers will understand that sinners can only be saved by the grace of God (Ephesians 2:8-9).

⑤ God rejected Cain's offering.

📖 Read Genesis 4:3 again. Then Read Genesis 4:5.

- **Cain brought the things that he had grown as an offering to God.**

    God did not accept Cain or his offering.

    Why do you think that God did not accept Cain's offering? Was it because the things Cain grew and brought to God were not good? Was it because God doesn't like things grown from the ground? No, those are not the reasons.

    Did God reject Cain's offering because Cain was a worse sinner than Abel? No, that wasn't the reason why God would not accept him. Both Cain and Abel were born sinners.

    God rejected Cain and his offering because Cain didn't come to God admitting he was a sinner and because he came to God in his own way, according to his own ideas, and not in the way that God had commanded. Cain did not believe God. He did not trust in God and in the way that God had told them to come. That is why God rejected him.

Teacher: You must emphasize faith as the reason for Abel's offering and unbelief as the reason for Cain's actions. If you emphasize obedience instead of faith, the people will be turned to doing rather than believing. According to Hebrews 11:4, God accepted Abel and his offering because Abel believed God. Faith was the great difference between Cain and Abel. Clearly teach that man must believe God (Hebrews 11:6). By laying this foundational truth, when you present the Gospel, the people will understand that it is only through faith that man can be accepted by God.

At the same time, you need to teach the balance between faith and works. Because Abel believed God, he offered sheep. Because Noah believed God, he built an ark. Because Abraham believed God, he went to the place of God's choice. Do not refer to Hebrews 11 as you teach the Old Testament, but read it as you prepare to teach and keep it in mind, using it to interpret the actions of the Old Testament characters.

- **Only God can provide the way so people can come to Him and be accepted.**

    Do you remember what happened when Adam and Eve made clothing for themselves out of leaves? God rejected that clothing, and God provided clothing for them. Why did God refuse to accept the clothing that Adam and Eve made? It was because God wanted to show them that they couldn't make themselves acceptable to Him by anything they could do. It had to be done in God's way. The animals had to die, and the animals' blood had to be shed so that Adam and Eve could be clothed.

    It was the same with Cain and Abel. God would not accept them unless they trusted in Him and came to Him in the way He had said. God would only accept them if they brought sheep and killed them, allowing their blood to flow out. Abel believed God and came God's way, so God accepted him. Cain came trusting in his own way, so God rejected him.

Teacher: Use the branch that you previously broke off from a tree to illustrate that people cannot do anything to restore their broken relationship with God. This illustration is especially useful when teaching people who have been deceived into thinking that they can bring themselves back into a right relationship with God through their own self-efforts.

- **God has not changed.**

    God is still the same today. Although He is not telling you to bring sheep and kill them, nevertheless, God is the One who says how you can come to Him. You must come God's way; otherwise, He will reject you as He rejected Cain. Listen carefully to God's message so that you will know the only way that you can come to God and be delivered from Satan's power and everlasting punishment.

Here is that same branch that I broke off and showed you previously. The branch is now dead because it has been separated a long time from the life it received from the tree. But I am going to join this branch back onto the tree so that once again it will be able to receive the life from the tree.

If I tie this limb back onto the tree, it will come back to life again, won't it? The leaves will turn green once again, and the limb will begin to grow, right? Do you think that I will be able to join the branch back on the tree so it will have life again?

No! I cannot join this limb back onto the tree so that it will live again. It is

impossible to restore life to this branch once it has been separated from the tree and is dead. Likewise, it is impossible for people to do anything to bring themselves into a right relationship with God.

- **Only God can bring us back into oneness with Himself**

    Because Adam and Eve disobeyed God, they were separated from God. Therefore, Cain and Abel were born outside of the garden and were also separated from God. They could not bring themselves back into fellowship with God.

    Adam and Eve made clothing to make themselves acceptable to God, but He rejected their clothing. Cain came to God in his own way, and God rejected him and his offering. Only God was able to provide the way so they could come back to Him and be His friends again.

    We, too, are all the descendants of Adam. We were all born sinners, separated from God because of our ancestor, Adam. We cannot make ourselves God's friends. Only God could provide the way for us to come back to Him.

6. Cain refused to listen to God.

- **God reasoned with Cain.**

    📖 Read Genesis 4:6-7.

    When Cain brought the incorrect offering, he was deliberately going his own way, and he became very angry when God did not accept him.

    Even though Cain refused to believe God and deliberately went his own way, God reasoned with him. Because of God's love and mercy, He talked to Cain and tried to get him to come the right way. God wanted Cain to know that he, too, would be accepted if he came as his brother, Abel, came. Cain would be accepted if he believed God's words, made the right offering and trusted in God and His promise of the Deliverer.

- **Cain would not listen to and believe God.**

    Cain was very angry. He refused to listen to and believe God. He was listening to Satan, just as his mother and father had done in the garden.

- **Don't be like Cain who refused to listen to God.**

    Refusing to listen to God always leads to trouble and death. It is very foolish to refuse to listen to God.

    God speaks to people today by His Word, the Bible. But Satan does not want you to listen to God. Satan may be using other people to try to trick you. They may say, "Don't listen to the Bible." Remember, refusing to listen to and believe God will lead to death. Don't be like Cain and refuse to listen to God.

    📖 Read Genesis 4:8.

☞ **Teacher:** Show a picture of Cain walking away from Abel's dead body.

- **Cain killed his brother, Abel.**

    Who was leading Cain? To whom was Cain listening? Who do you think put the idea into Cain's mind to kill his brother? Satan did. Satan is a murderer.

    Satan deceived Adam and Eve so that they would die. Satan told them that they wouldn't die if they ate the fruit from the tree of knowledge of good and evil, but he lied to them. Satan knew that Adam and Eve would die if they disobeyed God and ate the fruit. Satan wanted Adam and Eve to die so he lied to them.

    Satan wanted Cain to kill Abel so he put the idea in Cain's mind.

    Satan is a murderer. He hates all people. He lies and deceives because he wants all people to go to the place of everlasting punishment where he is going.

> **Teacher:** Even though Satan is not mentioned in these verses in Genesis, we know that he was involved. 1 John 3:12 says that Cain, "...*was of the wicked one and murdered his brother.*" John 8:44 describes Satan as a liar and "*a murderer from the beginning.*" Do not jump ahead and read these verses in the teaching session, but be aware of these truths as you teach from Genesis.

⑦ God judged Cain for killing Abel.

   📖 Read Genesis 4:9.

   God already knew that Cain had killed Abel. God saw him do it. God is everywhere and knows everything.

   So why do you think God asked this question when He already knew the answer? God was giving Cain an opportunity to admit what he had done.

   📖 Read Genesis 4:10-15.

- **God avenges evil done against other people.**

    God is the creator of all people. He had created Abel so he rightfully belonged to God. This is why God avenged Abel's death.

    God punishes anyone who says or does anything harmful to another person.

    God gave Abel life, and He gave life to each one of us. Even though we are separated from God, He still cares for us.

   Lesson Developer: Use an illustration to show that all people belong to God even though Satan has stolen them from the family of God. For example:

> 💡 *Think about this. If someone stole your pig, to whom would the pig belong? Has the pig become the property of the thief, or is it still your property? It still belongs to you! Even if the thief killed the pig, it would still be your pig.*

LESSON 16: GOD REJECTED CAIN AND HIS OFFERING, BUT HE ACCEPTED ABEL AND HIS OFFERING.

- **All people rightfully belong to God.**

    By deceit and lies, Satan stole Adam and Eve from God. And by stealing Adam, he also stole all of Adam's descendants. But because God has given life to all people, we all still rightfully belong to Him. Therefore, all evil done against another person is also sin against God. God will avenge all evil done against anyone.

    This doesn't mean that God will immediately avenge all evil; nevertheless, all sin will eventually be punished by God. The payment required for sin is death. Sometimes people try to make up for evil that they do against other people. They sin against others. God will eventually punish all evil done against other people, because God is the rightful owner of every person.

    📖 Read Genesis 4:16.

- **Cain would not repent.**

    Cain still would not listen to God. He chose to follow Satan. Cain refused to repent. Cain would not change his attitude and admit that everything God had said to him was right. He refused to acknowledge that he was a sinner and was unable to save himself from his sinful desires and ways which had control over him. He would not agree that he had done evil things that deserved God's judgment.

Teacher: We must be careful how we teach repentance. Many people teach that repentance means to leave, or promise to leave, all sin. But this is incorrect.

Repentance is a change of mind, a change of attitude toward God, oneself and one's own sin. Repentance is the sinner acknowledging before God, "God, You are right. I am wrong. Everything you commanded is good and righteous and holy. I have failed to obey You as I should. I have no hope in my own ability to save myself from the power of my sin or the judgment it deserves." That is true repentance which leads to the new birth and God's work of sanctification in the lives of His children (Ephesians 2:8-10).

Be sure to emphasize faith, rather than following or doing. If we stress obedience, we will have followers and doers rather than believers.

God doesn't ask a sinner to promise to leave his sin and "never do it again" before He will save him. God doesn't ask for the vain promises of helpless sinners. God doesn't strike a bargain with the sinner. He does not say, "You do this, and I will do that." God does not require reformation as a prerequisite for salvation. Eternal life is a gift given by God's grace alone (Romans 6:23; Ephesians 2:8-9).

Cain's descendants followed him in his rebellion against God. When Cain died, he went to everlasting punishment. So did Cain's descendants.

? Questions

1. Who gives every person his life?

   God gives life to every person.

2. Where were Cain and Abel born?

   Cain and Abel were born outside of the garden in Eden, away from the tree of life.

3. Why were Cain and Abel born sinners and separated from God?

   Cain and Abel were born sinners and separated from God because their father, Adam, was a sinner and was separated from God.

4. Why are all people born sinners and separated from God?

   All people are born sinners and separated from God because Adam is our ancestor.

5. What offering did Abel bring to God?

   Abel brought sheep, killed them and let their blood run out as an offering to God.

6. Why did God accept Abel and his offering?

   God accepted Abel and his offering because Abel believed God and trusted in God's promise to send the Deliverer. Abel came to God in the way God said to come.

7. What offering did Cain bring to God?

   Cain brought the things that he had grown as an offering to God.

8. Why did God reject Cain and his offering?

   God rejected Cain and his offering because Cain did not believe God and he did not trust in God's promise to send the Deliverer. Cain refused to bring the offering which God said they must bring.

9. Why did God reason with Cain?

   God reasoned with Cain because God loved Cain and wanted Cain to agree that he was a sinner and that he should bring the correct sacrifice.

10. Did Cain believe and agree with God?

    No. Cain refused to listen to God and believe Him.

11. What did Cain do to Abel?

    Cain killed Abel.

12. Who put the idea into Cain's mind to kill his brother?

    Satan put the idea into Cain's mind.

LESSON 16: GOD REJECTED CAIN AND HIS OFFERING, BUT HE ACCEPTED ABEL AND HIS OFFERING.

13. Why did Satan want Cain to kill Abel?

    Satan hates all people.

14. How did God know what Cain had done?

    God sees and knows everything.

15. Why will God punish us for saying and doing evil things to other people?

    God will punish those who say and do evil to other people because all people rightfully belong to God.

16. Sometimes people try to make up for evil that they do against other people. Does God forget about the evil that is done against other people if we make it right with the person we have wronged?

    No. Doing evil to people is a sin against God, who is the rightful owner of man, and all sin will eventually be punished by God.

17. Did Cain repent?

    No! Cain refused to change his attitude toward God and toward his sin.

18. What was the result of Cain's refusal to repent?

    Cain's descendants followed him in rebellion against God. They all lived and died separated from God.

LESSON 17: THE BIBLE TELLS ABOUT CAIN'S DESCENDANTS AND SETH'S DESCENDANTS.

Scripture

Genesis 4:16-26, Genesis 5:3-5, 22-32

Lesson Outline

1. Cain's descendants followed Cain's example and had no interest in God. (Genesis 4:16-24)

2. God gave Seth to replace Abel. (Genesis 4:25)

3. When Enosh, Seth's son, was born, people once again began to believe in God and to worship Him. (Genesis 4:26)

4. Adam died. (Genesis 5:3-5)

5. Enoch walked with God. (Genesis 5:22-24)

6. The Bible lists some of Enoch's descendants. (Genesis 5:25-32)

? Review Questions from Lesson 16.

Lesson Outline Developed

1. Cain's descendants followed Cain's example and had no interest in God.

Read Genesis 4:16-24.

- **The lives of Cain's descendants were filled with money and material things.**

    Cain's descendants followed Cain's example and had no interest in God. They filled their minds and time with doing the things they wanted to do. They built towns, raised cattle, and made tools and musical instruments. They had no interest in or time for God and the things He wanted them to know. They were under the control of Satan.

- **Think about what a terrible effect disobedience to God had already brought into the world.**
  - Because Adam and Eve sinned, all of their descendants were born sinners, separated from God and without oneness of mind with God.
  - Adam and Eve's first son, Cain, murdered their second son, Abel.
  - Cain turned away from God and would not listen to His words.
  - When Cain had children, he did not teach them about God. As a result, Cain's children did not know God and the truth.
  - Each generation of Cain's descendants lived according to their own sinful ways instead of God's way. They were guided by Satan and his lies.
- **This should be a warning to any of you who may refuse to take time to listen to God's Word.**

  Maybe you are more interested in working and making money than you are interested in listening to God's Word. It is good to work, but you should also take time to listen to God's Word so you can learn to know God and understand the way to be delivered from Satan's control and everlasting punishment.

  If you parents turn away from God's truth and refuse to listen to God, probably your children will never listen to the Word of God either. You are responsible, not only for yourselves, but for your children too. You should listen carefully to God's message and make sure your children also hear the truth.

  God's message should not only be important to you when we meet to read God's Word and to be taught, but it should also be the most important thing in every area of your lives. You can talk about God's message in your homes and when you work, fish or hunt.

② God gave Seth to replace Abel.

Read Genesis 4:25.

☞ **Teacher:** Point to the name, **"Seth,"** on the Chronological Chart.

In the Garden of Eden, God had promised that He would send a Deliverer who would overcome Satan. Satan knew that God's plan was to send the Deliverer as a descendant of Abel, so he guided Cain to kill Abel. In this way he was trying to hinder God's plan to send the Deliverer.

Did Abel's death mean the end of God's plan and promise to send the Deliverer? No! God always does what He promises. He doesn't give up or change because of the things Satan does.

LESSON 17: THE BIBLE TELLS ABOUT CAIN'S DESCENDANTS AND SETH'S DESCENDANTS.

In place of Abel, God gave Seth to Adam and Eve. Seth was also born separated from God, but he trusted in God just as Abel did. God planned that the Deliverer would come into the world through the line of Seth.

③ When Enosh, Seth's son, was born, people once again began to believe in God and to worship Him.

📖 Read Genesis 4:26.

Seth grew up and married. His wife gave birth to a son. They named him Enosh.

God's Book tells us that, when this child was born, Seth's family line began to remember God and their great need of Him. They began coming to God to worship, calling on Him to accept them.

- **Seth and his family line came to God just as Abel had come to God.**

    Think about what we've learned concerning how Abel came to God. What did Abel bring as an offering to God? Why did God accept Abel and his offering? God accepted Abel because he agreed with God that he was a sinner, he trusted in God's promise to send the Deliverer, and he brought the offering which God had told them they must bring.

    This is how Seth, his son Enosh, and their family line began to come to God. They came as Abel had come. They came to God in faith, bringing the sheep whose blood they had allowed to run out. God accepted them because they came to Him the way He had said.

- **Anyone who comes to God in the way He says to come will be accepted by God.**

    God always treats everyone alike – regardless of their color, or whether they are rich or poor, young or old, man or woman. God doesn't have any favorites.

    Even though people from Seth's line believed God, the majority of people did not come to God. They lived only for the things of this life. They didn't care that they were separated from God and that they would die and be separated from God forever.

④ Adam died.

📖 Read Genesis 5:3-5.

Adam lived until he was 930 years old. Both Adam and Eve died.

When God created Adam and Eve, God did not plan for them or their descendants to die. There was no death in the world in the beginning. But when Adam and Eve sinned, the result was death. Sin separated Adam and Eve from God. After Adam and Eve sinned, God removed them from the garden so that they couldn't eat from the tree of life and live forever. Their bodies eventually died.

People still continue to die because all people are the descendants of Adam, and all people sin.

(5) Enoch walked with God.

📖 Read Genesis 5:22-23.

One of Seth's descendants was a man named Enoch. Enoch was born a sinner, but he believed God and came to God in the way which God had said.

Enoch also obeyed and pleased God in the way he lived his life.

☞ **Teacher:** Point to the name, **"Enoch,"** on the Chronological Chart.

- **Enoch was God's messenger to the people of his time.**

  The Bible was not written at that time, so God told Enoch what to say to the people. Enoch warned them that God was going to judge and punish them for their unbelief and their evil ways. But the majority of the people did not believe God's message through Enoch.

Teacher: It is clear from Jude 14-15 that Enoch understood much more than what is recorded in Genesis. Enoch even foretold Christ's coming to judge the world.

- **God took Enoch.**

  📖 Read Genesis 5:24.

  Even though Enoch was a sinner and didn't deserve God's mercy, God loved and accepted Enoch. God took Enoch out of this world and into Heaven.

- **Heaven is the special, wonderful place where God lives.**

  Although God is everywhere, all of the time, Heaven is His home. Heaven is the place where all the spirits lived with God in the beginning and where the obedient angels are still living. Heaven is a beautiful place. There is no fear, sorrow, sickness, or death in Heaven. God provides everything for those who live in Heaven. Heaven is not here in this world. It is far away, past the moon, the sun and the stars. Heaven is a real place, even though none of us have been there or seen it.

Lesson Developer: To establish that Heaven is a real place, give an illustration of a town or capital city that they know about and yet have not seen. Choose a place where someone they know has been. For example:

> 🕯 *How many of you have been to Manila? Is Manila a real place? Yes, it is, even though many of you have never seen it. How do you know what Manila is like? People who have been there and know about Manila have told you. Even though you have never been there, it is a real place.*

LESSON 17: THE BIBLE TELLS ABOUT CAIN'S DESCENDANTS AND SETH'S DESCENDANTS.

Heaven is a real place, even though we have never seen it. In His Book, God, who lives in Heaven, tells us what it is like.

God took Enoch into Heaven. Enoch did not die physically.

- **All people rightfully belong to God.**

Because Enoch belonged to God, God had the authority to take him to Heaven. God can do what He wants with people. God doesn't need to ask anyone when He wants to do something. He wanted to take Enoch into Heaven, and so He did. God could do this because He is greater than everyone and everything.

6) The Bible lists some of Enoch's descendants.

Enoch was the only one taken to Heaven without dying at this time. Other people during those years lived for a long time, but they eventually died. Enoch's son, named Methuselah, lived longer than anyone else.

📖 Read Genesis 5:25-27.

Methuselah's grandson's name was Noah.

📖 Read Genesis 5:28-32.

☞ **Teacher:** Point to the names, **"Noah, Shem, Ham, Japheth,"** on the Chronological Chart.

Noah was a man who believed God. The story of Noah and his three sons, Shem, Ham and Japheth, is very important. We will learn about them in our next lesson.

❓ Questions

1. Cain and his descendants did not care about God and what He said. What were the things that interested them?

    Cain and his descendants were interested in money and material things.

2. It is good to work and to have money, but what is also very important for us to take time to do?

    It is important for us to take time to listen to God's Word.

3. Who did each generation of Cain's descendants follow?

    Each generation followed Satan.

4. Did Abel's death mean the end of God's plan to send the Deliverer?
   No! God always does what He promises.

5. Why did God give Seth to Adam and Eve?
   God gave Seth to replace Abel.

6. From what family line would the Deliverer be born?
   The Deliverer would come into the world through the line of Seth.

7. Why did Adam and Eve die?
   Adam and Eve died because they had sinned.

8. Why do people still die?
   People die because all people are the descendants of Adam, and all people sin.

9. How did Seth, Enosh, Enoch and others come to God?
   They came trusting in God and His promise. They killed sheep and shed their blood.

10. What unusual thing happened to Enoch?
    God took him to Heaven without dying.

11. What have we learned about Heaven?
    Heaven is the special, wonderful place where God lives. Heaven is where all the spirits lived with God in the beginning and where the obedient angels are still living. Heaven is a beautiful place. There is no fear, sorrow, sickness, or death in Heaven. Heaven is far away past the sun, moon and stars. Heaven is a real place, even though none of us have been there or seen it.

12. Why did God have the authority to take Enoch to Heaven without dying?
    God had the authority to take Enoch to Heaven without dying because Enoch belonged to God.

LESSON 18: GOD SAID HE WOULD PUNISH THE WORLD, BUT HE PROMISED TO SAVE NOAH AND ALL WHO ENTERED THE BOAT.

Scripture

Genesis 6:1-3, 5-22

Lesson Outline

(1) The population of the earth had greatly increased. (Genesis 6:1-2)

(2) God's Spirit was constantly telling the people to repent. (Genesis 6:3)

(3) The people became more and more wicked. (Genesis 6:5, 11)

(4) God saw how wicked the people had become. (Genesis 6:5, 11-12)

(5) God decided to destroy the people on the earth. (Genesis 6:6-7)

(6) God was gracious to Noah. (Genesis 6:8-10)

(7) God told Noah what was going to happen and what he must do. (Genesis 6:13-21)

(8) Noah obeyed God. (Genesis 6:22)

(9) Noah was God's messenger.

(?) Review Questions from Lesson 17.

Lesson Outline Developed

(1) The population of the earth had greatly increased.

📖 Read Genesis 6:1-2.

About 1,500 years had gone by since God created Adam, and many years had gone by since Adam had died. A large population lived on the earth.

The majority of the people were just interested in having what they thought was a good time. They were obsessed with sex and marrying. The majority did not think about God or about how they should please God.

> **Teacher:** As you prepare to teach, read Matthew 24:37-39. These verses describe the attitude of the people of Noah's day. Do not read these verses to the people, but be aware of them as you teach from Genesis 6.

② God's Spirit was constantly telling the people to repent.

God loved these people, but He hated their sin. God wanted them to repent – to change their minds, admit they were wrong and believe in Him.

- **God's Spirit used Noah.**

  God's Spirit guided a man named Noah who believed God to speak His words to the people. Noah told the people that God had commanded them to repent. Do you think that they listened to what God's Spirit told them through Noah? No! They would not repent.

> **Teacher:** As you prepare to teach, read 1 Peter 3:18-20 and 2 Peter 2:5, but do not read these verses to the people when you teach the lesson.

📖 Read Genesis 6:3.

- **God warned them that He would not always continue to tell them His message.**

  Because God is gracious and merciful, His Spirit would continue speaking through Noah to the people for 120 more years. If they refused to repent during this time, they could not expect God to show them mercy any longer.

- **God is speaking to you through us today.**

  God's Spirit guided Noah to tell the people the words of God at that time, and now we are telling you what God wants you to know from the Bible. Once you have heard God's message through us, God's Spirit will remind you of the things God wants you to know.

- **Satan will also speak inside your minds.**

  Sometimes it will seem to you as if a war is going on inside of you. The voice of God the Spirit will say to you, "Listen to God's message and trust in God." The voice of Satan will say, "Don't listen to God's message. Don't leave the beliefs and ways of your ancestors." Who will you listen to – God or Satan?

- **Don't turn away from listening to God's Word.**

LESSON 18: GOD SAID HE WOULD PUNISH THE WORLD, BUT HE PROMISED TO SAVE NOAH AND ALL WHO ENTERED THE BOAT.

If you continually refuse to agree with God and won't believe His message, then the time may come when you may no longer care what God says. If you don't listen to and believe God before you die, you will go to everlasting punishment to be separated from God forever.

③ The people became more and more wicked.

📖 Read Genesis 6:5, 11.

The majority of the people followed the ways of Cain, with no interest in God. The people refused to repent. They refused to believe God's message and trust in Him and His mercy. Instead of listening to God, the people became more and more sinful.

Listen to the things they were doing. How many of these are you guilty of?

- Their lives were controlled by things that were not right according to God.
- They were greedy for everything they saw and could imagine.
- They wanted what other people had.
- They were jealous and hateful to other people.
- They argued and fought all the time.
- They were cruel, and they murdered people.
- They tricked, lied to and deceived one another.
- They said evil things about others behind their backs.
- They were proud and always bragging about themselves.
- They were disobedient to their parents.
- They broke their promises to others and were without pity to people in need.
- They hated God and refused to obey the things He said.
- Although they knew that God's penalty for sin was death, they deliberately continued to sin.
- They encouraged others to also rebel against God and to live sinfully.

Teacher: This description of the moral conditions of the people is based on Romans 1:18-32. These verses aptly describe the attitudes and moral degradation of the people in Noah's day. Read these verses as you study, but do not read them to the people when you teach the lesson.

These people were born sinners because they were the descendants of Adam. In addition, they chose to sin. They loved their sin and deliberately refused to agree with God.

- **We, too, are descendants of Adam.**

  All people sin because all are born sinners separated from God. But people also sin because they love their sin. People choose to sin. No one can blame anyone else for having caused him to sin.

④ God saw how wicked the people had become.

📖 Read Genesis 6:5, 11-12.

- **God saw all their sin.**

  They may have hidden their lies, adultery, stealing and murder from others, but they could not hide it from God.

- **God still sees the sins that people do.**

  God always sees everything. No one can hide anything from Him. God is everywhere and sees everything at all times. Don't forget this when you are in the jungle or when it is very dark and you think that no one can see you. Remember, God sees everything, and He is Judge. He punishes all sin.

⑤ God decided to destroy the people on the earth.

📖 Read Genesis 6:6-7.

- **God decided to punish the unrepentant.**

  The people were so wicked that the Lord said He would destroy them and all animals on the earth.

  Do you think God really would destroy all who would not repent and trust in Him? Yes! We have already learned that God does what He says.

  ○ When Adam and Eve were in the garden, God had told them that if they disobeyed, they would die. They would be separated from God. They disobeyed, and they died just as God had said.

  ○ God made it clear to Cain and Abel that, if they wanted to approach Him and be accepted, they had to bring a sheep and shed its blood. Cain came his own way, so God rejected him. God did what He said.

  Would God also carry out His threat to the people in Noah's time if they did not repent? The Spirit of God endeavored to convince the people of Noah's time to repent. God waited for 120 years for them to repent. And He told them that He would punish them if they did not listen to and believe Him. The people refused to repent and they became more and more sinful. Do you think that God did what He said this time? Yes, God always does what He says.

LESSON 18: GOD SAID HE WOULD PUNISH THE WORLD, BUT HE PROMISED TO SAVE NOAH AND ALL WHO ENTERED THE BOAT.

- **God isn't like people who merely threaten.**

   Sometimes people threaten others when they become angry, but often they do not carry out their threats. Is God like people? Does He merely make threats? No! God always does what He says.

⑥ God was gracious to Noah.

Because of God's love and mercy, there was one man whom God was not going to destroy.

📖 Read Genesis 6:8-10.

- **Because of God's grace, He forgave and accepted Noah.**

   Noah was born a sinner and under Satan's control just like all the rest of Adam's descendants. Noah did not deserve to be saved by God. He, too, deserved to be punished.

   But Noah had listened to God the Spirit and had repented. Noah came to God in the way God required. He brought the animal sacrifices, just as Abel, Seth and Enoch had. Noah trusted God to save him through the coming Deliverer.

Lesson Developer: Tell a story to help the people understand what grace means. For example:

> 💡 *Here is a story about grace. There was a thief who stole many times from another man. One day the thief was caught in a flooded river and swept downstream. He was badly injured, and it looked as if he would drown. However, before this thief drowned, the man from whom he had stolen rescued him. Even though the man recognized the thief, he pulled him out of the river, carried him home and nursed him back to health and strength, never mentioning the man's evil deeds. The man rescued the thief, even though he did not deserve it because he had done wrong to him.*

This is how God treats those who agree with Him and depend only on Him. God saves those who deserve to be punished. They are saved by God's grace.

Noah was saved by God's grace. Noah didn't deserve to be saved. He did nothing to merit God's favor.

⑦ God told Noah what was going to happen and what he must do.

- **God told Noah that He was going to destroy those who did not believe in Him.**

   Because the people were so evil and would not change their minds and come to God, God had decided that He would destroy everyone on the earth.

But what about Noah and his family? How could they be saved?

Listen to what God told Noah.

📖 Read Genesis 6:13-17.

- **God planned to bring a flood of water on the earth.**

   God told Noah that He was going to bring a flood of water on the earth, enough to destroy every living thing.

   Lesson Developer: If the people have a story of the flood, then remind them of their story. For example:

   > 💡 *You have a story about a great flood, don't you? How did you learn your flood story? It was told to you, wasn't it? Your flood story has been passed down to you by word of mouth from generation to generation.*
   >
   > *The flood story you were told by your ancestors was originally the same story that is recorded in the Bible. However, your ancestors didn't have their story of the flood written down. Therefore, over many thousands of years, your story has slowly changed. Some parts were forgotten, and other details have been distorted.*

- **Details of past events are often distorted.**

   You know how stories about things that happen are so easily changed. If there is a big problem and an argument between lots of people, everyone will have their own personal version of the events. Everybody will tell the story of what happened and what was said from their own perspective. Some people will exaggerate, and others won't include all the details. The result is that many years later, the story of what happened is far from the truth and the people who were involved in the original events would not recognize that the story is about them.

- **The details of the great flood sent by God are all true.**

   The story of the flood that we will read in the Bible was written down so we have the exact account of what really happened. The story about the flood in the Bible is the true story because God guided chosen men to write down God's message so that it would not be distorted or forgotten.

   We read in the Bible that God told Noah that He was going to send a great flood which would cover the whole earth. All people and all animals would be drowned.

   But God planned to save Noah and his family from the flood. So God told Noah to build a large boat so that all those who trusted in God could be saved.

LESSON 18: GOD SAID HE WOULD PUNISH THE WORLD, BUT HE PROMISED TO SAVE NOAH AND ALL WHO ENTERED THE BOAT.

📖 Read Genesis 6:17-21.

God told Noah that he was going to judge the world by sending a great flood. But He did not just say to him, "Noah, I am going to judge the world. I am going to send a great flood. You had better do something about it. Now start building a boat." Noah couldn't just make up his own plans for this boat.

- **God gave Noah instructions about how to build the boat.**

  Noah had to follow God's instructions. He had to build the boat exactly according to God's plan.

  God always does things according to His own plan. Think about what we have already learned.

  - When Adam and Eve sinned, they made clothing, but their clothing was not acceptable to God. Their clothing had to be made according to God's plan.
  - For Cain and Abel to be accepted by God, their offerings had to be according to the way God had said.
  - The boat, too, had to be built according to God's plan.

- **God instructed Noah to put only one door in the boat.**

  This is a very important point you need to remember about the way this boat was to be built. There was to be only one way to get inside the boat. Every person and every animal that was to be saved from God's judgment had to enter by this door. There was only one boat in which people could be saved from God's wrath, and there was only one door to enter the boat.

Teacher: This emphasis on the "one boat" and "one door" is in preparation for the message of Christ and the Gospel. This point will be important as you go on in your teaching, so it needs to be carefully taught here. Do not brush over points like this lightly. They are necessary foundations on which to build later when you teach the Gospel in the death, burial and resurrection of the Lord Jesus Christ (1 Corinthians 15:1-4; Romans 1:1-4).

⑧ Noah obeyed God.

 Read Genesis 6:22.

Noah believed God. He trusted in and depended on God to save him and his family from the flood which God said He would send.

Remember, until this time, the world was watered by mist which rose up from the ground and by streams which were fed from underground lakes. No one had ever seen rain. Even though Noah had never seen rain, Noah believed God.

Teacher: As you prepare to teach, read Hebrews 11:7, but do not read this verse to the people when you teach the lesson.

Sometimes people will not believe because they have never seen God, Heaven and the place of punishment which God has prepared. But all that the Bible says is true.

Noah believed just because God said it. God said He would send a flood, and Noah believed God. He obeyed and built the boat just as God had said.

⑨ Noah was God's messenger.

- **While Noah was building the boat, he was also telling the people God's message.**

Noah warned them that God hated their wicked ways and that God was going to send a flood to destroy everything on the earth. He told them that, if they changed their attitude and came trusting in God and entered the boat which God had told Noah to make, they would be saved.

- **God's Spirit continually reminded the people of the things Noah said.**

The people didn't want to remember God's words, but God's Spirit wouldn't let them forget.

When you think about the things we are teaching you, God's Spirit wants you to carefully consider and believe God's message. God did not want the people in Noah's time to perish, nor does He want you to live and die still separated from Him.

The people in Noah's time would not listen to what God said to them through Noah. They loved their own sinful ways and would not repent. I hope that none of you are going to be like those foolish people.

❓ Questions

1. The majority of the people in Noah's time were only interested in having what they thought was a good time. What were the people not interested in?

   They were not interested in God or the things that would please Him.

2. Are many people today like the majority of people in Noah's time?

   Yes. The majority are like the people in Noah's time.

3. Who was speaking to the people's minds, telling them to repent?

   God's Spirit was constantly speaking to the people, endeavoring to convince them to repent.

LESSON 18: GOD SAID HE WOULD PUNISH THE WORLD, BUT HE PROMISED TO SAVE NOAH AND ALL WHO ENTERED THE BOAT.

4. Who speaks to our minds today to remind us of the Word of God?

   God's Spirit speaks to us today to remind us of the Word of God.

5. What did God say He was going to do because the people in Noah's time would not repent?

   God said He would destroy all people and animals on the earth.

6. Did Noah deserve to be delivered by God?

   No. Noah was also a sinner. He deserved to be destroyed in the flood like all the other people.

7. Noah was a sinner, but why did God plan to save him?

   God planned to save Noah because Noah had agreed with God that he was a sinner and had trusted God to save him through the coming Deliverer.

8. What did God tell Noah to build?

   God told Noah to build a big boat.

9. Did God allow Noah to build the boat however he thought best?

   No. The boat had to be built exactly as God commanded Noah.

10. How many doors did God tell Noah to put in the boat?

    God told Noah to put only one door in the boat.

11. Did Noah build the boat just as God said?

    Yes. Noah obeyed and built the boat just as God had said.

12. What else did Noah do at the same time as he was building the big boat?

    Noah told the people God's message and warned them that God was going to send a flood to destroy the world.

13. Had the people ever seen rain before?

    No. It had never rained before this time.

14. Did the people accept what Noah said and change their attitude?

    No. The people would not listen to what God said to them through Noah.

LESSON 19: GOD DESTROYED EVERYONE IN THE WORLD EXCEPT NOAH AND HIS FAMILY WHO WERE IN THE BOAT.

Scripture

Genesis 7:1-17, 21-23, Genesis 8:1-4, 14-22, Genesis 9:1-19

Lesson Outline

(1) God told Noah to bring his family, the animals and the birds into the boat. (Genesis 7:1-5)

(2) They all entered by one door. (Genesis 7:6-15)

(3) God shut them in. (Genesis 7:16)

(4) God destroyed all those outside the boat. (Genesis 7:17, 21-23)

(5) God remembered Noah and all those inside the boat. (Genesis 8:1-4, 14-19)

(6) God accepted Noah's offering. (Genesis 8:20-22)

(7) God gave His commands and promises to Noah. (Genesis 9:1-7)

(8) God gave the rainbow as the sign of His promise. (Genesis 9:8-17)

(9) Noah's sons were the ancestors of the human race. (Genesis 9:18-19)

(?) Review Questions from Lesson 18.

Lesson Outline Developed

(1) God told Noah to bring his family, the animals and the birds into the boat.

- **God does not overlook sin.**

    God had warned Noah that He was going to send a flood to destroy all who refused to repent. Do you think that God did what He said? Or do you think that God forgot about it?

We have learned many things about God. One thing we have learned is that God does what He says. Do you remember what God told Adam and Eve in the garden in Eden? God told them that they could eat the fruit from all the trees in the garden except the fruit from the tree of the knowledge of good and evil. God warned Adam that the day they ate the fruit of the tree of knowledge of good and evil, they would die. Adam and Eve disobeyed God, and they ate the fruit. Did they die? Yes! They died, just as God had said.

Lesson Developer: Use an illustration about how people threaten but often do not carry through. For example:

> *Sometimes, a person who is offended may threaten to do something bad to the offender. However, after some time goes by, his anger may subside, and he may eventually forget the whole incident.*

God is not like people. God always does what He says.

God will not overlook sin. He will not forget. Sin must be paid for. God's anger does not diminish against those who oppose Him. It grows stronger and stronger.

- **The people in Noah's time did not repent.**

    Read Genesis 7:1-4.

Since the creation of the world, there had never been rain. God watered the earth's surface by mist and the rivers and streams which fed from great lakes of water under the earth's surface. Even though Noah had never seen rain, he believed what God said to him.

Teacher: We know from other passages in Scripture that Noah had never seen rain. Hebrews 11:7 says that Noah was "divinely warned of things not yet seen." We also know from Genesis 2:6 that it had never rained prior to this time. Read these passages as you prepare to teach, but do not read these verses to the people when you teach the lesson.

Noah warned the people of God's coming judgment, but the people did not accept God's message. They refused to agree with God that they deserved His punishment. They would not trust in His promise to send the Deliverer. They didn't believe that God would destroy the world with a great flood.

God waited patiently for 120 years for them to change their minds, but He would wait no longer. It was time for God to punish them.

- **God still waits for people to repent.**

Just as God waited for the people to repent in Noah's day, so He is waiting for the people of the world today to listen to His words, to agree with Him and to trust Him. He has

LESSON 19: GOD DESTROYED EVERYONE IN THE WORLD EXCEPT NOAH AND HIS FAMILY WHO WERE IN THE BOAT.

not told us it will only be 120 years before He sends His judgment, but some day He is going to say, "That is long enough. I am not going to wait any longer." All those who refuse to believe God will then go to everlasting punishment.

- **Before it started to rain, God told Noah to take his family and the chosen animals into the boat.**

    📖 Read Genesis 7:5.

Noah believed that God was going to destroy the world. He also believed that he and his family could only be saved by God, so he did what God said. He built the boat just as God had instructed him. And he went into the boat when God told him to.

God didn't save Noah because of his good life. God saved him because Noah agreed with and trusted in God.

② They all entered by one door.

📖 Read Genesis 7:6-15.

Noah and his family all went into the boat through the one door which God had told Noah to make. This was the only way anyone could be saved from the flood and God's wrath against sin.

All the animals also came into the boat by the same door.

③ God shut them in.

📖 Read Genesis 7:16.

After Noah and his family and all the animals were inside the boat, God shut the door. Those inside the boat were safe because God had shut them in. But those outside the boat had no way to escape God's judgment because God had shut them out.

The people who had not repented did not have any more time to change their minds and believe. When God shut the door, it was too late for the people outside. Even if they cried or pleaded outside the door, they could not enter the boat. Noah could not let them in because God had shut them out. They had no way to be saved.

- ○ When God put Adam and Eve out of the garden, away from the tree of life, was there any way for them to get back in? No! There was no way they could get back to the tree of life.

- ○ The same was true in Noah's day. When God shut the people out of the boat, there was no way for them to get in.

When God decides it is time to punish sin, there is no escape from Him.

④ God destroyed all those outside the boat.

📖 Read Genesis 7:17, 21-23.

- **After God had shut the door of the boat, He sent the rain.**

    God controls the rain. He made the heavens and earth and He controls everything in them. God was the One who sent the rain.

    God sent the rain for 40 days and nights. It rained until the whole earth was covered with water, even the tallest trees and highest mountains.

    Where did all the water come from? We learned from an earlier lesson what the world was like when God first made it. The whole earth was in darkness and covered with deep water. On the first day, God created the light. On the second day, God created the air and the sky. Also, on the second day of creation, God placed much of the water which had been on the earth up above the sky. When God decided to flood the earth, He allowed the water which He had placed above the sky to fall back onto the ground.

    In addition to the water that fell from the sky, water gushed up from the springs deep in the earth.

Teacher: Originally the rivers and streams on the earth were fed from subterranean reservoirs and rivers of water. When God sent the flood, He may have caused great earthquakes and volcanic eruptions to open the earth's crust so that these great fountains of water gushed out onto the earth's surface (Genesis 8:2).

- **God can do anything He wants to do.**

    God made everything, and He controls everything. It was not hard for God to cause the water to flood the earth. Nothing is impossible to Him. He is almighty.

- **Everyone outside of the boat was destroyed by God.**

    Only Noah and his family had believed God and had entered the boat. All the other people had refused to believe, and they all died.

☞ **Teacher:** Show a picture of the people drowning in the flood.

- **The great majority of people today are like the people who died in the flood.**

    Most people have always refused to believe God. Most people love their sin and don't want to agree with God that they are wrong. Most people want to follow the crowd. They don't want to go against popular opinion.

LESSON 19: GOD DESTROYED EVERYONE IN THE WORLD EXCEPT NOAH AND HIS FAMILY WHO WERE IN THE BOAT.

If you go with the crowd who refuse to believe God, you will go to everlasting punishment. It is better to be like Noah. He didn't go along with what other people said. Noah believed God.

⑤ God remembered Noah and all those inside the boat.

📖 Read Genesis 8:1-4.

- **God's punishment by the flood was finished.**

   God stopped the rain. Then God sent a strong wind to dry up the water, and the dry land again appeared. God controls the rain and the wind.

   God, not the spirits, is in control of the world. You might think that the spirits have power over the wind and the rain. But the spirits have deceived you. They cannot do anything with the wind or rain unless God allows them.

Teacher: Read Job 1:9-19; Psalms 147:18; 148:8 before the teaching session to think about the truth that God is in control. However, do not read these verses to the people when you teach the lesson.

📖 Read Genesis 8:14-19.

- **God always does what He says.**

   Noah and his family and the animals were kept safe by God. No one who was in the boat died.

   God never forgets what He has said. He said He would save Noah and all inside the boat, and He did. He said He would destroy all outside of the ark, and He did. God is faithful to do all that He says He will do. God does not change

☞ **Teacher:** Point to **Mt. Ararat** (located in what is now the country of Turkey) on the map.

⑥ God accepted Noah's offering.

📖 Read Genesis 8:20-22.

☞ **Teacher:** Show a picture of Noah and his family bringing an offering to God.

God accepted Noah's offering just as He had Abel's. God accepted Noah and his family because they came God's way, trusting in Him to accept them. They killed animals and allowed their blood to flow out. The blood of the animals did not pay for their sin. The payment for sin is everlasting separation from God. The blood of animals just reminded those who offered it that sin brings death. God accepted them because of His grace.

7) God gave His commands and promises to Noah.

📖 Read Genesis 9:1-7.

God gave Noah and his sons, Shem, Ham and Japheth, authority over the animals, birds and fish. The world and everything in it belongs to God, and He had the authority to give it to Noah and his sons. He gave the world to them so that mankind could take care of it for Him.

8) God gave the rainbow as the sign of His promise.

📖 Read Genesis 9:8-17.

God gave the rainbow to show that He would never again destroy the earth by a flood. Many thousands of years have passed since the flood, and God has kept His Word.

When you see a rainbow, remember that God can be trusted. God gave the rainbow as a sign that He will never again destroy the world by a flood, and He has done what He promised.

9) Noah's sons were the ancestors of the human race.

📖 Read Genesis 9:18-19.

All the people of the world came from these three men. One of these men was your ancestor.

? Questions

1. How long did God wait for the people in Noah's time to agree with Him and to believe His message?
   God waited for 120 years.

2. Does God's anger subside against those who refuse to repent?
   No. God's anger does not subside against those who refuse to repent.

LESSON 19: GOD DESTROYED EVERYONE IN THE WORLD EXCEPT NOAH AND HIS FAMILY WHO WERE IN THE BOAT.

3. Who told Noah when to go into the boat?

   God told Noah when to go into the boat.

4. How did Noah and his family and the animals get into the boat?

   They all entered by the only door which God had told Noah to put in the side of the boat.

5. Who shut the door?

   God shut the door.

6. For what reason did God shut the door?

   God shut the door so that all those inside the boat would be safe and so that those outside the boat would no longer have the opportunity to enter and be saved.

7. Can anyone escape when God decides it is time to punish sin?

   No. When God decides it is time to punish sin, no one can escape from judgment.

8. Where did the water come from to be enough to cover even the tallest trees and highest mountains all over the whole earth?

   Some of the water came from up above the sky where God had placed it on the second day of creation, and some of the water gushed up from the springs deep in the earth.

9. Did anyone outside the boat escape from death?

   No. Everyone outside the boat died.

10. Did anyone inside the boat die?

    No. God kept everyone inside the boat safe.

11. Why did God accept the offering which Noah made when he came out of the ark?

    God accepted his offering because Noah trusted in God and offered the animals just like God had said.

12. Did the animals' blood pay for Noah's sins?

    No. It was not possible for the blood of animals to pay for Noah's sins. The payment for sin is everlasting separation from God.

13. Why could God give Noah and his sons control over all the animals, birds and fish?

    God could give Noah and his sons authority over all the animals, birds and fish because God created the world and everything in it belongs to God.

14. What did God put in the sky as a sign that He would never again destroy the whole earth by a flood?

    God put the rainbow in the sky as a sign of His promise.

15. Has God kept His promise to never again destroy the whole earth with a flood?

    Yes. God has kept His promise.

16. Who were the ancestors of the entire human race?

    Noah's sons, Shem, Ham and Japheth, were the ancestors of all people in the world.

LESSON 20: GOD SCATTERED THE REBELS AT THE TOWER OF BABEL.

Scripture

Genesis 11:1-9

Lesson Outline

(1) The descendants of Shem, Ham and Japheth were rebellious and proud. (Genesis 11:1-4)

(2) The people deliberately disobeyed God's command.

(3) God saw the people as they built the city and the tower. (Genesis 11:5)

(4) God scattered the people. (Genesis 11:6-9)

(?) Review Questions from Lesson 19.

Lesson Outline Developed

(1) The descendants of Shem, Ham and Japheth were rebellious and proud.

Read Genesis 11:1-4.

Many years had passed since God saved Noah and his family from the flood. Noah's three sons had children, and their children had children. Once again, many people lived on the earth.

- **The descendants of Shem, Ham and Japheth deliberately turned away from God.**

Although they knew about God, the majority of them refused to consider His will for them. They did not want to know and believe on the Lord as Abel, Seth, Enoch and Noah had. They did not want to obey God and come to Him the way He had said.

These people were under Satan's control and like Satan in their thinking. They wanted to be great and exalt themselves.

- **Let's think about what these people knew.**
    - They knew the truth about God because it was told from one generation to the next.
    - They knew that God was their creator. Every day and every night, they could see His mighty power revealed through all the things that He had created.
    - They knew that God had judged the world with a terrible flood, so they knew that God punished sin.
    - They also knew that God had given the rainbow as a sign that He would never again destroy the whole earth by a flood so they knew that God was faithful to keep His promise.
- **They turned away from the truth about God.**

    They did not have any excuse for not believing God. But they would not give God the place of honor which He deserves, and they would not thank Him for all He gave to them every day – life, health, sunshine, rain and food.

    They deliberately turned away from what they knew to be the truth about God, and their minds became more and more evil and foolish. They made images of people, animals, birds and reptiles, and they worshiped these images.

Teacher: The description of these people is based on Romans 1:18-25. Read this passage as you prepare to teach, but do not read it to the people when you teach the lesson.

Satan was leading these people to rebel against God and His will. Satan wants all people to turn away from God. Satan wants everyone to worship a false god like the sun, the moon, the stars, birds or animals. He doesn't want anyone to worship the only true and living God.

These people were the ancestors of all people who live today. Your ancestors and my ancestors were among these people who rebelled against God and worshiped images.

- **Nimrod was a powerful leader of the people.**

    The descendants of Shem, Ham and Japheth looked to men to lead them instead of God. One of the mighty leaders at this time was named Nimrod. He organized the building of many great cities. One of the cities he built was named Babel.

Teacher: As you prepare to teach, read Genesis 10:8-10, but do not read these verses to the people when you teach the lesson.

☞ **Teacher:** On the map, point to the area where Babel was situated in the Tigris-Euphrates plain.

LESSON 20: GOD SCATTERED THE REBELS AT THE TOWER OF BABEL.

👉 **Teacher:** Point to the word, "**Babel**," on the chronological chart.

② The people deliberately disobeyed God's command.

📖 Read Genesis 1:28.

God had told Adam and Eve to be fruitful and multiply and to fill the earth. After the flood, God gave this same command to Noah.

📖 Read Genesis 9:1.

The descendents of Shem, Ham and Japheth deliberately disobeyed the command given to Noah by God, their creator. They did not want to be separated by living in different parts of the world as God commanded. Instead, they gathered in one place, began to build a city and to erect a great, tall tower. They did not want to follow God's plans for them or the world. They wanted to exalt themselves.

③ God saw the people as they built the city and the tower.

Do you think God saw them? Did He know their thoughts and what they planned? Did He care about what they did?

📖 Read Genesis 11:5.

Yes, the Lord was interested in them even though they had deliberately dismissed Him from their minds.

- **God is interested in every person.**

God sees all people everywhere. He is interested in you, and He knows all about you. You cannot keep any secret from Him. God is your creator, and He owns you, even though you are separated from Him because of your sin. He has seen you, and He knows everything you have ever thought, said and done.

④ God scattered the people.

- **No one can fight against God and be the winner.**

When Satan was in Heaven, he tried to take God's place, but God would not allow him to do that. He removed Satan from his position of leadership over the other angels and would not allow him to continue to live in Heaven. Satan fought against God, but he lost. The spirits who followed Satan in his rebellion also lost in their fight against God.

We have already learned about people who tried to fight against God.

  ○ Adam and Eve chose to disobey God when they ate the fruit from the tree of knowledge of good and evil.

- Cain refused to obey God and come to God as He had said.
- The people who lived in Noah's time refused to repent.
- All of these lost in their fight against God.

What do you think happened this time? Did the people who disobeyed God and built the city and the tower win? No! God is greater than all.

- **God took control of the situation.**

    God knew that if all these sinful people remained in one place, they would become more and more evil and only become increasingly rebellious against God and His will.

    📖 Read Genesis 11:6-9.

☞ **Teacher:** Show a picture of the tower of Babel, with workers no longer able to understand each other.

- **The Lord caused the different families to speak different languages.**

    Because they could no longer understand one another, they stopped building the city, and they separated into their various families and moved away to different parts of the country. Over many years, they moved to other continents around the world, even traveling across the oceans.

    This is how the different nations and races began. Many people have stories about how languages and nations began, but the Bible tells the true story of how languages and people groups came into existence.

- **This is the beginning of the history of all people.**

    Our ancestors were at the tower of Babel. Your ancestors were also at the tower of Babel. They turned away from the truth of God which they knew, and they followed the ideas which Satan and his spirits put in their minds. Only a few people continued to worship the true and living God.

Teacher: At this stage in the teaching program, you will need to decide whether or not to state directly that their ancestors followed Satan. You do not want to needlessly offend so that they refuse to listen, yet you must reveal that their religious beliefs are based on the lies of Satan.

LESSON 20: GOD SCATTERED THE REBELS AT THE TOWER OF BABEL.

(?) Questions

1. Did the descendants of Shem, Ham and Japheth know the truth about God?
   Yes. They knew the truth about God.

2. How did these people know the truth about God?
   The truth about God was told from one generation to the next.

3. What did the world, the sun, the moon and the stars show these people about God?
   The world, sun, moon and stars showed them that God alone is the almighty creator of all things.

4. What fact about God did a rainbow in the clouds remind these people of?
   A rainbow reminded the people that God is faithful to do what He says.

5. Did the majority of these people worship God?
   No. The majority of them turned away from God.

6. Instead of worshiping God, what did these people worship?
   They worshiped images of people, animals, birds and reptiles. They also worshiped the sun, moon and stars.

7. Who were these people following?
   They were following Satan.

8. Who were the descendants of Shem, Ham and Japheth the ancestors of?
   The descendants of Shem, Ham and Japheth were the ancestors of all the people in the world.

9. What command had God given to Adam that He also gave to Noah?
   God commanded Adam and Noah to be fruitful and multiply and to fill the earth.

10. Instead of obeying God's command to Adam and Noah, what did these people do?
    They congregated in one place, began to build a city and to erect a great, tall tower.

11. Why did they begin to build the city and the tower of Babel?
    They did not want to be separated by living in different parts of the world. And they wanted to exalt themselves.

12. Did God know what the people were planning to do?
    Yes. God knew what they were planning to do.

13. Can anyone keep secrets from God?

    No. God knows all about every person. No one can keep a secret from Him.

14. What did the Lord do to stop the people who were building the city and the tower?

    The Lord caused different families to speak different languages so the people could no longer understand one another.

15. What happened when the different families started speaking different languages?

    They stopped building the city, and the various families separated from one another and moved to different places.

16. Where do we learn the true story of how the different languages and people groups began?

    The Bible tells the true story of how the languages and people groups began.

17. Were your ancestors among those who rebelled against God at the tower of Babel?

    Yes. Those were our ancestors who rebelled against God at the tower of Babel.

LESSON 21: GOD CHOSE ABRAM AND GUIDED HIM TO CANAAN.

Scripture

Genesis 11:27-32, Genesis 12:1-5

Lesson Outline

1. Abram was a descendant of Shem. (Genesis 11:27-32)

2. God told Abram to leave his country. (Genesis 12:1)

3. God chose Abram as part of His plan to save people from the punishment for sin.

4. God made promises to Abram. (Genesis 12:2-3)

5. Abram believed and obeyed God. (Genesis 12:4-5)

? Review Questions from Lesson 20.

Lesson Outline Developed

1. Abram was a descendant of Shem.

Noah had three sons. One of his sons was named Shem.

We are going to read in God's Book about one of the descendants of Shem. His name was Abram, and his father's name was Terah.

Abram lived many years after the descendants of Shem, Ham and Japheth had tried to build the tower of Babel.

📖 Read Genesis 11:27-30.

👉 **Teacher:** Point to the names, "Abraham and Sarah," on the chronological chart. Explain that they will learn later in the story how Abram's and Sarai's names were changed.

Abram married Sarai, but Abram and Sarai didn't have any children.

📖 Read Genesis 11:31-32.

☞ **Teacher:** Point to Ur, Haran and Canaan on the map as you teach the following section.

Abram lived in Ur, which is near where the people had begun to build the tower of Babel.

Abram's father, Terah, left Ur and moved to Haran. Terah took Abram and Sarai with him. Terah also took his grandson, Lot, because Lot's father had died in Ur.

☞ **Teacher:** Point to the name, "Lot," on the chronological chart.

They had planned to go into Canaan, but they only got as far as Haran. Terah died in Haran.

② God told Abram to leave his country.

📖 Read Genesis 12:1.

- **Before Abram moved with his father to Haran, God had spoken to Abram.**

Teacher: As you prepare to teach, read Acts 7:2-3, but do not read these verses to the people when you teach the lesson.

God had told Abram to leave his own country and go into the land of Canaan.

The Bible was not yet written in Abram's day, so God spoke directly to him and told him what he was to do.

God no longer speaks directly to people with a voice; He speaks through His Book, the Bible. The only way we can know about God and His message for us is through the words of this book, the Bible.

- **Abram was different from the people in his land.**

The people of Abram's land worshiped idols. They did not trust, love or obey God, the only true creator.

Teacher: As you prepare to teach, read Joshua 24:2, but do not read this verse to the people when you teach the lesson.

Abram was a descendant of Adam just as the people in his land were, and so Abram was a sinner just as they were. But Abram was different from the people in his land because he did not worship idols as they did. Abram believed in God and His promises, and Abram came to God in the way that God had said to come.

- **God told Abram to leave his country and his people.**

**LESSON 21: GOD CHOSE ABRAM
AND GUIDED HIM TO CANAAN.**

God's plan for Abram could not be achieved while Abram was living among his idolatrous countrymen. He must leave his homeland and go to the country to which God promised He would guide him.

God had the right to tell Abram what to do. God is greater than all. He is supreme.

③ God chose Abram as part of His plan to save people from the punishment for sin.

Ever since Adam disobeyed God when he disobeyed God by eating the fruit from the tree of knowledge of good and evil, people have been born separated from God and with sinful hearts.

- **Although all people were sinners, God never abandoned His plan to send the Deliverer.**

Think about the descendants of Shem, Ham and Japheth who were building the tower of Babel. These people, who were our ancestors, deliberately turned away from God and the truth. They worshiped the things God had created instead of their creator, and they rebelled against God. Yet, God still loved them and didn't forget His promise to send the Deliverer.

In the Garden of Eden, God had made a promise that He would send the Deliverer to rescue people from Satan's power and everlasting punishment. God never abandoned that plan. No one and nothing can stop God from carrying out His plans. Whatever He begins, He finishes. Choosing Abram was the next step in God's plan to rescue people.

- **God is still the same today as He was in the days of Abram.**

He is still loving, merciful and gracious. He never forgot His plan to save people from everlasting punishment. He wants all people – including you – to be saved from everlasting punishment and from Satan's power. It is very important for you to continue to listen carefully to God's message so that you can learn the only way that you can be saved.

④ God made promises to Abram.

📖 Read Genesis 12:2.

Even though Abram and Sarai did not have any children, God promised Abram that he would become the father of a great nation.

God also promised that He would protect and prosper Abram so that he would become an important man and that, through him, others would also receive great spiritual benefit and help.

📖 Read Genesis 12:3.

God promised that He would prosper those who helped Abram, but He would bring evil on anyone who treated Abram wrongly.

God also promised Abram that all families of the earth would be blessed through him. This is the greatest promise given to Abram because it is about the Deliverer.

- **God promised Abram that one of his descendants would be the Deliverer.**

    In the garden in Eden, God had told of One who would overcome Satan and deliver the world from his power. This Deliverer would make it possible for people to be in oneness again with God.

    All families of the earth would be blessed through the Deliverer who would be a descendant of Abram. This includes you and your people, me and my people, and all people in the world. The Deliverer whom God promised to send was for all people in every part of the world.

Teacher: If they ask you if the Deliverer has come, assure them that He has. Nevertheless, do not give the Gospel at this time. We need to wait until they have seen their great need as sinners and are truly prepared for the Gospel. Tell them to listen carefully in order to understand exactly what God wants them to know, and that, as they listen, they will hear how and when the Deliverer came.

⑤ Abram believed and obeyed God.

When God promised that one of Abram's descendants would be the promised Deliverer who would destroy Satan, Abram and Sarai didn't have any children. Nevertheless, Abram believed that God would send the Deliverer and that the Deliverer would be one of his descendants.

God told Abram to leave his home and go to the country to which God would guide him. Did Abram obey God? Yes, he believed God, so he obeyed God.

📖 Read Genesis 12:4-5.

☞ **Teacher:** Point on the map to the route Abram traveled, starting in Ur, then going to Haran, and arriving in Canaan as their final destination.

☞ **Teacher:** Show a picture of Abram and his household traveling to Canaan.

Abram was very rich and had many servants. He had many cattle, sheep and goats. He took all that he owned with him.

Abram and all those who traveled with him lived in tents.

Lot, Abram's nephew, went with Abram and Sarai. Lot also believed God and trusted in His promises.

The Lord faithfully guided Abram to the land of Canaan that He had promised to give to him.

LESSON 21: GOD CHOSE ABRAM AND GUIDED HIM TO CANAAN.

❓ Questions

1. God spoke directly to Abram, but God no longer speaks directly to people with a voice. How does God speak to people now?

   God speaks through the Bible.

2. The people of Abram's land worshiped idols. Whom did Abram worship?

   Abram worshiped the true God.

3. How did Abram come to God?

   Abram came to God in the way that God had said to come.

4. The descendants of Noah rebelled against God and built the tower of Babel. Did their rebellion cause God to abandon His plan to send the Deliverer?

   No. God never abandoned His plan to rescue people from Satan's power and everlasting punishment.

5. What was Abram's part in God's plan to send the Deliverer into the world?

   God chose Abram to be the ancestor of the Deliverer.

6. Where did God tell Abram to go?

   God told him to leave his own country and go to the land to which God promised to lead him.

7. What did God promise Abram would happen to his descendants?

   God promised that Abram's descendants would become a great nation.

8. What did God say He would do for people who helped Abram?

   God said that He would prosper those who helped Abram.

9. What did God say He would do to people who treated Abram wrongly?

   God said that He would bring evil on anyone who treated Abram wrongly.

10. Who did God promise would be blessed through the Deliverer, Abram's descendant?

    God promised that all the families of the earth would be blessed through the Deliverer, Abram's descendant.

11. How many children did Abram and Sarai have when God promised that the Deliverer would be one of Abram's descendants?

    They didn't have any children.

12. What did Abram do when God gave him the promises?

    He believed God. He left his own country and went where God guided him.

LESSON 22: GOD RENEWED HIS PROMISES TO ABRAM.

Scripture

Genesis 13:5-17, Genesis 15:5-6, 12-16, Genesis 17:1-5, 15-17

Lesson Outline

(1) Lot moved away from Abram. (Genesis 13:5-13)

(2) God renewed His promises to Abram.(Genesis 13:14-17; 15:5-6)

(3) God told Abram what would happen to his descendants. (Genesis 15:12-16)

(4) God gave new names to Abram and Sarai.(Genesis 17:1-5, 15-17)

(?) Review Questions from Lesson 21.

Lesson Outline Developed

(1) Lot moved away from Abram.

- **Abram and Lot settled together with all they owned in the land of Canaan.**

    Abram was very rich. He had many cattle, sheep and goats.

    Lot, Abram's nephew, was also rich like his uncle.

    Because Abram and Lot had many sheep and cattle, there wasn't enough grass and water for their animals.

- **Trouble developed between the servants taking care of Abram's and Lot's herds.**

    📖 Read Genesis 13:5-7.

- **Abram had a solution which he proposed to Lot.**

    📖 Read Genesis 13:8-9.

- **Lot chose to move to the fertile plain.**

    📖 Read Genesis 13:10-11.

Lot chose the grassy plain because it was well-watered and had plenty of grass for his animals.

Even though Lot believed and trusted in God, he didn't consider how this move to live with ungodly people would affect him and his family and their knowledge of God. Lot was thinking about how to make more money.

- **We have already learned that it is foolish to ignore God.**
  - Because Cain made a foolish decision to ignore God, all his descendants were drowned in the flood.
  - Because Lot chose prosperity, some terrible things later happened to him and his family.
- **Be careful of the choices you make.**

Don't be like Cain or Lot. You may have to make a choice between taking time to make money and taking time to listen to God's message. Which will you choose? If you choose to turn away from listening to God's Word, you will regret it forever when you are in the place of everlasting punishment. Riches will not help you if you die and go to the Lake of Fire.

- **Lot made the wrong choice.**

   Read Genesis 13:12-13.

Abram stayed up in the rocky, less fertile hills and mountains of Canaan. Lot moved down to the fertile plain and settled near the city of Sodom.

- **The people in the cities of Sodom and Gomorrah were very wicked.**

Sodom and Gomorrah were cities in this fertile plain that Lot had chosen. The people who lived in these cities didn't want to know about God or what He wanted them to do. They only thought of themselves and satisfying their evil desires. But even though the people in those cities weren't thinking about God, He saw all they did. He was their creator and He rightfully owned them, even though they were following Satan.

- **God is still the same.**

Just as God knew about the people in Sodom and Gomorrah, God knows all about people today. Although people may choose to reject God and follow Satan, they still rightfully belong to God. When He decides He has given people enough time to repent, He will judge and punish them.

Just as God was watching the wicked people of Sodom and Gomorrah to see if they would repent and believe in Him, God is also watching each one of you to see if you will repent and believe in Him.

② God renewed His promises to Abram.

After Lot moved away from Abram, the Lord spoke to Abram. The Lord encouraged

LESSON 22: GOD RENEWED HIS PROMISES TO ABRAM.

and reassured Abram that He, God, would be with him and that His promises to Abram would all be fulfilled.

- **God promised again to give Abram all of the land of Canaan.**

    📖 Read Genesis 13:14-17.

☞ **Teacher:** Point to the land of Canaan on the map.

- **God promised Abram that he would have many descendants.**

    📖 Read Genesis 15:5-6.

One night, God took Abram outside of his tent and told him to look up and count the stars if he could. God then promised Abram that his descendants would be as many as the stars, even though Abram did not have any children at this time.

Think about that. How many stars can you see in the sky on a cloudless night? There are so many stars that you cannot even count them.

How could Abram have so many descendants? Abram and Sarai had been married for many years and were old, but they had never been able to have a child.

Although it seemed impossible for Abram that his descendants would be unable to be counted just like the stars are unable to be counted, Abram believed God. Abram trusted that God would give him a child and that God would send the Deliverer as one of his descendants.

Because Abram believed God, God accepted Abram as if he had no sin. Abram was a sinner, but because of his trust in God, God accepted him as if he was perfectly righteous.

③ God told Abram what would happen to his descendants.

📖 Read Genesis 15:12-16.

God knew all that would happen to Abram's descendants before they were ever born.

Teacher: This prophecy about Abram's descendants did not reveal the location, so do not mention Egypt. Later, when you teach the story of the people of Israel going into Egypt, you will point back to this prophecy.

- **All of the future is known to God.**

    Do you know what will happen next week or next year or in ten years? Do you know what will happen in 100 years or 200 years? No person can tell what will happen in the future, but God knew what was going to happen to Abram's descendants. God knows everything. God knew about their future, and He knows all about your future as well.

> **Teacher:** Do not refer to the story of Hagar and Ishmael in Genesis 16. We are laying the foundations for the life of Christ told in the Gospels, and the story of Ishmael's birth is not a necessary part. God only recognized Isaac as Abraham's son (Genesis 17:18-21; 22:2). The story of Hagar and Ishmael will be taught in Phase 2 as preparation for teaching the Epistles.

④ God gave new names to Abram and Sarai.

📖 Read Genesis 17:1-5.

- **God changed Abram's name when he was 99 years old.**

  Not many people live to that age now, but in those days, people lived longer than they do today.

  God changed Abram's name to Abraham because God promised he would become the father of many descendants. Abraham means "father of a multitude of children."

  📖 Read Genesis 17:15-16.

- **God changed Sarai's name when she was 90 years old.**

  Even though Sarai was so old and had never been able to have a child, God promised she would have a son. God changed Sarai's name to Sarah because she would become the mother of many descendants. Sarah means "mother of nations."

  📖 Read Genesis 17:17.

- **Because God is almighty, He could give a son to Abraham and Sarah.**

  Abraham was 100 years old, and Sarah was 90 years old. They were too old to have a son, but nothing is impossible to God.

- **All life comes from God.**

  God gave life to the first man and woman. God created Adam and Eve out of the dust of the ground. He breathed into them and gave them life. He is the almighty God who gave life to you and your children. Because of His great power, He was able to give a son to Abraham and Sarah, even though they had passed the age of having children.

  Abraham believed God and he laughed with joy because he was so amazed that God was going to do this great thing. To man, it was impossible. But Abraham knew God could do anything He wanted, so he trusted in God.

LESSON 22: GOD RENEWED HIS PROMISES TO ABRAM.

? Questions

1. Why did Lot move away from Abram?

   Abram and Lot couldn't stay together in one place because there wasn't enough grass and water for all their animals.

2. Why did Lot choose to live on the plain near Sodom?

   Lot moved to the plain because it was well-watered and had plenty of grass for his animals.

3. Did Lot consider how this move would affect him and his family and their knowledge of God?

   No. Lot did not consider how his choice would affect him and his family.

4. If a person does not choose to listen to God, will he regret it?

   Yes. He will regret it forever when he is in the place of everlasting punishment.

5. How did God know about the wickedness of the people of Sodom and Gomorrah?

   God knew about their wickedness because God knows everything.

6. Can any person hide his thoughts, words or actions from God?

   No person can hide anything from God.

7. What land did God promise to give Abram?

   God promised to give Abram all the land of Canaan.

8. How many descendants did God promise to Abram?

   God promised that Abram's descendants would number more than the stars.

9. Why did it seem impossible that Abram's descendants would be unable to be counted?

   Abram and Sarai did not have a child.

10. What was Abram's response when God promised that he would have many descendants?

    Abram trusted that God would give him a child and that God would send the Deliverer as one of his descendants

11. Why did God accept Abram as if he had no sin?

    God accepted him because Abram believed God.

12. What did God say would happen to Abram's descendants?

    God said that Abram's descendants would go to live in another country and that they would be ill-treated for four hundred years, but after that time, God would bring them back to the land of Canaan which God had given to Abram.

13. Who knows the future of every person?
    God knows the future.

14. What new name did God give to Abram?
    God gave him the name, Abraham.

15. What does the name, Abraham, mean?
    Abraham means "father of a multitude of children."

16. What new name did God give to Sarai?
    God gave her the name, Sarah.

17. What does the name, Sarah, mean?
    Sarah means "mother of nations."

18. Why couldn't Abraham and Sarah have a child unless God performed a miracle?
    They were too old. Abraham was 100 years old, and Sarah was 90 years old.

19. Who gives life to every person?
    God gives life to every person.

20. Is anything impossible for God?
    No. God can do anything He wants to do.

LESSON 23: GOD DESTROYED SODOM AND GOMORRAH.

Scripture

Genesis 18:20-21, Genesis 19:1-17, 24-26

Lesson Outline

(1) God would not tolerate the wickedness of Sodom and Gomorrah. (Genesis 18:20-21)

(2) God's angels came to Sodom. (Genesis 19:1-3)

(3) The people who lived in Sodom were very sinful. (Genesis 19:4-9)

(4) God's angels rescued Lot, his wife and his daughters out of Sodom. (Genesis 19:10-17)

(5) God destroyed Sodom and Gomorrah. (Genesis 19:24-25)

(6) Lot's wife looked back. (Genesis 19:26)

(?) Review Questions from Lesson 22.

Lesson Outline Developed

(1) God would not tolerate the wickedness of Sodom and Gomorrah.

We learned in our last lesson that Lot, Abraham's nephew, had moved away from Abraham to the plain where there was plenty of grass and water for his animals. Sodom and Gomorrah were two of the cities on the plain. The people who lived in these cities were very wicked.

Read Genesis 18:20-21.

- **God saw the people of Sodom and Gomorrah.**

    Even though many people lived in the world at that time, God was able to see everything that every person did. God saw everything the people of Sodom and Gomorrah did, and He heard everything that they said. He knew all about them, and He was interested in them.

- **God is still interested in all people today.**

    Even though there are many millions of people in the world today, God still knows and is interested in every individual. Every person and thing is important to God.

    Think about this. Even though there are millions of birds in the world, God tells us in the Bible that He knows when one bird dies. He also tells us in the Bible that we are much more precious to Him than the birds.

- **God will punish every single person who refuses to believe His Word.**

    God is interested in every individual, and all are accountable to Him. You may think that God is not interested in your tribe because you are so few in number or that He does not care what you as an individual do. But that is not so. God will judge you too.

- **God was ready to judge the people of Sodom and Gomorrah.**

    God had been displeased with the wicked people from these cities for a long time, even before Lot first moved near them. The Lord had been patiently waiting for the people of Sodom and Gomorrah to repent. But the people would not change their minds and believe in God, so God decided that He would no longer tolerate their sinfulness. It was time for God to judge them.

    Think about the people in Noah's day. God patiently waited for them to repent, but the time came when God decided He had given the people sufficient time to repent. When God sent the flood, not one of those who refused to agree with God escaped from His punishment.

    God is supreme. He doesn't ask anyone what He should do. When He decides that it is time to punish sinners, no one can stop Him.

- **God does not always punish sin immediately.**

    Sometimes it may seem like God overlooks sin. But think about this: Did God overlook the sin of the people in Noah's day? No! Would God overlook the sin of the people of Sodom and Gomorrah? No! God will eventually punish all sin. No one can escape from God's judgment. He sees and will punish the sin of every person.

2) God's angels came to Sodom.

Read Genesis 19:1-3.

When Lot first moved to the plain, he lived near the city. We read in these verses that Lot had moved into the city of Sodom. Lot and his family were living in the same city as these wicked people.

God sent two of His angels into the city of Sodom for a special purpose. God sent them to warn Lot and his family that God was going to punish the people of Sodom and Gomorrah.

LESSON 23: GOD DESTROYED SODOM AND GOMORRAH.

③ The people who lived in Sodom were very sinful.

📖 Read Genesis 19:4-9.

- **The people of Sodom and Gomorrah were full of pride.**

    They didn't want to follow God's plan. They were gluttons, and they didn't care about the poor and needy. The Bible says that they were haughty and did detestable things before God.

Teacher: As you prepare to teach, read Ezekiel 16:49-50, but do not read these verses to the people when you teach the lesson.

As you teach this section about the sin of Sodom and Gomorrah, emphasize also the sins which are prevalent among the people whom you are teaching. Make sure they realize that they will be judged for their sins, whether or not their sin is the same as the sin of the people of Sodom and Gomorrah (John 3:18-19).

You would probably agree that the people of Sodom and Gomorrah were very wicked, wouldn't you? Perhaps you think that you have never done anything as wicked as those people did. But you need to know that all disobedience to God is sin, and the punishment for all sin is death. God judged the people of Sodom and Gomorrah for their sin, and God will judge you too unless you repent.

④ God's angels rescued Lot, his wife and his daughters out of Sodom.

📖 Read Genesis 19:10-17.

God was merciful to Lot and his family. Lot did not live a wicked life like the people of Sodom, but he was born a sinner, like all people on the earth. Lot, however, had agreed with God that he was a sinner, and he trusted in the coming Deliverer.

Before God destroyed Sodom and Gomorrah, God's angels led Lot out of the city to safety.

- **God always saves those who agree with Him and trust in Him.**
    - Abel agreed with God and trusted in Him, so God accepted Abel.
    - Noah agreed with God and trusted in Him, so God saved Noah from the flood.
    - Lot agreed with God and trusted in Him, so God delivered him before Sodom was destroyed.

⑤ God destroyed Sodom and Gomorrah.

📖 Read Genesis 19:24-25.

☞ **Teacher:** Show a picture of fire raining down on the cities of Sodom and Gomorrah.

After Lot was outside of the city, God rained fire down on Sodom and Gomorrah. God hates sin. He destroyed the world by a flood in the time of Noah. And He destroyed these cities by fire, along with the wicked people who lived in them.

- **God is still the same today.**

    He has not changed. He still sees and hates sin. No one can escape His judgment.

6) Lot's wife looked back.

- **Lot's wife disobeyed God's command.**

    Read Genesis 19:26.

    When the angels took Lot, his wife and his two daughters out of Sodom, they told them not to look behind them but to run to the mountains. Lot's wife disobeyed and looked back.

    God knew why Lot's wife looked back. Lot's wife was like Cain. She did not trust in God. She looked back because she liked the sinful ways of the people of Sodom. She didn't want to leave. She was very foolish to ignore God's warning because, when she looked back, God turned her into a pillar of salt.

- **God doesn't threaten to punish and then forget.**

    When God warned Lot and his family not to look back, He was not merely threatening them. People may threaten to do something, but they often forget and do not carry through with the threat. He remembers and keeps His promises to bless those who trust in Him and to punish those who disobey Him. God never forgets about sin until it is paid for in full. The punishment for sin is death, separation from God forever in the Lake of Fire.

? Questions

1. Did God know about the wickedness of the people who lived in Sodom and Gomorrah?

    Yes. God knew about their wickedness.

2. Is God interested in people today?

    Yes. Every person is important to God.

3. If people refuse to believe God's Word, will God bypass them and not punish them?

    No. God will judge every person.

4. The people of Sodom and Gomorrah had been wicked for a long time. Why had God waited to punish them?

    God was patiently waiting for the people to repent.

**LESSON 23: GOD DESTROYED
SODOM AND GOMORRAH.**

5. Does God merely threaten but never punish sinners?

   No. Even though God is patient, He will eventually punish sinners.

6. Can anyone stop God from punishing people when He decides they have had sufficient time to repent?

   No. God is supreme. When He decides that it is time to punish sinners, no one can stop Him.

7. Whom did God send to rescue Lot and his family from Sodom?

   God sent His angels to rescue Lot and his family.

8. Why did the Lord plan to rescue Lot?

   God planned to rescue Lot because Lot agreed with God that he was a sinner and trusted in God's promises to send the Deliverer. God always saves those who agree with Him and trust in Him.

9. What happened when Lot's wife disobeyed God's command and looked back?

   God turned Lot's wife into a pillar of salt when she disobeyed the command of the Lord.

LESSON 24: GOD GAVE ISAAC AND DELIVERED ISAAC FROM DEATH.

Scripture

Genesis 21:1-3, Genesis 22:1-19

Lesson Outline

(1) God fulfilled His promise to give Abraham and Sarah a son. (Genesis 21:1-3)

(2) God commanded Abraham to sacrifice Isaac. (Genesis 22:1-2)

(3) Abraham believed God. (Genesis 22:3-5)

(4) Abraham and Isaac went to make the sacrifice to God. (Genesis 22:6-10)

(5) God provided a ram to take Isaac's place. (Genesis 22:10-13)

(6) Abraham trusted God to send the Deliverer. (Genesis 22:14-19)

(?) Review Questions from Lesson 23.

Lesson Outline Developed

(1) God fulfilled His promise to give Abraham and Sarah a son.

- **Nothing is too hard for God.**

    Even though Abraham and Sarah were too old to have children, God had promised to give them a son. By this time, Abraham was 100 years old and Sarah was 90. Sarah had never had a child, and it was naturally impossible for her to have a child at her age. But nothing is impossible with God. God does everything He wants to do.

- **God keeps His promises.**

    Many years had passed since God first promised to give Abraham a son, but God had not forgotten His promise. God did not change His mind.

    Sarah had a son just as God had promised.

    Abraham and Sarah named their son Isaac.

Building on Firm Foundations
- Volume 2: Evangelism:
Genesis to The Ascension

📖 Read Genesis 21:1-3.

👉 **Teacher:** Point to the name, "Isaac," on the chronological chart.

- **God gives life to all people.**

    God had the authority and God had the authority and power to give Abraham and Sarah a son because He is the creator of all people and all things. He gave life to your ancestors, and He gave life to you and your children. Because God gives life to everyone, everyone rightfully belongs to God.

② God commanded Abraham to sacrifice Isaac.

- **Many years passed, and Isaac grew to be a young man.**

    Isaac's father and mother loved him.

    Abraham believed that all of God's promises about the coming Deliverer would be fulfilled through Isaac and his descendants.

    One day, God told Abraham to do something very astonishing; His command was out of the ordinary and would be very difficult to obey.

    📖 Read Genesis 22:1-2.

- **God had the authority to command Abraham to sacrifice Isaac.**

    To whom did Isaac belong? Perhaps you think that Isaac belonged to Abraham, because he was Abraham's son. But think about this: Who gave Isaac his life? Who gave Isaac to Abraham and Sarah? God did! Therefore, Isaac belonged to God.

    God gave Isaac his life, and God gave you life. You men, you women, you children – God gave each of you life. In addition, God sustains your life. He makes trees grow so you can build houses. He makes fruit and vegetables grow so you can eat. God gives life to every person and every living thing so God has authority over all people and all things.

- **God was testing Abraham.**

    📖 Read Genesis 22:1-2 again.

Teacher: If the people have heard of Ishmael and wonder why God referred to Isaac as Abraham's only son when he already had Ishmael, explain that God only recognized Isaac as Abraham's son because he was the one who was born in fulfillment of God's promise. God intended that Isaac would follow Abraham as the next descendant in line through whom the Deliverer would be born. Ishmael was not born according to God's plan but because Sarah and Abraham tried to fulfill God's promise of a son by following their own wisdom. Remember, the story of Ishmael is not included in Phase 1 lessons, so do not bring up this topic unless you are questioned about it.

LESSON 24: GOD GAVE ISAAC AND DELIVERED ISAAC FROM DEATH.

What a shock this must have been to Abraham!

Whom did Abraham love the most – God or Isaac? Would Abraham obey God? Or would he protect his son?

③ Abraham believed God.

Think about this: If Abraham obeyed God and sacrificed Isaac, how could God fulfill His promises to Abraham? Isaac would be dead, and if Isaac was dead, he would not have any descendants. Had God decided that the Deliverer would not be one of Isaac's descendants? Had God changed His mind?

Abraham did not doubt or question God. He knew that God would not lie. He knew that God would not make promises and then change His mind. Abraham trusted God and believed that God would still keep His word.

God is not like people who make promises but easily break them. You know that people often make promises but do not keep them.

Lesson Developer: Give an illustration based on the local setting to contrast God's faithfulness and trustworthiness to man's changeableness and failure to keep his word. For example:

> *When someone borrows something from you, he may promise to return the next week to bring the article back to you. But instead of coming next week to return the article, he begins to avoid you. When you happen to meet him on the path or in some other place, he is embarrassed and tells lies to cover his failure to do what he promised. He may say, "I am sorry I did not come as I said I would, but I have been sick. I will definitely come to return your article tomorrow." But he still doesn't come. Even after many weeks, he hasn't come to return your article. He failed to do what he promised to do.*

God is not like people. He always does what He promises to do, and He does it completely and exactly at the time He said He would.

Abraham believed that God would do what He said. Abraham believed that even if he did kill Isaac in obedience to God, God would raise Isaac from the dead. He trusted God to do this even though it is impossible to man.

Teacher: As you prepare to teach, read Hebrews 11:17-19, but do not read these verses to the people when you teach.

Abraham responded differently than Adam and Eve had. In the garden in Eden, God had told Adam that he must not eat the fruit from the tree of the knowledge of good and evil. God said that if Adam did eat it, he would die. When Satan said that they wouldn't die, Adam and Eve believed Satan. They doubted the word of God, and they disobeyed Him.

Adam and Eve did not believe God, but Abraham did. Abraham believed God would do exactly as He promised.

Because Abraham believed and trusted in God, he immediately made preparations to go and sacrifice Isaac in the place where God promised to lead him.

📖 Read Genesis 22:3-5.

④ Abraham and Isaac went to make the sacrifice to God.

- **Isaac questioned Abraham.**

    📖 Read Genesis 22:6-8.

    Isaac knew that they were going to make a sacrifice to God, but he could not understand why they had not taken a sheep withthem to sacrifice.

    Abraham had not told Isaac what God had told him to do.

- **Abraham answered Isaac.**

    📖 Read Genesis 22:8 again.

    Abraham trusted God to provide a suitable animal to be sacrificed.

    Believing God is the most important thing that we can do. Just listening to God's message will not help us. We must accept God's words by believing them with our hearts and trusting in Him.

Lesson Developer: Use the following illustration to show that merely listening to God's Word will not save us. We must take it to heart and believe.

> 🕯 If you were sick and came to me for medicine, would it help you if you only listened to me tell you about the medicine and how it could heal you? No! You would have to take the medicine to be healed.

- **Merely listening to God's Word will not help you.**

    You must accept God's Word in your heart and believe it.

    If you merely listen to God's words but do not believe them, you are showing that you think that God is a liar. When Satan spoke to Eve in the Garden of Eden, he deceived her into thinking that God was a liar. God had said that Adam would die if he ate the fruit from the tree of the knowledge of good and evil. Satan said that Adam would not die. When Adam and Eve ate the fruit, they were showing that they thought God was a liar.

    God will never accept those who refuse to believe Him. God accepts those who believe what He says and trust only in Him, as Abraham did.

- **Abraham bound Isaac.**

  📖 Read Genesis 22:9-10.

- **Isaac could not escape.**

  He was tied to the altar, and Abraham had lifted up the knife to kill him. God had commanded Abraham to offer Isaac as a sacrifice, and there was no way for Isaac to escape after he was bound to the altar.

- **There is no escape from God's judgment, unless God provides the way of escape.**

  We have already learned that this is true through the true stories we have read in the Word of God.

  - In the days of Noah, the people who did not believe God could not escape from the flood after God shut the door of the boat. But Noah and his family and all the animals and birds were safe inside the boat because God had provided the only way they could be saved. Only God could save Noah and his family from the flood.

  - In the same way, the wicked people in the cities of Sodom and Gomorrah could not escape when God rained down fire on them. There was no escape for Lot's wife when she disobeyed God and looked back at the city of Sodom. But Lot and his daughters were safe because God provided the way for them to escape before He rained down fire on the cities. Only God could save Lot and his daughters from the fire which destroyed Sodom and Gomorrah.

- **God is the only Savior.**

  - God saved Noah and his family from the flood.

  - God saved Lot from the fire which destroyed Sodom and Gomorrah.

  - God was the only One who could save Isaac from death on the altar of sacrifice.

- **We cannot save ourselves.**

  Think about this: Is there any way that we can save ourselves from death? Can we save ourselves from God's judgment? No! We are sinners, and God will punish all sin. We cannot escape from God's judgment unless God provides the way, just as Isaac could not escape unless God provided the way.

  Isaac was bound on the altar and Abraham was ready to kill him. Isaac could not escape. Do you think God saved Isaac? Let's read God's Book to see what happened.

⑤ God provided a ram to take Isaac's place.

📖 Read Genesis 22:10-12.

- **God saved Isaac.**

  God told Abraham not to kill Isaac.

Isaac couldn't be saved, however, unless there was another suitable sacrifice to offer to God. Abraham and Isaac hadn't brought an animal with them to sacrifice. Abraham could not provide a sacrifice to take the place of Isaac, but God could!

- **God graciously provided a ram for Abraham to offer as a sacrifice instead of Isaac.**

  Read Genesis 22:13.

> **Teacher:** Show a picture of Isaac, bound to the altar, with Abraham holding a knife poised to kill him, and with a ram in the thicket.

God caused the ram to be caught by its horns in the bush. If it had been caught by any other part of its body, it would have injured itself by struggling to get free. If it had been injured, it would not have been an acceptable offering to God. God would only accept a healthy, strong animal as a sacrifice. Because God is perfect, He will only accept what is perfect.

- **The ram became Isaac's substitute.**

  Abraham took Isaac off the altar and put the ram on the altar. Abraham killed the ram and burned it as an offering to God. God saved Isaac by providing the ram to die instead of him.

  God kept His promise to Abraham. Through Isaac, God would give Abraham many descendants.

(6) Abraham trusted God to send the Deliverer.

- **Abraham believed God would provide the Deliverer.**

  Read Genesis 22:14-19.

  Abraham named the place where God provided the ram "The Lord will provide." God had provided a ram to die instead of Isaac, and Abraham believed that God would also provide the Deliverer to rescue mankind from the power of Satan and from the punishment of sin.

(?) Questions

1. Why was God able to give Abraham and Sarah a son even though it was naturally impossible for them to have children at their age?

   God was able to give them a son because He is the creator of all people.

LESSON 24: GOD GAVE ISAAC AND DELIVERED ISAAC FROM DEATH.

2. Why did God have the authority to command Abraham to offer Isaac as a sacrifice?

   God had the authority to command Abraham to offer Isaac because He had given life to Isaac and Isaac belonged to Him.

3. Did Abraham think that God had changed His mind about Isaac being the father of a great nation and the forefather of the Deliverer?

   No. Abraham believed and trusted in God because he was convinced that God would not make a promise and then change His mind.

4. What did Abraham think God would do after Isaac had been sacrificed?

   Abraham thought that God would raise Isaac from the dead.

5. Once Abraham had bound Isaac to the altar, was there any way Isaac could escape from death?

   No. Isaac could not escape from death.

6. Is there any way you can save yourself from the payment of death and everlasting punishment which you deserve because of your sins?

   No. No one can save himself from God's punishment.

7. Who saved Isaac from death?

   God saved Isaac from death.

8. Could anyone else have saved Isaac from death?

   No. Only God could save Isaac from death.

9. Who provided a sacrifice to take Isaac's place?

   God provided a sacrifice to take Isaac's place.

10. Why was it important that the ram was held in the bush by its horns so that it would not be injured?

    Because God is perfect, He would only accept a sacrifice that was strong and healthy.

11. Why did Abraham name the place where God provided the ram "The Lord will provide"?

    Abraham named it "The Lord will provide" because, just as the Lord provided the ram instead of Isaac, Abraham believed that the Lord would provide the Deliverer to rescue mankind from Satan's power and everlasting punishment.

LESSON 25: GOD CHOSE JACOB AND REJECTED ESAU.

Scripture

Genesis 24:67, Genesis 25:20-34, Genesis 27:41-44, Genesis 28:10-15, Genesis 29:1, Genesis 31:13, Genesis 32:28

Lesson Outline

1. Isaac married Rebekah. (Genesis 24:67; 25:20)
2. Isaac and Rebekah had two sons, Esau and Jacob. (Genesis 25:21-27)
3. God chose Jacob to be the next in line as the ancestor of the Deliverer. (Genesis 25:28-34; 27:41-44; 28:10)
4. God spoke to Jacob in a dream. (Genesis 28:11-12)
5. God gave Jacob the same promises He had given to Abraham and Isaac. (Genesis 28:13-15; 29:1; 31:13; 32:28)

(?) Review Questions from Lesson 24.

Lesson Outline Developed

Teacher: As you teach this lesson and other lessons, do not merely teach history. Continue to emphasize the truths about God's character and man's need to have faith. Remember to apply truth to your hearers. Your hearers must face up to the truth about God and their own spiritual condition before Him if they are going to be prepared to believe the Gospel.

1 Isaac married Rebekah.

Abraham's wife, Sarah, grew old and she died.

Isaac mourned for his mother, but he was comforted when Rebekah became his wife.

📖 Read Genesis 24:67; 25:20.

Rebekah was born in the land where Abraham had lived before the Lord led him to Canaan.

☞ **Teacher:** Point to Mesopotamia on the map.

Abraham also died. Isaac inherited the promises about the land of Canaan and the coming Deliverer that God had given to his father Abraham.

② Isaac and Rebekah had two sons, Esau and Jacob.

📖 Read Genesis 25:21-23.

- **God knew all about Isaac's sons before their birth.**

  Even before they were born, the Lord knew what kind of people Isaac's two sons would grow up to be.

  The Lord knows all about us even when we are in our mother's womb. He knows everything about all people. Nothing is hidden from Him.

  📖 Read Genesis 25:24-27.

☞ **Teacher:** Point to the names, "Esau and Jacob," on the chronological chart.

- **Esau did not believe God's promises.**

  Esau had the same attitude as Cain had. Esau refused to admit that he was a sinner and needed to be accepted by God. He went his own way and lived only for the things of this world. His own desires were more important to him than the things which God wanted to give him and teach him. Esau did not value God's promises.

- **Jacob believed God's promises.**

  Jacob had the same attitude as Abraham and Isaac had. Jacob believed God. He admitted that he was a sinner and needed God to send the Deliverer. He cherished God's promises and wanted God's mercy and care.

③ God chose Jacob to be the next in line as the ancestor of the Deliverer.

📖 Read Genesis 25:28-34.

LESSON 25: GOD CHOSE JACOB AND REJECTED ESAU.

- **Esau was Isaac's firstborn son.**

  In those days, the firstborn had a right to a double portion of the inheritance from his father, and he would become the head of the family group at the death of his father. Because Esau was Isaac's firstborn son, he should have received the rights of the firstborn. As firstborn, Esau was also destined to become the guardian of the promises from God which his father had inherited from Abraham. The Deliverer from God would have been one of Esau's descendants. But Esau was not interested in the promises of God. Esau gave away all his rights and privileges as the firstborn son to Jacob in exchange for a bowl of food.

  ☞ **Teacher:** Show a picture of Esau, looking hungry, wanting the bowl of stew more than his birthright.

- **Esau was like Cain.**

  Esau did not believe, and he did not follow the ways of God.

  Teacher: As you prepare to teach, read Hebrews 12:16, but do not read this verse to the people when you teach the lesson.

  Think about this: Are you like Cain and Esau? Are your own desires more important to you than God and what God has to teach you about the Deliverer? Are you also going to turn away from God's truth and follow your own way like Cain and Esau? Or are you going to be like Abel, Enoch, Noah, Abraham, Isaac and Jacob who admitted their sin and trusted in God to provide the Deliverer?

  Teacher: Questions such as these help the people to consider the truth of Scripture in relationship to their own lives. Do not make them feel they must publicly declare their inner thoughts. Instead, allow the Lord to use the truth in their hearts to bring them to a genuine heart conviction and faith.

- **Jacob inherited the promises instead of Esau.**

  Although Jacob was the second son, he wanted to inherit the promises which his father, Isaac, had inherited from Abraham. Jacob believed God and trusted Him to send the Deliverer.

  Even before Esau and Jacob were born, God had decided that Jacob would be given the privilege to be the ancestor of the Deliverer. Eventually, just as God planned, Jacob was given the position of the firstborn.

- **Esau was not interested in the promises of the Deliverer.**

  Although Esau did not care about the promises of the Deliverer, he did want the position and the privileges which came with being the firstborn. Therefore, when he knew that Jacob had been given the blessing that he should have received as the firstborn, Esau became angry.

- **Esau planned to kill Jacob just as soon as their father died.**

  📖 Read Genesis 27:41.

  Rebekah, Jacob and Esau's mother, heard about Esau's plan to kill Jacob. She advised Jacob to go far away to her brother's home in Haran.

  📖 Read Genesis 27:42-44.

  Jacob left his father and mother's home and began the long trek to the land of Mesopotamia. This is the land where his grandfather, Abraham, and his mother, Rebekah, had lived.

> 👉 **Teacher:** Show on the map Jacob's journey from Beersheba in the south of Canaan to Haran.

📖 Read Genesis 28:10.

4) God spoke to Jacob in a dream.

It was a long way from Canaan to Mesopotamia, so on the way, Jacob had to sleep out in the mountains.

📖 Read Genesis 28:11.

- **One night as Jacob slept, God gave him a dream.**

  Occasionally during those times, God would speak to people through dreams, but ever since God's message to all people has been completely written down, God's usual way to tell us what He wants us to know is through the Bible.

  📖 Read Genesis 28:12.

  Through this dream, God was showing Jacob something important about the coming Deliverer.

- **The Deliverer would become the way for people to come to God.**

> 👉 **Teacher:** Show a picture of Jacob dreaming about a ladder that reached from earth to heaven.

LESSON 25: GOD CHOSE JACOB AND REJECTED ESAU.

Lesson Developer: Use an illustration to show how a ladder provides a way for entry to an inaccessible place. For example:

> *Because your houses are built up high off the ground, you need a ladder to be able to enter your home. When you leave your house, you remove the ladder so that your dogs cannot enter and steal your food. The ladder is the way into the house. Without the ladder, there is no way to enter your house.*

Through Jacob's dream, God was showing that the Deliverer would be like a ladder reaching from earth to heaven.

Teacher: As you prepare to teach, read John 1:51, but do not read this verse to the people when you teach the lesson.

Think about this: Why was it necessary that the Deliverer be like a ladder? It was necessary because all people are separated from God. In the beginning, Adam and Eve were in oneness with God. But when they disobeyed, they were separated from God, and as a result, all of us who are Adam's descendants have also been born separated from God. There was no way that people could come to God and be in oneness with Him unless God provided the way. In the garden in Eden, He promised that the Deliverer would come to destroy Satan and reconcile people to God. And through Jacob's dream, God showed that the Deliverer would be like a bridge between God and man. Through the Deliverer, people would once again be able to be in oneness with God.

Teacher: Tell the following story to help the people understand what God was teaching Jacob through this dream. Do not develop the story further than what is given in the example below. In addition, do not give the Gospel message to the whole group because you have not yet taught on the life of the Lord Jesus. Even though the story ends with the "son" restoring a friendship, you need to be careful not to jump ahead in the teaching program. If you do need to take an awakened and repentant individual on ahead of the main group you are teaching, this type of illustration can be a good introduction to the story of the Redeemer.

> *Let me tell you a story as an example: There were once two very good friends who had a common enemy. This enemy was jealous of their friendship, and he was determined to destroy the companionship which they enjoyed.*
>
> *In order to do this, the enemy went to one of the men and told him that his friend was plotting evil against him. The man was deceived by his enemy, and he believed the lie that the enemy had told him. He stopped associating with his friend. He broke the friendship.*
>
> *But the other man wanted to restore the friendship. He still loved his friend, even though his friend had believed the enemy. So he sent his son to speak with his former friend. The man listened to the words of the son, and through the son, the friendship was reestablished.*

This is what God was showing Jacob: Even though all people have been separated from God because of Satan's lies and Adam's disobedience to God, God planned to send the Deliverer who would make it possible for God and man to be reconciled and reunited.

5) God gave Jacob the same promises He had given to Abraham and Isaac.

📖 Read Genesis 28:13-15.

- **God was continuing to work out His plan to send the Deliverer.**

  Although many years had passed since God gave the first promise of the Deliverer in the garden in Eden, and although Abraham, whom God had chosen to be the forefather of the Deliverer, was now dead, God had not forgotten His plan. God is faithful to do whatever He says He will do.

- **God promised Jacob that the coming Deliverer would be one of his descendants.**

  One of Jacob's descendants would become the ladder that would make it possible for people to be in friendship with God. When Jacob woke from his dream, he knew that God had given him the same promises that He gave to his grandfather, Abraham, and his father, Isaac.

  📖 Read Genesis 29:1.

  Jacob lived in the land of Mesopotamia for many years. Then God spoke to Jacob again and told him to return to his own country, the land that God had given to Abraham.

  📖 Read Genesis 31:13.

  Jacob had married two sisters, and he had become the father of twelve sons.

  During his stay in Haran, God had protected Jacob because it was through one of his descendants that God's promise of the Deliverer was to be fulfilled.

- **During Jacob's journey to return to the land of Canaan, God changed Jacob's name.**

  From this time forward, Jacob would have a more important name than the name, Jacob. His new name was to be Israel. This new name which God gave to Jacob meant that through the difficult experiences Jacob had been through, God had taught Jacob not to depend on himself but only to depend on God. The name, Israel, also meant that because Jacob no longer depended on himself but on God, God would fight for him.

  📖 Read Genesis 32:28.

LESSON 25: GOD CHOSE JACOB AND REJECTED ESAU.

? Questions

1. How did God know, even before they were born, what type of people Jacob and Esau would be?

    God knew what type of people they would be because God knows everything about all people.

2. Did Esau admit that he was a sinner?

    No. Esau did not admit he was a sinner and needed to be accepted by God.

3. What was more important to Esau than the things which God wanted to give him and teach him?

    Esau's own desires were more important to him than the things which God wanted to give him and teach him.

4. Did Jacob admit that he was a sinner?

    Yes. Jacob admitted that he was a sinner.

5. Did Jacob value God's promises to send the Deliverer?

    Yes. Jacob valued God's promises to send the Deliverer.

6. Did God choose Jacob or Esau to be the ancestor of the Deliverer?

    God chose Jacob to be the ancestor of the Deliverer.

7. What did Jacob see in the dream given to him by God?

    Jacob saw a ladder resting on the earth with its top reaching to heaven. God's angels were walking up and down the ladder, and God stood above the ladder.

8. What did this dream mean?

    The dream meant that the Deliverer would be like the ladder connecting the earth to heaven. Through the Deliverer, people could be brought into oneness with God.

9. After Jacob had spent many years in the land of Mesopotamia, where did God tell him to go?

    God told him to return home to Canaan, the land which God had given to his grandfather, Abraham.

10. How many sons did Jacob have?

    Jacob had twelve sons.

11. What new name did God give to Jacob?

    God gave him the name, Israel.

LESSON 26: GOD GUIDED AND PROTECTED JOSEPH.

Scripture

Genesis 37:1-35, Genesis 39:1-23

Lesson Outline

(1) Jacob lived in Canaan. (Genesis 37:1)

(2) Joseph believed God. (Genesis 37:2-3)

(3) Joseph was hated by his older brothers. (Genesis 37:4)

(4) Joseph dreamed about his future. (Genesis 37:5-11)

(5) Joseph was sold and taken into Egypt. (Genesis 37:12-35)

(6) Joseph worked in Potiphar's house. (Genesis 39:1-19)

(7) Joseph was put into prison. (Genesis 39:20-23)

(?) Review Questions from Lesson 25.

Lesson Outline Developed

Teacher: The story of Joseph is included in the teaching program as a connecting story to show how the Israelites got into Egypt. You may teach most of this lesson by carefully reading the story from the Scriptures. To make certain that your hearers understand the story, however, be sure to ask questions and discuss the story with them as you read the Scriptures.

(1) Jacob lived in Canaan.

After Jacob had lived in the land of Mesopotamia for many years, God had brought him safely back to the land of Canaan. God kept all His promises to Jacob.

📖 Read Genesis 37:1.

God had given Jacob the same promises He had given to Abraham and Isaac. He had promised that the coming Deliverer would be one of Jacob's descendants. He had also promised that Jacob and his descendants would inherit the land that God had given to Abraham.

② Joseph believed God.

📖 Read Genesis 37:2-3.

Teacher's note: Do not read the following Scriptures to your students or make a point of explaining about the two women, Bilhah and Zilpah, who are mentioned in Genesis 37:2 unless you are asked. Bilhah was a servant-girl given to Rachel at her marriage by her father, Laban (Genesis 29:29). This girl took the place of her mistress and bore Dan and Naphtali on her behalf to Jacob (Genesis 30:1-8). The circumstances relating to Zilpah are similar (Genesis 29:24). She took the place of her mistress, Leah, and bore Gad and Asher with Jacob as their father (Genesis 30:9-13).

Jacob had twelve sons. Joseph was his favorite son, because he had been born to Jacob in his old age.

☞ **Teacher:** Point to the name, **"Joseph,"** on the chronological chart.

Joseph knew he was a sinner and could only be forgiven by God's mercy. He trusted in God's promises just as Abraham, Isaac and Jacob had.

Teacher: As you prepare to teach, read Hebrews 11:22, but do not read this verse to the people when you teach the lesson.

③ Joseph was hated by his older brothers.

📖 Read Genesis 37:4.

When Joseph's brothers did things which were wrong, Joseph reported that to his father.

Because Joseph told his father about the evil things his brothers did and because Joseph was his father's favorite son, his older brothers hated him.

People get angry and hate one another because everyone has been born separated from God and has an evil heart. This is why there is anger, hatred and evil things in your hearts and minds. You were all born separated from God, and there is no way you can change yourselves.

④ Joseph dreamed about his future.

📖 Read Genesis 37:5-11.

LESSON 26: GOD GUIDED AND PROTECTED JOSEPH.

God knew exactly what was going to happen to Joseph and to the rest of Jacob's family. Joseph did not know how his dreams would be fulfilled, but God made it clear that Joseph would become the leader and ruler over his family.

God knows the future of all people. He knows your future just as He knew Joseph's future.

5) Joseph was sold and taken into Egypt.

📖 Read Genesis 37:12-28.

👉 **Teacher:** Show a picture of Joseph being sold into slavery.

📖 Read Genesis 37:29-35.

👉 **Teacher:** Point to Canaan and then to Egypt on the map.

6) Joseph worked in Potiphar's house.

📖 Read Genesis 39:1-19.

7) Joseph was put into prison.

📖 Read Genesis 39:20-23.

Even though Joseph was hated by his brothers and lied about by Potiphar's wife, he still trusted in the only true and living God.

God did not fail Joseph even when he was in prison. God took care of him because He had a wonderful plan for Joseph's life.

Through Joseph's dreams, God had made it clear that Joseph would become the leader and ruler over his family. With Joseph in prison, it seemed impossible that he would ever become the leader and ruler of his family. But God never changes. He always does everything that He promises. He is not like people who change their minds, forget their promises, or tell lies. God would take care of Joseph and fulfill His promise to make him the leader of his family.

? Questions

1. Who protected Jacob and brought him back safely to the land of Canaan?
   God protected Jacob and brought him back safely to the land of Canaan.

2. Who was Jacob's favorite son?
   Joseph was Jacob's favorite son.

3. Did Joseph believe God's promises about the Deliverer?
   Yes. Joseph believed God's promises about the Deliverer.

4. How did Joseph's older brothers react to their father's love for Joseph?
   They hated Joseph.

5. What did Joseph dream about sheaves of grain?
   Joseph dreamed that he and his brothers were binding sheaves of grain and that his sheaf stood upright while his brothers' sheaves bowed down to it.

6. What did Joseph dream about the sun, moon and stars?
   Joseph dreamed that the sun, moon and eleven stars bowed down to him.

7. What did Joseph's dreams mean?
   These dreams meant that Joseph would become the leader and ruler over his family.

8. Who knew Joseph's future and showed it to him through his dreams?
   God knew Joseph's future and revealed it through Joseph's dreams.

9. How much of your future does God know?
   God knows everything about the future.

10. What did Joseph's older brothers do to Joseph?
    They sold Joseph to become a slave in Egypt.

11. What happened to Joseph in Egypt?
    The wife of his owner lied about him, and Joseph was put into prison.

12. Who took care of Joseph in prison?
    God did.

13. Why did God take care of Joseph?
    God took care of him because He had a wonderful plan for Joseph's life.

LESSON 27: GOD PROMOTED JOSEPH. GOD TOOK JACOB'S FAMILY INTO EGYPT.

Scripture

Genesis 41:1-8, 14-16, 25-49, Genesis 42:1-20, Genesis 43:1-5, 11-17, Genesis 45:1-11, 25-28, Genesis 46:5-7

Lesson Outline

(1) God spoke to Pharaoh through dreams. (Genesis 41:1-8)

(2) Joseph interpreted Pharaoh's dreams. (Genesis 41:14-16, 25-37)

(3) God put Joseph in a position of leadership in Egypt. (Genesis 41:38-49)

(4) Joseph's brothers came to Egypt for food. (Genesis 42:1-20)

(5) Joseph revealed his true identity. (Genesis 43:1-5, 11-17; 45:1-11)

(6) Jacob's family went down to Egypt. (Genesis 45:25-28; 46:5-7)

(7) Abraham's descendants became known as Israelites.

(?) Review Questions from Lesson 26.

Lesson Outline Developed

(1) God spoke to Pharaoh through dreams.

📖 Read Genesis 41:1-8.

- **Pharaoh was the king of Egypt.**

Teacher: Explain the position of a king and tell the people that the kings of Egypt were known as Pharaoh.

- **God spoke to Pharaoh about the future through dreams.**

In the dreams, God showed Pharaoh what was going to happen in the land of Egypt.

Pharaoh didn't understand the meaning of the dreams and was troubled because he knew that the dreams were showing him something important.

Although God spoke to people in the past through dreams, that is no longer His usual way of speaking to people. Why do you think God no longer speaks through dreams? Ever since God's Word has been completely written down, God has spoken through the Bible.

Does God still know what will happen in the future? Yes! God still knows everything about the future. He teaches what He wants us to know about the future through the Bible.

- **Pharaoh did not know or worship the true and living God.**

The Egyptians worshiped the things God created instead of God. They worshiped the sun, moon and stars, as well as animals and creeping creatures. They also worshiped the Nile River which was a large river in their country. But even though the Egyptians did not worship Him, God planned to use this king and his people to fulfill the purposes of God.

God is Ruler over all people even though they may not know or worship Him. He can use anyone in whatever way He chooses to fulfill His purposes.

Lesson Developer: Use an illustration to show that the owner of an object has the right to use that object in whatever way he chooses. For example:

> *Does your spear have the authority to tell you how you should use it? What about your canoe or your basket? Can they tell you how you should or should not use them? No! You can use them for whatever you wish because you made them. You are their owner.*

God is the Creator of all people. He is the giver and sustainer of our life. He has made us, and we rightfully belong to Him. God can do whatever He wishes with us. But because God is righteous, everything that He does to people is always right.

(2) Joseph interpreted Pharaoh's dreams.

Read Genesis 41:14-16, 25-37.

Joseph did not have the ability to interpret Pharaoh's dreams, but he trusted in the Lord to give him the interpretation. God never fails those who trust in Him. God gave Joseph understanding of the dreams so he could explain to Pharaoh what would happen in Egypt.

LESSON 27: GOD PROMOTED JOSEPH. GOD TOOK JACOB'S FAMILY INTO EGYPT.

③ God put Joseph in a position of leadership in Egypt.

God had shown Joseph through his dreams as a youth that he would become a leader and ruler. Joseph was still a prisoner in Egypt, so it seemed impossible that he would ever become a leader. But God was in control, and He had not forgotten Joseph.

📖 Read Genesis 41:38-49.

When it was time for God to do what He planned, God brought Joseph out of prison and gave him a high position of leadership. God used Pharaoh to put Joseph in charge of the whole land of Egypt. He was second-in-command to Pharaoh. God always does what He plans. No one can hinder Him.

④ Joseph's brothers came to Egypt for food.

📖 Read Genesis 42:1-20.

☞ **Teacher:** Show a picture of Joseph's brothers bowing before him.

⑤ Joseph revealed his true identity.

📖 Read Genesis 43:1-5, 11-17; 45:1-11.

Teacher: Read these Scriptures clearly, precisely and with animation so your hearers will understand and so their imaginations will be captured by the unfolding drama.

⑥ Jacob's family went down to Egypt.

📖 Read Genesis 45:25-28; 46:5-7.

Many years before, God had told Abraham that his descendants would go into a country that was not their own. Let's read what God had told Abram.

Read Genesis 15:13.

Even though many hundreds of years had passed, God did what He had promised. All that God says in His Word will happen just as God has said.

⑦ Abraham's descendants became known as Israelites.

From the time Jacob and his family settled in Egypt, they became known as Israelites. They were called Israelites because Jacob's other name was Israel. You will remember that when Jacob was returning to the land of Canaan from Mesopotamia, God gave him the new name, Israel. From this time on, the Bible often refers to Israel's descendants as the children of Israel or Israelites.

⟨?⟩ Questions

1. God revealed some future events in Egypt to Pharaoh. How did God reveal these events?

   God revealed these future events by giving Pharaoh dreams.

2. Who gave Joseph the ability to interpret Pharaoh's dreams?

   God gave Joseph the ability to interpret Pharaoh's dreams.

3. What did Pharaoh's dreams mean?

   Pharaoh's dreams meant that Egypt would have seven years of very good harvest, followed by seven years of drought.

4. What did Pharaoh and the people of Egypt worship?

   Pharaoh and the people of Egypt worshiped things God created, such as the sun, moon, stars, animals and the Nile River.

5. Why was God able to use Pharaoh and his people to fulfill the purposes of God, even though the people of Egypt did not worship Him?

   God was able to use Pharaoh and his people because God is ruler over all people.

6. Why is it right for God to have the authority to rule over all mankind?

   God has the right to have authority over all mankind because He is the creator and owner of every person.

7. What had God shown Joseph in his dreams as a youth?

   God had shown Joseph that he would become a leader and ruler.

8. How did God fulfill the dreams which He had given to Joseph as a youth?

   The Lord gave Joseph wisdom to interpret the king's dreams so that Pharaoh would give Joseph a high position of leadership in Egypt.

9. Why did Jacob take all of his family down to live in Egypt?

   Jacob took his family to Egypt because Jacob had heard that his son, Joseph, was alive and living in Egypt and because there was plenty of food in Egypt.

LESSON 28: GOD PRESERVED THE ISRAELITES AND PROTECTED MOSES.

Scripture

Exodus 1:1-22, Exodus 2:1-22

Lesson Outline

(1) Joseph and his generation died in Egypt. (Exodus 1:1-6)

(2) The people of Israel increased in number and in riches. (Exodus 1:7)

(3) The new king wanted to destroy the people of Israel. (Exodus 1:8-11)

(4) God took care of the people of Israel. (Exodus 1:12-22)

(5) Moses was born. (Exodus 2:1-4)

(6) Moses was adopted by Pharaoh's daughter. (Exodus 2:5-10)

(7) Moses tried to help his fellow Israelites. (Exodus 2:11-22)

(?) Review Questions from Lesson 27.

Lesson Outline Developed

(1) Joseph and his generation died in Egypt.

Read Exodus 1:1-6.

Joseph, his brothers and their families continued to live in Egypt after their father's death even though the drought had ended. They did not return to Canaan, the land which God had given to Abraham, Isaac and Jacob. The Bible says that Joseph and all his generation died in Egypt.

Teacher: Point to Egypt on the map.

Building on Firm Foundations
- Volume 2: Evangelism:
Genesis to The Ascension

② The people of Israel increased in number and in riches.

📖 Read Exodus 1:7.

The people of Israel had lived in Egypt for about 350 years. During that time, their numbers increased rapidly and they became very rich. They had many cows, goats and sheep. They enjoyed living in Egypt because there was plenty of grass for their animals and the king was very good to them. But things were soon to change.

③ The new king wanted to destroy the people of Israel.

📖 Read Exodus 1:8-11.

- **The Egyptian king made the Israelites slaves.**

    He made them slaves because the Israelites had become many in number. The new king was afraid that they might join with the Egyptians' enemies and take control of Egypt. This king forced the Israelites to be slaves because he wanted to destroy them.

👉 **Teacher:** Show a picture of the Israelites working as slaves in Egypt.

- **Satan was guiding the king in his evil plan.**

    Think about this: Why would Satan want to destroy the people of Israel? Satan wanted to destroy them because Satan did not want the Deliverer to be born.

- **Satan knew the Deliverer would be an Israelite.**

    Satan knew that God had promised that the Deliverer would be a descendant of Abraham. Satan wanted to destroy the people of Israel because they were God's chosen people to fulfill His plan to send the Deliverer into the world.

- **Satan knew the Deliverer would destroy him.**

    Satan didn't want the Deliverer to come. He had not forgotten the promise that God had given in the garden in Eden. God had promised that the Deliverer would destroy Satan.

- **Satan knew that the Deliverer would deliver people from Satan's power**

    Satan didn't want the Deliverer to deliver people from his power. He wanted everyone to go into everlasting punishment.

- **Satan has not changed.**

    Satan wants to keep people in his power, and he wants people to go to everlasting punishment. Satan doesn't want anyone to be brought into oneness with God. Satan hates God and the people God created. Satan hates you. Just as Satan used Pharaoh to try to

LESSON 28: GOD PRESERVED THE ISRAELITES AND PROTECTED MOSES.

destroy the people of Israel, so Satan will try to destroy you by keeping you from hearing and believing God's message.

4) God took care of the people of Israel.

God had not forgotten the people of Israel. He was faithfully watching over them. He would not let Satan destroy them.

📖 Read Exodus 1:12-22.

Teacher: As you read this passage, explain any portion which may not be clear.

Even though the Egyptians oppressed them and worked them ruthlessly, and even though the king ordered all the baby boys to be killed, the people of Israel continued to multiply and prosper. God protected His people from the evil king and Satan. Satan planned to destroy them, but God planned to deliver them from slavery and take them back to the land that He had promised to give them for their own. God had not forgotten His promise to Abraham, Isaac and Jacob.

5) Moses was born.

📖 Read Exodus 2:1-4.

The parents of this child trusted in God. They trusted God to take care of their baby son.

6) Moses was adopted by Pharaoh's daughter.

📖 Read Exodus 2:5-10.

☞ **Teacher:** Point to the name, **"Moses,"** on the Chronological Chart.

God used the wicked king's daughter to protect Moses because God planned to use Moses to deliver the Israelites from slavery. No one and nothing can stop God from doing whatever He plans. God is greater than Satan. God is greater than everyone and everything.

Pharaoh's daughter adopted Moses. God knew that Moses would be safer in Pharaoh's house than anywhere else. He also knew that Moses would learn many things in the king's house that would be important for him to know for his future work as the leader of his people. God put Moses in a place where he could be trained for the work God had for him. God is wise, and He knows what is best.

God cared for the people of Israel, and He had a plan to deliver them from slavery in Egypt. God also cares for you. Continue to listen to His Word so you will understand His plan to deliver you from the power of Satan and bring you into oneness with God.

⑦ Moses tried to help his fellow Israelites.

The next part of the story tells us what happened when Moses grew into manhood.

📖 Read Exodus 2:11-22.

The Israelites were held captive by the wicked king, and they couldn't escape. Moses tried to help them, but he failed. No person could rescue them from the wicked king.

Just as the Israelites were held captive by the king, you are held captive by Satan and his evil spirits. You cannot deliver yourselves. I cannot deliver you, and no other person can deliver you. Only God can deliver you!

❓ Questions

1. Of what was the king of Egypt afraid concerning the people of Israel?

   The king was afraid that the Israelites might join with the Egyptians' enemies and take control of Egypt.

2. What did the king do so that the Israelites would not continue to increase in number?

   He forced them to become slaves, he made them endure hard labor, and he ordered that the baby boys be killed.

3. Who was guiding the king in his evil plan to destroy the people of Israel?

   Satan was guiding the king.

4. Why would Satan want to destroy the Israelites?

   Satan knew that God had promised Abraham that one of his descendants would be the Deliverer, and Satan did not want the Deliverer to be born.

5. Why did God protect the people of Israel in Egypt?

   God protected them so that He could keep His promise to send the Deliverer into the world through Abraham's descendants.

6. Who adopted Moses?

   Pharaoh's daughter adopted Moses.

7. What did God plan to do through Moses?

   God planned to deliver the Israelites from slavery through Moses.

LESSON 28: GOD PRESERVED THE ISRAELITES AND PROTECTED MOSES.

8. What were the advantages that Moses had by living in Pharaoh's house?
   Moses was safer in Pharaoh's house than anywhere else, and he would be trained there as a leader.

9. Can Satan, the spirits, people, or anything hinder God from doing what He plans?
   No. God does everything He plans to do.

10. Could the Israelites deliver themselves from slavery, or could Moses deliver them?
    No. They could not deliver themselves, and no other person could rescue them from slavery.

11. Can you deliver yourself from Satan's control?
    No. No one can deliver himself from Satan's control.

12. Who is the only one who can deliver you from Satan's control?
    God is the only one who can deliver people from Satan's control.

LESSON 29: GOD CHOSE MOSES TO LEAD THE ISRAELITES OUT OF SLAVERY.

Scripture

Exodus 2:23-25, Exodus 3:1-20, Exodus 4:1-20

Lesson Outline

1. God saw the people of Israel in slavery and heard their cries. (Exodus 2:23-25)
2. God spoke to Moses from the burning bush. (Exodus 3:1-6)
3. God told Moses that He had chosen him to lead the people of Israel out of slavery. (Exodus 3:7-12)
4. God is the "I AM." (Exodus 3:13-18)
5. God knew what the king would do. (Exodus 3:19-20)
6. Moses was reluctant to go back to Egypt. (Exodus 4:1-17)
7. Moses obeyed the Lord. (Exodus 4:18-20)

(?) Review Questions from Lesson 28.

Lesson Outline Developed

1. God saw the people of Israel in slavery and heard their cries.

- **The people of Israel had been in slavery for four hundred years.**

    Read Exodus 2:23.

    The king of Egypt died, but the king that followed also kept the Israelites as slaves. The Israelites must have often wondered if they would ever be delivered from their suffering. Although many years passed, the Israelites continued to cry to God to deliver them.

- **The Lord loved the Israelites, and He heard their cries for help.**

    Read Exodus 2:24-25.

God had not forgotten the promises which He had made to Abraham, Isaac and Jacob hundreds of years before. He had promised them that the Deliverer would be one of their descendants, and He had promised to give them the land of Canaan.

When Abraham was alive, God had told him that his descendants would leave the land that God had given to them and be made slaves in another country. God had promised Abraham that, after 400 years, He would deliver them from slavery and bring them back to the land of Canaan.

Read Genesis 15:13-15.

It seemed impossible for the Israelites to be set free and return all the way to Canaan, but God is faithful to His promises. Whatever He says, He does. The time had come for God to fulfill His promise to bring Abraham's descendants out of slavery and back to their own country.

Because the Israelites had been in slavery for many years, it may have seemed to them that God had forgotten His promises. But God never forgets. God is never in a hurry. He never begins something and then abandons it. He will do all that He planned and promised.

2) God spoke to Moses from the burning bush.

Read Exodus 3:1-4.

Teacher: Show a picture of Moses standing barefoot in front of the burning bush.

This bush was an ordinary bush. The extraordinary thing was that the bush was burning and yet it was not being burned up. Because God was in the bush, the bush wasn't consumed.

God is almighty. Nobody can do the things which God can do.

- **The burning bush was like the people of Israel who were suffering.**

As Moses looked at the burning bush, he may have been reminded of the terrible conditions of his fellow Israelites. They, like the burning bush, were in danger of being totally destroyed. But, just as God was in the bush and kept it from being consumed, so He was with the Israelites and would not let them be destroyed. Neither Satan nor Pharaoh could destroy the Israelites because God was with them.

- **God spoke to Moses from the burning bush.**

Moses didn't know that God was in the bush until God spoke to him from within the bush.

God knew Moses' language. Moses didn't speak English. God knows all languages, including your language. God hears and understands everything which you think and say. Even if you whisper, God still hears and understands.

📖 Read Exodus 3:5-6.

God told Moses to take his shoes off as a sign of respect to God who is perfect and is the great Creator. In those days, to be barefoot was a sign of humility and submission.

③ God told Moses that He had chosen him to lead the people of Israel out of slavery.

📖 Read Exodus 3:7-10.

God told Moses that He had chosen him to lead the Israelites out of slavery in Egypt and take them back to the land which God had given to Abraham.

The Lord chooses whomever He pleases to do His will, and when the time comes for the Lord to fulfill His plans, no one can stop Him.

📖 Read Exodus 3:11.

Moses had failed when he had tried to help his people previously so he knew that he was not able to confront the king and deliver the Israelites from slavery by his own strength.

📖 Read Exodus 3:12.

God told Moses that He would be with him, and He gave Moses a sign. God promised Moses that He would bring him back to the mountain on which he was standing. This mountain was named Mount Sinai or Mount Horeb.

④ God is the "I AM."

Lesson Developer: If the people's names have meanings, you can use their names as an illustration and introduction for these next verses.

📖 Read Exodus 3:13.

- **Moses wanted to know God's name.**

Because his own people had rejected him when he had tried to assist them previously, Moses did not think that they would believe him when he went to them and told them that the God of Abraham, Isaac and Jacob had sent him to deliver them from slavery. So he asked God His name. Moses intended to use the name of God as proof to the Israelites that God had sent him.

- **Names in the Bible have meanings.**

    A person's name emphasized some personal characteristic or quality. For example, Moses' name meant "to draw out of" because he was taken out of the water when the king's daughter found him.

    What name could God use that would express His characteristics? Think about the characteristics of God.

    - God is supreme; He is greater than everyone and everything.
    - He is the mighty and holy Creator.
    - He is everywhere and sees everything.
    - He knows everything.
    - He is almighty.
    - He is faithful and unchanging.
    - He is the judge and avenger of all evil.
    - He is loving, kind and gracious.

    God has all of these characteristics and many others.

    Therefore, what one name could God use to identify Himself that would tell the Israelites all of His characteristics? It could not be done.

    📖 Read Exodus 3:14.

- **God told Moses to tell the Israelites that "I AM" had sent him.**

    This name, "I AM," includes so much that we cannot understand it completely. But, we do know that it means that God never had a beginning and cannot have an end. God has always lived and will always live completely by His own power and wisdom. He never has been nor will He ever be dependent on anyone or anything. The name "I AM" means that God is the self-existent One.

    The first words in the Bible are, "In the beginning God." God was already there in the beginning. He had no beginning and will have no end.

    God was never dependent on anyone or anything, and He will never be dependent on anyone or anything. He created everything and everyone, and all depend on Him for everything.

    God has control over the heavens and the earth. He has control over all things.

    Because God is the great "I AM," He is greater than all.

    Pharaoh, the Egyptians, and even Satan could not hold God's people when the Lord, the "I AM," decided to deliver them.

LESSON 29: GOD CHOSE MOSES TO LEAD THE ISRAELITES OUT OF SLAVERY.

📖 Read Exodus 3:15-18.

⑤ God knew what the king would do.

📖 Read Exodus 3:19-20.

God knew exactly how the king of Egypt would react.

God knows our thoughts, words and actions before we ever think or do them. He knows everything about us from birth to death and even what will happen to us after death.

⑥ Moses was reluctant to go back to Egypt.

📖 Read Exodus 4:1.

Moses remembered how his people had rejected him when he was in Egypt, when he tried to help them. He didn't think they would believe that the God of Abraham, Isaac and Jacob had sent him to be their leader and deliverer.

📖 Read Exodus 4:2-9.

God gave Moses miraculous signs for him to show as proof that he had been sent by God.

But Moses was still reluctant to return to Egypt, so he tried another excuse. Listen to what Moses said and what God answered.

📖 Read Exodus 4:10-12.

All things are under the Lord's control. He is the great Creator and is therefore King over the whole earth. All people, including Moses, were created by Him.

Even though God promised to help him, Moses was still reluctant so he suggested that the Lord send someone who was more suitable than he was.

📖 Read Exodus 4:13.

The Lord was angry with Moses for continuing to argue, but He promised to send Aaron, Moses' older brother, to assist him.

📖 Read Exodus 4:14-17.

👉 **Teacher:** Point to the name, **"Aaron,"** on the Chronological Chart.

⑦ Moses obeyed the Lord.

📖 Read Exodus 4:18-20.

The Lord assured Moses that the king and all others who had previously planned to harm him were now dead. When Moses heard that, he obeyed the Lord and began his journey back to Egypt.

? Questions

1. Did God hear the Israelites when they cried out to Him, asking for help?
   Yes. God heard their cries for help.

2. What had God told Abraham would happen to his descendants?
   God had told Abraham that his descendants would go to a country that was not their own where they would be enslaved for 400 years, and that they would return to the land God had given to Abraham.

3. Had God forgotten the promises that He made to Abraham, Isaac and Jacob?
   No. God will always do all that He has promised.

4. What unusual thing did Moses see?
   Moses saw a bush that was burning but was not being burned up.

5. Why was the bush not being consumed even though it was burning?
   The bush was not consumed because God was in the bush.

6. How were the people of Israel like the burning bush?
   The people of Israel, like the burning bush, were in danger of being totally destroyed, but just like God was in the bush and kept it from being consumed, so He was with the Israelites and would not let them be destroyed.

7. What does the name of God, "I AM," mean?
   It means that God is the self-existent One.

8. Did God know how the king of Egypt would react?
   Yes. God knew exactly how he would react.

9. What did God give Moses to show to the Israelites as proof that he had been sent by God?
   God gave Moses miraculous signs to prove that he was God's messenger.

10. What happened to Moses' rod when God used it as a sign?
    Moses' rod became a snake when Moses threw it on the ground, and it turned back into a rod when he picked the snake up by the tail.

LESSON 29: GOD CHOSE MOSES TO LEAD THE ISRAELITES OUT OF SLAVERY.

11. What happened to Moses' hand when God used it as a sign?

    Moses' hand became covered with leprosy when he placed his hand inside his coat, but the leprosy was gone when he put his hand back inside his coat again.

12. Whom did God promise to send to speak on Moses' behalf?

    The Lord promised to send Aaron, Moses' brother, to speak on his behalf.

LESSON 30: THE LORD SENT PLAGUES ON THE EGYPTIANS.

Scripture

Exodus 4:27-31, Exodus 5:1-2, Exodus 6:1-8, Exodus 7:4-5, 20-21, Exodus 8:5-6, 16-17, 24, Exodus 9:3, 6-7, 10, 23-26, Exodus 10:13-15, 21-23, 28-29

Lesson Outline

(1) Moses and Aaron went to Egypt together. (Exodus 4:27-29)

(2) The Israelites believed that the Lord sent Moses. (Exodus 4:20-31)

(3) Pharaoh refused to obey God's command given through Moses and Aaron. (Exodus 5:1-2)

(4) Through Pharaoh's rebellion, the Lord planned to show the Israelites that He was their God. (Exodus 6:1-8)

(5) Through Pharaoh's rebellion, the Lord planned to show the Egyptians that He alone was the true and living God. (Exodus 7:4-5)

(6) The Lord sent nine plagues on the Egyptians. (Exodus 7:20-21; 8:5-6, 16-17, 24; 9:3, 6-7, 10, 23-26; 10:13-15, 21-23)

(7) God protected the Israelites from the nine plagues. (Exodus 9:6-7; 10:22-23)

(8) Pharaoh hardened his heart. (Exodus 10:28-29)

(?) Review Questions from Lesson 29.

Lesson Outline Developed

(1) Moses and Aaron went to Egypt together.

Read Exodus 4:27-29.

The Lord sent Aaron to meet his brother, Moses. God had promised Moses that Aaron would assist him in demanding the release of the Israelites from the king of Egypt.

Moses and Aaron went back to Egypt. They called together their own people, the Israelites, and told them what the Lord had said to Moses.

② The Israelites believed that the Lord sent Moses.

📖 Read Exodus 4:30-31.

The Israelites believed God's Word given through Moses. They were thankful that the Lord had heard their cries for deliverance.

The Israelites were wise to listen to and believe God's message given through Moses. When people don't believe the Word of God, they are showing that they think God is a liar. The Lord is unable to help those who refuse to believe His Word.

③ Pharaoh refused to obey God's command given through Moses and Aaron.

📖 Read Exodus 5:1-2.

God used Moses and Aaron to speak His message to the king of Egypt, but the king refused to obey the Lord's command to let the people of Israel go. Pharaoh did not know the only true and living God.

- **The Egyptians worshiped the things that God had created instead of the Creator of the whole earth.**

The Egyptians worshiped the Nile River, which is the largest river in their country. They also worshiped the sun and moon, as well as many different kinds of animals. In addition, the Egyptians worshiped Pharaoh, their king, as a god. The Egyptians had turned away from the true understanding of God, and they worshiped many false gods.

- **When people don't want to know God, He allows them to worship things that are false gods.**

When people deliberately turn away from the true knowledge of God, they become foolish in their understanding about God.

Your ancestors and my ancestors also turned away from the true understanding of God. Satan led them to worship things which are false gods, and he controlled them through fear of the spirits.

- **The truth about God is in the Bible which God gave through the Israelites.**

Because most people in the world had turned away from the true understanding of God, God chose Abraham and his descendants, so that, through them, He could preserve the true knowledge of God. Through Abraham's descendants, God planned to make known the truth to all other people of the world.

God would have taught the king of Egypt that the gods he and his people worshiped

**LESSON 30: THE LORD SENT
PLAGUES ON THE EGYPTIANS.**

were false and that the God of the Israelites is the only true and living God, but this king refused to listen to God's message through Moses.

I hope that none of you will take the same attitude as the foolish king of Egypt. I hope you will continue to listen to God's message in the Bible.

4) Through Pharaoh's rebellion, the Lord planned to show the Israelites that He was their God.

Read Exodus 6:1-8.

The generation of Israelites living in Egypt when Moses returned there had heard about the Lord and what He had done for Abraham, Isaac, Jacob and Joseph, but they had never personally experienced the Lord's greatness and power. The Lord was going to use this wicked king and his rebellion to display His power and wisdom to this generation of Israelites. God planned to show them that He was still almighty and that He cared about them. God wanted them to know that the God of Abraham, Isaac and Jacob was also their God.

5) Through Pharaoh's rebellion, the Lord planned to show the Egyptians that He alone was the true and living God.

Do you think God was surprised when the king of Egypt refused to obey Him? No! God was not surprised. He knew what the king would say and do. When God talked with Moses from the burning bush, He had told Moses that the king would not let the Israelites go.

Because Pharaoh was determined to fight against God, God planned to use this proud and wicked king to display His mighty power. God was going to show the Israelites and the Egyptians that He is the true and living God and that He has power over the whole earth. God was also going to show them that all who rebel against Him will suffer terrible judgment.

Read Exodus 7:4-5.

No one who ignores God or fights against Him can escape from God's punishment. Pharaoh could not fight against God and win, and people today cannot fight against God and win.

Lesson Developer: It is not necessary to include the story about the contest between Moses and Pharaoh's magicians from Exodus 7:10-12, 22; 8:7, 18. This story does not add any further details to what we have already learned about God, man or Satan and adds no necessary foundations for teaching the life of Christ and the Gospel. We want to move as quickly as possible to the story of Christ, and we don't want to add stories unless they are a necessary part of the teaching program.

But should you decide to include this story, you need to be very careful that your hearers don't misunderstand this story so that it becomes a hindrance rather than a help at this stage of their understanding of the truth. Be sure to emphasize that, although Satan does have some power, God is greater in power than Satan. However, be careful how strongly you emphasize the truth that God's power is greater than Satan's power. Animistic people battle for survival throughout their whole lives by appeasing, bribing and endeavoring not to offend the spirits. They are looking for escape from those things which threaten the life, health, crops and the daily welfare of their families and communities. Remember that you do not want the people to think that you are merely offering God as an alternative to the spirits. Since it will be obvious to the hearers by this point in the teaching program that God is loving and yet much more powerful than all other spirits, they may profess faith in God without really facing the true issues of sin, righteousness and judgment. Consequently, there will be no true faith, for there has been no true repentance, that is, a true change of mind toward God, sin and themselves. We must make sure the people understand that their true need is deliverance from sin and death, not simply deliverance from dependence upon the spirits.

(6) The Lord sent nine plagues on the Egyptians

Because the king of Egypt refused to release the Israelites, the Lord began to show His great power by sending plagues on the Egyptians.

- **The Lord turned the water in the Nile River into blood.**

    Read Exodus 7:20-21.

- **The Lord sent a plague of frogs.**

    Read Exodus 8:5-6.

- **The Lord sent lice.**

    Read Exodus 8:16-17.

- **The Lord sent flies.**

    Read Exodus 8:24.

- **The Lord sent a plague on all the Egyptians' livestock so that all their animals died.**

    Read Exodus 9:3, 6-7.

- **The Lord caused all the Egyptians to have terrible boils.**

    Read Exodus 9:10.

- **The Lord sent a destructive hailstorm on Pharaoh and his people.**

    📖 Read Exodus 9:23-26.

- **The Lord sent locusts.**

    📖 Read Exodus 10:13-15.

- **The Lord blotted out all light over all of the land where the Egyptians were living.**

    📖 Read Exodus 10:21-23.

- **Pharaoh and the Egyptians could not save themselves from these terrible plagues sent by the Lord.**

⑦ God protected the Israelites from the nine plagues.

Even though the Israelites were living nearby in the same country, they did not suffer from the plagues that God sent upon the Egyptians.

📖 Read Exodus 9:6-7; 10:22-23 again.

- **The Lord protected the Israelites because He loved them.**

    The Lord didn't protect them because they were without sin or because they deserved His care. He protected them because of His love, mercy and grace.

- **God protected the Israelites because of His promises to Abraham, Isaac and Jacob.**

    God chose Abraham and promised to bless him and to make his descendants into a great nation. Although hundreds of years had passed and the Israelites were now slaves in Egypt, the Israelites were still God's special people because they were the descendants which God had promised to Abraham.

- **God protected the Israelites from the plagues to demonstrate that He was the only true and living God in the whole earth.**

    God wanted Pharaoh and the people of Egypt to know that He is supreme and sovereign and can do whatever He chooses to do.

⑧ Pharaoh hardened his heart.

Each time the Lord sent a plague on the Egyptians, Pharaoh called for Moses and asked him to remove the plague. Pharaoh claimed that he would let the people of Israel go as soon as the plague was over. As soon as the Lord removed the plague, however, Pharaoh hardened his heart and would not let the Israelites leave. Every time Pharaoh did this, he became harder and more proud.

After the Lord had removed the last plague of thick darkness, Pharaoh was very arrogant. Listen to what he said to Moses.

📖 Read Exodus 10:28.

Pharaoh was angry and he told Moses that he would kill him if he ever dared to come and ask him again to let the Israelites go. Nevertheless, Moses still believed that the Lord would deliver the Israelites. His faith and trust was in the power of God. This is how Moses answered the king.

📖 Read Exodus 10:29.

Was this the end? Does this mean that Pharaoh had won and God had lost?

Teacher: As you ask questions like these, allow time for the people to answer. Their responses will help you to ascertain what the people understand and believe about the God of the Bible.

Even after going through these nine terrible plagues, Pharaoh still refused to allow the Israelites to go. He still refused to obey the Lord.

Think about this: Can anyone fight against God and win? Do you think God was defeated by this proud man? After all God had done to make Pharaoh release the Israelites, did they remain in slavery? We will see what happened when we have the next lesson.

⑦ Questions

1. What had God promised Moses that his brother, Aaron, would help him to do?

    God had promised that Aaron would assist Moses in demanding the release of the Israelites from the king of Egypt.

2. When Moses and Aaron spoke to the Israelites, did the people believe God's message?

    Yes. They believed God's message.

3. Will God accept those who do not believe what He says?

    No. God rejects all who do not believe what He says.

4. When people don't believe the Word of God, what are they showing that they think about God?

    They are showing that they think God is a liar.

5. What did Pharaoh say when Moses told him that the Lord commanded him to let the Israelites go?

LESSON 30: THE LORD SENT PLAGUES ON THE EGYPTIANS.

Pharaoh said that he didn't know the Lord and wouldn't let the Israelites go.

6. Did the king's answer surprise the Lord?
   No. The Lord knew that Pharaoh would not let the Israelites go immediately.

7. Does anything you say, think, or do surprise the Lord?
   No. He knows everything before it ever happens.

8. For what purpose did God plan to use this proud king?
   God planned to display His power to this proud king so everyone would know that the God of Israel is the only true and living God and that He is almighty.

9. What did God do to show His power?
   The Lord sent plagues on the Egyptians.

10. What were the plagues that the Lord sent on the Egyptians?
    The Lord turned the river to blood. He sent frogs, gnats and flies. He destroyed the Egyptians' livestock. He also sent boils, hail storms, locusts and total darkness.

11. Could the Egyptians save themselves from these terrible plagues sent by the Lord?
    No. The Egyptians could not save themselves from the plagues.

12. Did the Israelites suffer from the plagues as the Egyptians did?
    No. Even though the Israelites were living nearby in the same country, they did not suffer from the plagues that God sent upon the Egyptians.

13. Who protected the Israelites from the plagues?
    God protected them.

14. Did the Israelites deserve to be protected from the plagues?
    No. God protected the Israelites because of His love and grace.

15. Had God forgotten the promise that He made to Abraham to bless his descendants and make them into a great nation?
    No. Although hundreds of years had passed and the Israelites were now slaves in Egypt, the Israelites were still God's special people because they were the descendants which God had promised to Abraham.

16. What did God's protection of the Israelites from the plagues reveal to Pharaoh and the people of Egypt?
    God's protection of the Israelites revealed that the God of Israel was the only true and living God and that He can do whatever He chooses.

17. What did Pharaoh do each time the Lord sent a plague?

    Pharaoh promised to let the people of Israel go, and he asked Moses to remove the plague.

18. What did Pharaoh do each time the Lord removed the plague?

    Pharaoh hardened his heart and refused to allow the people of Israel to leave.

19. Can anyone fight against God and win?

    No! No one can fight against God and win.

LESSON 31: GOD KILLED THE FIRSTBORN OF THE EGYPTIANS, BUT HE SAVED THE FIRSTBORN OF THE ISRAELITES.

Scripture

Exodus 11:1, 4-7, Exodus 12:1-7, 12-14, 22-23, 28-33, 46, 51

Lesson Outline

1. The Lord planned to send one last plague on the Egyptians. (Exodus 11:1, 4-7)
2. God told Moses how the Israelites must prepare for the final plague. (Exodus 12:1-7, 22-23, 46)
3. God promised the Israelites that He would protect their firstborn if they believed and obeyed Him. (Exodus 12:12-14)
4. The Israelites believed God and obeyed Him. (Exodus 12:28)
5. All the Egyptians' firstborn died. (Exodus 12:29-30)
6. Pharaoh told the Israelites to go. (Exodus 12:31-33, 51)

? Review Questions from Lesson 30.

Lesson Outline Developed

1. The Lord planned to send one last plague on the Egyptians.

Although the Lord had already sent nine terrible plagues on the rebellious Egyptians, the king of Egypt refused to obey the Lord and let the Israelites go free.

Do you think that God had to give up and let the Israelites remain in slavery? No! God knew all along that the king would be stubborn and refuse to release the Israelites. Even before He sent Moses back to Egypt, God had told him that this would happen.

God is never surprised by what people do. He always knows everything before it happens, and He always has His plan worked out so that He wins, no matter what people say or do.

The Lord knew that Pharaoh would release the Israelites after one final plague. The wicked king could not stop God from delivering the descendants of Abraham.

📖 Read Exodus 11:1, 4-7.

② God told Moses how the Israelites must prepare for the final plague.

We learned previously that the Israelites did not suffer from the nine plagues that God had sent upon the Egyptians. God had protected them because He loved them and because the Israelites were His special people, the descendants which God had promised to Abraham.

Although the Israelites had not suffered from the other plagues, they would have suffered through this last terrible judgment along with the Egyptians, unless God made the way for them to escape. Because of God's mercy and grace, He told Moses what the Israelites must do in order to save their firstborn children from death.

- **They must choose a lamb without blemish.**

  📖 Read Exodus 12:1-5.

  Do you remember the ram that God provided to die instead of Isaac? The ram was caught by its horns in the bush so that it could not injure itself by struggling to get free. If it had been injured, it would not have been an acceptable offering to God. God would only accept a healthy, strong animal as a sacrifice.

  Because God is perfect, He will only accept what is perfect. He would never accept an animal that was sick or hurt, so He told the Israelites that the head of each home was to choose a lamb without blemish.

- **They must kill the lamb and catch its blood in a basin.**

  📖 Read Exodus 12:6.

  The lamb was to be kept until the fourteenth day of the month. They were to kill the lamb in the evening of that day.

- **The lamb had to die.**

  The lamb's blood, on which its life depended, had to flow out. This was to remind the Israelites that the punishment for sin is death.

  Before Adam and Eve sinned, there was no death in the world. But when Adam and Eve disobeyed God, they were immediately separated from God, and someday their bodies would also die. All of Adam and Eve's descendants have been born sinners, separated from God. This is why all people die physically and why people who do not believe God will be separated from God forever in the place of eternal punishment. Because there is sin in the world, there is death.

LESSON 31: GOD KILLED THE FIRSTBORN OF THE EGYPTIANS, BUT HE SAVED THE FIRSTBORN OF THE ISRAELITES.

When the Israelites killed the lambs, they were reminded that the punishment for sin is death. The lambs died instead of the firstborn of the Israelites, just as the ram died instead of Isaac. A perfect lamb had to die so that the Israelite's firstborn would not die.

- **They must place the blood on the doorposts and above the doors of their homes.**

  📖 Read Exodus 12:7.

  God told the Israelites that they were to put some of the blood on the sides and tops of the door frames on the outside of each of their houses. If their firstborn was to be saved from God's judgment, they must apply the blood of the lamb as God commanded.

☞ **Teacher:** Show a picture of the Israelites applying the lamb's blood on the sides and tops of the door frames on the outside of each of their houses.

- **They must stay inside the house on which they had placed the blood.**

  📖 Read Exodus 12:22-23.

  God told the Israelites that, when they killed the lamb, they were to catch the blood in a basin. Then they were to take a branch from a particular bush, dip it into the blood, and use it to apply the blood to their doorposts.

  After they applied the blood to the doorposts, the Israelites were to stay inside their houses until the morning. It was just as if they were to hide behind the blood of the lamb which God said they must kill in order to save their firstborn.

- **They must not break any of the lamb's bones.**

  📖 Read Exodus 12:46.

  They were not to break the bones of the animal when they killed it or ate it.

③ God promised the Israelites that He would protect their firstborn if they believed and obeyed Him.

📖 Read Exodus 12:12-14.

God promised the Israelites that, when He saw the blood on the doorposts of their houses, He would not allow the plague to enter and kill their firstborn.

- **The Israelites had to do everything exactly as the Lord had instructed Moses.**

  God has always required that people believe what He says and come to Him according to His way. We have already learned that God does not accept what people try to do to be acceptable to Him.

  ○ Do you remember that Adam and Eve made clothing for themselves after they had disobeyed God? Did God accept the clothing that they made? No, He refused to accept what they had made, and He killed animals and made clothing for them.

- ○ Do you remember the offering that Cain brought to God? Was that offering according to God's instructions? No, it was not, so God refused Cain's offering.
- ○ Do you remember the boat that Noah built? Who gave him the instructions about how to build that boat? God did! Noah had to follow God's instructions exactly.

In the same way, the Israelites also had to do everything according to God's instructions.

- **God is still the same.**

We cannot come to God according to our own ideas or the ideas of any other person. We can only come to God according to God's way. If we don't believe what God says and come the way He says, then He will never accept us.

- **What would have happened if the Israelites did not do what God said?**

What do you think would have happened if an Israelite had said, "I don't believe what God said. I'm not going to kill one of my good lambs. I have a sick one. I'll kill that one instead"? Would God have accepted the blood of a sick lamb? No! God would only accept a lamb without blemish.

What do you think would have happened if an Israelite had said, "I don't believe what God said. I do not want to kill this good lamb. I will just tie it up at the door. God will see the living lamb, and He will not kill my child by the plague"? Would

God have accepted a lamb whose blood had not been shed? No! The lamb had to die, and the blood had to be shed so that the firstborn could live. The Israelites must not forget that the punishment for sin is death.

The Israelites had to follow God's instructions exactly. If they did not, their firstborn would have been killed.

④ The Israelites believed God and obeyed Him.

Do you think the Israelites would have said, "Oh, well, only our firstborn will die. We have other children. It doesn't matter. We won't bother to kill the lamb and put the blood on the doorposts"? No! The Israelites loved their children just as you love your children. And the only way their children could be saved was if the Israelites trusted God who had told them that, when He saw the blood on the doorposts of their houses, their firstborn children and the firstborn of their livestock would not die.

Do you think the Israelites trusted God? Yes! They did. They believed what God had told them, and they obeyed Him.

📖 Read Exodus 12:28.

LESSON 31: GOD KILLED THE FIRSTBORN
OF THE EGYPTIANS, BUT HE SAVED THE
FIRSTBORN OF THE ISRAELITES.

⑤ All the Egyptians' firstborn died.

📖 Read Exodus 12:29-30.

The Lord passed through Egypt just as He said He would. He always does what He says. He doesn't merely threaten and then not carry out His threats. When God decides to punish sinners, there is no way to escape.

☞ **Teacher:** Show a picture of an Egyptian weeping over his dead child.

Every firstborn Egyptian child and the firstborn of all the Egyptians' livestock died. But because the Israelites had put the blood on their houses in obedience to the Lord, not one of their firstborn children or livestock died.

God always does what He says. He said He would destroy the firstborn in the Egyptian homes, and He did. He said He would pass over every house where He saw the blood, and He did. The Lord can be trusted to do everything He says.

⑥ Pharaoh told the Israelites to go.

📖 Read Exodus 12:31-33.

Pharaoh told Moses that very night to take the Israelites out of Egypt. The Lord delivered His people just as He had promised He would.

Pharaoh had thought that he could fight against God and that he would not have to give in, but no one can fight against the Lord and win. God will send punishment on those who fight against Him, but He will give His mercy and peace to those who trust Him.

📖 Read Exodus 12:51.

❓ Questions

1. Could Pharaoh stop God from delivering the Israelites?
   No. Pharaoh was not able to stop God from delivering the Israelites.

2. Can anyone fight against God and win?
   No. No one can fight against God and win.

**Building on Firm Foundations
- Volume 2: Evangelism:
Genesis to The Ascension**

3. What was the last plague which God sent on the Egyptians?

   God sent a plague which killed the firstborn in every Egyptian family and the firstborn of all their livestock.

4. Who was the only One who could save the Israelites from suffering from this plague?

   God was the only One who could save the Israelites from this plague.

5. Did God tell the Israelites what to do so their firstborn children would not die?

   Yes. God told them exactly what to do.

6. What kind of a lamb were the Israelites to choose?

   They were to choose a lamb without blemish.

7. The Israelites were to keep the lamb until the fourteenth day of the month. What were they to do with the lamb after this time?

   They were to kill it.

8. When they shed the blood of the lamb, what were the Israelites reminded of?

   They were reminded that the punishment for sin is death.

9. Where did God tell the Israelites to place the blood from the lamb after they killed it?

   God told them to put the blood on the sides and tops of the door frames on the outside of each of their houses.

10. After they applied the blood to the doorposts, where did God tell the Israelites to stay?

    God told the Israelites to stay inside their houses.

11. Were the Israelites allowed to break the bones of the lamb when they killed it or ate it?

    No. God told them not to break the bones of the lamb.

12. What did God promise the Israelites that He would do when He saw the blood on the doorposts of their houses?

    God promised them that when He saw the blood on the doorposts of their houses He would not allow the plague to enter and kill their firstborn.

13. What would have happened if the Israelites had not done everything exactly as God instructed Moses?

    If the Israelites had not done exactly as God said, their firstborn children would have been killed.

14. Who is the only One who can tell us how we can come to God and be accepted by Him?

    God is the only One who can tell us how we can come to Him and be accepted by Him.

LESSON 31: GOD KILLED THE FIRSTBORN OF THE EGYPTIANS, BUT HE SAVED THE FIRSTBORN OF THE ISRAELITES.

15. What happened in the Egyptian homes on that night when God said that He would kill the firstborn of every family?

    God killed the Egyptian's firstborn just as He said He would.

16. What happened to the firstborn of the Israelites?

    All of the firstborn of the Israelites were safe. None of them died.

17. Why didn't the firstborn of the Israelites die?

    The firstborn of the Israelites did not die because the Israelites had believed God and had put the blood on their houses in obedience to the Lord.

18. Does God always do what He says?

    Yes. God always does what He says.

19. What did Pharaoh tell Moses after the Egyptians' firstborn children died?

    Pharaoh told Moses to take all the Israelites out of Egypt.

LESSON 32: GOD DELIVERED THE ISRAELITES AT THE RED SEA.

Scripture

Exodus 13:21-22, Exodus 14:1-31

Lesson Outline

① God led the Israelites by a cloud. (Exodus 13:21-22)

② The Israelites camped near the sea. (Exodus 14:1-4)

③ Pharaoh decided to recapture the Israelites. (Exodus 14:5-9)

④ The Israelites were afraid, and they blamed Moses. (Exodus 14:10-12)

⑤ Moses trusted in the Lord and told the Israelites to believe God. (Exodus 14:13-14)

⑥ God opened the sea. (Exodus 14:15-18)

⑦ God led the Israelites through the sea. (Exodus 14:19-25)

⑧ God drowned the Egyptian army in the sea. (Exodus 14:26-31)

(?) Review Questions from Lesson 31.

Lesson Outline Developed

Teacher: As you teach this lesson, point out on the map the areas where the various events took place. Emphasize to your hearers that these events are actual history.

① God led the Israelites by a cloud.

- **God delivered the Israelites from slavery.**

    When God delivered the Israelites from slavery in Egypt, He was showing His almighty power to the Egyptians and to the Israelites.

- **God was keeping His promise to Abraham, Isaac and Jacob.**

    God had promised that Abraham's descendants would inherit the land of Canaan. God delivered the Israelites from the land of Egypt, and He planned to take them back to the land He had promised to them, the land where their ancestors had lived.

- **God preserved the people of Israel so that the Deliverer would be born into the world.**

    God had also promised Abraham that one of his descendants would be the Deliverer. The Israelites are the descendants of Abraham. God protected the Israelites while they were in Egypt, and He delivered them from slavery.

- **The Lord protected the Israelites because He was entrusting His Word to them to give to the world.**

    The words of God that we have been studying in the Bible were originally given to the Israelites. God wanted all people in the world to be able to learn the truth about God and come to know Him so He gave the people of Israel His message for all mankind.

- **God began leading the Israelites towards the land of Canaan.**

    The land of Canaan is the land which God had promised to Abraham, Isaac and Jacob. It was the land where Jacob and Joseph's brothers had lived before they went down into Egypt to be with Joseph.

    When the Israelites first went into Egypt, there were only seventy of them. When they left Egypt, there were about two-and-a-half million of them.

    📖 Read Exodus 13:21-22.

- **God directed the Israelites where to go by a pillar of cloud.**

    God kept the cloud before them at all times. They would have gotten lost in the desert and would have eventually died if the Lord had not directed them. God loved the Israelites, and so He took care of them.

② The Israelites camped near the sea.

📖 Read Exodus 14:1-4.

God led the Israelites up to the sea, and they camped near it. This sea is named the Red Sea.

☞ **Teacher:** Point to the Red Sea on the map.

God brought the Israelites to this place because He planned to demonstrate again to them and to the Egyptians that He is the almighty, sovereign God. God was going to show them again that He is greater than all.

LESSON 32: GOD DELIVERED THE ISRAELITES AT THE RED SEA.

God knew what Pharaoh would think and plan. How did God know what Pharaoh would think? God knew because God knows everything that people are going to say or think or do, even before it happens. The Lord was with the Israelites at the Red Sea, and He was also in Egypt. He knew what Pharaoh was planning to do.

3. Pharaoh decided to recapture the Israelites.

Read Exodus 14:5-9.

Pharaoh was guided by Satan. He was not going to give up and let the Israelites go. He planned to go after them and recapture them.

4. The Israelites were afraid, and they blamed Moses.

What do you think the Israelites did when they saw the Egyptians coming after them? Do you think they trusted in the Lord and asked Him to deliver them?

Read Exodus 14:10-12.

Even though the Israelites had seen all the great and mighty things the Lord had done in Egypt, they did not trust in the Lord to save them from Pharaoh and his army.

Just like the Israelites, people today have to decide if they will believe God. Are you willing to believe God's Word and trust only in Him even though Satan, the spirits, and maybe some people do not want you to believe?

Teacher: Don't require the people to respond to questions like these. However, if someone wants to express their thoughts, you should let them.

5. Moses trusted in the Lord and told the Israelites to believe God.

Read Exodus 14:13-14.

Even though the Israelites sinned by not trusting in the Lord, He was merciful and planned to deliver them. They couldn't deliver themselves. The sea was in front of them, mountains were around them, and their enemies were behind them.

- **Only God could save them.**

We have already learned that God is the only One who can provide the way for people to be saved.

  - Only God could provide the way for Adam and Eve to be accepted by Him after they had sinned. They could not make things right between them and God, but God provided the way.

- Only God could provide the way so that Abel could be accepted by God.
- Only God could save Noah and his family from the flood.
- Only God could save Isaac when he was tied to the altar and his father had the knife raised above him.
- Only God could provide the way so the firstborn children of the Israelites could be saved from death.

Likewise, only God could provide the way so the Israelites could escape from the Egyptians at the Red Sea.

- **Only God can save sinners!**

  People cannot provide the way to escape the wrath of God. You cannot make things right between you and God by the things you do. Only God can save you from everlasting punishment. Continue to listen carefully to God's Word so you will learn the way God has provided to save sinners.

⑥ God opened the sea.

📖 Read Exodus 14:15-16.

- **God created the sea, so He had complete control over it.**

  In the beginning, when the whole earth was covered with water, the Lord caused the water to move back so there was dry ground. God had not changed – He could move the waters of the Red Sea. God is still the same today – He has complete control over the whole earth.

- **God commanded the Red Sea to move back.**

  God planned that His people would walk on dry land to the other side. It was not difficult for God to open the sea so that the Israelites could walk through to the other side. The Lord is almighty. Nothing is too hard for Him.

☞ **Teacher:** Show a picture of the Israelites crossing the Red Sea.

📖 Read Exodus 14:17-18.

The Lord knew that the Egyptians would follow the Israelites into the sea. The Lord planned to destroy Pharaoh's army in the sea.

LESSON 32: GOD DELIVERED THE ISRAELITES AT THE RED SEA.

⑦ God led the Israelites through the sea.

📖 Read Exodus 14:19-22.

The Lord did not forsake His people. He promised to lead them safely out of Egypt and into the land He had promised to Abraham. The Lord guided the Israelites into the path which He had made through the sea.

The Lord moved the cloud that was leading the Israelites and placed it between them and the Egyptians. Behind the Israelites, the cloud was bright and shining like a large fire, giving light so the Israelites could see where they were going. Before the Egyptians, however, the cloud was black. There was only darkness in front of them. Nevertheless, the Egyptians continued to follow the path that God had made through the sea.

📖 Read Exodus 14:23-25.

⑧ God drowned the Egyptian army in the sea.

📖 Read Exodus 14:26-29.

- **The Egyptian army was drowned by God in the sea.**

  No one can fight against God and succeed. He punishes all those who fight against Him, but He is merciful to all those who believe His Word and come to Him in the way He says.

  📖 Read Exodus 14:30.

- **The Lord protected all of the Israelites.**

  Not one of them was drowned, and the Egyptians did not catch any of them. The Lord saved them because of His love for them and because He had promised to save them.

  📖 Read Exodus 14:31.

  When the Israelites saw the great things which the Lord did, they believed in Him.

- **God tells us to believe His Word and to trust in Him.**

  Some people say they will only believe if they can see God do some great and wonderful thing. But God has not promised that He will do great miracles so that people will believe. If we refuse to believe what He has written in His Word, then we will be separated from God forever when we die and we will go to everlasting punishment.

Building on Firm Foundations
- Volume 2: Evangelism:
Genesis to The Ascension

? Questions

1. How did the Lord direct the Israelites where He wanted them to go?

   God directed them by a cloud during the day, which became a pillar of fire at night.

2. What would have happened to the Israelites in the desert if the Lord had not directed them where to go?

   The Israelites would have gotten lost in the desert and would have eventually died if the Lord had not directed them.

3. Why did God protect the Israelites?

   God protected them because He loved them, because of His promises to their ancestors, Abraham, Isaac and Jacob, because He had promised that the Deliverer would be born into the world through them, and because He had entrusted His Word to them.

4. To which land was God leading the Israelites?

   God was leading the Israelites to Canaan, the land which God had promised to give to Abraham, Isaac and Jacob.

5. What did God plan to demonstrate to the Israelites and to the Egyptians at the sea?

   God planned to demonstrate to the Israelites and to the Egyptians that He is the sovereign, almighty God.

6. What did the Israelites do when they saw Pharaoh's armies coming behind them?

   They blamed Moses for bringing this trouble on them and said he should have left them in Egypt.

7. What should the Israelites have done when they saw Pharaoh's armies coming?

   They should have asked God to help them and trusted Him to rescue them.

8. Was there any way the Israelites could save themselves?

   No. Only God could save them.

9. What did God command the sea to do?

   God commanded the sea to move back so His people could walk on dry land to the other side.

10. Was it difficult for God to open up the sea?

    No! God created the sea so He could control it. Nothing is too hard for Him.

11. What did God do to protect the Israelites from the Egyptians when they were walking through the sea?

    God placed the cloud between the Israelites and the Egyptians. The cloud shone brightly to show the way to the Israelites, but it was a dark, black cloud in front of the Egyptians.

LESSON 32: GOD DELIVERED THE ISRAELITES AT THE RED SEA.

12. What happened to the Egyptian army in the sea?
    The Egyptian army was drowned by God in the sea.

13. Why couldn't the Egyptians escape from God?
    No one can fight against God and win.

14. Can you make a way to deliver yourself from God's punishment for your sins?
    No. Only God can save people from everlasting punishment

LESSON 33: GOD GAVE FOOD AND WATER TO THE ISRAELITES.

Scripture

Exodus 16:1-3, 11-16, 35, Exodus 17:1-6

Lesson Outline

① The Israelites complained. (Exodus 16:1-3)

② God provided food for them. (Exodus 16:11-16, 35)

③ The Israelites complained again. (Exodus 17:1-4)

④ God provided water for them. (Exodus 17:5-6)

⑤ God provided what the Israelites needed because He is merciful.

(?) Review Questions from Lesson 32.

Lesson Outline Developed

① The Israelites complained.

📖 Read Exodus 16:1-3.

- **The Israelites were in the wilderness, and there was no food for them.**

  Without food, the Israelites would starve to death. They couldn't provide food for themselves, and Moses couldn't provide it for them.

Teacher: Take the time to explain what a wilderness is like. Show pictures of a wilderness, and stress that it was impossible for the Israelites or for Moses to provide food in this setting. Help your students to realize that only God could save the Israelites by providing food for them. Through these stories, we want to teach that "Salvation is of the LORD" (Jonah 2:9). Our main objective in teaching the Old Testament is to show man's helplessness and God's salvation so that, when we present the Gospel, our hearers will turn to Christ alone.

Although the Israelites and Moses couldn't provide food, the Lord could. Nothing is impossible to the Lord.

- **The Israelites should have trusted in the Lord to give them food.**

  They already knew that God was all-powerful. The Lord had delivered them from the Egyptians when He had commanded the Red Sea to move back so they could walk on dry land to the other side. But even though they had seen God do miraculous things, they did not trust in Him. They did not ask God to help them; instead, they blamed Moses and Aaron because there was no food.

② God provided food for them.

📖 Read Exodus 16:11-12.

The Israelites didn't deserve for God to provide for them, but in mercy the Lord promised to give them food.

📖 Read Exodus 16:13-16.

- **God delivers those who have no way of escape.**

  God saved the Israelites by providing food for them. The Israelites were helpless to provide food for themselves, but God helps those who are helpless.

  We have already learned that God shows mercy to people.

  - When Adam and Eve sinned against God and were therefore separated from Him, God promised to send a Deliverer.
  - When Adam and Eve tried to make clothing from leaves, God provided them with the skins of animals.
  - When Abel brought God a sacrifice from his flock, God accepted his offering.
  - When God sent a flood and destroyed all people and animals outside the ark, God saved Noah and his family.
  - When Abraham was living among people who worshipped idols, God chose him to be an ancestor of the Deliverer.
  - When Jacob's family would have died from starvation during the severe famine, God provided for them through Joseph.
  - When the Israelites were suffering from slavery in Egypt, God rescued them.
  - When the Israelites were trapped beside the Red Sea, God moved the water so that they could walk across on dry ground.
  - And we learned today that, when the Israelites would have died because they did not have anything to eat, God provided food for them.

LESSON 33: GOD GAVE FOOD AND WATER TO THE ISRAELITES.

None of these people deserved the things that God did for them. He did it all because of His mercy.

The same is true today. No one deserves God's mercy. We all deserve everlasting punishment.

📖 Read Exodus 16:35.

☞ **Teacher:** Show a picture of the Israelites gathering manna.

- **The Lord provided all that the Israelites needed.**

   He faithfully provided food for the Israelites all of the time they were in the wilderness. He never failed them.

   God is faithful. He can be trusted to do everything He has said in His Word.

③ The Israelites complained again.

Although the Israelites were thankful when the Lord provided food for them, they soon forgot about His great power, and they began to complain again.

Teacher: As you prepare to teach, read Psalm 106:7, 13, but do not read these verses to the people when you teach the lesson.

Listen to what happened this time.

📖 Read Exodus 17:1-4.

The Israelites complained because there was no water. Why was there no water? It was because they were in the wilderness. There was nowhere to get water in the wilderness. Without it, they would have died.

Who is the only One who could help them? Yes, the Lord.

Do you think that God could give them water even in the wilderness? Where could God get water in that dry, barren place?

Do you think that God helped them, or did God let them die?

Teacher: Give the people time to answer these questions because their answers will reveal their understanding about God's nature and character.

④ God provided water for them.

God would not let the Israelites die of thirst. Even though they did not deserve to have God give them water, God provided what they needed because He is loving, merciful and gracious.

📖 Read Exodus 17:5-6.

God told Moses to strike the rock with his rod. God promised that He would give water out of the rock when Moses struck it.

- **Moses had to do exactly as God said.**

Every time the Israelites were in an impossible situation, God told them exactly what they must do to escape

- **The same is still true – people can only come to God according to God's way.**

God does not leave it up to us to work out a way to escape from our sin, Satan's power and everlasting punishment. God delivers all who will turn from trusting in themselves and trust only in Him.

📖 Read Exodus 17:6 again.

- **Moses obeyed the Lord and struck the rock.**

Immediately, a great stream of water flowed out. The Israelites numbered two and a half million, and they had many animals, but there was enough water for all of them.

- **God is almighty.**

He has the power to cause water to come from a rock. Only God could give water from a rock in the wilderness.

☞ **Teacher:** Show a picture of Moses striking the rock and water gushing out.

⑤ God provided what the Israelites needed because He is merciful.

- **God gave the Israelites food and water.**

They didn't deserve for God to give them this food and water. They didn't work for it. They didn't pay for it. God gave them food and water because He is loving and merciful. He didn't ask for anything in return.

- **No person deserves God's love and mercy.**

No one can gain acceptance with God by the things that he does. God's forgiveness to sinners is a gift.

- **God faithfully provided everything that the Israelites needed.**

He provided food and water so they could survive in the wilderness. Many years previously, God had promised that He would bless Abraham's descendants. God always does what He says.

LESSON 33: GOD GAVE FOOD AND WATER TO THE ISRAELITES.

? Questions

1. What problem did the Israelites face as they began their journey through the wilderness?
   They didn't have any food.

2. Did the Israelites remember all the great things that God had already done for them?
   No. The Israelites did not remember all the great things God had done for them.

3. Did the Israelites trust God to provide food for them?
   No. The Israelites complained. They blamed Moses and Aaron because there was no food.

4. Did the Israelites deserve to be given food by God?
   No. They did not deserve anything from God.

5. Is there any person who deserves to be rescued from everlasting punishment?
   No. All people deserve to be punished by God.

6. The Israelites complained because there was no water. Why couldn't they get water?
   They couldn't get water because they were in the wilderness.

7. What did God tell Moses to do in order to provide water for the Israelites?
   God told Moses to hit the rock with his rod.

8. Can people come to God in their own way?
   No. People can only come to God according to God's way.

LESSON 34: GOD MADE AN AGREEMENT TO BLESS THE ISRAELITES IF THEY OBEYED HIM.

Scripture

Exodus 19:1-25

Lesson Outline

(1) God directed the Israelites to Mt. Sinai. (Exodus 19:1-2)

(2) The Lord planned to make an agreement with the Israelites. (Exodus 19:3-6)

(3) The Israelites promised to obey the Lord. (Exodus 19:7-8)

(4) The Israelites prepared for the Lord's presence on the mountain. (Exodus 19:9-15)

(5) God spoke to the Israelites from Mt. Sinai. (Exodus 19:16-19)

(6) God told Moses to warn the Israelites again not to touch the mountain. (Exodus 19:20-25)

(?) Review Questions from Lesson 33.

Lesson Outline Developed

Teacher: As you teach this portion of Scripture, you will be emphasizing God's righteousness and holiness along with His terrible wrath and certain judgment against all sin. The boundaries that God set for the people and animals around Mt. Sinai show the holiness of God, the sinfulness of man and the certainty of judgment on all who dare to come into God's presence while their sins remain unforgiven.

(1) God directed the Israelites to Mt. Sinai.

After God delivered the Israelites from Egypt, He directed them where He wanted them to go by a pillar of cloud by day and a pillar of fire by night. During the whole time that they were in the wilderness, God guided them with the cloud. The Israelites did not decide when they would travel or where they would go. God made these decisions for them. He wanted them to accept Him as their ruler, protector and provider.

📖 Read Exodus 19:1-2.

- **God brought the Israelites to Mount Sinai in the Desert of Sinai.**

    This was the same mountain where Moses had seen the burning bush. When God talked to Moses out of the burning bush, He had promised Moses that He would bring him and the Israelites back to this mountain.

    📖 Read Exodus 3:12.

☞ **Teacher:** Point to Egypt and then to Mt. Sinai on the map.

- **God is trustworthy.**

    He had protected Moses from Pharaoh's anger and had delivered the Israelites from slavery in Egypt. He had opened the Red Sea and provided the Israelites with food and water. He did all this so that He could bring them to Mt. Sinai just as He had promised Moses.

    You can trust God to do everything He promises.

② The Lord planned to make an agreement with the Israelites.

God brought Moses and the Israelites to this mountain because it was in this place that God intended to teach them what they must do if they were to have a right relationship with God.

📖 Read Exodus 19:3-6.

- **The Lord promised to bless the Israelites if they obeyed Him perfectly.**

    If they did everything that He told them, then He would accept them and give them prosperity in every part of their lives.

Teacher: This is the second time in Scripture when God's acceptance has been linked with complete obedience. The first was when Adam was in the garden. The second is this promise by God to bless the Israelites if they obeyed the Law. If they kept their part of the covenant by obeying perfectly, then they would be a peculiar treasure to God and they would serve Him as a kingdom of priests. (See Deuteronomy 26:16-19; 28:1-68.)

As you teach this lesson and the next few lessons, emphasize that the Law promises blessing to those who obey, but it also promises a curse to those who depart in heart or action from its holy demands. (See Galatians 3:10.) Through these lessons on the Law, your students should begin to realize that, because we are helpless sinners, it is absolutely impossible to be accepted or blessed by God by obeying the Law.

As you prepare to teach, read the Scripture listed in this teacher's note, but do not read these verses to the people when you teach the lesson.

LESSON 34: GOD MADE AN AGREEMENT TO BLESS THE ISRAELITES IF THEY OBEYED HIM.

③ The Israelites promised to obey the Lord.

📖 Read Exodus 19:7-8.

- **The Israelites promised to obey the Lord in everything.**

  They had forgotten that they had doubted God at the Red Sea when the Egyptian army was behind them. They had forgotten that they had complained when they didn't have food and water.

- **Most of the Israelites were self-confident.**

  They thought that they could obey God well enough so that He would prosper them in everything. They didn't realize that their thoughts and their desires were all tainted by sin. The Israelites needed to realize that they were totally unacceptable to God and that they could never please God by their own efforts. They were like Cain who thought that he could please God by the things which he gave to God.

  Under this new agreement, the Israelites had to obey God perfectly so that He would accept them and bless them. If they disobeyed, they would be punished by God.

- **The Lord knew that, in a very short time, the Israelites would disobey Him.**

  Even though God knew that the Israelites were not capable of keeping their side of the bargain, God made this agreement with them. Why do you think He would do that?

- **God made this agreement with the Israelites because He wanted them to understand that they were sinners.**

  Through the agreement, the Lord was going to teach them that they could not become His friends and earn His blessings and merit His acceptance by their own efforts.

Lesson Developer: Use a story to illustrate what God wanted to teach the Israelites. For example:

> 🕯 Let me tell you a story to show you what God wanted to teach the Israelites. A man was swimming across a river, but he became tired and was caught in the swift-flowing current. He was going to drown.
>
> A group of people were on the bank of the river watching. They were not strong swimmers so they could not help the drowning man. However, one of the men was very strong and was an excellent swimmer.
>
> The people on the bank kept urging the strong swimmer to help the man who was drowning in the river. But he didn't go. Instead, he stood watching while the struggling man became weaker and weaker.
>
> Finally, when the drowning man became so tired that he gave up his struggle, the strong swimmer dived in and rescued him. When the people criticized the strong swimmer for waiting so long before he helped the drowning man, he told them, "The drowning man would never have allowed me to help him as long as he still had strength of his own. I could only help him when he gave up trying to help himself."

God planned to give His commandments to show the Israelites that they were unable to please God and make themselves acceptable to Him. When they gave up trying to make themselves acceptable to Him and trusted in Him, then He would be able to save them from everlasting punishment.

- **God saves those who realize they cannot save themselves.**

    God will only deliver those who agree with Him that they are sinners and that they are under the control of Satan, sin and death. This is what God wants you, also, to understand. You are a helpless sinner, and you cannot deliver yourself from sin, Satan or death. Only God can save you.

④ The Israelites prepared for the Lord's presence on the mountain.

📖 Read Exodus 19:9-11.

- **God told the Israelites to prepare themselves to see His presence displayed on the mountain.**

    The Lord planned to display His great glory, power and holiness so that the Israelites would realize that He is a holy God who hates sin and will not accept those who disobey Him.

    📖 Read Exodus 19:12-13.

- **God told them to set a boundary around the mountain.**

    This boundary was to keep them from coming near to or touching the mountain when God's presence was displayed there. If an Israelite or animal were even to touch the mountain when God was on it, they were to be killed.

- **God will not accept anyone or anything that is not perfect.**

    By the boundary they were to set on the mountain, God was reminding them that God is absolutely holy; therefore, sinners cannot come near to Him. Think about what happened when Adam and Eve sinned. They were immediately separated from God, and God put them out of the garden. God hates disobedience to His commands, and He will not accept people whose sins have not been fully paid for.

    📖 Read Exodus 19:14-15.

    Moses had the people prepare themselves, just as God had instructed. They had to do everything God's way; otherwise, they would have died.

⑤ God spoke to the Israelites from Mt. Sinai.

📖 Read Exodus 19:16-19.

LESSON 34: GOD MADE AN AGREEMENT TO BLESS THE ISRAELITES IF THEY OBEYED HIM.

- **The people were afraid when God spoke to them.**

    There was thunder and lightning. The mountain was covered with billowing smoke, and it shook. It was a terrifying sight. It was not surprising that the Israelites were frightened.

Teacher: As you prepare to teach, read Hebrews 12:18-21, 29, but do not read these verses to the people when you teach the lesson.

☞ **Teacher:** Show a picture of Mount Sinai, with the boundary around it and the fire and smoke on it.

- **God hates sin, and He will always punish sinners.**

    Through the thunder and lightning, the billowing cloud of smoke, and the earthquake, God was showing the Israelites that He is almighty and that He is a God of wrath who hates and punishes all sin.

    We have already learned that God hates sin. Can you think of other times when God demonstrated His mighty power and His hatred of sin?

    - He destroyed the whole world by a flood during Noah's time.
    - He rained fire and brimstone upon the wicked cities of Sodom and Gomorrah.
    - He sent many terrible plagues on the Egyptians and drowned their army in the sea.

⑥ God told Moses to warn the Israelites again not to touch the mountain.

📖 Read Exodus 19:20-25.

God told Moses to go down to the people and warn them again in case they were foolish enough to think that they could come up onto the mountain to see God. Because the Israelites were sinners and God was holy, they would die if they came up onto the mountain.

- **God chose Moses to be His messenger.**

    God allowed Moses to go up onto the mountain because He wanted to give His message to Moses. Moses did not deserve to go up onto the mountain to talk to God. Moses was also a sinner, just as the other Israelites, but God accepted him because he trusted in God's mercy and came to Him in the way God had said.

    If the Israelites refused to listen to Moses, they would be refusing to listen to God, and they would be punished.

- **The Bible is God's message to all people in the world.**

    God wants people today to hear His message. The Bible is God's message to you. God wants you to know that all who refuse to listen to and obey God's message in the Bible will be punished by God forever.

    Teacher: As you prepare to teach, read Hebrews 2:1-3, but do not read these verses to the people when you teach the lesson.

(?) Questions

1. What had God promised when Moses saw the burning bush at Mount Sinai?

    God had promised Moses that He would bring Moses back to this mountain, accompanied by the Israelites.

2. Did God do what He promised to Moses?

    Yes. God did what He promised to Moses. God always does what He says.

3. What was the agreement that God planned to make with the Israelites?

    The agreement was that God promised to bless the Israelites if they obeyed Him perfectly.

4. When the Israelites promised to obey God completely, what was their attitude?

    The Israelites were self-confident. They thought that they could obey God well enough for Him to bless them.

5. Could the Israelites keep their part of the agreement?

    No. Because the Israelites were sinners, it was impossible for them to obey God completely.

6. Why did God make this agreement with the Israelites, knowing that they would disobey Him?

    God made this agreement with the Israelites because He wanted to prove to them that they were sinners and could not earn His acceptance and gifts by their own efforts.

7. What did the boundary around the mountain show the Israelites?

    The boundary showed them that because God is holy, sinners cannot come near to Him.

8. Why were the people so frightened when God spoke to them from the mountain?

    The people were frightened because there was thunder and lightning, a billowing cloud of smoke and a violent earthquake.

LESSON 34: GOD MADE AN AGREEMENT TO BLESS THE ISRAELITES IF THEY OBEYED HIM.

9. What was God showing to the Israelites through the thunder and lightening, the smoke and the earthquake?

   God was showing that He is almighty and that He is a God of wrath who hates and punishes sin.

10. Who was God's messenger to the Israelites?

    Moses was God's messenger.

11. How do we hear God's message today?

    We hear God's message through the Bible.

LESSON 35: GOD GAVE THE TEN COMMANDMENTS. (PART 1)

Scripture

Exodus 20:1-11

Lesson Outline

① God spoke His commandments. (Exodus 20:1-2)

② God gave the first commandment. (Exodus 20:3)

③ God gave the second commandment. (Exodus 20:4-6)

④ God gave the third commandment. (Exodus 20:7)

⑤ God gave the fourth commandment. (Exodus 20:8-11)

⑥ God is supreme and sovereign.

(?) Review Questions from Lesson 34.

Lesson Outline Developed

① God spoke His commandments.

- **God spoke to the Israelites from the mountain.**

    After Moses had returned to the bottom of the mountain, God spoke to the Israelites from the mountain.

    The mountain was still shaking. It was still covered with smoke, and there was still thunder and lightning and the loud sound of a trumpet. God was showing the Israelites that He is almighty and that He is a God of wrath who hates and punishes all sin. The people did not come close to the mountain or climb it because they were afraid.

    📖 Read Exodus 20:1-2.

    When God spoke to the Israelites from the mountain, He reminded them that He was the God who delivered them from slavery in Egypt. Then He told them His commandments.

- **God gave His commandments to teach the Israelites that they were sinners.**

    When the Lord gave His commandments to the Israelites, He knew that they would not be able to obey them perfectly all of the time. God gave His commandments to the Israelites because God wanted them to understand that they were sinners. Through His commandments, God intended to teach the Israelites that they could not obey God perfectly and that, therefore, they could never be accepted by God through their own efforts. God wanted them to learn that they needed to trust in Him because He was the only one who could save them from everlasting punishment.

- **God wants all people to realize that they are sinners.**

    God gave His commandments to the Israelites to teach them that they were sinful, but God's commandments also teach **all people** that they are sinful and that, therefore, no one can become acceptable to God by the things which he does. God wants **all people** to learn to trust only in His mercy to be saved from everlasting punishment.

Teacher: Be careful how you state the truths in this section. God's commands were not given to the Gentiles, although God's standard for righteousness is the same for Gentiles as it was for the Israelites. As you teach the lessons about the Ten Commandments that God gave to Israel, be sure to clearly state that the commands were given to the Israelites but that God demands the same standard of perfection from all people, Jew or Gentile. When God's commandments are applied to the Gentiles, they teach them that they too have sinned and cannot please God, but the Ten Commandments were given to Israel, not to the Gentiles.

Although you as the teacher are aware of the difference between Jew and Gentile and of God's different way of dealing with Jews and Gentiles, do not teach these things to your students. Only teach what is actually in the text. What is written in these teacher's notes is only meant for you as the teacher.

Lesson Developer: Give an illustration to show that when the Ten Commandments are applied to the Gentiles, they too are proven to be sinners, just like the Jews. For example:

> The daughter of a rich man had two suitors. When she chose one over the other, the rejected suitor became very angry. On the day before the wedding, large pots of food were prepared for the marriage feast. During that night, the rejected suitor crept in and added bitter herbs to all the pots of food. On the next day, all the wedding guests sat down to eat. When they took the first mouthful, they all spat the food out. It was bitter. The father of the bride ordered that all the food be thrown out. He didn't need to taste the remainder of the food to know that it had all been spoiled. The father in that story knew that all the food was bitter, even though he didn't test it all.

LESSON 35: GOD GAVE THE TEN COMMANDMENTS. (PART 1)

- **God knows that all people are sinners.**

    God gave the Ten Commandments to the Israelites to prove to them that they were helpless sinners, but He didn't test all the other people of the world by giving them the Ten Commandments. He gave the Ten Commandments only to the Israelites. But God knew that if the same Ten Commandments were given to the other people of the world, they would also be proven to be just as sinful and unable to please Him as the Israelites were

- **The commandments of God are like a mirror.**

    Just as we cannot see our dirty face until we look into a mirror, so we cannot see our sinful hearts until God's commandments show them to us. As we learn what God's commandments say a person must do if he is to be completely acceptable to God, we will see that we have all failed to please God. Not one of us has reached the standard of goodness that God requires.

Teacher: As you prepare to teach, read James 1:22-25; 2:10-11, but do not read these verses to the people when you teach the lesson.

- **God will only accept those who have never sinned.**

    Do you think that God would accept people who tried to do their best and obeyed as many of God's commandments as they could? No! The only way anyone could make himself acceptable to God would be to obey God's commandments perfectly all of the time. But no one can. It is not sufficient to obey just some of the commandments. Even if a person were able to obey God's commandments most of the time, but failed to obey just one time, that person would still have broken God's laws and would be guilty of sin.

- **God punishes sinners even if they only disobey one of His commandments one time.**

    How many times did Adam and Eve disobey God before they were separated from God and put out of the garden? Adam and Eve disobeyed only once, and they received the punishment of death. The punishment for disobedience to even one of God's commandments is death and everlasting separation from God in the place of terrible punishment which God prepared for Satan and his demons.

Lesson Developer: Use an illustration about a chain with a broken link to show what it means to break only one of God's commandments. For example:

Building on Firm Foundations
- Volume 2: Evangelism:
Genesis to The Ascension

> 🕯️ *Is a chain still strong if one of its links is broken? Would you trust a chain with a broken link to hold your water buffalo?*
>
> *Would you go near a wild bull if it were tied with a chain which had one broken link? No, of course not! Could I convince you to go near that wild bull if I said, "What are you afraid of? The chain has nine strong links, do not be afraid. Only one link in the chain is broken"? I'm sure you wouldn't risk your life by going near a wild bull if you knew that one of the ten links was broken. A chain is only strong if all of the links are unbroken.*
>
> *If one link in the chain is broken, the whole chain is broken.*

If we break only one of God's commandments, we are guilty of breaking all of them. God says that death is the punishment for disobeying even one of His commandments.

- **No one can keep God's commandments perfectly.**

God wants everyone to realize that they can never be good enough to please Him and be accepted by Him. Because we were all born sinners and separated from God, it is impossible for us to keep God's commandments perfectly.

This is true for every person, including us teachers. We have broken God's commandments, and we deserve to go to everlasting punishment just as all people do. All of us were born sinners. All of us were born separated from God without the ability to know, love and obey God. We cannot do anything to make ourselves pleasing or acceptable to God.

- **We are going to read each of God's Ten Commandments and explain each one to you.**

As we read each commandment, think about your own life and whether you have obeyed that commandment perfectly. God wants you to admit that you are a sinner and that you are unable to obey His commandments. He wants you to realize that you cannot save yourselves from everlasting separation from God in the Lake of Fire.

Remember, you cannot please God by what you do. You cannot remove your own sins from before God's eyes. Your sin must be paid for by death.

Teacher: Do not be in a hurry while teaching this lesson because "by the law is the knowledge of sin" (Romans 3:20). You need to clearly teach what God requires so that the people will realize that they are sinners and that they cannot please God by what they do.

As you teach each commandment, you will be emphasizing that God is supreme and sovereign. He had the right to set these standards, and He has the right to demand complete obedience. No one should challenge God's commandments. In addition, you will be making it clear that it is not possible for anyone to be accepted by God because of his obedience to the commandments of God, for no one is able to obey any one of God's commandments perfectly.

LESSON 35: GOD GAVE THE TEN COMMANDMENTS. (PART 1)

② God gave the first commandment.

📖 Read Exodus 20:3.

- **God said that He and only He should be the God of the Israelites.**

    This means that there is only one true and living God and that because He created all people, only He should be worshipped. God will not allow anyone or anything to share His place as God. God is supreme and sovereign. He is the only true God.

    If people were able to worship God the way He commanded, they would not depend on anyone except Him for everything they need in this life and for eternity. They would give God the highest place in their thoughts and give Him praise and thank for everything.

- **If we were able to obey this commandment, we would allow God to be the ruler of every part of our lives.**

    Nothing and no one would take God's place in our lives. When a person puts anyone else in God's place, it is rebellion and sin. When we say with our lips that God is our ruler, yet we do not give Him the first place in our hearts all of the time, we have broken this commandment.

    Adam deliberately turned away from giving God first place in his life. Adam went his own way instead of God's way. Because of Adam's sin, all of his descendants were born sinners and have also gone their own way. No one has allowed God to rule every part of his life.

- **All people have disobeyed this first commandment.**

    My ancestors disobeyed it, and so did yours. Your ancestors put the spirits in God's place, and by doing that, they followed Satan.

    None of us has obeyed this commandment of God. The punishment for disobeying this commandment is separation from God.

Teacher: Expand this point as necessary to make sure your students clearly understand these truths. To agree that God is truly God means to listen to, obey, exalt, and worship Him and Him alone in every situation. In addition, it means that we will not attribute His power to anyone else or give His glory to anyone else.

Do not teach this point, or any of the commandments, as things they must try to do. Instead, help them understand that they are not capable of doing what God commanded.

③ God gave the second commandment.

📖 Read Exodus 20:4-6.

- **God said that the Israelites should not make any image as an object of worship.**

They must not make an image of something or worship trees, rocks, or anything else which God has made as if they represented Him. The Israelites were told that they must not put anything, even things which God created, in the place of God, the creator.

- **No one knows what God looks like.**

The Bible tells us that God is Spirit and does not have a body like man or anything which has been created. The only way we can know what God is like is through the Bible. All ideas about God that are different to what the Bible says are the lies of Satan.

- **All over the world, Satan has led people away from the true knowledge of God.**

Satan has led people to follow their own ideas and other people's ideas concerning what they think God might be like. For example, some people think God looks like a man or a bird or an animal or a fish or a snake, and they have made idols to represent what they think God is like. They worship those idols, instead of worshiping the true and living God.

All people who worship images claiming that they represent God have already broken this commandment and are condemned. They will be punished by separation from God forever in the Lake of Fire.

Teacher: As you prepare to teach, read Romans 1:18-23, but do not read these verses to the people when you teach the lesson.

④ God gave the third commandment.

Read Exodus 20:7.

- **God said that that the Israelites must never speak or use God's name in a careless way.**

God commanded the Israelites to respect Him and to acknowledge that He was their creator and rightful ruler.

Everyone should fear God and realize that He has the power to take our lives and to send us into everlasting punishment.

Respect is very important. You know that. A child should show respect for his parents. A wife and husband should show respect for one another. A young person should show respect for his elders. People should show respect for their leaders. Saying something evil about someone or insulting someone shows a lack of respect.

- **To disrespect any person is bad, but it is much more evil to show disrespect for the true and living God.**

When we use the name of God in an incorrect way, we are showing disrespect to God.

Each person who has not given God the respect He deserves is condemned.

⑤ God gave the fourth commandment.

📖 Read Exodus 20:8-11.

- **God told the Israelites to keep the seventh day as a special day of rest.**

    The seventh day of each week was to be the time when the Israelites rested in honor of God as the creator of the heavens and the earth.

    In the beginning, God created all things in six days. Do you remember what God did on the seventh day, the day after He finished creating everything? God rested. Do you remember why God rested? God rested because He had finished creating everything that He had planned to create.

    God told the Israelites to rest every seventh day so they would remember that God alone created the earth and everything in it. All people need to recognize that God is the creator and that He is the one they should worship.

    Because God created the world, He is the only rightful owner of this world. Satan and His demons have taken control over the people in this world, but the world still belongs to God.

    Not only did God create the world in the beginning, but He also continues to give life to all living things. For example, He gives the rain and the sunshine on the earth so everything will grow.

- **This commandment reminds us that God alone is the creator, owner and provider of all things.**

    If a person depends on anyone other than God as the creator and giver of all things, he is disobeying God's commandment and will be punished.

Teacher: If you are working in an area where there is an emphasis on observing the Sabbath, you may need to explain that God is not commanding your hearers to rest on the seventh day, just as He is not commanding them to offer sacrifices of sheep or other animals. Nevertheless, God does expect them to recognize that He alone is creator of all things and that there is no other God.

If some of your students believe that they must observe the Sabbath, try to avoid making this a point of controversy or becoming the main subject. But, be sure they understand that their Sabbath observance will not make them acceptable to God. Because they have not obeyed perfectly all of the other nine commandments every moment of their lives, resting on the seventh day will not make them acceptable to God. (See James 2:9-11.)

Building on Firm Foundations
- Volume 2: Evangelism:
Genesis to The Ascension

(6) God is supreme and sovereign.

- **The commandments that we studied in this lesson remind us that God is supreme and sovereign.**

    He alone is the true God, the creator and owner of all. Because He is God and our creator, He had the right to set these standards and He has the right to demand our complete obedience.

- **Remember that these commandments teach us that we are sinners.**

    Because we are sinners, only God can deliver us from sin, Satan and death.

    In our next lesson, we will study the rest of God's Ten Commandments.

(?) Questions

1. When God gave His Ten Commandments to the Israelites, did He think that they would be able to obey them?

    No. God knew that no one would be able to obey His commandments perfectly.

2. Why is it impossible for any person to obey God's commandments perfectly?

    It is impossible for any person to obey God's commandments perfectly because all people are born sinners.

3. What is the main lesson that the Ten Commandments teach all people?

    God's Ten Commandments teach all people that they are sinful and cannot become acceptable to God by the things they do.

4. If a person were able to obey God's commandments most of the time, but failed to obey just one time, would that person be punished?

    Yes. If a person failed to obey God just one time, he would be punished.

5. What is the punishment for disobeying even one of God's commandments?

    The punishment for disobedience of even one of God's commandments is death and everlasting separation from God in the place of terrible punishment which God prepared for Satan and his demons.

6. God said, "You shall have no other gods before me." According to this commandment, who should people worship?

    People should worship only God.

LESSON 35: GOD GAVE THE TEN COMMANDMENTS. (PART 1)

7. Will God share His position as ruler with anyone else?

    No. God will not allow anyone or anything to share His place as God.

8. If people do not give God first place in their lives, have they broken this commandment?

    Yes. God said that people should give God first place in their lives.

9. Is it right for people to worship an image?

    No. Worshiping any image is a sin against God.

10. Is it right to worship trees, rocks, or anything else which God has made?

    No. No one should put the things which God created in the place of God.

11. God said that people should not misuse God's name. When people misuse the name of God, what are they showing?

    When people misuse the name of God, they are showing disrespect to God.

12. Why should all people have respect to God?

    People should have respect to God because He is their creator and rightful ruler.

13. If a person misuses God's name or shows disrespect to God, has he broken God's commandment?

    Yes. Each person who misuses God's name or shows disrespect to God has broken God's commandment and is condemned.

14. God told the Israelites to keep the seventh day as a special day of rest. By giving them this commandment, what did God want the Israelites to remember about Him?

    God wanted them to remember that He alone is the creator, owner and provider of all things.

15. If a person depends on anyone other than God as the creator and giver of all things, has he broken God's commandment?

    Yes. A person who depends on someone other than God the creator has disobeyed God's commandment.

16. Does God have the right to demand our complete obedience?

    Yes. God had the right to demand our complete obedience because He is God and our creator.

LESSON 36: GOD GAVE THE TEN COMMANDMENTS. (PART 2)

Scripture

Exodus 20:12-17

Lesson Outline

① God gave His commandments.

② God gave the fifth commandment. (Exodus 20:12)

③ God gave the sixth commandment. (Exodus 20:13)

④ God gave the seventh commandment. (Exodus 20:14)

⑤ God gave the eighth commandment. (Exodus 20:15)

⑥ God gave the ninth commandment. (Exodus 20:16)

⑦ God gave the tenth commandment. (Exodus 20:17)

⑧ God's commandments teach us all that we are sinners.

(?) Review Questions from Lesson 35.

Lesson Outline Developed

Teacher: Do not be in a hurry while teaching this lesson. Remember, *"…by the law is the knowledge of sin"* (Romans 3:20). You need to clearly teach what God requires so that the people will realize that they are sinners and that they cannot please God by what they do.

Be sure that you teach these commandments as things your hearers have not done and not as laws that they should try to keep. They need to realize they are already condemned because by sinning they have broken all the commandments of God.

As you teach each commandment, you will be emphasizing that God is supreme and sovereign. He had the right to set these standards and He has the right to demand complete obedience. No one should challenge God's commandments. In addition, you will be making it clear that, if we were to try to obey God's commandments, then we would have to obey them perfectly in our hearts and minds and not just outwardly.

1 God gave His commandments.

In our last lesson we learned that God gave His commandments to the Israelites. We also learned that those commandments teach all people that they are sinners and deserve God's punishment.

We studied the first four commandments that God gave. Those commandments teach us that we have failed in our relationship with God. We will look at the next six commandments today. These commandments teach us that we have failed in our relationship with other people.

2 God gave the fifth commandment.

Read Exodus 20:12.

- **God said that children should respect and obey their parents.**

Lesson Developer: Give culturally appropriate examples to show how the people have not honored their parents. For example:

> *Here are some examples of how children do not honor their parents: They are disrespectful to their parents. They mock their parents. They refuse to do what their parents have told them to do. They refuse to submit when their parents correct them. They go their own way instead of listening to their parent's advice. They ignore what their parents tell them. They criticize their parents. They do not help their parents or comfort them when they are old.*

- **No person has honored his parents completely as God requires.**

If we have disobeyed or dishonored our parents in any way, we have disobeyed God's commandment. Remember, if we have disobeyed God's commandment just one time, then the punishment is everlasting separation from God.

Do you think it is possible to obey this commandment to honor our parents? No! We have all broken this commandment. Even if we obeyed each of the other commandments, if we disobey just this one, we are condemned by God.

LESSON 36: GOD GAVE THE TEN
COMMANDMENTS. (PART 2)

③ God gave the sixth commandment.

📖 Read Exodus 20:13.

- **God said that people should not murder another person.**

    God is the creator of all people. Because God gives life to every person, no one has the right to take another person's life. To commit a murder is sin against God.

Teacher: God does give governments the authority to take the life of a murderer (Genesis 9:6; Romans 13:1-4). As you prepare to teach, read these verses, but do not read them to the people when you teach the lesson.

- **To God, a person's attitude and motives are as important as his actions.**

    God makes it very clear in His Word that He judges us, not just by what we do, but also by what we really want to do. God knows the motives in a person's heart.

    God says that if a person hates someone, he has already committed murder in his heart. If a person wants to kill someone, he has already committed murder. If a person curses someone else, hoping they will die, he has already committed murder.

Teacher: As you prepare to teach, read Matthew 5:21-26, but do not read these verses to the people when you teach the lesson.

A person might think, "I have never murdered anyone." But if a person has hated someone or cursed someone hoping they will die, he has broken God's commandment. All who have broken this commandment are condemned by God.

④ God gave the seventh commandment.

📖 Read Exodus 20:14.

- **God said that people should not have any sexual relationship with anyone except one's own wife or husband.**

    After God created Adam, He created Eve and gave her to Adam to be his wife. God said that, because they were married, He considered that they were no longer two people but were like one person. Husband and wife belong to one another, and they must only have sexual relations with each other.

- **The Bible tells us that adultery and all types of sex sins can be committed in the mind.**

    God says that, if we look at someone else other than our own husband or wife and want to have any type of sex relationship with that person, then we have already broken this commandment.

Building on Firm Foundations
- Volume 2: Evangelism:
Genesis to The Ascension

> **Teacher:** As you prepare to teach, read Matthew 5:27-28, but do not read these verses to the people when you teach the lesson.

We may be able to hide adultery or other types of sexual sins from people, but we cannot hide this sin from God. God is present everywhere and sees us all the time, so He knows if we have committed adultery. Even if we have not broken this commandment by a physical act, God knows our thoughts, so He knows if we have broken this commandment in our minds.

The punishment for all sexual sin is everlasting separation from God.

(5) God gave the eighth commandment.

📖 Read Exodus 20:15.

- **God said that people should never take anything which belongs to someone else.**

    God is the One who gives each person the right to own and to keep his own property. If a person takes something which belongs to someone else, then he has sinned against God.

    Sometimes a thief steals something, but no person ever knows about it. Do you think that a thief could hide what he has done from God? No! God knows everything.

    Sometimes a thief gets caught and the authorities may make him give back the thing he stole or pay compensation for what he stole. Do you think that God would agree that the full payment for sin has been made if a thief pays back the person? No! Even if a person pays the wronged party back for stealing, he still owes the payment for sin to God. When a person steals, he is breaking God's commandment, and the punishment for breaking God's commandments is everlasting separation from God.

- **God judges what a person wants to do in his heart.**

    Sometimes a person may think about stealing or make plans to steal something but not do it because he is afraid of being caught. Do you think that person is still guilty of stealing before God? Yes, he is. God will punish all sinners for the evil things which they planned to do even though they were not able to do them.

Lesson Developer: Use a story to illustrate that the intent to steal is stealing. For example:

> *A man saw a very good fighting cock at another man's house. He knew that the owner would not sell it to him, and even if he would, he didn't have sufficient money to buy it. So he planned to steal it. He watched carefully to see where the owner kept the cock at night, and he planned to return late at night when the owner was sleeping soundly.*

LESSON 36: GOD GAVE THE TEN COMMANDMENTS. (PART 2)

Later that night, he quietly crept from his house and started toward the house of the cock's owner. He knew that it was kept in a cage close by. He didn't use a light lest someone see him and be able to identify him. Reaching the house, he crept through the darkness on his hands and knees toward the cage. He reached out his hand and was just going to open the door of the cage when the cock took fright and began to squawk. Jumping up, the man ran as hard as he could back through the jungle to his own house.

The owner of the cock never did know who almost stole his prize bird that night, but God saw it all. The man who planned to steal had disobeyed God's commandment, "You shall not steal." He had sinned and the punishment for his sin is everlasting separation from God.

God demands death as the payment for stealing.

⑥ God gave the ninth commandment.

📖 Read Exodus 20:16.

- **God said that the Israelites should always tell the truth about everyone and everything.**

    Satan is a liar. Satan lied to Adam and Eve in the garden, and he has continued to tell lies throughout history and even today. He told lies to your ancestors and even tells lies to you, because he wants to trick and deceive people so that they will not believe God. All who lie are following the ways of Satan.

    Lesson Developer: Give culturally appropriate examples to show reasons why and ways that people lie. For example:

    > 💡 *Some people tell lies about other people because they are jealous or angry or because they hate the other person. They tell lies to harm the other person.*
    >
    > *Some people tell lies to cover up the wrong things they have done.*
    >
    > *Some people tell lies by starting rumors or by gossiping.*

    God said that people must not lie; therefore, all lying is sin against God.

- **God knows every lie.**

    We may be able to hide the fact that we are lying from other people, but we can't hide our lies from God. God always speaks the truth, and He knows the truth about everyone and everything.

    Even if we have lied only one time, we have broken God's commandment and will be punished. God demands death as the punishment for lying.

(7) God gave the tenth commandment.

📖 Read Exodus 20:17.

- **God said that the Israelites should not want what other people have.**

    This was Satan's sin. He was envious of God's position, and he wanted to be like God.

    Lesson Developer: Give culturally appropriate examples to show ways in which people express their covetousness. For example:

    > 💡 Some people are greedy and want another person's possessions. Such people are never satisfied with what they have. They might think that they deserve to have those same possessions, and they might be angry because they don't have what someone else has.
    >
    > Some people are jealous of another person's position. They might wish that they were a leader or a teacher or someone else who is respected.

- **God looks on the heart, and He knows what we truly desire in our hearts.**

    We may be able to hide our covetousness from other people, but we can't hide it, from God.

    If we have broken this commandment even once, we have broken God's law, and God will punish us.

(8) God's commandments teach us all that we are sinners.

- **God's standard is the same for all people, no matter where they are.**

    God gave the Ten Commandments to the Israelites to prove to them that they were sinners, and they also prove that we are sinners. God has not changed His mind about the standards that He gave.

- **Because God is holy and righteous, He will not tolerate disobedience to His commandments.**

    Disobedience is sin, and God demands death as the payment for sin. Even if we make payment for our sin and put things right with the person we have wronged, we still have a sin debt before God. The payment for sin is death, everlasting separation from God in the place of punishment which He prepared for Satan and his demons.

- **Whoever disobeys one of God's commandments, even one time, is guilty of sinning against God.**

    The only way we could please God is if we were able to perfectly obey all of God's commandments from the time we were born to the time we die.

LESSON 36: GOD GAVE THE TEN COMMANDMENTS. (PART 2)

A person cannot choose which of God's commands he will obey and which ones he will disobey. No person has ever been able to keep God's commandments perfectly. I haven't. Have you?

Even though God knew that no one would be able to keep His commandments perfectly, He still gave them. Why did He do this? God gave the Ten Commandments to the Israelites to teach them that they were sinners and that they were unable to please God by their own efforts. These same commandments teach us also that we are sinners who cannot please God by what we do and that we need God's mercy to be saved from everlasting punishment.

? Questions

1. Will God punish children who do not respect and obey their parents?
   Yes. God will punish all who do not respect and obey their parents.

2. Why should people not commit murder?
   People should not murder because God gives life to all people.

3. What does God say that a person has done if he hates someone else?
   God says that if a person hates someone, he has committed murder in his heart.

4. What is God's attitude toward adultery?
   God condemns all sexual relationships except between a man and his wife.

5. Can we hide adultery or other types of sexual sins from God?
   No! We cannot hide sexual sin from God because He is present everywhere and sees us all of the time.

6. Who gives each person the right to own his own property?
   God gives each person the right to own his own property.

7. If a person takes something which belongs to someone else, against whom has he sinned?
   He has sinned against God.

8. Is a person guilty of stealing if he plans to steal but does not do it because he is afraid of being caught?
   Yes! A person is guilty if he only makes the plan to steal because God judges a person by the things he wants to do in his heart.

9. What is God's command about telling lies?

   God said that people should not tell lies, but always tell the truth.

10. Who knows the truth about everything?

    God knows the truth about everything.

11. Does God care if we are envious of other people and want what they have?

    Yes. God commands us that we should not covet.

12. Does God judge a person by just the actions he does?

    No! God makes it very clear in His Word that He judges us, not just by what we do, but also by what we really want to do.

13. Can a person hide his actions or thoughts from God?

    No! God knows everything.

14. If a person makes things right with the person he has wronged, will God also agree that the full payment for sin has been made?

    No. Even if a person makes things right with the person he has wronged, he still owes the payment for sin to God.

15. What is the payment for all sin?

    The payment for sin is death, everlasting separation from God in the place of punishment which He prepared for Satan and his demons.

16. Will a person be accepted by God if he obeys only some of God's commandments?

    No. God will only accept those who perfectly obey all of His commands.

17. Could the Israelites decide which of God's commandments they would obey?

    No. God required them to obey all His commandments all of the time.

18. Do you think that God would accept people who tried to do their best and obeyed as many of God's commandments as they could?

    No! The only way we could make ourselves acceptable to God would be to obey His commandments perfectly all of the time.

LESSON 37: GOD TOLD THE ISRAELITES TO BUILD THE TABERNACLE.

Scripture

Exodus 24:12-18, Exodus 25:1-11, 17-22, Exodus 26:31-33, Exodus 27:1-2, 9, Exodus 28:1, Leviticus 1:1-5, Leviticus 16:2-3, 15

Lesson Outline

1. The Lord planned to give Moses two flat stones on which God had written the Ten Commandments. (Exodus 24:12-18)
2. God commanded Moses to have the Israelites build the Tabernacle. (Exodus 25:1-8)
3. The Tabernacle had to be built exactly as God commanded Moses. (Exodus 25:9)
4. The Tabernacle was to be transportable.
5. The Tabernacle was to have two rooms.
6. The ark and the mercy seat were to be made and put in the Most Holy Place. (Exodus 25:10-11, 17-22)
7. A curtain was to hang between the Holy Place and the Most Holy Place. (Exodus 26:31-33)
8. The Tabernacle was to have a courtyard. (Exodus 27:9)
9. The brazen altar was to be set up inside the courtyard. (Exodus 27:1-2; Leviticus 1:1-5)
10. God chose Aaron and his sons to serve Him as priests. (Exodus 28:1; Leviticus 16:2-3, 15)

(?) Review Questions from Lesson 36.

Building on Firm Foundations
- Volume 2: Evangelism:
Genesis to The Ascension

Lesson Outline Developed

Teacher: Teach this lesson with visual aids if possible. A simple model of the Tabernacle would be best, but you could also use a picture and diagram of the layout of the Tabernacle. Because this lesson does not teach about every part of the Tabernacle, include in your model or picture only the parts listed below:

- The outer fence
- The brazen altar
- The Holy Place
- The Most Holy Place
- The curtain
- The ark
- The mercy seat

Point to each part of the Tabernacle as you teach about it.

1) The Lord planned to give Moses two flat stones on which God had written the Ten Commandments.

📖 Read Exodus 24:12.

- **It was important that the Israelites didn't forget God's laws.**

    When God first gave His commandments to the Israelites from Mt. Sinai, they heard Him speaking to them. God did not want the Israelites to forget His laws, so He planned to write His Ten Commandments on two flat stones.

    God told Moses to come up onto the mountain again. God was going to give Moses the two flat stones on which He had written His Ten Commandments so that Moses could teach God's laws to the Israelites.

    📖 Read Exodus 24:13-18.

- **Moses obeyed the Lord and went up onto the mountain.**

    A young man named Joshua went with Moses up onto the mountain. Joshua was Moses' assistant.

    👉 **Teacher:** Point to the name, "Joshua," on the chronological chart.

    They stayed on the mountain for forty days and forty nights.

LESSON 37: GOD TOLD THE ISRAELITES TO BUILD THE TABERNACLE.

While Moses was on the mountain, the Lord gave him the Ten Commandments, written on two flat stones. The Lord also explained to Moses other rules and customs that He commanded the Israelites to follow. God was their king, so He told them what He wanted them to do.

② God commanded Moses to have the Israelites build the Tabernacle.

- **The Israelites were to make God a special building.**

  While Moses was on the mountain, the Lord told Moses to have the Israelites build a special place where God would live with the Israelites. They would bring their sacrifices and worship Him in this special building.

  It is important for us to understand God's purpose for telling them to make this building. So I will explain.

- **The Lord promised to bless the Israelites if they obeyed Him perfectly.**

  We have already learned that the Lord had given His Ten Commandments to the Israelites. If they did everything that He told them, then He would be with them, protect them and give them prosperity in every part of their lives. But if they disobeyed His laws, God would not prosper them as a nation and, for those who disobeyed, the punishment would be death.

- **The Lord knew that the Israelites would disobey Him because they were sinners.**

  The Israelites had promised to obey God in everything. However, because of their sinfulness, they would certainly disobey. Unless God provided the way for them to come to Him, they could not escape the punishment for their disobedience. The punishment for sin is death and eternal separation from God in the Lake of Fire.

- **God provided the way so their sins could be forgiven.**

  Because the Lord loved the Israelites, He did not want to destroy them. Therefore, He told them to build a special place where He would live among them and where they could come to Him to receive His forgiveness and mercy and be saved from the punishment which they deserved for breaking His laws.

  📖 Read Exodus 25:1-8.

- **God did not need a house to live in.**

  We need houses to live in. Houses help us stay dry when it rains and give us a place to sleep. But God does not need the things that people need because God does not have a body like people do. God is Spirit. God does not need a place where He could stay dry when it rains. God does not need a place to sleep because He never gets tired. God did not tell them to build this house for Him because He needed a house to live in.

Because God is Spirit, He would continue to be everywhere even after He came to live in the house which He told Moses to have the Israelites build.

3) The Tabernacle had to be built exactly as God commanded Moses.

📖 Read Exodus 25:9.

- **Everything had to be done God's way.**

    The Israelites had to build the Tabernacle and everything in it exactly as the Lord instructed Moses when he was up on the mountain.

    We have already learned that God requires people to come to Him according to His way.

    ○ Do you remember the man who refused to follow God's way and bring the correct sacrifice to Him? Cain refused to bring the sacrifice that God told him to bring, and so God would not accept him.

    ○ Do you remember that God gave Noah specific instructions about how to build the big boat? Did Noah believe God and obey Him? Yes, he did. Noah believed God so he built the big boat exactly the way God had told him, and God saved him from the flood.

    We cannot tell God how we will come to Him. We must come to God in the way He teaches us in the Bible.

4) The Tabernacle was to be transportable.

Teacher: You may lead a short discussion on the type of materials that the people use to build their houses. This can help keep their attention, and it will also help them to understand as you explain the materials used in the Tabernacle.

Because the Israelites would be walking many miles to go back to the land from which their ancestors had come, they could not carry a building made of heavy materials. The Lord told them to build most of the Tabernacle with materials made from animal skins and materials made from the hair of goats. The Israelites lived in tents while they were traveling, and their tents were also made of these materials.

During their stops on the journey, the Tabernacle was to be set up in the center of the

☞ **Teacher:** Show a model or a picture of the two rooms in the Tabernacle. If possible, the picture or model should only include the Holy Place, the Most Holy Place, the curtain, the ark and the mercy seat. If your picture or model includes the other pieces of furniture in the Holy Place, explain that you will teach about these items later. You will be teaching about these other items in Phase 2.

LESSON 37: GOD TOLD THE ISRAELITES TO BUILD THE TABERNACLE.

- **The first room was the Holy Place.**

   God said that the Holy Place was to be used only for Him. The only people who could enter this room were God's chosen priests. They were to come into the Holy Place when they were serving God. The priests would enter this room from the courtyard.

Teacher: If they ask about the priests, explain that you will be teaching about the priests later in this lesson.

- **The second room was the Most Holy Place.**

   The second room would be the most important part of the Tabernacle. The Most Holy Place was to be set apart just for God. It was the special room in the Tabernacle where God would live.

   On one special day every year, the high priest would be allowed to enter the Most Holy Place. This room was an inner room, and the High Priest would only be able to enter it from the Holy Place.

6) The ark and the mercy seat were to be made and put in the Most Holy Place.

- **God commanded the Israelites to make a box.**

   📖 Read Exodus 25:10-11.

   The Lord directed Moses to have the Israelites make a box out of the wood of a particular tree. After they made the box, they were to cover it with gold. This box would be put inside the Most Holy Place. The Bible calls this box the "ark."

Teacher: If your hearers do not know what gold is, show them an object made of gold, such as a wedding ring.

- **God commanded the Israelites to build a lid for the box.**

   📖 Read Exodus 25:17-20.

   The lid of the box was to be made of gold. The lid was called the mercy seat. It was the most important piece of furniture in the whole Tabernacle because this was the place where God promised to live and where He would show mercy to the sinful Israelites.

   The Israelites were to make two gold statues of cherubim and place one at each end of the mercy seat, facing each other. The cherubim's wings were to be made so they would stretch out toward one another over the mercy seat. Their faces were to be looking downwards onto the mercy seat.

Some of God's angels are cherubim. They do special work for God. Do you remember when we last heard about cherubim? God placed cherubim at the entrance to the garden in Eden to prevent Adam and Eve from returning and eating the fruit from the tree of life. Those cherubim were real live cherubim, but these which looked down on the mercy seat were gold statues.

- **God commanded the Israelites to place the box and the lid in the Most Holy Place.**

    📖 Read Exodus 25:21-22.

    The Lord told Moses to put inside the ark the two flat stones on which He had written the Ten Commandments. They were to place the mercy seat on top of the ark and put them in the Most Holy Place.

☞ **Teacher:** Point to the ark and the mercy seat on a model or picture of the Tabernacle. Explain that these were the only items in the Most Holy Place.

God promised that, when every part of the Tabernacle was built and set up just as He had commanded, He would come into the Most Holy Place. His presence would be evidenced by a very bright light between the cherubim.

⑦ A curtain was to hang between the Holy Place and the Most Holy Place.

📖 Read Exodus 26:31-33.

God told Moses that the Israelites were to hang a beautiful, thick curtain as a divider between the two rooms of the Tabernacle. This curtain was to remind the Israelites that they were separated from God because of their sin.

☞ **Teacher:** Point to the curtain between the Holy Place and the Most Holy Place on a model or picture of the Tabernacle.

⑧ The Tabernacle was to have a courtyard.

📖 Read Exodus 27:9.

God told Moses to have the Israelites make a courtyard for the Tabernacle. The courtyard was to be enclosed with a fence of cloth curtains which were held upright between posts. God told them exactly how big to make the courtyard.

☞ **Teacher:** Point to a picture of the Tabernacle and its enclosed courtyard.

LESSON 37: GOD TOLD THE ISRAELITES TO BUILD THE TABERNACLE.

There was only one entrance to the courtyard.

⑨ The brazen altar was to be set up inside the courtyard.

📖 Read Exodus 27:1-2.

Just inside the entrance to the courtyard, the Israelites were to place an altar. This altar was to be made of wood and covered with brass, and it was named the brazen altar.

📖 Read Leviticus 1:1-5.

When a person brought an offering to be burnt before the Lord, he was to bring it to the brazen altar. God said that the Israelites could bring sheep, goats, bulls, or birds as sacrifices.

☞ **Teacher:** Show a picture of an offering at the brazen altar.

When the person brought an animal to the brazen altar, he was to place his hand on the head of the animal and then kill it. By doing this, he was admitting to God that he was a sinner and that he deserved to die, but he was asking God to accept the animal's death instead of his. God forgave the sins of those who came trusting in God and bringing the offering He had commanded.

Do you think that the blood of animals could pay for sin? No! Sin must be paid for by the sinner's death. The blood of the animals was only a picture of the punishment which had to be paid for sin. Separation from God is the only just payment for sin.

⑩ God chose Aaron and his sons to serve Him as priests.

📖 Read Exodus 28:1.

The Lord told Moses that Aaron was to be the high priest and that his sons were to be priests. The priests were to serve God in the Tabernacle, and they helped with the sacrifices.

- **God said who could enter the Most Holy Place.**

    📖 Read Leviticus 16:2-3.

    Only Aaron, the high priest, was allowed to go into the Most Holy Place where God was. If anyone else went behind the curtain and entered the Most Holy Place, he would die.

    Aaron was allowed to go into this room where God was only on one day of each year. The special day each year when God said Aaron could go into the inner room was called the Day of Atonement.

Teacher: As you prepare to teach, read Leviticus 16:34; 23:26-32, but do not read these verses to the people when you teach the lesson.

- **Aaron must take the blood of an animal into the Most Holy Place.**

    📖 Read Leviticus 16:15.

    Before Aaron was allowed to enter the Most Holy Place, he had to kill an animal and catch its blood in a basin. He was to take the blood with him as he went behind the thick curtain which hung between the two rooms. Then Aaron was to sprinkle the blood on the mercy seat.

- **Aaron was to enter the Most Holy Place and sprinkle the blood on the mercy seat.**

    God promised to forgive the sins of the people of Israel for the past year. But He would forgive them only if Aaron did everything exactly the way the Lord had instructed Moses.

    Could the blood of animals that Aaron brought into the Most Holy Place pay for their sins? No! The blood of the animals could not pay for their sins. The punishment for sin is death, and that includes the separation of the sinner from God forever in the Lake of Fire. Sin must be paid for in full. Nevertheless, God promised to hold off the judgment they deserved and forgive their sins for the past year if they came to Him in faith and according to the way He had told them to come. God will only accept those who come to Him in the way He says in the Bible.

Teacher: You are teaching the doctrine of atonement. During the Old Testament, those who came in faith and according to God's way were fully forgiven and released from the judgment due to their sins (Psalm 103:3,12). God did this only because He intended to deal with their sin righteously and completely through the sacrificial blood and death of the Lord Jesus Christ on the cross. When the Lord Jesus died, God laid on Him the sins of the Old Testament believers which, in the forbearance of God, He had left unpunished (Romans 3:25; Hebrews 9:15).

Do not jump ahead and explain this to your hearers. If they ask, explain that they will understand later how the sins forgiven in the Old Testament times were paid for fully.

❓ Questions

1. On what did God write His Ten Commandments?

    God wrote His Ten Commandments on two flat stones.

2. What was the name of Moses' assistant who went with Moses up onto the mountain?

    His name was Joshua.

3. What did God tell Moses that he and the Israelites must build?

**LESSON 37: GOD TOLD THE ISRAELITES
TO BUILD THE TABERNACLE.**

God told them to build a tabernacle where He would live among them and where they could come to bring their sacrifices to Him.

4. Why does God not need a house, as we people do?

   God does not need a house because God is Spirit.

5. Why did God tell the Israelites to build the Tabernacle?

   God knew that the Israelites would disobey the Ten Commandments which He had given them. Therefore, He told them to build a special place where He would live among them and where they could come to Him to receive His forgiveness and mercy and be saved from the punishment of death which they deserved for breaking His laws.

6. Were the Israelites allowed to make the Tabernacle according to their own ideas?

   No. They were to make everything exactly as God had instructed Moses when he was up on the mountain.

7. How many rooms were to be in the Tabernacle?

   The Tabernacle was to have two rooms.

8. What were the names of the two rooms?

   The first room was the Holy Place, and the second room was the Most Holy Place.

9. Which room was the special room where God would live?

   The Most Holy Place was where God would live.

10. What did God have the Israelites make to be placed in the Most Holy Place?

    God had them make the ark and the mercy seat.

11. Describe the ark.

    The ark was a box made of a special kind of wood and covered with gold. The flat stones with the Ten Commandments written on them were put inside the ark.

12. Describe the mercy seat.

    The mercy seat was the lid of the box which was made of gold. Two gold statues of cherubim faced each other from each end of the mercy seat. The cherubim's wings stretched out toward one another over the mercy seat, and their faces looked down onto the mercy seat.

13. After every part of the Tabernacle was built and set up, God said that He would come into the Most Holy Place. What would be seen to show that He was there?

    God's presence would be seen by a very bright light on the mercy seat between the cherubim.

14. What was to be hung between the Holy Place and the Most Holy Place?

    A beautiful, thick curtain was to be hung as a divider between the two rooms of the Tabernacle.

15. What did the curtain remind the Israelites of?

    The curtain reminded the Israelites that they were separated from God because of their sin.

16. How many entrances were there to the courtyard of the Tabernacle?

    There was only one entrance to the courtyard.

17. What was to be set up just inside the entrance to the courtyard?

    The brazen altar was to be set up just inside the courtyard.

18. What sacrifices did the Israelites bring to the brazen altar?

    The Israelites brought sacrifices of sheep, goats, bulls, or birds.

19. When the person brought an animal to the brazen altar, he was to place his hand on the head of the animal and then kill it. By doing this, what was he admitting to God?

    He was admitting that he was a sinner and that he deserved to die, but he was asking God to accept the animal's death instead of his.

20. Who did God chose to serve Him as priests?

    God chose Aaron and his sons to serve Him as priests.

21. Who was the only one who could go behind the thick curtain into the Most Holy Place?

    Only Aaron, the high priest, was allowed to go into Most Holy Place where God was.

22. How often was the high priest allowed to go into the Most Holy Place?

    The high priest was allowed to go into the Most Holy Place only on one day of each year on the Day of Atonement.

23. What must the high priest take with him?

    The high priest was to take the blood of an animal which he had killed.

24. What was the high priest to do with the blood?

    He was to sprinkle it on the mercy seat.

25. What did God promise He would do if the high priest did this?

    God promised that He would forgive the sins of the Israelites and hold off His judgment on them for one more year.

26. Did the blood of animals satisfy God as a payment for sin?

    No. The blood of animals could never pay for sin.

27. What is the only payment for sin?

    The sinner must die. The sinner must be separated from God and punished by Him forever in the Lake of Fire.

LESSON 38: THE ISRAELITES WORSHIPED A GOLDEN CALF.

Scripture

Exodus 32:1-20, Exodus 34:1-2, Exodus 39:42-43, Exodus 40:17, 34-35

Lesson Outline

(1) The Israelites made a golden calf to worship. (Exodus 32:1-6)

(2) The Lord saw that the Israelites had made and worshiped a golden calf. (Exodus 32:7-8)

(3) Moses pleaded for the Lord not to destroy all the Israelites. (Exodus 32:9-14)

(4) Moses broke the two flat stones on which the Ten Commandments were written. (Exodus 32:15-19)

(5) Moses destroyed the golden calf. (Exodus 32:20)

(6) The Lord again wrote the Ten Commandments on two flat stones. (Exodus 34:1-2)

(7) God came to live in the Tabernacle. (Exodus 39:42-43; 40:17, 34-35)

(?) Review Questions from Lesson 37.

Lesson Outline Developed

(1) The Israelites made a golden calf to worship.

- **Moses was up on the mountain for forty days and forty nights.**

  During that time, God gave Moses the Ten Commandments and other instructions for the Israelites to follow.

  While Moses was up on Mt. Sinai, the Israelites were waiting at the bottom of the mountain. What do you think the Israelites were doing while they waited for Moses?

Listen to what they did.

📖 Read Exodus 32:1-6.

- **The Israelites told Aaron that they wanted to make gods to worship.**

  They gave Aaron their gold jewelry, and he made an idol for them in the shape of a calf. They said that this image was the god who had brought them out of Egypt.

  Was that true? Did the golden calf bring them out of Egypt? No! Only the true and living God could deliver the Israelites out of Egypt.

  Think about all the wonderful and miraculous things the Israelites had seen God do for them.

  - He had sent plagues on the Egyptians.
  - He had killed the Egyptians' firstborn but passed over the Israelites' children when He saw the blood on their houses.
  - He had opened up the sea so the Israelites could escape from the army of Egypt.
  - He had drowned the whole Egyptian army in the sea.
  - He had provided food from heaven and water from the rock.
  - He had shown His almighty power and holiness by the lightning, fire, thunder and smoke when He spoke to them from Mount Sinai.

  In spite of all of these incredible things which the Israelites had seen the Lord do, they chose to turn away from believing in Him. They chose to worship an image of a calf as the god who brought them out of Egypt.

- **The Israelites disobeyed God's command.**

  When God gave His commandments from the mountain, He told the Israelites that they must not have any other gods before Him and that they must never make any type of image and worship it.

  📖 Read Exodus 20:3-4.

  The Israelites had promised to obey God's commands perfectly, but they quickly turned away from obeying God. They disobeyed God when they made and worshiped this golden calf.

② The Lord saw that the Israelites had made and worshiped a golden calf.

📖 Read Exodus 32:7-8.

Could Moses see what the Israelites were doing? No! Could the Lord see them? Yes! He saw everything the Israelites did.

We have already learned that God sees and knows everything.

LESSON 38: THE ISRAELITES WORSHIPED A GOLDEN CALF.

- God saw Adam and Eve when they disobeyed Him and ate the forbidden fruit.
- God saw Cain kill Abel.
- God saw the wicked things the people did in the days of Noah.
- God saw the wicked people of Sodom and Gomorrah.
- God saw Joseph down in Egypt, even when Jacob, his father, thought that he was dead.
- God saw the Israelites in Egypt, and He saw the wicked king who kept them as slaves.

Nothing is hidden from God. He knows all about each one of us. Even when we are hidden from other people, the Lord still sees everything that we do.

God saw the Israelites at the bottom of the mountain. He told Moses that the Israelites had made a golden calf and were worshiping it.

3) Moses pleaded for the Lord not to destroy all the Israelites.

📖 Read Exodus 32:9-14.

God had made an agreement with the Israelites. If they obeyed Him perfectly, He would accept them and bless them, but if they disobeyed, they would be punished. Had they disobeyed God's commands? Yes! They disobeyed Him when they made the golden calf and worshiped it. They disobeyed Him when they said that the golden calf had delivered them from slavery in Egypt. They disobeyed; therefore, they deserved to be punished by God.

When Moses was on the mountain, the Lord told him that He was going to destroy the Israelites. Moses pleaded for the Lord to forgive them. He reminded the Lord that the Egyptians would hear about it and think that God had delivered the Israelites from slavery just to destroy them.

Moses also reminded God that He had promised Abraham, Isaac and Jacob that their descendants would more than the stars Abraham could see in the sky and that He would give them the land of Canaan. Moses knew that the Lord would never break His promise.

Teacher: If a student asks if God forgot His promise, assure them that God never forgets. The Lord put the thoughts in Moses' mind so he would pray this prayer. Do not raise this question unless they do.

The Lord did not destroy the Israelites.

4) Moses broke the two flat stones on which the Ten Commandments were written.

📖 Read Exodus 32:15-19.

When Moses went to the bottom of the mountain and saw what the Israelites had done, he was angry. He broke the two flat stones on which God had written His commandments.

> ☞ **Teacher:** Show a picture of the Israelites worshiping the golden calf and of Moses with the broken stones on which God's commandments were written.

(5) Moses destroyed the golden calf.

📖 Read Exodus 32:20.

Moses destroyed the calf idol which the Israelites had made from gold.

(6) The Lord again wrote the Ten Commandments on two flat stones.

📖 Read Exodus 34:1-2.

The Lord still wanted the Israelites to remember His commands and to obey His law. He told Moses to prepare two flat stones to replace the ones which he had broken and to bring them up onto the mountain. The Lord wrote the Ten Commandments on these flat stones.

(7) God came to live in the Tabernacle.

After Moses came down from Mount Sinai with the two flat stones on which the commandments were written, he told the Israelites all the commands the Lord had given him on Mount Sinai. He also told them that God wanted them to build a house so that He could live with them.

- **The Israelites built the house for God and erected it exactly as the Lord had instructed Moses.**

  📖 Read Exodus 39:42-43; 40:17.

  If they had not made it exactly as God told them, God would not have come to live with them. But because they made the Tabernacle exactly as God instructed, He came to live in the center of the Israelites' camp in the Most Holy Place.

  📖 Read Exodus 40:34-35.

  The Israelites could now come to God in the way that He had taught them through Moses. Each year, Aaron, the high priest, could enter the Most Holy Place and sprinkle the blood on the mercy seat under the cherubim.

- **We cannot decide how we will come to God.**

  He is perfect, and He will only accept us if we come to Him in the way He tells us in His

LESSON 38: THE ISRAELITES WORSHIPED A GOLDEN CALF.

Word. Continue to listen carefully as we teach you God's message so you can learn the only way that sinners can come to Him.

? Questions

1. What did the Israelites do while they were waiting for Moses to come back down from the mountain?

   They made an image of a calf out of gold, and they began to worship it as the god which had brought them out of Egypt.

2. Which of God's commandments did the Israelites disobey when they built and worshiped the golden calf?

   They disobeyed God's commandments that they must not have any other gods before Him and that they must never make any type of image and worship it.

3. Could the Lord see what the Israelites were doing?

   Yes! He saw everything the Israelites did.

4. Did the Israelites deserve to be punished by God for breaking His commandments?

   Yes. The Israelites deserved to be punished by God.

5. When God told Moses that He was going to destroy the Israelites, what did Moses plead for the Lord to do?

   Moses pleaded for the Lord to forgive the Israelites for their disobedience.

6. Why didn't God destroy the Israelites?

   God did not destroy the Israelites because He remained faithful to His promises to Abraham, Isaac and Jacob.

7. When Moses saw what the Israelites had done, what did Moses do with the two flat stones on which God had written His commandments?

   Moses broke them.

8. What did Moses do to the golden calf?

   Moses destroyed the golden calf.

9. What did God tell Moses to do to replace the two flat stones on which God had written the Ten Commandments?

   God told Moses to cut two flat stones and bring them up onto the mountain so God could give the Israelites another written copy of the Ten Commandments.

10. What did God want the Israelites to build for Him?

    God wanted them to build a tabernacle so that He could live with them.

11. Would God have come to live in the house which the Israelites made if they had not done everything exactly as God had instructed Moses?

    No. They had to make the tabernacle exactly as God instructed.

12. Can sinners come to God in whatever way they wish?

    No. In order to be accepted by God, we must come to God in the way that He says.

13. How can we learn the way to God?

    God tells us the way to Him through the Bible.

LESSON 39: THE ISRAELITES DID NOT BELIEVE THAT GOD WOULD GIVE THEM THE LAND OF CANAAN.

Scripture

Exodus 40:36-38, Numbers 13:1-3, 17-21, 23-33, Numbers 14:1-10, 26-32

Lesson Outline

1. Moses was God's prophet.
2. God guided the Israelites by the cloud. (Exodus 40:36-38)
3. The Lord told Moses to send spies into the land of Canaan. (Numbers 13:1-3, 17-20)
4. The men spied out the land and returned with their report. (Numbers 13:21, 23-29)
5. Caleb and Joshua believed God. (Numbers 13:30)
6. Ten of the spies did not believe God. (Numbers 13:31-33)
7. The Israelites did not believe God. (Numbers 14:1-10)
8. God told them that they would all die in the wilderness. (Numbers 14:26-32)

? Review Questions from Lesson 38.

Lesson Outline Developed

1 Moses was God's prophet.

During the time that Moses was leader of the Israelites, he was God's messenger. God guided Moses to tell the Israelites exactly what God wanted them to know.

God also guided Moses to write down exactly what God wanted him to write. Moses wrote the first five books in the Bible. We have taught you from four of the books Moses wrote, and we will soon teach from the other book he wrote.

☞ **Teacher:** Show them in your Bible the five books which Moses wrote (Genesis through Deuteronomy).

② God guided the Israelites by the cloud.

After the Israelites were delivered from slavery in Egypt, the Lord led them through the Red Sea and to Mount Sinai. Do you remember how God directed them where He wanted them to go? He directed them with a pillar of cloud.

After the Lord had given His laws at Mount Sinai and after the tabernacle was built and God had come to live with them, it was time for the Israelites to travel to the land of Canaan which God had promised to give to their ancestor, Abraham.

But the Israelites had never traveled to Canaan before. They did not know the way to go, and there weren't any roads for them to follow. How do you think they knew which way to go? God guided them with the cloud.

📖 Read Exodus 40:36-38.

When God wanted them to stop, the cloud would stand still. When He wanted them to start traveling again, the cloud rose up and moved out in front of them.

God showed the Israelites by the cloud during the day and by the fire at night that He was always with them as their guide. God never deserted them even though they often doubted and disobeyed Him.

③ The Lord told Moses to send spies into the land of Canaan.

The Lord led the Israelites from Mount Sinai to the border of the land of Canaan. He had promised to give the land of Canaan to them.

There were already people living in Canaan. Because these people were very wicked and worshiped idols, the Lord planned to have them destroyed and to give their land to the Israelites.

☞ **Teacher:** The Israelites were at Kadesh Barnea in the Desert of Paran. Point to Kadesh on the map.

When the Israelites arrived at the border of Canaan, the Lord told Moses to choose one man from each of the twelve tribes. These twelve men were to go and spy out the land before the Israelites entered.

**LESSON 39: THE ISRAELITES DID NOT
BELIEVE THAT GOD WOULD GIVE
THEM THE LAND OF CANAAN.**

📖 Read Numbers 13:1-3, 17-20.

Moses obeyed the Lord and sent the twelve men into the land of Canaan to look at the land and the people who were living there.

④ The men spied out the land and returned with their report.

📖 Read Numbers 13:21, 23-25.

After exploring the land for forty days, the twelve men returned to the Israelite people who were camped in the desert. They reported to Moses and the Israelites.

📖 Read Numbers 13:26-29.

These men were telling the truth. There were strong walls around the cities, and the land was owned by strong people. There were even giants in the land.

⑤ Caleb and Joshua believed God.

📖 Read Numbers 13:30.

Two of the spies, however, did believe that God was able to give them the land. Their names were Caleb and Joshua.

☞ **Teacher:** Point to the name, "Joshua," on the chronological chart.

Caleb and Joshua had also seen the strong walls surrounding the cities in Canaan. They had also seen the strong men and the giants. But Caleb and Joshua had not forgotten that their God was almighty and that He could do anything that He wants to do. They remembered the many miracles that God had already done for them, and they believed that He would drive out the people of Canaan and give the land to the Israelites as He had promised.

⑥ Ten of the spies did not believe God.

📖 Read Numbers 13:31-33.

Ten of the spies said that it was impossible for the Israelites to conquer the land of Canaan. These men had forgotten that God can do anything. They had forgotten all the great and mighty things that the Lord had done for them. Can you remember some of the miracles they had seen God do?

- He had sent plagues on the Egyptians.

- He had delivered the Israelites from slavery in Egypt.
- He had led them through the Red Sea.
- He had provided manna in the wilderness
- He had provided water from a rock.

Even though the spies had seen all these miracles, ten of them didn't believe that God was strong enough to overcome the people of Canaan and give the land to the Israelites.

7) The Israelites did not believe God.

Who do you think the Israelites followed? Do you think that they followed the ten men who didn't believe God? Or do you think that they followed Caleb and Joshua who believed God would give them the land?

📖 Read Numbers 14:1-10.

The Lord heard everything the Israelites said. He knew that they did not believe that God would give them the land. By choosing not to believe God, they were showing that they thought God lied to them when He promised to give them the land.

If someone tells you something and you don't believe him, isn't that calling him a liar? Yes, it is. If you hear God's Word but do not believe it, then you, too, are showing that you think God is a liar.

Even though Joshua and Caleb urged them to believe that the Lord was with them and that He had promised to give them the land, the people refused to believe God and they rebelled against Him.

☞ **Teacher:** Show a picture of the unbelieving Israelites wanting to kill Joshua and Caleb.

8) God told them that they would all die in the wilderness.

The Lord was very angry that the Israelites refused to believe Him.

📖 Read Numbers 14:26-32.

Because the Israelites did not believe God, He told them that all the adults would die in the wilderness, except for Joshua and Caleb who had believed God. God said that, after 40 years, when they had all died, then He would take their children and Joshua and Caleb into the land of Canaan and give it to them.

It is a very evil thing not to believe God. We have already learned that God punishes all those who refuse to believe Him.

LESSON 39: THE ISRAELITES DID NOT BELIEVE THAT GOD WOULD GIVE THEM THE LAND OF CANAAN.

- God had told Adam and Eve that they would die if they ate the fruit from the tree of knowledge of good and evil. Satan told Eve that she would not die. Satan called God a liar, and Eve believed him. Adam and Eve ate the fruit in disobedience to God. Therefore, they were immediately separated from God, just as He had warned them.

- Cain did not believe God. God had explained how people were to come to Him if they wanted to be accepted by Him. Cain came to God in his own way. Therefore, God rejected him and his offering.

- The people in Noah's day refused to believe that God would punish the earth with a flood. Even though God the Spirit was trying to convince them, they refused to believe God's message given though Noah. Therefore, they were all destroyed in the flood.

- The Egyptians would not believe that the God of Israel was the only true God. They trusted in their idols to deliver them. Therefore, God destroyed their land, killed their firstborn and drowned their armies in the sea.

- The Israelites refused to believe that God would fulfill His promise and give them the land of Canaan. Therefore, God told them that all the adults would die in the wilderness, except for Joshua and Caleb.

God will punish all those who refuse to believe Him. He always speaks the truth, and He tells us in His Word that all who refuse to believe Him will go to the place of everlasting punishment prepared by God for Satan and his demons.

? Questions

1. How many books in the Bible did Moses write?
   Moses wrote five books in the Bible.

2. How did Moses know what to write?
   God guided him to write down exactly what God wanted him to write.

3. How did the Israelites know where to go as they traveled to the land of Canaan?
   The Lord guided them by a cloud.

4. When the Israelites arrived at the border of Canaan, what did God tell Moses to do?
   God told Moses to send twelve men into Canaan as spies.

5. What did ten of the spies report when they got back from spying out the land of Canaan?

   The ten spies reported that the land was good but that Canaan had walled cities and strong men, including giants. They also reported that it was impossible for the Israelites to conquer the land of Canaan.

6. Did these ten spies believe that God was strong enough to overcome the people of Canaan and give them the land?

   No. They did not believe that God would give them the land.

7. What were the names of the two spies who believed that God was able to give them the land?

   Their names were Caleb and Joshua.

8. Caleb and Joshua urged the Israelites to believe that the Lord was with them and that He had promised to give them the land. Did the people listen to Caleb and Joshua?

   No. The people refused to believe that God would give them the land, and they rebelled against God.

9. By refusing to believe God, what were the Israelites showing that they thought God had done?

   They were showing that they thought God had lied to them.

10. If you do not believe God's Word and trust in Him, what are you showing that you think about God?

    We are showing that we think God is a liar.

11. Will God accept anyone who does not believe what He says?

    No. All who do not believe God will go to everlasting punishment.

12. What was God's punishment on the Israelites because they did not believe His promise to give them the land?

    God said all the adults who did not believe Him would die in the wilderness and would not enter Canaan.

13. To whom was God going to give the land of Canaan?

    God was going to give the land to the children of the Israelites and to Caleb and Joshua.

LESSON 40: THE LORD GAVE THE ISRAELITES WATER FROM THE ROCK. HE HEALED THOSE WHO LOOKED AT THE BRONZE SNAKE.

Scripture

Numbers 20:1-12, 23-25, 28, Numbers 21:4-9

Lesson Outline

1. The Israelites blamed Moses and Aaron because they didn't have any water. (Numbers 20:1-5)
2. Moses and Aaron asked the Lord for help. (Numbers 20:6)
3. God commanded Moses to speak to the rock. (Numbers 20:7-8)
4. Moses disobeyed and struck the rock. (Numbers 20:9-11)
5. The Lord punished Moses and Aaron. (Numbers 20:12)
6. Aaron died. (Numbers 20:23-25, 28)
7. The Israelites murmured again. (Numbers 21:4-5)
8. God sent poisonous serpents. (Numbers 21:6-7)
9. God healed those who looked at the snake on the pole. (Numbers 21:8-9)

(?) Review Questions from Lesson 39.

Lesson Outline Developed

1. The Israelites blamed Moses and Aaron because they didn't have any water.

📖 Read Numbers 20:1-5.

Because there was no water, the Israelites grumbled against Moses and Aaron. They blamed Moses for bringing them out into the desert and complained because there was no water.

- **The Israelites that God brought out of Egypt had complained when they were traveling to Mount Sinai.**

  They didn't have any water and they grumbled against Moses. They said, "Why did you bring us up out of Egypt to make us and our children and livestock die of thirst?" Do you remember what the Lord did that time? He told Moses to strike the rock with his staff. Moses did exactly as God said, and God caused water to flow from the rock, enough for the Israelites and all their animals.

- **The Israelites had seen many miracles, but they still didn't look to the Lord for help.**

  Although it was many years later, the Israelites knew that the Lord had given water from the rock when they needed it before. So why do you think the Israelites didn't ask the Lord for water this time? The reason the Israelites didn't ask the Lord to help them was because they did not truly trust in Him even though He had done so much for them.

- **The majority of people today are like the Israelites.**

  Every day and night, the Lord shows all people that He is the almighty God. He shows us who He is by the things that He has made. Look around at all that God created. He made the sun, the moon and the stars. He sends the rain and the wind. He causes the trees, the fruit and your crops to grow. All these things that we see around us are under His control. He has given all of these things so that we will believe on Him. God has also given His Word so that we can know the truth.

- **Most people ignore the evidence that God gives all the time.**

  Even though we can know that God exists by the things that He created and even though we can read the truth of God in the Bible, the majority of people in the world are like the Israelites were; they will not believe God. But, we hope you will not follow the majority of the people of this world. We hope you will believe God's message in the Bible and that, as you look at the things God has made, you will realize that He is everywhere and that He is all powerful.

Teacher: As you prepare to teach, read Romans 1:18-23, but do not read these verses to the people when you teach the lesson.

② Moses and Aaron asked the Lord for help.

📖 Read Numbers 20:6.

Moses and Aaron knew that they could not find water in the wilderness, but they knew that God could provide water. Because Moses and Aaron trusted in the Lord, they asked Him for help. Without the Lord's help, the Israelites would have all died of thirst.

3) God commanded Moses to speak to the rock.

📖 Read Numbers 20:7-8.

Previously, when they needed water, the Lord had told Moses to strike the rock. This time, the Lord told him to just speak to the rock. Each time, it had to be done the way the Lord said.

4) Moses disobeyed and struck the rock.

📖 Read Numbers 20:9-11.

Moses and Aaron were angry with the Israelites. They did not completely depend on the Lord in this situation as they had when faced with other problems. Moses disobeyed the Lord and struck the rock.

5) The Lord punished Moses and Aaron.

The Lord provided water for the Israelites, but because Moses and Aaron had disobeyed, the Lord told them that they would be punished. Because Moses and Aaron had not acted as God wanted them to, they would not be allowed to enter the land of Canaan.

📖 Read Numbers 20:12.

6) Aaron died.

📖 Read Numbers 20:23-25, 28.

Aaron died and was buried on the mountain in the wilderness. He never entered into the land which God had promised to Abraham and his descendants. God always does what He says. God said that He would not allow Aaron to enter the land of Canaan so Aaron died before entering the promised land. Aaron's son became high priest in place of his father.

7) The Israelites murmured again.

The Lord had provided so many things for the Israelites. He gave them water from the rock, and He provided the manna which they ate every day. But the Israelites still did not trust and depend on Him. They soon became impatient and began to complain again.

📖 Read Numbers 21:4-5.

8) God sent poisonous serpents.

When they complained this time, the Lord punished the Israelites so that many of them died.

📖 Read Numbers 21:6.

God punished them for their sin against Him by sending poisonous snakes among them. Many of the Israelites died because they were bitten by the snakes.

The Israelites could not escape the serpents sent by the Lord. The snakes were everywhere.

- **When God decides to punish sinners, there is no place where they can hide from Him.**
  - In the days of Noah, was there any place where the people could escape the judgment of God after God shut the door of the big boat and sent the flood?
  - Could the people of Sodom and Gomorrah escape the judgment of God when He sent fire and brimstone on them?
  - Did Lot's wife escape the judgment of God when she disobeyed Him and looked back?

When God decides that it is the time to punish people, there is no place where they can go to escape from God.

What do you think the Israelites did when God sent the poisonous snakes as His judgment on their sin? They quickly changed their attitude toward God and acknowledged their sin.

📖 Read Numbers 21:7.

They realized that only the Lord could save them from punishment, and so they asked Moses to ask the Lord for His help.

They could not help themselves, and Moses could not save them from the snakes. Only the Lord could save them.

⑨ God healed those who looked at the snake on the pole.

The Lord told Moses what to do so the Israelites could be saved from death. The Lord didn't leave it up to them to find their own way to be saved.

- **God told Moses to make a bronze snake and put it up on a pole.**

Those who were bitten by the snakes would not die if they looked at the snake on the pole.

📖 Read Numbers 21:8-9.

Because the Lord is merciful, He decided to forgive and save them. They didn't deserve God's help, but He saved all those who put their trust in Him by looking at the snake on the pole.

☞ **Teacher:** Show a picture of the bronze snake on the pole, with some of the Israelites looking at it and some looking away from it.

LESSON 40: THE LORD GAVE THE ISRAELITES WATER FROM THE ROCK. HE HEALED THOSE WHO LOOKED AT THE BRONZE SNAKE.

- **The Israelites were healed by God's power.**

  The snake didn't have any power. The power of God healed every Israelite who showed they trusted in God by looking at the snake on the pole.

  The reason the Lord healed those who looked at the snake on the pole was because they believed in Him.

- **They could only be healed if they did what God said.**

  Do you think people would have been healed if they had called to God for help but had not looked at the snake on the pole? No! Do you think the people would have been healed if they had offered God a gift but had not looked at the snake on the pole? No! They had to look at the bronze snake, just as the Lord said. It had to be done God's way.

- **God kept His promise to all who looked at the snake on the pole.**

  God always keeps His promises. God immediately healed all who looked at the snake on the pole. God can be trusted to do everything He says.

Teacher: Make certain your students understand that the snake had no power to heal. Emphasize that the Lord saved those who trusted in Him by looking at the bronze snake.

? Questions

1. What did the Israelites do when they did not have water?

   They complained because there was no water, and they blamed Moses for bringing them out into the desert.

2. What should the Israelites have done when they needed water?

   They should have trusted in the Lord.

3. What did God tell Moses to do to provide water for the people?

   God told Moses to speak to the rock.

4. Instead of speaking to the rock, what did Moses do?

   Moses struck the rock.

5. What did God tell Moses and Aaron would happen to them because they did not act as God wanted them to?

   The Lord told them that they would not be allowed to enter the land of Canaan.

6. What happened to Aaron?
   Aaron died and was buried on the mountain in the wilderness.

7. Who became the high priest in place of Aaron?
   Aaron's son became the high priest in place of Aaron.

8. After God provided water from the rock, did the Israelites trust God?
   No. They did not trust God. They became impatient and complained again.

9. What did the Lord do to punish the Israelites for their unbelief?
   The Lord sent poisonous snakes which bit and killed many people.

10. What did God tell Moses to do to save the Israelites from death?
    The Lord told Moses to make a snake and put it on a pole.

11. What did those who had been bitten by a snake have to do in order to be healed so that they did not die from the snake bites?
    They had to look at the snake on the pole.

12. Did the snake on the pole have magical power to heal those who looked at it?
    No. The snake on the pole did not have power to heal people.

13. Who healed those who looked at the snake on the pole?
    The Lord healed them.

14. Did the Israelites deserve to be healed so that they did not die from the snake bites?
    No. The Israelites were sinners and deserved to die.

15. What do we learn about God's character when we read from the Bible that He saves sinners who deserve to die?
    We learn that God is merciful.

16. What were the Israelites showing when they looked at the snake on the pole?
    The Israelites were showing that they believed God.

17. Did anyone die if he was bitten by a snake but looked at the snake on the pole?
    No. God healed each one who looked at the snake on the pole.

18. Can God be trusted to do what He says?
    Yes. God always does what He says.

LESSON 41: GOD TOOK THE ISRAELITES INTO CANAAN. GOD CHOSE THEIR LEADERS AND THEIR KING.

Scripture

Numbers 27:18-23, Deuteronomy 34:1-5, 9, Joshua 1:1-2, Joshua 11:23, Joshua 23:14-16, Judges 2:7-19, 1 Samuel 8:1-7, 1 Samuel 11:14-15

Lesson Outline

1. The unbelieving Israelites died in the wilderness.
2. God chose Joshua to take Moses' place. (Numbers 27:18-23)
3. Moses died. (Deuteronomy 34:1-5)
4. Joshua led the Israelites into Canaan. (Deuteronomy 34:9; Joshua 1:1-2; 11:23; 23:14-16)
5. The Israelites turned to idols after Joshua's death. (Judges 2:7-15)
6. God chose judges to lead the nation of Israel. (Judges 2:16-19)
7. Samuel was the last judge. (1 Samuel 8:1-7)
8. God appointed Saul to be the first king of the nation of Israel. (1 Samuel 11:14-15)

? Review Questions from Lesson 40.

Lesson Outline Developed

1. The unbelieving Israelites died in the wilderness.

We learned earlier that the Israelites, except for Caleb and Joshua, had refused to believe that God would give them the land of Canaan. Do you remember what happened? God had led the Israelites to the border of the land of Canaan, and God had told Moses to send twelve spies to check out the land. When they came back, ten of the spies said that it was impossible for the Israelites to conquer the land of Canaan. Even though Joshua and Caleb urged the Israelites to believe that the Lord was with them and that He had promised to give them the land, the people refused to believe God and they rebelled against Him. Because the Israelites did not believe God, He told them that all the adults would die in the wilderness, except for Joshua and Caleb who had believed.

- **The Israelites wandered for 40 years in the wilderness.**

   Because of their unbelief, God punished them by not allowing them to enter the land of Canaan.

   In the same way as Moses gave God's words to the Israelites, we are teaching you God's words which are written in the Bible. God will punish all who refuse to believe His Word. All unbelievers will die and be separated from God forever.

- **The generation of Israelites who had refused to believe God died in the wilderness.**

   The children of those who didn't believe had grown up and were now adults. The time had come for God to fulfill His promise and give them the land of Canaan. So God led this new generation of Israelites to the border of Canaan.

2) God chose Joshua to take Moses' place.

- **The old leader of Israel would not lead the new generation into Canaan.**

   Moses was still their leader at this time, but we have already learned that God was not going to allow Moses to enter the land that God had promised to give the Israelites. Do you remember why? Moses had acted in a way that displeased the Lord, and he struck the rock instead of speaking to it, so God would not allow him to enter Canaan.

- **A new leader was to be appointed to lead the new generation of Israelites.**

   Because the time had come for the Israelites to enter the land that God had promised to give them and because the Lord would not allow Moses to enter, the Israelites needed a new leader. Therefore, the Lord told Moses to appoint Joshua as the new leader of the nation of Israel.

   📖 Read Numbers 27:18-23.

   Joshua was Moses' helper. He was the man who had gone up into the mountain with Moses when God gave Moses the Ten Commandments written on the flat stones. Joshua was also one of the spies who had believed that God would give the Israelites the land of Canaan. Joshua was a man who trusted in God.

3) Moses died.

After Joshua was appointed as the new leader of the Israelites, the Lord told Moses to go up onto a high mountain which was close to the border of Canaan. From the top of this mountain, the Lord showed Moses the land that He had promised to Abraham, Isaac, Jacob and their descendants.

📖 Read Deuteronomy 34:1-5.

Moses died on the top of the mountain. God did what He said – He did not allow Moses to enter into the land that God had promised to give to the Israelites. God is greater than everyone, and He does whatever He wants to do.

④ Joshua led the Israelites into Canaan.

📖 Read Deuteronomy 34:9.

- **Joshua was the new leader of Israel.**

   📖 Read Joshua 1:1-2.

   Joshua led the Israelites into Canaan, and God gave them the land that He had promised to Abraham and his descendants.

   📖 Read Joshua 11:23.

- **No one could hinder God from fulfilling His plan for the Israelites.**

   God always does what He says He will do. Satan tried to keep the Israelites enslaved in Egypt. The king of Egypt tried to stop the Israelites from leaving Egypt. But neither Satan nor the king of Egypt could prevent God from doing what He said.

   Even though the Israelites doubted God many times, He still did what He had promised. He provided the way for them through the Red Sea. He led them, protected them, and provided water and food for 40 years while they wandered in the wilderness. The Lord did not fail to do any of the things He had promised them.

- **Joshua reminded the Israelites of all God had done for them.**

   Joshua was old and knew he was going to die, so he called the Israelites together and spoke to them. He reminded the Israelites of God's faithfulness to them. Joshua also warned them that if they disobeyed the Lord, they would be punished.

   📖 Read Joshua 23:14-16.

⑤ The Israelites turned to idols after Joshua's death.

While Joshua was alive, the Israelites followed the Lord. But after Joshua and the generation who had seen the Lord's miracles in the wilderness had died, the Israelites forsook the Lord. They followed the ways of the nations living near to their country who did not know the true and living God and did not have His Word. The Israelites made idols and worshiped them instead of the Lord.

☞ **Teacher:** Show a picture of the Israelites worshipping idols.

📖 Read Judges 2:7-13.

The wicked people who continued to live near to the Israelites worshiped false gods named Baal and the Ashtaroths. Satan had deceived these people into thinking that they were worshiping real and living gods. The people did not know that they were really worshiping Satan and his demons.

Teacher: As you prepare to teach, read 1 Corinthians 10:19-20, but do not read these verses to the people when you teach the lesson.

- **Satan disguises himself.**

  When people worship anything other than the true and living God described in the Bible, they are really worshiping Satan. Satan disguises himself. When Satan tempted Eve in the garden in Eden, he disguised himself by using the snake. He disguises himself today by using idols, the spirits, ancestral spirits and other things which people worship or depend on. Satan hates God and doesn't want anyone to worship God. Because Satan doesn't want anyone to trust in God and be delivered from death, he disguises himself so people will not realize that he is trying to trap them and keep them under his control.

- **God punished the Israelites**

  Because the Israelites forsook God and worshiped idols, the Lord punished them. God allowed surrounding nations who hated Israel to overcome the Israelites and make them their servants.

  📖 Read Judges 2:14-15.

  The Lord had warned the Israelites that this would happen to them if they did not obey and worship only Him.

  God does not change. He always does what He says no matter how many years pass. When He makes a promise, He keeps it. When He warns people that unless they repent, He will punish them, He will do it.

⑥ God chose judges to lead the nation of Israel.

The Israelites were conquered on many occasions by their enemies. Each time this happened, the Israelites repented – they turned back to God and agreed with Him that they had sinned. They cried out to God for His help. Each time they repented, God chose a man or woman to lead them and deliver them from their enemies. These people chosen by God to lead Israel were called judges.

LESSON 41: GOD TOOK THE ISRAELITES INTO CANAAN. GOD CHOSE THEIR LEADERS AND THEIR KING.

☞ **Teacher:** Point to the word, **"Judges,"** on the chronological chart.

- **The Israelites disobeyed the Lord many times.**

  This happened over and over again. The Israelites would rebel against God and worship idols. God would allow their enemies to conquer them. When the Israelites were in distress because of being conquered, they would repent and ask God for help. God would choose another judge to deliver them from their enemies. But when the judge died, the Israelites would again forsake the Lord.

  📖 Read Judges 2:16-19.

- **God protected Israel so His plans would be fulfilled through them.**

  Even though the Israelites were disobedient to God and He had to punish them, His love and care for them never changed.

- **God protected Israel because the Deliverer would be an Israelite.**

  In the garden in Eden, the Lord had promised that He would send a Deliverer who would destroy Satan and deliver the world from his power. The Deliverer would provide the way so that people could come back into a right relationship with God. God also promised that the Deliverer would be the descendant of Abraham, Isaac and Jacob. Therefore, God protected the people of Israel because it was through them that God planned to fulfill all His promises to send the Deliverer.

- **God protected Israel because He had entrusted His Word for the world to them.**

  God wanted all people to know Him, so God used chosen Israelites to record His message in the Bible. God wants you to hear His Word so that you, too, can hear the story of the Deliverer and be able to come to God.

⑦ Samuel was the last judge.

One of the messengers of God to Israel at this time was a man named Samuel. Samuel was the last judge of Israel. He was a judge for many years.

When Samuel grew old, there was no one to take his place. His sons were not obedient to the Lord.

📖 Read 1 Samuel 8:1-3.

- **The Israelites wanted a king to lead them.**

  The nation of Israel was unlike the other nations because they did not have a man who ruled them as king. From the time God delivered the Israelites from slavery in Egypt, God had been their sovereign ruler.

At this time, however, the Israelites wanted a king to rule over them, just as the other countries around them had. By wanting a man as their king, the Israelites were rejecting God as their ruler.

📖 Read 1 Samuel 8:4-7.

⑧ God appointed Saul to be the first king of the nation of Israel.

God gave the Israelites a man to be their king. His name was Saul. He was the first man to be king over the nation of Israel.

📖 Read 1 Samuel 11:14-15.

☞ **Teacher:** Point to the name, "Saul," on the chronological chart.

- **God continued to take care of the nation of Israel.**

    Although the Israelites rejected God as their only king and wanted a man to be their leader, God did not forsake them. He continued to speak to them through his chosen servants and to protect the nation of Israel. God would not allow anything to hinder His great purpose for calling Abraham and taking care of His descendants. It was through this nation that God had promised to send the Deliverer into the world.

❓ Questions

1. Who was the leader of Israel after Moses died?

    Joshua was the leader of Israel after Moses died.

2. After the generation of Israelites who had refused to believe God died in the wilderness, where did God lead the new generation of Israelites?

    God led the new generation of Israelites to the border of Canaan.

3. Did God give Abraham's descendants the land which He had promised them?

    Yes. God kept His promise and gave them the land.

4. While Joshua was alive, the Israelites followed the Lord, but what did they do after Joshua died?

    They forsook the Lord and worshiped idols.

LESSON 41: GOD TOOK THE ISRAELITES INTO CANAAN. GOD CHOSE THEIR LEADERS AND THEIR KING.

5. Who deceives people so they worship and obey idols, spirits, ancestral spirits and other created things?

   Satan deceives people so that they worship idols, spirits and other created things.

6. If we worship anyone or anything else other than the true and living God, whom are we really worshiping?

   We are worshiping Satan and his demons.

7. Why does Satan deceive people into worshiping idols, spirits, ancestral spirits and other false gods?

   Satan hates God and people. He doesn't want anyone to trust in God and be delivered from eternal punishment.

8. How did God punish the Israelites for worshiping idols?

   God allowed their enemies to conquer them.

9. What did God do when the Israelites repented and asked God to deliver them?

   Each time they repented, God chose a man or woman to lead them and deliver them from their enemies.

10. Who was the last judge over Israel?

    Samuel was the last judge.

11. Before Samuel died, what did the Israelites ask him to do?

    They asked him to appoint a man to be their king.

12. By asking for a man to be their king, who were the Israelites rejecting as their king?

    They were rejecting God as their king.

LESSON 42: GOD CHOSE DAVID TO BE KING. GOD CHOSE SOLOMON TO BUILD THE TEMPLE.

Scripture

1 Samuel 13:13-14, 1 Samuel 16:1-5, 11-13, 2 Samuel 5:1-4, 2 Samuel 7:1-3, 12-17, 1 Chronicles 22:5-6, 1 Chronicles 29:26-28, 2 Chronicles 2:1, 2 Chronicles 5:1

Lesson Outline

(1) Saul disobeyed the Lord. (1 Samuel 13:13-14)

(2) God chose David to be king. (1 Samuel 16:1-5, 11-13; 2 Samuel 5:1-4)

(3) David planned to build the temple. (2 Samuel 7:1-3)

(4) God gave promises to David. (2 Samuel 7:12-17)

(5) Solomon built the temple. (1 Chronicles 22:5-6; 29:26-28; 2 Chronicles 2:1; 5:1)

(6) Many kings ruled over the Israelites after Solomon died.

(?) Review Questions from Lesson 41

Lesson Outline Developed

(1) Saul disobeyed the Lord.

The Lord Himself had chosen Saul to be king over Israel. Saul's responsibility was to obey the Lord, but Saul disobeyed the Lord. Therefore, the Lord chose another man to take Saul's place as king over the nation of Israel.

📖 Read 1 Samuel 13:13-14.

(2) God chose David to be king.

After Saul's death, David became the second man to be king over Israel.

👉 **Teacher:** Point to the name, **"David,"** on the chronological chart.

📖 Read 1 Samuel 16:1-5, 11-13; 2 Samuel 5:1-4.

- **David had a different attitude than Saul had.**

    David believed the Lord and wanted to obey Him in everything.

    David, like all of us, was born a sinner and was separated from God. But David knew that he was a sinner and that the punishment for sin is death. He knew his only hope was in God's mercy and forgiveness. In obedience to God, David offered blood sacrifices for his sins. Because David trusted in the Lord, he was accepted and forgiven just like Abel, Enoch, Noah, Abraham, Isaac, Jacob, Moses, Joshua and many others who had trusted in the Lord.

- **David was also one of God's prophets.**

    David wrote many things that are in the Bible. David wrote many songs of praise to God for His love and mercy.

☞ **Teacher:** Show the book of Psalms and point to some of David's writings.

☞ **Teacher:** Show a picture of David as a shepherd who sang songs to God.

③ David planned to build the temple.

Because David was the king, he was very rich. David ordered people to build him a beautiful house of timber, stone, gold and silver. One day as David was thinking about his beautiful house, he realized that the Lord's house was still the same one which the Israelites had made from animal skins and curtains of cloth. It was the house that the Israelites had made for the Lord when they were at Mount Sinai and which they had carried as they wandered through the wilderness.

- **David decided to build a permanent and beautiful house for the Lord.**

    He planned to build it out of stone, timber, silver and gold.

    Does the Lord need a house to live in? No! God is Spirit and He is present everywhere. But David wanted the Lord to have a permanent house where the people could come to worship Him and offer their sacrifices.

    The Lord was very pleased with David for wanting to do this, and so the Lord sent one of His prophets to tell David that He was in agreement with his plan that a permanent stone and timber house should be built for the Lord.

    📖 Read 2 Samuel 7:1-3.

LESSON 42: GOD CHOSE DAVID TO BE KING. GOD CHOSE SOLOMON TO BUILD THE TEMPLE.

④ God gave promises to David.

- **God promised David that his son would build a house for God.**

    The Lord told David that he would not be allowed to build the house of the Lord. However, David's son would build this new place where Israel could bring their sacrifices and worship God.

    📖 Read 2 Samuel 7:12-17.

- **The Lord promised David that the Deliverer would be one of his descendants.**

    God gave David the same promise that He had given to Abraham, Isaac and Jacob. God also told David that the Deliverer would rule as king forever. God had not forgotten His promise to send the Deliverer.

⑤ Solomon built the temple.

David had his men prepare the materials for the house of the Lord which was to be built in Jerusalem.

Jerusalem is a big city in the mountains in the country of Israel. Jerusalem, like all the cities at that time, was surrounded by great walls of stone. The walls helped to protect the city and those who lived within it from their enemies.

☞ **Teacher:** Point to the location of Jerusalem on the map. Show a picture of Jerusalem and a picture of a city's stone walls.

Before David died, he gave his son Solomon the responsibility to build the house of the Lord.

☞ **Teacher:** Point to the name, **"Solomon,"** on the chronological chart.

📖 Read 1 Chronicles 22:5-6.

Solomon became king over all Israel after his father David had died.

📖 Read 1 Chronicles 29:26-28.

Solomon ordered his people to build the house of the Lord in Jerusalem.

☞ **Teacher:** Show a picture of Solomon's temple.

📖 Read 2 Chronicles 2:1; 5:1.

- **God's new house that Solomon built was called the temple of the Lord.**

    As soon as the house of the Lord was built in Jerusalem, God came to live there. Therefore, there was no further need for the building made of skins and cloth which the Israelites had made in the wilderness.

- **The temple's rooms and furniture were similar to the tabernacle's rooms and furniture.**

    The temple had two inner rooms just like the tabernacle had. A thick curtain hung between the Holy Place and the Most Holy Place just like one had hung between the two rooms in the tabernacle. This curtain kept everybody except the high priest from entering into God's presence. God's dwelling place was behind the curtain in the Most Holy Place. The bright light which showed God was in the inner room of the tabernacle moved into the inner room of the temple. This became God's special place on earth.

- **The priests offered sacrifices in the temple just as they did in the tabernacle.**

    Only the high priest was allowed to enter the inner room of the temple, and he could only enter it once a year on the Day of Atonement. The Israelites could not come to God themselves. The only way they could be accepted by God was to depend on the high priest and the animal blood he offered for them. Every year, the high priest took the blood of animals into Most Holy Place in the temple and sprinkled it on the mercy seat.

- **The priests had to continually offer sacrifices year after year.**

    The sacrifices had to be offered continually so the Israelites would never forget these things:
    - They were never to forget that they were sinners.
    - They were never to forget that because God is perfect He cannot accept sinners unless the full payment for sin is made.
    - They were never to forget that the punishment for sin is death.
    - They were never to forget that the death of an animal could never pay for their sin.
    - They were never to forget that God had promised to send the Deliverer.

    Because the blood of animals could not pay for their sin, the priests had to offer sacrifices to God every day, and the high priest had to enter the Most Holy Place once each year to place the blood of an animal before God. This special day each year when God said the high priest could go into the inner room was called the Day of Atonement. If the high priest did everything the way God had commanded, God promised to forgive the Israelites for the past year and to hold off His judgment until a perfect and complete payment for sin could be made.

LESSON 42: GOD CHOSE DAVID TO BE KING. GOD CHOSE SOLOMON TO BUILD THE TEMPLE.

⑥ Many kings ruled over the Israelites after Solomon died.

- After Solomon's death, the Israelites argued over who should be king, and they split into two kingdoms.

    The ten northern tribes were named Israel, and the two southern tribes were named Judah.

    Through the years, many kings ruled over Judah, while other kings ruled over Israel.

    ☞ **Teacher:** Point to the word, **"Kings,"** on the chronological chart.

    Some of these kings believed God's words and trusted in Him, but the majority of them did not believe God's words. They worshiped idols and led the people of Judah and Israel to sin against the commandments of God.

❓ Questions

1. After King Saul disobeyed the Lord, whom did the Lord appoint to be king over the nation of Israel?

    God appointed David to be king over the nation of Israel.

2. How was David different from Saul?

    David believed and obeyed God.

3. David agreed with God that he was a sinner, therefore, what did he bring to God?

    David brought the blood of animals to show that he was trusting in God to forgive his sins and accept him.

4. What important promise did God make to David?

    God promised David that one of his descendants would be the Deliverer and would rule as king forever.

5. After David had finished his own house, what did he decide to build?

    David decided to build a house for the Lord in Jerusalem.

6. Did David build this temple for the Lord?

    No. David's son, Solomon, had his men build the temple.

7. What building did the temple replace?

   The temple replaced the tabernacle which the Israelites had built at Mount Sinai and which they carried with them through the wilderness.

8. How many inner rooms did the temple have?

   The temple had two inner rooms – the Holy Place and the Most Holy Place.

9. What hung in front of the entrance to the Most Holy Place?

   A heavy curtain hung in front of the entrance to the Most Holy Place.

10. Who was the only one allowed into the Most Holy Place?

    The high priest was the only one allowed to enter the Most Holy Place.

11. How often was the high priest permitted to enter the Most Holy Place?

    The high priest was allowed to enter the Most Holy Place on one day of each year.

12. What did the high priest do when he entered the Most Holy Place?

    The high priest sprinkled the blood of animals on the mercy seat.

13. Could the blood of animals pay for the sin of the Israelites?

    No. Sin must be paid for by the death of the sinner.

14. What did God promise to do when the high priest sprinkled the animals' blood on the mercy seat?

    God promised to forgive the sins of Israel committed during the past year and to hold off His punishment until a perfect and complete payment for sin could be made.

15. What happened after King Solomon died?

    The Israelites argued over who should be king, and they split into two kingdoms.

LESSON 43: GOD CHOSE JONAH AND OTHER MEN TO BE HIS MESSENGERS.

Scripture

Jonah 1, Jonah 2:1, 10, Jonah 3:1-5, 10, Psalm 139:1-18, Isaiah 10:5-6, Jeremiah 20:5

Lesson Outline

1. God has communicated with people from the beginning.
2. God told Jonah what He wanted him to do. (Jonah 1:1-2)
3. Jonah disobeyed the Lord. (Jonah 1:3-10; Psalm 139:1-18)
4. A great fish swallowed Jonah. (Jonah 1:11-17)
5. The Lord delivered Jonah. (Jonah 2:1, 10)
6. God repeated His command to Jonah. (Jonah 3:1-2)
7. Jonah obeyed, and Nineveh repented. (Jonah 3:3-5, 10)
8. The prophets warned Judah and Israel of God's coming judgment. (Isaiah 10:5-6; Jeremiah 20:5)

(?) Review Questions from Lesson 42.

Lesson Outline Developed

1) God has communicated with people from the beginning.

- **God wants everyone everywhere to know the truth.**

    God created all people, and God loves all people. He wants everyone to be delivered from the power of Satan, sin and death. Therefore, from the very beginning of the world, God has communicated with people so they would know His will. We learned that God spoke to Adam and Eve, to Cain, to Noah and to many others.

God also chose messengers to speak His words to the people. We have learned about some of God's messengers.

- Noah was God's messenger. While he was building the boat, he was also telling people God's message. He warned them that God hated their wicked ways and that He was going to send a flood to destroy everything in the world. He told them that God commanded them to repent and to believe only in Him.

- Moses was also God's messenger. God gave His message to Moses, and Moses gave it to Pharaoh and to the Israelites. God continued to speak to Moses, and Moses told God's message to the Israelites during the time when God was leading the Israelites toward the land He had promised to give them. God also used Moses as His messenger to the nation of Israel when He gave them His commandments at Mt. Sinai.

God continued to send messengers to Israel and Judah to teach them His ways and to warn them of His judgment on sin. God also sent His messengers to other nations who were living near the land of Israel.

② God told Jonah what He wanted him to do.

One day, God spoke to an Israelite named Jonah. God told him to take God's message to the wicked people in the city of Nineveh.

📖 Read Jonah 1:1-2.

☞ **Teacher:** Point to the name, **"Jonah,"** on the chronological chart.

☞ **Teacher:** Point to Nineveh on the map.

③ Jonah disobeyed the Lord.

- **The Assyrians were the enemies of the Israelites.**

    The people of Nineveh were not the descendants of Abraham, Isaac and Jacob.

    Jonah did not want to take God's message to the people of Nineveh because He did not want the enemies of Israel to repent and so escape from God's judgment. So Jonah disobeyed the Lord.

    📖 Read Jonah 1:3-10.

    Jonah tried to flee from God's presence. Could Jonah really flee from God's presence by going out onto the ocean? No! God is everywhere.

- **God is the maker, owner and controller of the whole earth.**

LESSON 43: GOD CHOSE JONAH AND OTHER MEN TO BE HIS MESSENGERS.

God is near every person. No one can escape from Him. Not even Satan or the spirits can hide from God.

King David wrote in the Bible that God is near every person and that no one can escape from Him.

📖 Read Psalm 139:1-18.

④ A great fish swallowed Jonah.

Let's read what happened to Jonah.

📖 Read Jonah 1:11-17.

It was not hard for God to prepare a fish that could swallow Jonah. God had created all things in the beginning, and there isn't anything too hard for Him to do.

- **Jonah was in the belly of the fish for three days and three nights.**

Teacher: As you prepare to teach, read Matthew 12:39-40, but do not read these verses to the people when you teach the lesson.

He could not get out. Only God could save him

- **Jonah's helpless condition is similar to your condition as sinners.**

Just as Jonah could not deliver himself from the belly of the fish, you cannot deliver yourself from Satan's power, from the sin which controls your lives, or from the judgment of God. Only God can save you.

⑤ The Lord delivered Jonah.

📖 Read Jonah 2:1.

- **Jonah admitted to the Lord that he couldn't save himself.**

He knew that he couldn't deliver himself from the belly of the fish. Jonah repented of his disobedience and called out to the Lord, asking to be delivered.

📖 Read Jonah 2:10.

- **The Lord saved Jonah from dying inside that great fish.**

☞ **Teacher:** Show a picture of Jonah on the shore after God rescued him from the great fish.

- **God is the only Savior.**

    God is the Savior of all those who agree with Him, trust in Him, and admit that they cannot escape from His judgment. We have already learned this.

    - God saved Noah from drowning in the flood because he trusted in Him.
    - God saved the Israelites every time they repented and trusted Him to rescue them from their enemies.
    - God saved Jonah from the belly of the fish when he repented and trusted in God.

(6) God repeated His command to Jonah.

📖 Read Jonah 3:1-2.

Even though Jonah had disobeyed Him, God had not changed His mind about what He wanted Jonah to do. God told Jonah again to go to Nineveh.

- **God does not change.**

    He is the same today as He was in the days of Jonah. Sometimes people ignore God's Word, thinking that they can escape God by refusing to listen to His message. But no one can escape. God said He will judge and punish all sinners, and God always does what He says.

(7) Jonah obeyed, and Nineveh repented.

Jonah obeyed the Lord this time and went to Nineveh to preach God's message.

📖 Read Jonah 3:3-5, 10.

- **The people of Nineveh believed and repented because of God's message through Jonah.**

    They showed that they were repenting of their sin by wearing sackcloth which was a coarse black cloth, usually made of goat's hair. The people of Nineveh agreed with God and asked for His mercy.

- **God wants you to be like the people of Nineveh.**

    He wants you to believe His message, repent and trust in Him to show you the way to be saved from His judgment.

LESSON 43: GOD CHOSE JONAH AND OTHER MEN TO BE HIS MESSENGERS.

Teacher: We must be careful how we teach repentance. Many people teach that repentance means to leave, or promise to leave, all sin. But this is incorrect.

Repentance is a change of mind, a change of attitude toward God, oneself and one's own sin. Repentance is the sinner acknowledging before God, "God, You are right. I am wrong. Everything You commanded is good and righteous and holy. I have failed to obey You as I should. I have no hope in my own ability to save myself from the power of my sin or the judgment it deserves." That is true repentance which leads to the new birth and God's work of sanctification in the lives of His children (Ephesians 2:8-10).

God doesn't ask a sinner to promise to leave his sin and "never do it again" before He will save him. God doesn't ask for the vain promises of helpless sinners. God doesn't strike a bargain with the sinner. He does not say, "You do this, and I will do that." God does not require reformation as a prerequisite for salvation. Eternal life is a gift given by God's grace alone (Romans 6:23; Ephesians 2:8-9).

⑧ The prophets warned Judah and Israel of God's coming judgment.

- **Jonah was one of God's messengers.**

    God chose other men in addition to Jonah to be His messengers. Some of them spoke God's message to Israel and to Judah, and some of them spoke God's message to the surrounding countries.

- **God's messengers warned of God's coming judgments.**

    These messengers were called prophets because they spoke God's message and told what God said would happen in the future. The prophets told the people to repent, that is, to agree with God that they had sinned against Him and deserved His judgment.

☞ **Teacher:** Point to the word, **"Prophets,"** on the chronological chart.

- **The prophets said that God will not accept worship from anyone who follows any other spirit or god.**

    Many of the Israelites who worshiped in the temple also worshiped idols. Through the prophets, God told the Israelites that they must choose whom they were going to serve. They could not be God-worshipers if they were idol worshipers. Those who worship God must do so from their hearts, and their worship must be according to God's Word. God is the only true God

- **God's prophets also reminded the Israelites of God's laws given to them through Moses.**

    Many of the Israelites had disobeyed these laws. The prophets told the people that the Lord said they must repent or He would punish them by sending their enemies to fight against them. These enemies would conquer them and lead them away captive to foreign lands.

- **The prophet Isaiah warned Israel, the northern ten tribes.**

    Isaiah said that the Lord would send the Assyrians to fight against them and capture them if they didn't repent. Although the Assyrians had repented when God sent Jonah to them, they did not continue to follow the God of Israel.

    📖 Read Isaiah 10:5-6.

    👉 **Teacher:** Point to Assyria on the map.

- **God sent Jeremiah to warn the people of Jerusalem and Judah.**

    Jeremiah said that if they did not repent, the Lord would send the Babylonians to fight against them and capture them.

    📖 Read Jeremiah 20:5.

    👉 **Teacher:** Point to Babylon on the map.

- **God has not changed.**

    Just as God warned Israel and Judah through the prophets that He would punish them for sinning by worshiping idols, so He warns people today through the Bible that He will punish those who sin by worshiping or serving anyone or anything other than Him. God wants all people to repent and to trust only in Him.

❓ Questions

1. Why does God communicate with people?

    God communicates with people because He loves them and wants everyone to know the truth and be delivered from the power of Satan, sin and death.

2. Whom did God chose to speak His words to people?

    God chose messengers (prophets) to speak His words to people.

3. Why did God want Jonah to tell the people of Nineveh to repent?

    God wanted Jonah to tell the people of Nineveh to repent so that they could be saved from God's judgment.

LESSON 43: GOD CHOSE JONAH AND OTHER MEN TO BE HIS MESSENGERS.

4. Instead of going to Nineveh, what did Jonah try to do?

   Jonah tried to flee from God's presence by getting on a ship.

5. Can anyone flee from God's presence?

   No. No one can escape from God because God is everywhere.

6. What did the Lord do when Jonah disobeyed Him?

   The Lord prepared a large fish to swallow Jonah.

7. Could Jonah save himself from death in the belly of the fish?

   No. Jonah could not save himself.

8. Is there any way you can save yourself from the power of Satan, from the control of sin and from God's judgment?

   No. We cannot save ourselves.

9. Who was the only One who could rescue Jonah?

   Only God could rescue Jonah.

10. Who is the only One who can rescue you from Satan's power, from the control of sin and from God's punishment?

    Only God can rescue us.

11. What did the Lord do when Jonah repented and trusted in the Lord?

    The Lord made the big fish vomit Jonah up onto dry land.

12. Had God changed His mind and decided that Jonah did not need to go to Nineveh?

    No. God had not changed His mind. He still wanted Jonah to go to Nineveh.

13. Did the people of Nineveh repent when Jonah told them God's message?

    Yes. The people of Nineveh repented.

14. Did the Lord destroy the people of Nineveh?

    No. The Lord did not punish them at that time.

15. What was God's message to Israel and Judah through the prophets?

    The prophets told Israel and Judah to repent, to destroy their idols, and to trust only in the Lord.

16. What did the Lord say He would do if Israel and Judah refused to repent?

    The Lord said that He would punish them by sending their enemies to conquer them and lead them away captive to foreign lands.

17. Will God still punish those who worship or serve anyone or anything other than Him?

    Yes. God will punish all who sin by worshiping or serving anyone or anything other than Him.

18. God communicated with Israel and Judah through His prophets. How does God communicate with people today?

    God communicates with us through the Bible.

LESSON 44: GOD TOLD THE PROPHETS TO WRITE MANY THINGS ABOUT THE COMING DELIVERER.

Scripture

Psalm 16:10, Psalm 22:6-8, 16, 18, Psalm 27:12, Psalm 41:9, Psalm 68:18, Psalm 69:4, Isaiah 7:14, Isaiah 9:7, Isaiah 11:2, Isaiah 50:6, Isaiah 53:3-5, 7, 9, 12, Jeremiah 6:13-14, Hosea 11:1, Micah 5:2, Zechariah 11:12-13

Lesson Outline

(1) God had not abandoned His promise to send the Deliverer.

(2) God told the prophets to write down many things about the coming Deliverer. (See chart.)

(3) Most of the Israelites refused to obey God's message through His prophets. (Jeremiah 6:13-14)

(?) Review Questions from Lesson 43.

Teacher: For this lesson, you will need to prepare a chart which lists Old Testament prophecies concerning Christ. (See sample on the next page.) Write the Old Testament prophecies along with the Old Testament references on the chart, and leave a blank place to write in the New Testament references when you come to each fulfillment in the life of Christ. You will be told in the New Testament lessons when to write in the fulfillment. The Old Testament references are arranged by the order in which they are fulfilled in the lessons on the life of Christ.

Make the chart large enough to be clearly seen by everyone. You can also make smaller charts to carry and use in house meetings.

If you have a regular meeting place, leave the chart up on the wall so that the people can refer to it. When you teach from the life of Christ, this chart will be a constant reminder of the main events as well as a testimony of the faithfulness of God to do all that He says.

What God said about the Deliverer He would send		How God's Word Came True
Isaiah 9:7	David's descendant	
Isaiah 7:14	Born of a virgin	
Micah 5:2	Born in Bethlehem	
Hosea 11:1	Be brought out of Egypt	
Isaiah 11:2	Some of His characteristics	
Isaiah 53:4-5	Suffer for others	
Psalm 41:9	Betrayed by a friend	
Zechariah 11:12-13	Sold for 30 pieces of silver	
Psalm 27:12	Accused by false witnesses	
Isaiah 50:6	Smitten and spat upon	
Isaiah 53:7	Silent when accused	
Isaiah 53:3	Rejected by Jews	
Psalm 69:4	Hated without a cause	
Psalm 22:16	His hands and feet pierced	
Psalm 22:18	His clothing gambled for	
Isaiah 53:12	Die with the wicked	
Psalm 22:6-8	Mocked and insulted	
Isaiah 53:9	Buried with the rich	
Psalm 16:10	Rise again	
Psalm 68:18	Go back to Heaven	

Lesson Outline Developed

1) God had not abandoned His promise to send the Deliverer.

- **God gave the first promise of the Deliverer in the garden in Eden.**

    God promised that the Deliverer would destroy Satan, deliver people from sin, Satan and

LESSON 44: GOD TOLD THE PROPHETS TO WRITE MANY THINGS ABOUT THE COMING DELIVERER.

death, and make it possible for people to again be in a right relationship with God.

- **God promised individuals that the Deliverer would be one of their descendants.**

  God told Abraham, Isaac and Jacob that the Deliverer would be one of their descendants. Later, the Lord promised David that the coming Deliverer would be of his family line and would rule as king forever. All through the years, God repeatedly reminded the Israelites about the promised Deliverer.

- **Because God loved people, He never forgot His promise to send the Deliverer.**

  Even though thousands of years had passed since God first promised to send the Deliverer, God had not forgotten His promise. Even though the majority of people were not interested in His will for them and did not care about His promises, God never abandoned His promise. Because God loved the world and did not want anyone to go to everlasting punishment, He planned to send the Deliverer.

- **God foretold many things about the Deliverer.**

  Hundreds of years before the Deliverer came, God foretold many things about Him. God was able to tell what the Deliverer would be like because God knows everything before it happens.

- **God chose prophets to write down what He told them about the Deliverer.**

  The prophets wrote as God directed them, and the words they wrote are recorded in the Bible.

  In our lesson today, we are going to read some of the things that God told the prophets to write about the Deliverer.

- **Many of the things written by the prophets had two meanings.**

  The first meaning was about something that had already taken place historically or would happen in the prophet's lifetime. The other meaning was about an event that would happen to the Deliverer in the future.

Teacher: As you teach about each prophecy, point to it on the chart.

Do not explain the New Testament fulfillment of these prophecies at this time. For example, when you teach the prophecy from Psalm 22:16 that the Deliverer's hands and feet would be pierced, do not explain that the Savior will be crucified. When you teach the fulfillment from the New Testament, you will point back to this chart and write in the New Testament fulfillment of each prophecy.

Building on Firm Foundations
- Volume 2: Evangelism:
Genesis to The Ascension

② God told the prophets to write down many things about the coming Deliverer.

- **The Deliverer would be David's descendant.**

    📖 Read Isaiah 9:7.

    The prophet Isaiah wrote that the Deliverer would be one of David's descendants and that the Deliverer would rule as king forever. God had made this same promise to King David when he was alive.

- **The Deliverer would be born of a virgin.**

    Isaiah also wrote that the Deliverer would not have a human father. His mother would be a virgin.

    📖 Read Isaiah 7:14.

    God had foretold in the garden in Eden that a child who would be born of a virgin woman would destroy Satan.

- **The Deliverer would be born in Bethlehem.**

    The prophet Micah wrote that the Deliverer would be born in the town of Bethlehem.

    📖 Read Micah 5:2.

☞ **Teacher:** Point to Bethlehem on the map.

- **God would bring the Deliverer out of Egypt.**

    📖 Read Hosea 11:1.

    We have already learned that God loved the Israelites and brought them out of slavery in Egypt. The prophet Hosea wrote about this historical event, but although he probably didn't know it, what he wrote also pointed forward to an event in the life of the Deliverer. Later we will learn how God brought the Deliverer out of Egypt.

☞ **Teacher:** Point to Egypt on the map.

- **The prophet Isaiah wrote about some of the Deliverer's characteristics.**

    📖 Read Isaiah 11:2.

- **The Deliverer would suffer for others.**

    📖 Read Isaiah 53:4-5.

- **The Deliverer would be betrayed by a friend.**

LESSON 44: GOD TOLD THE PROPHETS TO WRITE MANY THINGS ABOUT THE COMING DELIVERER.

📖 Read Psalm 41:9.

When David wrote this, he was talking about one of his close friends who betrayed him. But God guided David to write these words because God knew that the same thing would happen to the Deliverer. One of the Deliverer's friends, a man who would often eat meals with the Deliverer, would turn against Him and betray Him.

- **The Deliverer would be sold for 30 pieces of silver.**

    📖 Read Zechariah 11:12-13.

    Although these verses are referring to an event at the time of the prophet Zechariah, later we will learn that God was also foretelling that the coming Deliverer would be sold for 30 pieces of silver.

- **The Deliverer would be accused by false witnesses.**

    📖 Read Psalm 27:12.

    David was asking God to deliver him from his enemies who told lies about him. God knew that people would also tell lies about the Deliverer.

- **The Deliverer would be beaten and spit upon.**

    📖 Read Isaiah 50:6.

    Isaiah wrote these words as though these things happened to him, but God knew they would happen to the Deliverer. Not only would the Deliverer be beaten and spit upon, but He would humbly allow people to do these things to Him. He would patiently endure suffering and disrespect.

- **The Deliverer would be silent when accused.**

    📖 Read Isaiah 53:7.

    Sheep are not like other animals. Other animals make lots of noise when they are being held. However, even when their wool is being cut off, sheep don't usually cry out. The Deliverer would be silent when people told lies about Him.

- **The Deliverer would be rejected by the Jews.**

    📖 Read Isaiah 53:3.

    The prophet wrote as though this was already happening, but later we will learn that these words were pointing forward to what would happen to the Deliverer.

- **The Deliverer would be hated without a cause.**

    📖 Read Psalm 69:4.

    The verses are written as though they were already happening, but later we will learn that they were pointing forward to what would happen to the Deliverer.

- **The Deliverer's hands and feet would be pierced.**

  📖 Read Psalm 22:16.

  The Israelites did not keep dogs as pets or use them for hunting. Dogs were usually savage and would attack people. The Bible often uses the word "dog" to refer to wicked, vicious people. Wicked people would surround the Deliverer, and they would pierce His hands and feet.

- **The Deliverer's clothing would be gambled for.**

  📖 Read Psalm 22:18.

- **The Deliverer would die with the wicked.**

  📖 Read Isaiah 53:12.

  This verse says several things about the Deliverer, but we want to notice one particular thing. The Deliverer will be treated as if He is a wicked man and will die with wicked men.

- **The Deliverer would be mocked and insulted.**

  📖 Read Psalm 22:6-8.

- **The Deliverer would be buried with the rich.**

  📖 Read Isaiah 53:9.

  The Deliverer will die with wicked men, but because He will be a good man, He will be buried in the grave of a rich man.

- **The Deliverer would rise again.**

  📖 Read Psalm 16:10.

  This verse was written as though the Deliverer Himself was speaking to God. Although the Deliverer will die, He will be sure that God will not allow His body to decompose but that God will raise Him from the dead before this can happen.

- **The Deliverer would go back to Heaven.**

  📖 Read Psalm 68:18.

  Later you will understand that this verse is saying that, after the Deliverer is raised from the dead, He will go up into Heaven.

③ Most of the Israelites refused to obey God's message through His prophets.

- **Most of the Israelites did not believe God in their hearts.**

  We learned in our last lesson that God's prophets told the people they must repent, destroy their idols and obey only the Lord. If they refused, then the Lord said He would

LESSON 44: GOD TOLD THE PROPHETS TO WRITE MANY THINGS ABOUT THE COMING DELIVERER.

allow their enemies to conquer them and take them as slaves to faraway countries.

Most of the Israelites refused to repent and put their trust in the Lord alone. They persecuted and killed God's messengers. They continued to worship idols. They followed the wicked ways of the surrounding nations.

☞ **Teacher:** Show a picture of a prophet being stoned.

Most of the Israelites continued to go to the temple to worship the Lord and to offer sacrifices, but they did not obey the commandments of God. Even most of the priests and leaders of the Israelites were evil men. They did not trust in the Lord or obey His commands. Although the Israelites said many good things to God, He did not accept them because He knew that they did not believe Him in their hearts. They were worshiping God with their lips, but in their hearts, they were unrepentant and they didn't trust in God.

- **Only God knows our thoughts and knows what we are really like in our hearts.**

    No one can fool God. Other people can hear what we say and see what we do, but they do not know our thoughts. God says that we are all sinners. None of us pleases God by what we do.

- **False prophets told lies to the Israelites.**

    False prophets claimed to be the messengers of God, but they were the servants of Satan. They spoke lies to the people. They told the people that everything would be all right and that God would not punish them for their sins.

    📖 Read Jeremiah 6:13-14.

- **Satan still uses people to speak lies.**

    People may tell you that God's Word is not true, or they may say that God will not punish sin. They may tell you that you must continue to follow the ways of your ancestors instead of listening to God's Word. Every person must make a choice either to believe the words of men or the Word of God. Beware of the lies of Satan which he speaks through people.

- **Some of the Israelites believed God and were waiting for the Deliverer to come.**

    Among the Israelites, there were always a few who believed God's words given through the prophets. They trusted in the Lord and tried to follow His commands. They were accepted by the Lord because of their faith in Him. They were like Abel, Noah, Abraham and others who realized they were sinners and trusted in the Lord for His mercy and forgiveness. They were waiting for the coming Deliverer whom God had promised would save them from Satan and the punishment for their sins.

Teacher: It is clear from what Zacharias said that the Old Testament saints at this time had a clear understanding of the redemptive purpose of the coming Savior (Luke 1:76-79).

Who are you like? Are you like the Israelites who refused to believe God, or are you like those who believed His words and trusted only in Him?

❓ Questions

1. Although thousands of years had gone by since God first promised to send the Deliverer, had God forgotten His promise?
   No. God had not forgotten His promise to send the Deliverer.

2. Whom did God choose to write down information about the coming Deliverer?
   God chose prophets to write down what He told them about the Deliverer.

3. Where are the words that the prophets wrote about the Deliverer recorded?
   The words of the prophets are recorded in the Bible.

4. Did the Israelites listen to the prophet's message to repent, destroy their idols and put their trust in God alone?
   No. Most of the Israelites refused to repent, destroy their idols and trust in God alone.

5. What did the Israelites do to the prophets?
   They persecuted and killed the prophets.

6. Did the Israelites continue to go to the temple, offer sacrifices and worship God?
   Yes. They continued to go to the temple, offer sacrifices and worship God.

7. Did He accept their worship and their sacrifices?
   No. God did not accept their worship and sacrifices.

8. Why didn't God accept the worship and sacrifices of many of the Israelites?
   God did not accept them because they were worshiping Him only with their lips, but they were unrepentant in their hearts.

9. Who knows our thoughts and knows what we are really like in our hearts?
   God knows our thoughts and He knows what we are really like in our hearts.

10. Which Israelites did God accept?
    God accepted the Israelites who agreed with Him that they were sinners and trusted in Him for His mercy and forgiveness.

11. For whom were these believing Israelites waiting?
    They were waiting for the Deliverer whom God had promised would save them from Satan and the punishment of their sins.

LESSON 45: GOD PUNISHED ISRAEL AND JUDAH, BUT HE BROUGHT SOME OF HIS PEOPLE BACK FROM ASSYRIA AND BABYLON.

Scripture

2 Kings 17:1-8, 2 Kings 25:1-12

Lesson Outline

(1) God judged Israel and Judah. (2 Kings 17:1-8; 25:1-12)

(2) Some of the exiles returned from Assyria and Babylon.

(3) God allowed other nations to conquer the Jew's land.

(4) The scribes, Pharisees and Sadducees were the religious leaders of the Jews.

(5) The Jews built synagogues where they read and taught God's Law.

(6) Some of the Jews believed God.

(?) Review Questions from Lesson 44.

Lesson Outline Developed

(1) God judged Israel and Judah.

- **God is patient. He does not immediately punish sinners.**

    We already learned that God is patient. Do you remember how God was patient with the people in Noah's time? God the Spirit tried to convince those people to repent but they would not. God waited for 120 years before He sent the flood to destroy them.

    In the same way, God was patient with Israel and Judah. For many hundreds of years, He sent His prophets to warn the Israelites of God's anger because of their sin and His coming punishment on them if they did not repent.

    Do you think that the Israelites believed that God would punish them by allowing their enemies to fight against them, conquer their land and make them captives? No! The

Israelites would not believe God, and they did not repent of their sin. Therefore, God allowed their enemies to fight against them and conquer them.

- **The Assyrians conquered the ten northern tribes and took them away captive.**

    📖 Read 2 Kings 17:5-8.

    Do you remember the story of Jonah? The Assyrians were the people to whom God sent Jonah. When Jonah went to the city of Nineveh, the people repented, but later they turned away from following God.

☞ **Teacher:** Point to Assyria on the map.

The Assyrians came and fought against the people of the ten northern tribes of Israel and took many of them away to Assyria.

The Assyrians then brought people from other countries to live in the northern part of the land of Israel. These people worshiped idols. They did not know the true and living God.

Many of the Israelites from the northern tribes who were not taken to Assyria intermarried with these people who had been brought there from other countries. The descendants of these mixed marriages were known as Samaritans. The Samaritans claimed to worship the Lord, but they worshiped Him according to their own ways and not according to the way God had told Moses. They refused to go up to God's temple in Jerusalem to worship, so the Lord would not accept their worship.

Teacher: As you prepare to teach, read John 4:20-22, but do not read these verses to the people when you teach the lesson.

- **The Babylonians conquered the two southern tribes and took them away captive.**

    The two southern tribes also refused to repent, so God allowed the Babylonians to take them captive into the land of Babylon.

    The Babylonians smashed down the stone walls of Jerusalem. They also tore down and burned the temple of God which Solomon the king had built.

    📖 Read 2 Kings 25:1-12.

☞ **Teacher:** Show a picture of the Israelites being taken away as slaves and the destruction of the walls of Jerusalem.

LESSON 45: GOD PUNISHED ISRAEL AND JUDAH, BUT HE BROUGHT SOME OF HIS PEOPLE BACK FROM ASSYRIA AND BABYLON.

- **No one can escape God's judgment.**

    God did what He said. He had warned the Israelites that He would send other nations to fight against them and conquer them if they did not repent. The people would not believe His Word so He punished them.

    God will always punish those who refuse to believe Him. All unbelievers will be thrown into the place of punishment prepared for Satan and his evil spirits. No one can escape from God's judgment.

2) Some of the exiles returned from Assyria and Babylon.

After many years, some of the Israelites who had been taken away to Assyria returned to their own land, and the people of Judah who had been taken captive to Babylon repented and asked the Lord to take them back to their own land. The Lord heard their cries for His help, and He brought many of them back to Jerusalem. Those who returned from Babylon rebuilt Jerusalem as well as the stone walls around the city.

They also rebuilt the temple in Jerusalem.

☞ **Teacher:** Show a picture of the Israelites rebuilding the temple.

When the Israelites returned to their land, they started to be known by a different name. They were called Jews. The Israelite people are still known as Jews or as Israel. Their land is called the land of Israel.

3) God allowed other nations to conquer the Jew's land.

The Jews continued to worship the Lord, although the majority did not do it from their hearts. They went to the temple with their sacrifices, but most of them did not really believe they were sinners and needed God's mercy. Therefore, the Lord punished them once again by allowing other nations to conquer them.

- **The Greeks took control of the Jews' country.**

    Although the Greeks took control of the land of Israel, they allowed the Jews to continue to live there. The Jews learned to speak the Greek language.

☞ **Teacher:** Point to Greece on the map.

- **The Romans took control of the Jews' country.**

    After some time had gone by, the Romans conquered the Greeks, and they took control of Jerusalem and the land of Israel.

☞ **Teacher:** Point to Rome on the map.

The Romans made the Jews obey them and pay taxes.

☞ **Teacher:** Show a picture of the Romans collecting taxes from the Jews.

If anyone disobeyed, the Romans punished him. They killed many Jews with swords and spears, and they crucified other Jews.

Teacher: Make sure the people know what swords, spears and crucifixion are. Show pictures and explain as necessary.

The king of the Romans, known by the name Caesar, lived in the city of Rome. Caesar appointed men to rule for him over the countries which he had conquered.

The Romans worshiped many false gods. They also worshiped their king, Caesar, because they thought he was a god. Nevertheless, they permitted the Jews to continue worshiping the Lord by going to the temple in Jerusalem.

④ The scribes, Pharisees and Sadducees were the religious leaders of the Jews.

- **The scribes copied the words of God.**

  We have learned that God chose men to write His words down so that all people could know the truth about God. Moses and the prophets wrote on long pieces of paper what God told them to write.

  In those days, they did not have books with pages. The writing in my Bible was done by a machine, but there were no printing machines in the days when the Bible was first written. Moses and the prophets wrote by hand what God told them.

  To preserve the words of God and to make the Scriptures widely available, the scribes copied what had been written on other scrolls. The scribes meticulously copied every little mark from the original Scriptures. To make sure they had not forgotten anything, they counted each letter and each word in the original writings, and when they had finished the copy, they checked to see that the copy had the same number of letters and words as were in the original. If the number of letters and words in the copy was incorrect, they destroyed the copy and began again.

LESSON 45: GOD PUNISHED ISRAEL AND JUDAH, BUT HE BROUGHT SOME OF HIS PEOPLE BACK FROM ASSYRIA AND BABYLON.

We can trust the Bible because God has preserved the message of the original writers.

The men who copied the words of God were known as "scribes." They were also known as "lawyers" and "teachers of the Law" because they were the men who were supposed to know and be able to explain the real meaning of the words of God.

Many scribes were very proud because of their knowledge of the Word of God. They thought they were pleasing to God just because they knew what God's Word said. They didn't realize that it is more important to God that we believe His Word and obey it.

- **The Pharisees were leaders of the Jews.**

The Pharisees thought they could please God and be accepted by Him by obeying many different rules. Although they knew God's commandments, they did not teach them correctly because they added their own interpretation and rules. They taught that a person must follow their rules to be accepted by God.

The Pharisees did not think that they were sinners like other people. They kept themselves separate from anyone who was not a Pharisee. They were proud and thought that they were good enough to be accepted by God because of the things that they did.

- **The Sadducees were also leaders of the Jews.**

The Sadducees went to the temple and claimed to worship God. However, they did not believe many things which God had written in His Word.

Instead of being interested in what God had said, the Sadducees were more interested in their political position. They wanted to please the Roman rulers and make sure that they kept their position as leaders of the Jews. They did not truly trust in God from their hearts.

(5) The Jews built synagogues where they read and taught God's Law.

During these times, the Jews built meeting houses [synagogues] in every town and city.

On the last day of the week, the Jews met in their synagogues, and the religious teachers and leaders read and explained the writings of Moses and the prophets. However, often their explanations were not the true message that God had spoken and which Moses and the prophets had written in the Bible.

The Jews worshiped and offered animal sacrifices in the temple, and they also met in their synagogues to hear the Scriptures read and explained. However, most of them did not truly trust in the Lord or obey His Word.

(6) Some of the Jews believed God.

Even though most of the Jews did not trust God, there were always some Jews who believed. They were like Abraham, Isaac, Jacob, Moses and David who realized that they were sinners and needed God's mercy. These believing Jews knew that their sin would separate them forever from God, so they came to God in the way that He had said in His Word. By faith, they trusted God to accept their sacrifice of animals and the blood of the animals.

These Jews were waiting for the promised Deliverer to come. They believed that God is faithful and that He always does what He says. Thousands of years had passed since God had first promised to send the Deliverer, but these believing Jews knew that He would come at the exact time which God had planned.

Questions

1. What did the Lord allow to happen to the ten northern tribes of Israel?

   The Lord allowed the Assyrians to take them as captives.

2. What did the Lord allow to happen to the two southern tribes?

   The Lord allowed the Babylonians to take the two southern tribes captive into the land of Babylon.

3. Did any of the Israelites return to their own land?

   Yes. Some who were taken into Assyria returned, and the Lord brought back those who repented from Babylon.

4. What did they do when they returned to Jerusalem?

   They rebuilt the city and its stone walls, and they rebuilt the temple of the Lord.

5. What new name was given to the Israelites?

   The Israelites were called "Jews."

6. What other nations did God allow to conquer the Jews' land?

   God allowed the Greeks and the Romans to conquer the Jews' land.

7. Whom did the Romans worship?

   The Romans worshiped many false gods and also their king, Caesar.

8. Who were the scribes?

   The scribes were the Jewish religious leaders who made the hand-written copies of the Scripture.

9. Of what were the scribes proud?

   The scribes were proud of their knowledge of the Word of God.

10. Who were the Pharisees?

    The Pharisees were some of the religious leaders of the Jews.

11. What did the Pharisees add to God's law?

    The Pharisees added many of their own rules to God's law.

12. What did the Pharisees think made them acceptable to God?

    The Pharisees thought that obeying the rules would make them acceptable to God.

13. Who were the Sadducees?

    The Sadducees were some of the religious leaders of the Jews.

14. Did the Sadducees believe all of God's Word?

    No. The Sadducees did not believe many of the things that God had written in His Word.

15. Instead of being interested in what God had said, what were the Sadducees interested in?

    The Sadducees were interested in pleasing the Roman rulers and making sure that they kept their position as rulers over the Jews.

16. Did the Sadducees trust God?

    No. Even though the Sadducees went to the temple and seemed to worship God, they did not truly trust God in their hearts.

17. What were synagogues?

    Synagogues were buildings which the Jews erected in all their towns as places to teach the laws of God given through Moses and the writings of the prophets.

18. How often did the Jews meet in the synagogues?

    The Jews met in the synagogues one day each week.

19. Were there any Jews who believed God?

    Yes. Some of the Jews realized they were sinners and trusted in God.

20. How did the believing Jews demonstrate their faith in God?

    They came to God in the way He had told Moses, bringing animals and blood sacrifices.

21. What were these believing Jews waiting for God to do?

    They were waiting for God to send the Deliverer.

Teacher: This is the last Phase 1 lesson from the Old Testament. Continue directly into the Phase 1 lessons from the New Testament without mentioning it to your students. The Old Testament and New Testament lessons are to be taught as one unit. No break should be allowed in the chronological teaching program. Continue to build in evangelism by going directly into the New Testament lessons.

LESSON 46: GOD FORETOLD THE BIRTHS OF JOHN AND OF JESUS.

Scripture

Luke 1:5-17, 24-38

Lesson Outline

(1) Malachi was one of God's prophets.

(2) God promised that Zacharias and Elizabeth would have a son. (Luke 1:5-14)

(3) God gave John the work of preparing the way for the Deliverer. (Luke 1:15-17, 24-25)

(4) God promised Mary a son. (Luke 1:26-31)

(5) Jesus would be both man and the Son of God. (Luke 1:32-33)

(6) Jesus, the Deliverer, would not have a human father. (Luke 1:34-38)

(?) Review Questions from Lesson 45.

Lesson Outline Developed

(1) Malachi was one of God's prophets.

- **God's prophets told God's message to the people.**

    In the Bible times, God spoke His message to prophets, and they told God's message to the people. Malachi was one of God's prophets.

- **Malachi told the people that another prophet would come to prepare them for the Deliverer.**

    Malachi reminded the Jews that God's promised Deliverer would come to save them. Malachi also told them that, before God sent the Deliverer, He would send another prophet. This prophet would teach the people so that they would be ready for the Deliverer to come.

> **Teacher:** As you prepare to teach, read Malachi 3:1, but do not read this verse to the people when you teach the lesson.

After Malachi died, God did not speak His word through His prophets for four hundred years.

- **Some of the Jews believed that God would send the Deliverer, but most did not believe.**

During those four hundred years while God did not speak through a prophet, the Jews continued to go to the temple and offer sacrifices. They also went to the synagogues each week to hear the Word of God. However, very few of the Jews were waiting and watching for the Deliverer to come.

Even though most of the Jews did not trust God, there were always some who believed God. They were like Abraham, Isaac, Jacob, Moses and David who realized that they were sinners and needed God's mercy. They believed that God was going to send the Deliverer, and they were waiting for Him to come.

② God promised that Zacharias and Elizabeth would have a son.

📖 Read Luke 1:5-14.

- **Zacharias and his wife, Elizabeth, were Jews who trusted in God and believed His Word.**

Zacharias and Elizabeth came to God in the way God had instructed the Jews through Moses, bringing the animals to be killed and offering the blood sacrifices. Because they trusted in God and came to Him the way He had told them, God accepted them. God has always accepted those, like Abel, who trusted in Him and came the way He said.

- **Zacharias and Elizabeth were childless.**

Both Zacharias and Elizabeth were old, and they had never been able to have children.

- **God's angel spoke to Zacharias.**

> ☞ **Teacher:** Show a picture of Zacharias in the temple.

Zacharias was one of the priests who served in the temple in Jerusalem. While he was doing his work as a priest, God's angel spoke to him.

- **God's angel promised Zacharias that he and Elizabeth would have a son.**

The angel told Zacharias that he must name his son, John.

LESSON 46: GOD FORETOLD THE BIRTHS OF JOHN AND OF JESUS.

☞ **Teacher:** Point to the name, **"John,"** on the chronological chart.

③ God gave John the work of preparing the way for the Deliverer.

📖 Read Luke 1:15-17.

- **God's angel told Zacharias what John would be like and what he would do.**

  The Lord knew all about Zacharias' son even before he was conceived. God knows everything before it ever happens.

- **God had foretold about Zacharias' son through the prophet Malachi.**

  God had guided Malachi to write that God would send a prophet. He would be God's messenger to prepare the people for the Deliverer who would come. The angel told Zacharias that his son would go before the Lord to prepare the way for Him. John was the messenger that Malachi had written about.

- **Zacharias' son would prepare the people "for the Lord."**

  The angel told Zacharias that his son would prepare the people to recognize and believe in the Lord their God. The coming Deliverer was to be the Lord Himself.

- **Elizabeth became pregnant.**

  📖 Read Luke 1:24-25.

  God made it possible for Elizabeth to become pregnant, even though she had never been able to have a child. God always does what He says He will do.

④ God promised Mary a son.

- **Everything was ready for God to fulfill all of His promises regarding the Deliverer.**

  It was time for God to send the Deliverer!

  Listen to what God did next.

  📖 Read Luke 1:26-31.

- **God chose Mary to be the mother of the Deliverer.**

☞ **Teacher:** Show a picture of Gabriel announcing to Mary that she would be the mother of the Deliverer.

God sent an angel to tell a virgin named Mary that God had chosen her to be the mother of the Deliverer. Mary was just an ordinary young woman who, although she was a sinner, trusted in God to send the Deliverer.

☞ **Teacher:** Point to the name, **"Mary"** on the chronological chart.

God chose Mary to be the mother of the Deliverer because God does whatever He wants to do. He doesn't have to ask anyone for permission for what He does. God is supreme and sovereign.

- **God had never forgotten His promise to send the Deliverer.**

Mary was to name her son, "Jesus," which means Savior or Deliverer.

God loves all people in the whole world, and He wants sinners to be delivered from death and everlasting punishment with Satan and his demons.

☞ **Teacher:** Point to the name, **"Jesus,"** on the chronological chart.

⑤ Jesus would be both man and the Son of God.

The angel who told Mary that she was to be the mother of the Deliverer also told her some things about her future son.

- **The angel told Mary that the child she would give birth to would be God's Son.**

    📖 Read this portion of Luke 1:32, *"He will be great, and will be called the Son of the Highest...."*

Mary's son was going to be her son, but He would also be the "Son of the Highest." Jesus would be the Son of God.

In a previous lesson, we learned that, although there is only one God, there are three persons who are the one God: God the Father, God the Son and God the Spirit. These three are equal in every way

We have also learned that God is spirit. God the Father, God the Son and God the Spirit never had a body as we humans do. The Deliverer, however, had to be a human being, just as we are human beings, except that He must be sinless. Therefore, so that God's plan regarding the Deliverer could be fulfilled, God the Son, who was spirit, had to be born as a human being.

God chose Mary to be the mother of the Deliverer. The Deliverer, who was God the Son, had to come down from Heaven to be born on the earth as the child of Mary. Mary's son would be both God and man.

LESSON 46: GOD FORETOLD THE
BIRTHS OF JOHN AND OF JESUS.

- **The angel told Mary that her son would reign as king forever.**

    📖 Read Luke 1:32-33.

    Because the Deliverer would be a direct descendant of David the king, He was to be king over Israel. He was to be king forever.

    God was going to do what He had promised King David. God keeps His promises.

⑥ Jesus, the Deliverer, would not have a human father.

- **Mary could not understand how she could have a child who wouldn't have a human father.**

    📖 Read Luke 1:34-35

    The angel explained to Mary that God the Spirit would perform this miracle.

    This does not mean that the Holy Spirit would have intercourse with Mary.

Teacher: Be sure that the people clearly understand that the Holy Spirit did not have intercourse with Mary. This is especially important if they believe that the spirits can have intercourse with humans.

- **Jesus would not inherit Adam's sinfulness.**

    Because Jesus would not have a human father, He would be born sinless. All people are born sinners because the sin of Adam was passed down to us. But Jesus would be different. He would not have a human father. His Father would be God. Therefore, Jesus would not inherit Adam's sinfulness like every other person born into the world. He would be a perfect man, the Son of God.

- **God is almighty.**

    📖 Read Luke 1:36-37.

    It is impossible for a virgin to have a child! We all know that, and Mary knew that. It is also impossible for a woman to have a child after the age of childbearing has passed. But God can do the impossible. God had already performed a miracle for Elizabeth – she was pregnant with John even though she was past the age of childbearing. God was also going to perform a miracle so that Mary, a virgin, could have a child.

    With God, all things are possible. God can do anything.

    God had created the first man, Adam, out of the dust of the ground. God gives life to every person. It was not difficult for God to cause Mary to conceive a son without the child having a human father, and it was not difficult for God to give Elizabeth a child in her old age. Nothing is impossible with God.

- **Mary trusted in the Lord.**

    Mary accepted that the Lord's will for her to be the mother of the Deliverer was good.

    📖 Read Luke 1:38.

❓ Questions

1. What work did God plan to give to John, the son of Zacharias and Elizabeth?
    John's work would be to prepare the Jews to receive and trust in the Deliverer.

2. Was John the prophet that Malachi had written about?
    Yes. John was the prophet who would go before the Lord to prepare the way for Him.

3. Whom did God choose to be the mother of the Deliverer?
    God chose a virgin named Mary to be the mother of the Deliverer.

4. What was Mary to name her son?
    Mary was to name her son, Jesus.

5. What does the name, Jesus, mean?
    The name, Jesus, means Savior or Deliverer.

6. Would Jesus be just human?
    No. He would be both God and man.

7. What king would Mary's son be a descendant of?
    Mary's son would be a descendant of King David.

8. What did God promise to King David about the Deliverer?
    God had promised that the Deliverer would be a direct descendant of King David.

9. Would Jesus be conceived by a human father?
    No. Jesus would not be conceived by a human father.

10. How could Jesus be conceived without a human father?
    God was going to perform a miracle. God is almighty and can do anything He wishes to do.

11. Was Jesus to be the promised Deliverer?
    Yes. Jesus was to be the Deliverer whom God first promised in the garden in Eden.

LESSON 46: GOD FORETOLD THE BIRTHS OF JOHN AND OF JESUS.

12. Would Jesus inherit Adam's sinfulness?

    No. Because Jesus did not have a human father, He would not inherit Adam's sinfulness like every other person born into the world.

LESSON 47: GOD FULFILLED HIS PROMISE IN THE BIRTH OF JOHN.

Scripture

Luke 1:57, 67-79

Lesson Outline

(1) John was born. (Luke 1:57)

(2) Zacharias spoke a message from God about the Deliverer and about John. (Luke 1:67-79)

(?) Review Questions from Lesson 46.

Lesson Outline Developed

(1) John was born.

- **God fulfilled His promise to Zacharias.**

    📖 Read Luke 1:57.

☞ **Teacher:** Show a picture of Zacharias and Elizabeth, with Zacharias writing down the name of his son, John.

God did what He had promised Zacharias. His wife, Elizabeth, had a son, just as God said. They named him, John.

- **God always does what He says.**

    Can you think of some of the instances when God did what He said?

Teacher: Give the people time to answer. Guide them to think through and discuss the truth that God always does what He says.

- God warned Adam and Eve that they would die if they ate the fruit from the tree of the knowledge of good and evil. When they disobeyed God, they were separated from

Him, and after many years, their bodies also died.

- God warned the people in Noah's day that He would punish them if they did not repent. Because the people would not repent, God sent a flood to destroy everyone on the earth except Noah and his family.
- God promised to preserve the Israelites in Egypt while they were in slavery. God preserved the Israelites while they were slaves in Egypt.
- God promised to lead the Israelites out of Egypt after 400 years. God led them out.
- God promised to bring the Israelites to the land of Canaan, the land that God had promised would belong to Abraham's descendants. God brought them to the land of Canaan.
- God warned Israel and Judah that they would be taken captive by other nations if they did not repent of their sin. They did not repent, and they were taken captive by other nations.

God did all He promised from the beginning of the world, and He also fulfilled His promise to Zacharias and Elizabeth by giving them a son.

(2) Zacharias spoke a message from God about the Deliverer and about John.

Read Luke 1:67-79.

God the Spirit guided Zacharias to speak this message.

- **Zacharias said that God's promises concerning the Deliverer would soon be fulfilled.**

  Read Luke 1:67-71 again.

  Zacharias believed God's promises which were given through the prophets and written in the Bible. Zacharias knew that God's promised Deliverer would soon be coming to deliver mankind from Satan, sin and death.

  Each of you needs to be delivered from Satan, from the sinful things that control your lives, and from death and separation from God. Because all were born sinners, we all need God's deliverance. That is why God planned to send the Deliverer into the world.

- **Zacharias said that God was going to fulfill His promise to Abraham.**

  Read Luke 1:68, 72-75 again.

  Do you remember the promise that God made to Abraham? God had promised Abraham that one of his descendants would be the Deliverer. Even though at least 2,000 years had passed since God made that promise to Abraham, God had not forgotten. God always remembers and always does what He says.

LESSON 47: GOD FULFILLED HIS PROMISE IN THE BIRTH OF JOHN.

- **Zacharias said that John would prepare the people of Israel to believe on the Deliverer.**

    📖 Read Luke 1:76 again.

    In this part of his message, Zacharias was speaking about his son, John.

    When the angel spoke to Zacharias in the temple, he told him that his son was the prophet who would go ahead of the Lord to prepare the way for Him. Zacharias believed what God had told him through the angel. He believed that John was the prophet who was to speak God's Word to Israel and tell them that the Deliverer would soon come to them.

- **Zacharias said that the Deliverer was the Lord.**

    📖 Read Luke 1:76 again.

    It was "the Lord" who was coming as the Deliverer. John was to prepare the people so they would recognize that God was the Deliverer and so each person would put his trust in "the Lord" as his own personal deliverer.

    No ordinary man could deliver us from Satan, sin and death. The Lord, who is God, is the great Deliverer of all who trust in Him.

    We have already learned that God delivers those who trust in Him.

    ◦ Who delivered Noah and his family from the flood?
    ◦ Who delivered Isaac from death and provided a ram to die in his place?
    ◦ Who delivered Lot from the destruction of Sodom and Gomorrah?
    ◦ Who delivered Joseph from prison in Egypt?
    ◦ Who delivered the Israelites from slavery in Egypt?
    ◦ Who delivered the Israelites from Pharaoh's army at the Red Sea?
    ◦ Who delivered the Israelites from death by providing them with water and food in the desert?
    ◦ Who delivered Jonah from death in the belly of the great fish?

    The Lord is the great Deliverer. There is no Savior other than God.

- **Zacharias said that the Deliverer would show His people how their sins could be forgiven.**

    📖 Read Luke 1:68, 77 again.

    God cannot and will not forgive sins unless the full price for sin is paid. What is the payment for sin? We know that the payment for our sin is death – separation from God forever. We also know that the payment must be made if we are to be delivered. But, think about this, how can our payment be made so that we will be delivered from death?

The Deliverer would make it clear how sin could be paid for and how sinners could be forgiven and saved from separation from God forever in the Lake of Fire.

- **Zacharias said that the Deliverer would come like the sun rising in the morning.**

  📖 Read Luke 1:78-79 again.

  Think about this. How would you feel if you were lost on a dark night in a thick jungle where you had never been before? Would you be eager for the sun to rise in the morning? Of course, you would. You would feel great relief when the sun came up.

- **Everyone in the world has been born in spiritual darkness.**

  This means we were all born separated from God and unable to know God or how to come to God. We were all born into this world without God and without hope. When Adam and Eve sinned against God in the garden in Eden, they were separated from God. It was like they had become lost in a thick darkness without any light. If God did not show them the way back to Him, they would be lost forever.

  Because Adam and Eve are the ancestors of all people, all people have been born into the darkness. Cain and Abel were born in that darkness because their parents were in the darkness. Your ancestors were also born in darkness. They could not find their way out of the darkness and back to God. Satan told them many lies, and they believed him. You, too, were born in that darkness with no way to escape Satan, sin and everlasting separation from God.

- **There is a light which can lead you out of the darkness of Satan's control.**

  Zacharias said that the Deliverer would come into this world to be the light to all people. The Deliverer would come just as the sun rises after a dark night and gives light to all people everywhere.

  How many suns are there in the world? There is only one. The same sun gives light all over the world.

- **God only sent one Deliverer into the world.**

  God did not send different deliverers, one for the Jews and another one for you. God only promised one Deliverer who would make it possible for all people in the world to come to God.

LESSON 47: GOD FULFILLED HIS PROMISE IN THE BIRTH OF JOHN.

? Questions

1. Did God keep His promise to give Zacharias a son?
   Yes. Zacharias' wife, Elizabeth, had a son, just as God said.

2. Who guided Zacharias to speak a message about the Deliverer?
   God the Spirit guided Zacharias to speak a message about the Deliverer.

3. Zacharias said that God's promises which were given through the prophets and written in the Bible would soon be fulfilled. Who did Zacharias say would fulfill those promises?
   The Deliverer would fulfill God's promises.

4. What work did God plan for John to do?
   God planned for John to precede the Deliverer to prepare the people to receive and trust in Him.

5. Who did Zacharias identify the Deliverer to be?
   Zacharias identified the Deliverer as "the Lord."

6. Could an ordinary man deliver us from Satan, sin and death?
   No. Only the Lord could deliver us from Satan, sin and death.

7. To people who lived in spiritual darkness, Zacharias said that the Deliverer would be like what?
   Zacharias said that the Deliverer would be like the sun rising in the morning.

8. How many people were born in spiritual darkness?
   Everyone in the world has been born in spiritual darkness.

9. What does the Bible mean when it says that people are in darkness?
   The Bible means that all people are without God and without hope. Because all people have been born separated from God, everyone is lost and with no way to escape Satan, sin and everlasting separation from God.

10. How did Zacharias know what the Deliverer would do?
    Zacharias read and believed what God had said through the prophets.

LESSON 48: GOD'S ANGEL EXPLAINED TO JOSEPH HOW JESUS WOULD BE BORN.

Scripture

Matthew 1:1-2, 18-25

Lesson Outline

(1) Jesus was born in fulfillment of God's promises. (Matthew 1:1-2)

(2) Jesus was to be the Christ.

(3) Mary was engaged to be married to Joseph. (Matthew 1:18-19)

(4) God's angel explained to Joseph that Mary's baby was the Deliverer. (Matthew 1:20-23)

(5) Joseph did what the angel told him. (Matthew 1:24-25)

(?) Review Questions from Lesson 47.

Lesson Outline Developed

(1) Jesus was born in fulfillment of God's promises.

📖 Read Matthew 1:1-2.

Jesus, the coming Deliverer, was to be a descendant of Abraham, Isaac, Jacob and David. God had promised each of these men that the Deliverer would be one of their descendants, and God fulfilled this promise.

God had also said through the prophet Isaiah that the Deliverer would be David's descendant.

★ Tell them God's words written by Isaiah were fulfilled. Then read Isaiah 9:7 and Matthew 1:1 to them. Then point to the Prophetic Chart, and write Matthew 1:1 opposite Isaiah 9:7. (See example below.)

What God said about the Deliverer He would send		How God's Word Came True
Isaiah 9:7	David's descendant	Matthew 1:1

Jesus would be David's descendant. What God said about the Deliverer He would send did happen, just as God said. God fulfilled His promise to David and His prophecy through Isaiah.

2) Jesus was to be the Christ.

Jesus, who would also be called Christ, was being sent by God the Father to do three special things.

- **Jesus would be God's final prophet to tell the world the truth.**

  God the Father was sending Jesus into the world to tell the way for all people to be delivered from Satan, sin and everlasting punishment.

- **Jesus was sent as God's final priest to make a way back to God.**

  Do you remember what the high priest did once a year in the temple? The high priest took the blood of animals into the inner room of the temple and sprinkled it on the mercy seat as God instructed so that the sins of the people could be forgiven. Jesus was going to be the final high priest.

- **Jesus would be God's final king to rule over Israel and the whole world.**

  God the Father was sending Jesus to become the King and to rule as the descendant of King David. God's plan is that Jesus will become the king of the whole world.

- **Jesus was the only One promised by God to be the final prophet, priest and king.**

  No other person could rightfully claim these positions. Jesus Christ was promised by God to be the only Deliverer of sinners.

3) Mary was engaged to be married to Joseph.

We learned previously that the angel told Mary that God had chosen her to be the mother of the Deliverer. Now let's learn what happened next.

- **Mary's future husband, Joseph, found out that Mary was pregnant.**

☞ **Teacher:** Point to the name, **"Joseph,"** on the chronological chart.

LESSON 48: GOD'S ANGEL EXPLAINED TO JOSEPH HOW JESUS WOULD BE BORN.

Remember that Mary was a virgin. Joseph had never had sexual relations with her. But before Mary and Joseph were married, she became pregnant.

What would you young men think if this happened to you? Imagine that you were engaged to be married to a girl who was supposed to be a virgin, but then you found out that she was pregnant. What would you think?

- **Joseph thought that Mary had had sexual relations with another man.**

  Had Mary been with a man? No! How had she become pregnant? The baby in her had been given by God the Spirit. Her baby was the God the Son who had come down from Heaven to become a human baby so He could be the Deliverer of sinners.

  Joseph didn't know that Mary was carrying God the Son in her womb. He thought she was pregnant with another man's baby.

- **Let's read from the Bible what Joseph decided to do.**

  📖 Read Matthew 1:18-19.

  Joseph decided that he would not get married to Mary.

4) God's angel explained to Joseph that Mary's baby was the Deliverer.

- **Joseph was a man who trusted in God.**

  He was a sinner, but he came to God the way God said, bringing the blood of animals.

- **God wanted Joseph to marry Mary.**

  God planned for Joseph to marry Mary so that Jesus would have a good earthly father. Therefore, God sent one of His angels to tell Joseph the truth about Mary. The angel spoke to Joseph in a dream.

👉 **Teacher:** Show a picture of the angel speaking to Joseph.

- **The angel explained the truth to Joseph.**

  📖 Read Matthew 1:20-23.

  The angel explained to Joseph that Mary's baby was conceived by the power of the Holy Spirit. The angel told Joseph to marry her and, when the baby was born, to name the baby, Jesus.

- **The name, Jesus, means Savior.**

  Jesus was to be born into this world to save sinners from God's punishment for their sins. He was to come to save all those who agree with God that they are sinners and need a Savior.

- The prophets had said that the promised Savior would be born of a virgin.

★ Tell them God's words written by Isaiah were fulfilled. Then read Isaiah 7:14 and Matthew 1:22-23 to them. Then point to the Prophetic Chart, and write Matthew 1:22-23 opposite Isaiah 7:14. (See example below.)

What God said about the Deliverer He would send		How God's Word Came True
Isaiah 7:14	Born of a virgin	Matthew 1:22-23

- The Deliverer would be Emmanuel.

  The Deliverer was to have many names. We have already learned that one of His names was to be Jesus, and another name was to be Christ. He was also called Emmanuel. This name means "God with us." Jesus would be Emmanuel because He was God the Son who was coming down from Heaven to live with people here in this world.

5) Joseph did what the angel told him.

📖 Read Matthew 1:24-25.

When Mary gave birth to the baby, Joseph named Him, Jesus, which means "the One who will save sinners."

? Questions

1. What Jewish king was an ancestor of Jesus?
   King David was an ancestor of Jesus.

2. As the Christ, Jesus was being sent by God the Father to do what three things?
   Jesus was being sent by God the Father to be the final prophet, priest and king.

3. To whom was Mary engaged to be married?
   Mary was engaged to be married to Joseph.

4. What did Joseph think when he found out that Mary was pregnant?
   Joseph thought that Mary had had sexual relations with another man.

5. Whom did God send to tell Joseph the truth about Mary and the baby she was pregnant with?

LESSON 48: GOD'S ANGEL EXPLAINED TO JOSEPH HOW JESUS WOULD BE BORN.

God sent one of His angels to tell Joseph the truth about Mary and the baby.

6. What did the angel tell Joseph?

   The angel explained to Joseph that Mary's baby was conceived by the power of the Holy Spirit. The angel told Joseph to marry her and, when the baby was born, to name the baby, Jesus.

7. Why was Jesus to come into this world?

   Jesus was to come into this world in order to save sinners from God's punishment for their sins.

8. What does Emmanuel mean?

   Emmanuel means "God with us."

9. Why was Jesus to have the name, Emmanuel?

   Jesus was to have the name, Emmanuel, because He was God the Son who was coming down from Heaven to live with people on earth.

LESSON 49: GOD FULFILLED HIS PROMISES BY SENDING JESUS, THE DELIVERER. JESUS GREW INTO MANHOOD.

Scripture

Matthew 2, Luke 2:40-52

Lesson Outline

(1) Jesus was born in Bethlehem. (Matthew 2:1-2)

(2) Wise men came to worship Jesus. (Matthew 2:1-11)

(3) God protected Jesus from King Herod. (Matthew 2:12-18)

(4) Joseph, Mary and Jesus returned to Nazareth. (Matthew 2:19-23)

(5) Jesus grew into a strong and wise boy. (Luke 2:40)

(6) Jesus went to Jerusalem. (Luke 2:41-45)

(7) Jesus stayed behind in the temple. (Luke 2:46-51)

(8) Jesus grew into manhood. (Luke 2:52)

(?) Review Questions from Lesson 48.

Lesson Outline Developed

(1) Jesus was born in Bethlehem.

📖 Read Matthew 2:1-2.

Many years earlier, God had said through the prophet Micah that the Deliverer would be born in Bethlehem.

Jesus was born in Bethlehem just as God had foretold.

★ Tell them that God's words written by Micah were fulfilled. Then read Micah 5:2 and Matthew 2:1 to them. Then point to the Prophetic Chart and write Matthew 2:1 opposite Micah 5:2. (See example below.)

What God said about the Deliverer He would send		How God's Word Came True
Micah 5:2	Born in Bethlehem	Matthew 2:1

② Wise men came to worship Jesus.

- **Wise men came to Jerusalem, looking for the King of the Jews.**

    📖 Read Matthew 2:1-2 again.

    The men who came looking for the King of the Jews were not Jews. They had come from their country which was a long way from Israel.

    These men were called wise men because they had studied and learned many things. They had seen a new star shining over the land of Israel. God had shown these men that the new star was a sign that the King of the Jews had been born in the country of Israel. These learned men decided to go to Israel to worship the new King.

    They did not know in which town the King of the Jews was living, so they went to Jerusalem, looking for Him.

- **King Herod did not want anyone to be king instead of him.**

    📖 Read Matthew 2:3.

    King Herod was troubled to hear that a child had been born who might be the King of the Jews. Herod was afraid that he would lose his position as king when this baby grew into manhood. King Herod did not want anyone to rule over him.

- **The chief priests and scribes knew where the Deliverer was to be born.**

    📖 Read Matthew 2:5-6.

    The chief priests and scribes knew the Scriptures, and they knew that God had foretold that the Deliverer would be born in Bethlehem. They read what the prophet Micah had written, just as I read it to you earlier.

- **King Herod sent the wise men to Bethlehem.**

    📖 Read Matthew 2:7-8.

- **The wise men found Jesus and worshiped Him.**

    📖 Read Matthew 2:9-11.

LESSON 49: GOD FULFILLED HIS PROMISES BY SENDING JESUS, THE DELIVERER. JESUS GREW INTO MANHOOD.

☞ **Teacher:** Show a picture of the wise men worshiping Jesus. Be sure your picture does not depict them in the stable.

Do you remember the first commandment in the Law that God gave through Moses? God had said that they should have no other gods before Him. Only God should be worshiped.

So do you think it was right for these wise men to worship Jesus? Do you think that God was angry with these men for worshiping Jesus? No. God was not angry with them. The baby Jesus was human, but He was also God, so it was right for the wise men to worship Him. Jesus is both God and man.

③ God protected Jesus from King Herod.

- **God knew that King Herod wanted to kill Jesus.**

  When the wise men were in Jerusalem, King Herod had told them to return after they found the King of the Jews. King Herod had said that he wanted to worship Him, too, but he lied. He did not really want to worship Jesus. He planned to kill Jesus.

  God knew what King Herod was really planning. God knows everything. God knows what people think, even if they do not say it out loud.

  God wasn't going to allow anyone to hinder His plans that Jesus should be the Deliverer of sinners. He had promised that He would rescue sinners from Satan's power, and God always keeps His promises. He would not let King Herod kill Jesus.

- **God told the wise men not to go back to Jerusalem.**

  📖 Read Matthew 2:12.

  The wise men returned to their country without going back to tell King Herod that they had found Jesus.

- **God told Joseph to take Mary and Jesus and to flee to Egypt.**

  📖 Read Matthew 2:13-15.

  Joseph took Mary and Jesus into Egypt to protect Jesus from King Herod. They stayed there until God told them that King Herod had died.

☞ **Teacher:** Show a picture of Joseph and Mary fleeing into Egypt with Jesus.

- **King Herod commanded that all the baby boys who were in or near Bethlehem be killed.**

    Read Matthew 2:16-18.

    Do you remember how God protected the baby Moses when the wicked king of Egypt commanded that all the baby boys be killed? Just as God protected baby Moses from the King of Egypt, so God protected the baby Jesus from King Herod.

    Who was guiding the wicked king of Egypt when he killed the baby boys in Moses' time? Satan was guiding him. Satan didn't want Moses to save the Israelites from slavery because Satan wanted them all to die. Satan knew that one of the Israelites' descendants would be the Deliverer who would overcome him, destroy him and bring deliverance for the world.

- **Satan tried to have Jesus killed by King Herod.**

    Satan knew that Jesus was born to save sinners, so he wanted to kill Jesus while He was still a baby.

- **Satan has not changed.**

    Although Satan wasn't able to kill the Deliverer through King Herod, he still hasn't stopped fighting against God and the truth. Satan does not want you to believe in the Deliverer. Satan wants you to go to everlasting punishment. Satan will try to stop you from believing God's Word.

(4) Joseph, Mary and Jesus returned to Nazareth.

   Read Matthew 2:19-23.

The Lord sent one of His angels to tell Joseph to take Mary and Jesus out of Egypt and back to the land of Israel.

Many years previously, God had foretold through the prophet Hosea that the Deliverer would be called out of Egypt.

★ Tell them that God's words written by Hosea were fulfilled. Then read Hosea 11:1 and Matthew 2:14-15 to them. Then point to the Prophetic Chart and write Matthew 2:14-15 opposite Hosea 11:1. (See example below.)

What God said about the Deliverer He would send		How God's Word Came True
Hosea 11:1	Be brought out of Egypt	Matthew 2:14-15

God's words given through His prophets were fulfilled. God always does what He says.

LESSON 49: GOD FULFILLED HIS PROMISES BY SENDING JESUS, THE DELIVERER. JESUS GREW INTO MANHOOD.

As a boy, the Deliverer lived in the town of Nazareth.

☞ **Teacher:** Point to Nazareth on the map.

⑤ Jesus grew into a strong and wise boy.

📖 Read Luke 2:40.

Jesus was God, but He was also a human being who grew physically and mentally like every other normal child. God, His Father, protected and guided Jesus in everything that He thought, said and did.

- **Jesus never sinned.**

Because Jesus was not just a human being but also God, He always did what was right. All of Adam's descendants have been born as sinners, separated from God, because Adam was a sinner. But Jesus was not born as a sinner. Jesus is God, and God is completely holy and righteous.

Every other person who has ever lived has disobeyed God's commands, but Jesus perfectly obeyed every command of God.

⑥ Jesus went to Jerusalem.

📖 Read Luke 2:41-45.

- **Jesus went with His parents, Joseph and Mary.**

Joseph was not Jesus' father, but he cared for Jesus just as if He were his own son.

- **They went to Jerusalem for the Feast of the Passover.**

Jerusalem was a very long way from Nazareth. Joseph, Mary and Jesus walked from Nazareth to Jerusalem. They went up to Jerusalem to worship God in the temple.

- **After the Feast was over, Mary and Joseph left Jerusalem to walk back home.**

Joseph and Mary did not realize that Jesus was not with them when they left Jerusalem to return to Nazareth. They were traveling with many of their friends.

In those days, there were many robbers on the roads, so it was much safer if many people traveled together.

Because there were so many people traveling together, Mary and Joseph thought Jesus was among their relatives and friends who were also on their way back to Nazareth. What a surprise when they found out that He wasn't traveling with them!

As soon as they realized that He wasn't with the group, Mary and Joseph went back to Jerusalem to look for Him.

Where do you think Jesus was?

⑦ Jesus stayed behind in the temple.

- **Jesus was sitting with the teachers in the temple.**

    📖 Read Luke 2:46-47.

    These religious teachers did not know that Jesus was the promised Deliverer, and they didn't know that He was God the Son. They were amazed that a 12-year old boy understood the Scriptures so thoroughly.

    ☞ **Teacher:** Show a picture of Jesus as a boy in the temple.

- **Mary questioned Jesus to find out why He stayed in Jerusalem.**

    📖 Read Luke 2:48-50.

    Jesus knew that God was His Father even when He was only twelve years old. He obeyed everything that God His Father told Him to do. Jesus never thought, said, or did anything that was wrong. He was perfect.

- **Jesus returned to Nazareth with Mary and Joseph.**

    📖 Read Luke 2:51.

    Jesus was always obedient to Mary and Joseph, His earthly parents. He loved and respected them.

⑧ Jesus grew into manhood.

📖 Read Luke 2:52.

Even though Jesus was God, He was also a real human being. Jesus grew, just as your children grow physically and in their understanding.

- **Jesus grew to be a wise man.**

    God was pleased with Jesus, and people liked Him.

    Many years earlier, God's prophet Isaiah said that the Deliverer would be wise and would have great knowledge because He would be in oneness with God the Spirit.

LESSON 49: GOD FULFILLED HIS PROMISES BY SENDING JESUS, THE DELIVERER. JESUS GREW INTO MANHOOD.

What God said through Isaiah was fulfilled. God always remembers what He says. Everything happens just as He says.

★ Tell them that God's words written by Isaiah were fulfilled. Then read Isaiah 11:2 and Luke 2:52 to them. Then point to the Prophetic Chart and write Luke 2:52 opposite Isaiah 11:2. (See example below.)

What God said about the Deliverer He would send		**How God's Word Came True**
Isaiah 11:2	Some of His characteristics	Luke 2:52

? Questions

1. In what town did the prophet Micah say that Jesus would be born?
   The prophet Micah foretold that the Deliverer would be born in Bethlehem.

2. Why did the wise men want to find Jesus?
   They wanted to worship Him.

3. Why was it right for the wise men to worship Jesus?
   It was right for the wise men to worship Jesus because Jesus was God the Son.

4. To which country did God tell Joseph to take Jesus in order to escape from King Herod?
   God told Joseph to take Jesus into Egypt.

5. Why did Satan try to have the baby Jesus killed?
   Satan tried to have the baby Jesus killed because Satan knew that Jesus was born to save sinners.

6. Although Jesus looked like other children, what great difference was there?
   Jesus was God as well as a human being.

7. Did Jesus ever do anything wrong?
   No. Jesus never sinned, even as a child. He never thought, said or did anything which displeased God His Father.

8. Has any other person been sinless as Jesus was?
   No. All of Adam's descendants have been born as sinners, separated from God, because Adam was a sinner. Every other person who has ever lived has disobeyed God's commands.

9. What was Jesus doing in the temple when Mary and Joseph found Him?

   Jesus was asking questions and answering the questions asked of Him by the men who were the teachers of the Scriptures.

10. What was Jesus' answer to Mary when she questioned Him?

    Jesus asked Mary if it wasn't right that He should be doing what God His Father wanted Him to do.

11. What was Jesus' attitude toward Mary and Joseph as He was growing up?

    Jesus obeyed, loved and respected them in everything.

LESSON 50: GOD SENT JOHN TO TEACH AND TO BAPTIZE. JOHN BAPTIZED JESUS.

Scripture

Matthew 3:1-17, John 1:29-34

Lesson Outline

(1) John was God's messenger to Israel. (Matthew 3:1-4)

(2) Many of the Jews believed God's message which John told them. (Matthew 3:5-6)

(3) John spoke to the proud and unrepentant. (Matthew 3:7-10)

(4) John taught the people about the Deliverer. (Matthew 3:11-12)

(5) John baptized Jesus. (Matthew 3:13-17)

(6) John told the people who Jesus was. (John 1:29-34)

(?) Review Questions from Lesson 49.

Lesson Outline Developed

(1) John was God's messenger to Israel.

We learned earlier that God was going to send a prophet to prepare the people for the coming Deliverer. Who was the prophet who was chosen by God to prepare the Jews to receive the Deliverer? It was John.

As John grew into manhood, he was waiting for the time when he would begin preparing the people of Israel to trust in the coming Deliverer.

John believed God. He knew that he was a sinner, but he came to God with animal sacrifices and offered their blood. He trusted in God to save him from everlasting punishment. John trusted in the coming Deliverer.

The time had come for John to begin teaching the people.

- **John taught the people that they must repent.**

    📖 Read Matthew 3:1-2.

    The people needed to change their attitude toward God, about themselves and about sin. John told them to change their minds so that they would be ready to receive the Deliverer.

    - They needed to change their minds about God. They needed to understand and agree that God is the only true God and that they should serve and worship only Him.
    - They needed to change their minds about themselves. They needed to understand and agree that they had sinned against God by disobeying His laws and that they were unable to make themselves acceptable to Him.
    - They needed to change their minds about sin. They needed to understand and agree that all sin is against God and that God hates sin and will always punish it by sending the unrepentant and unbelieving sinner to the everlasting fire.

    God wants each of you to understand and agree with these same truths.

Teacher: Go back over these three points and apply them directly to your students so they will realize that each of us needs to change our minds about God, about ourselves and about sin.

- **John was the one whom the prophet Isaiah had said would precede the promised Deliverer.**

    📖 Read Matthew 3:3.

Teacher: As you prepare to teach, read Isaiah 40:3, but do not read this verse to the people when you teach the lesson.

- **John was a poor man.**

    📖 Read Matthew 3:4.

    Being God's prophet did not make John a rich man. John ate food that he found in the wilderness, and he wore the clothing of a very poor man.

- **God does not promise that a person will become rich if he believes Him and obeys His Word.**

    Some people think that if they follow the ways of the Bible, God is obligated to give lots of things to them. That way of thinking is wrong. Many people who are written about in the Bible who believed God and obeyed Him were very poor. Later you will see that even Jesus, God's Son, was a very poor man when He was here in the world.

Teacher: Many people throughout the world believe that if they become a Christian, they will probably become rich. Be sure your hearers understand that this is not one of God's promises to those who trust in Him.

LESSON 50: GOD SENT JOHN
TO TEACH AND TO BAPTIZE.
JOHN BAPTIZED JESUS.

② Many of the Jews believed God's message which John told them.

📖 Read Matthew 3:5-6.

- **Many of the Jews repented when they heard what John told them.**

  They changed their mind about God, about themselves and about sin. They agreed with God that they were sinners, and they believed that God was going to send the Deliverer.

- **John baptized those who repented.**

  John said that all who repented and believed that God would send the Deliverer were to obey God's command to be baptized by being dipped under water. By being baptized, they were showing everyone that they agreed with God that they deserved death for their sins but that they were trusting in God to send the Deliverer to save them.

- **Baptism does not make people acceptable to God.**

  Baptism does not wash away sin before the eyes of God. Baptism cannot pay God for sins, because the payment for sin is death.

  Baptism is a public way to show others that a person agrees with God's message and that he is trusting only in God's deliverance from the punishment he deserves for his sin.

③ John spoke to the proud and unrepentant.

- **The religious leaders who came to see John were proud people.**

  📖 Read Matthew 3:7.

  Most of the Pharisees and Sadducees were proud. They thought that they were good enough for God to accept them, and they refused to admit that they were sinners.

  Because the Pharisees and Sadducees were so proud, John's words to them were very strong.

- **God's words are very strong to those who are proud and refuse to listen to His message.**

  God is the enemy of proud people and will fight against them unless they change their attitude and agree with Him, but God will deliver those who agree that they are sinners and that only He can help them.

- **John taught that people who believe will do good actions.**

  📖 Read Matthew 3:8.

  John told the Pharisees and the Sadducees that, if they really repented and believed God, then they must show it by their actions.

- **The Pharisees and Sadducees were proud that Abraham was their ancestor.**

  📖 Read Matthew 3:9.

  Many of the Jews were proud that Abraham was the father of their nation. They thought that God would accept them because they were the descendants of Abraham. Has the Bible said that God would accept them because Abraham was their ancestor? No! No one is accepted by God because of his parents.

- **Some people still think that God will accept them because their parents agree with and trust in God.**

  But this is not true. No one is accepted by God because of his parents. God judges each person individually.

  John told the Pharisees and Sadducees not to trust in the fact that they were Abraham's children. Because God can do anything, He could even make children for Abraham out of stones if He wanted to.

- **John gave an illustration about a tree that produces bad fruit.**

  📖 Read Matthew 3:10.

Lesson Developer: Use an illustration about a tree or plant that produces bad fruit. For example:

> 💡 *What would you do if you found a tree bearing inedible fruit growing among your good fruit trees?*
>
> *Could you make the tree bear edible fruit by cutting off some of its branches? No.*
>
> *Could you make the bad tree good if you picked all its bad fruit and threw it away? No.*
>
> *If a tree produces bad fruit, you cut it down right from the roots and burn it because the whole tree is bad.*

All people are like bad trees because we all descended from Adam who disobeyed God. The bad things we think, say and do are like the useless fruit of a wild tree. Just as it is not possible to make a bad tree good by picking off and throwing away its bad fruit, we cannot make ourselves pleasing to God by removing from our lives the bad things which we think, say and do. No matter how hard we might try to be good, we are still like bad trees before God.

All who refuse to agree with God and trust only in Him to deliver them are like bad trees which God is going to cut down. They will die and be thrown into the everlasting fire to be punished.

LESSON 50: GOD SENT JOHN TO TEACH AND TO BAPTIZE. JOHN BAPTIZED JESUS.

④ John taught the people about the Deliverer.

- **John knew that the coming Deliverer was more important than John was.**

    📖 Read Matthew 3:11.

    John was God's prophet who had been sent to prepare the people to receive and trust in the Deliverer. John reminded them that he was just a man and that the coming Deliverer was the Son of God.

    During the time when John lived, important men had servants to do all of their work. The important man would not even put his own shoes on or take them off. That was the work of servants. John said that he wasn't even worthy to be the servant who would take off the Deliverer's shoes. The Deliverer was the Son of God. He was the Creator of the world. He was greater than John because He had given John his life.

- **John said that the Deliverer would do something greater than baptizing people in water.**

    John baptized all those who said that they agreed with God and were trusting in God to send the Savior. John explained that the coming Deliverer would do something greater than just baptizing those who believed. The coming Deliverer would give God the Spirit, who is also called the Holy Spirit, to all who trusted in Him.

- **John said that the Deliverer would separate the chaff from the grain.**

    📖 Read Matthew 3:12.

Lesson Developer: Use an illustration that will show that chaff is useless. For example:

> 💡 After you pound your rice, you place it in a winnowing basket and toss it into the air so the wind will blow the chaff away. The chaff is useless. It cannot be eaten. Later, when there is much chaff, you rake it together and burn it.

John said that all those who refuse to agree with the words of God through the Deliverer are like chaff. The Deliverer will separate those who do not believe from those who do believe His Word and trust in Him. The Deliverer will throw all those who are like the chaff into the everlasting fire to be punished.

Teacher: The "fan" was a long, wooden fork used by threshers to toss grain into the air so that the chaff would be blown away.

⑤ John baptized Jesus.

- **Jesus came to be baptized.**

    📖 Read Matthew 3:13-17.

    Jesus was about 30 years old when He came to John to be baptized.

    Teacher: As you prepare to teach, read Luke 3:23, but do not read this verse to the people when you teach the lesson.

- **Although Jesus came to John to be baptized, it was not because He was a sinner.**

    All the other people who came to be baptized by John did so because they wanted to show that they agreed that they were sinners and needed the Deliverer. Jesus was born perfect and lived in full agreement with God. Jesus did not need a Deliverer – Jesus was the Deliverer!

- **Jesus came to be baptized to show that He accepted John as God's prophet.**

    It was God's will that all who accepted John as God's prophet be baptized. If Jesus wasn't baptized, people would think that He did not obey God's commands or that He did not believe that John was sent by God.

    Teacher: As you prepare to teach, read Luke 7:29-30, but do not read these verses to the people when you teach the lesson.

- **God the Spirit came to guide Jesus in His future work.**

    When Jesus came up out of the water after John baptized Him, God the Spirit came to be with Jesus to guide and empower Him for the work God planned for Him to do. Jesus was almighty God, but when He became a man, He chose to depend on God the Spirit for power to do the work of the Deliverer here on earth.

- **God the Father was pleased with His Son.**

    📖 Read Matthew 3:17 again.

    God the Father called Jesus, His Son. Jesus was a man, but He was also God the Son who had come down from Heaven.

    God was fully satisfied with Jesus. Jesus was the only man who did everything that pleased God. Jesus did not have any sin before God.

⑥ John told the people who Jesus was.

- **John said that Jesus was the Lamb of God.**

LESSON 50: GOD SENT JOHN TO TEACH AND TO BAPTIZE. JOHN BAPTIZED JESUS.

📖 Read John 1:29.

☞ **Teacher:** Show a picture of John the Baptist introducing Jesus as the Lamb of God.

We have learned that, since the time when Adam sinned, God required the people to bring a sacrifice and kill it so that its blood ran out. They offered the sacrifice to die for their sins as their substitute. They had to bring a sacrifice in order to be accepted by God.

- Think about Abel. Abel offered sheep when he came to God, and God accepted him.
- Think about Isaac. When Isaac was just about to be killed by Abraham in obedience to God, God stopped Abraham. When Abraham looked up, what did he see caught in a bush by its horns? Yes, he saw a ram. Who put the ram there to be offered instead of Isaac? God did. God provided the ram offering to take the place of Isaac so that Isaac could be saved from being killed.
- Think about when the Israelites escaped from Egypt. God had told each family to kill a lamb and put the lamb's blood on the sides and tops of the door frames on the outside of each of their houses. God did not kill the firstborn of any family who did what God said. The lamb died in place of the firstborn.

Teacher: When you refer back to Old Testament characters or incidents, be sure that your hearers remember clearly what you are referring to. You could show the appropriate picture that will remind them of the story and/or point to the chronological chart.

The blood of animals could not pay for sin, so God sent Jesus into the world to completely pay for sin and deliver all those who put their trust in Him. Just as God provided the ram to die instead of Isaac, so God sent His Son to be the Lamb who would die in the place of sinners.

- **John said that Jesus was the promised Deliverer.**

  📖 Read John 1:30-34.

- **God gave John this special sign so he would know that Jesus was the Son of God and the promised Deliverer.**

  John did not know who the Deliverer would be, but God had told him that the one on whom the Spirit of God would descend like a dove was the Deliverer. So when John saw this sign from God, he knew for certain that Jesus was the Son of God and the Savior of the world.

- **We no longer need miraculous signs.**

    We have the Word of God, the Bible. God wants you to trust in His words which are written in the Bible. If you refuse to believe God's words, then you will never be made acceptable to Him.

⟨?⟩ Questions

1. What did John teach that the people should do?

    John taught the people that they should repent and be baptized.

2. What does it mean to repent?

    To repent means to change our minds about God, about ourselves and about sin.

3. When we repent, in what way do we change our mind about God?

    We agree with God that He is the only true and living God, our Creator, and that we should serve and worship Him completely.

4. When we repent, in what way do we change our mind about ourselves?

    We agree with God that we are sinners, that we have disobeyed His laws and that we are unable to make ourselves acceptable to God.

5. When we repent, in what way do we change our mind about sin?

    We agree with God that sin is wrong because it is against God and that it deserves to be punished by God.

6. Whom was John preparing the people to receive?

    John was preparing the people to receive the promised Deliverer.

7. Does baptism make people acceptable to God?

    No! Being dipped under the water cannot make us acceptable to God.

8. What did the Pharisees and Sadducees think made them acceptable to God?

    They thought they were acceptable to God because of the things which they did and because they were the descendants of Abraham.

9. What did John say that the Deliverer would do to those who refused to repent and believe?

    John said that the Deliverer would throw those who did not believe into the everlasting fire.

LESSON 50: GOD SENT JOHN TO TEACH AND TO BAPTIZE. JOHN BAPTIZED JESUS.

10. Jesus came to be baptized by John. Was that because Jesus was a sinner?

    No! Jesus was not a sinner. He was born perfect and lived in full agreement with God.

11. Why did Jesus come to be baptized by John?

    Jesus came to be baptized by John to show that He accepted John as God's prophet.

12. When Jesus came up out of the water after John baptized Him, who came to be with Jesus?

    God the Spirit came to be with Jesus.

13. Did anyone else ever please God like Jesus?

    No. No one ever pleased God in every way as Jesus did.

14. John called Jesus "the Lamb of God." In what way was Jesus the Lamb of God?

    Just as God provided the ram to die instead of Isaac, so God sent His Son to be the Lamb who would die in place of sinners.

LESSON 51: JESUS RESISTED SATAN'S TEMPTATIONS.

Scripture

Matthew 4:1-11

Lesson Outline

(1) Satan tempted Jesus. (Matthew 4:1)

(2) Satan tempted Jesus to prove that He was the Son of God. (Matthew 4:2-4)

(3) Satan tempted Jesus to prove that God would take care of Him. (Matthew 4:5-7)

(4) Satan tempted Jesus to worship him. (Matthew 4:8-10)

(5) Jesus defeated Satan every time He was tempted. 6. Satan left Jesus for a short time. (Matthew 4:11)

(?) Review Questions from Lesson 50.

Lesson Outline Developed

(1) Satan tempted Jesus.

- **Do you remember who God's great enemy is?**

  God's great enemy is Satan. Satan hates God, and he hates the people whom God created. Satan has fought against God from the beginning. He had tried to take God's place, and God cast him out of Heaven. He tried many times to prevent God's plan to send the Deliverer. He even tried to destroy Jesus when He was a baby. Satan had not won, but do you think that Satan gave up fighting against God? No!

- **Satan tempted Jesus to rebel against God.**

  Read Matthew 4:1.

☞ **Teacher:** Show a picture of Jesus in the desert.

Satan, or the Devil as he is sometimes called, wanted Jesus to sin against God. Satan knew that if Jesus sinned, He would be under Satan's control and He would not be able to be our Deliverer.

Satan tempted Jesus to rebel against God, just as he had tempted Adam. Adam had sinned, and his sin put all of his descendants under Satan's control. Would Jesus rebel against God like Adam did? Let's read from the Scripture and see what happened.

② Satan tempted Jesus to prove that He was the Son of God.

📖 Read Matthew 4:2-3.

- **Jesus was hungry.**

  Although Jesus is God, He was also a real man. He became hungry just as we become hungry.

- **Satan tried to make Jesus prove that He was the Son of God.**

  Satan told Jesus to prove that He was the Son of God by turning stones into bread.

  Jesus was the Son of God, and He had the power to turn stones into bread. However, God the Father had not told Jesus to turn the stones into bread. Jesus came down to earth from Heaven to do only what His Father wanted Him to do.

  Jesus was not going to obey Satan. He would not do anything that Satan told Him to do.

- **Jesus answered Satan by quoting from the Bible.**

  📖 Read Matthew 4:4.

  Satan had told Jesus to turn the stones into bread, but Jesus knew that obeying God's Word was more important than eating.

  Food is very important, isn't it? We need food to keep our bodies alive.

Lesson Developer: Remind your students that food is important to them as seen by the time and effort they devote to providing food for their families. For example:

> 💡 You work hard to clear the land to make a rice field or to make a vegetable garden. You work hard to care for your crops and to harvest them. You spend time and effort to provide food for your family because food is important.

Our bodies need food, for without it they will die. Did you realize, though, that God's Word is even more important than food? We need God's Word to show us the truth and the way to everlasting life.

Food will help anyone to have a healthy body, but what benefit will it be to anyone if he has a healthy body but dies still separated from God and goes to everlasting punishment? We need to eat food so our bodies will live, but we also need to hear and believe God's words so that we will be able to live forever with God.

③ Satan tempted Jesus to prove that God would take care of Him.

📖 Read Matthew 4:5-6.

- **Satan tried to make Jesus prove that God would take care of Him.**

  Satan told Jesus to throw Himself down from the temple to test if God would take care of Him.

- **Satan used God's words incorrectly.**

  Satan quoted the words of God in the Bible to try to get Jesus to do something that was wrong.

  Satan knows the words of God, but he uses them in the wrong way.

  We have already learned that Satan changes God's words in order to trick people. Do you remember how Satan tricked Eve? Satan asked her, "Did God say that you aren't allowed to eat any of the fruit from the trees in the garden?" Satan knew that God had told Adam that he must not eat the fruit from one of the trees in the garden. Satan changed what God had said in order to trick Eve.

  Satan is a liar and a deceiver.

- **Jesus answered Satan by quoting from the Bible.**

  📖 Read Read Matthew 4:7.

  Jesus obeyed the Bible by refusing to test His Father. God the Father had promised to take care of His Son, so Jesus simply trusted His Father's Word. He did not need further proof of God's loving care. What was written in the Bible was sufficient proof.

- **We do not need proof that God will do what He has promised.**

  God's Word is trustworthy. We have learned that God always does what He has promised. We should believe that the Lord will do everything that He has written in the Bible.

④ Satan tempted Jesus to worship him.

📖 Read Read Matthew 4:8-9.

- **Satan controls the people of this world.**

  Satan could offer Jesus control over the people in this world because Satan is the god of this world. When Adam rebelled against God and followed Satan, Satan took control of the human race.

All people who have not been delivered by God from Satan's control are worshiping and serving Satan instead of God. Satan leads those under his control to do the evil things he has planned, and he tries to keep them from believing God.

Teacher: As you prepare to teach, read Ephesians 2:1-2; 2 Corinthians 4:3-4; 2 Timothy 2:26; 1 John 5:19, but do not read these verses to the people when you teach the lesson.

- **Satan tried to get Jesus to worship him.**

    In the beginning, Satan tried to take God's position as the ruler of the whole universe. Although Satan failed in that attempt to take God's position, many angels followed him in his rebellion against God. After Satan and the rebellious angels were thrown out of Heaven, they continued to fight to take God's position. Satan tempted Adam, and when Adam rebelled against God and followed Satan, Satan took control of the human race.

    Satan never gave up trying to take God's position. Satan knew that Jesus was God's Son so Satan tried to take God's place by trying to get Jesus to worship him.

- **Jesus answered Satan by quoting from the Bible.**

    📖 Read Matthew 4:10.

    Jesus refused to worship Satan. Jesus answered Satan by telling him that the Bible says to worship and serve only God. Jesus chose to obey the Bible. He refused to worship Satan.

⑤ Jesus defeated Satan every time He was tempted.

- **Jesus defeated Satan by quoting God's Word and by obeying God.**

    Every time that Satan tempted Jesus, Jesus answered by telling him what God really says in the Bible. Jesus did not change God's words as Satan did.

    Jesus did only what God told Him to do. Jesus did not obey Satan as Adam did in the garden in Eden. Jesus obeyed God His Father.

- **Because Jesus is God, He has authority over Satan.**

    In the beginning, Jesus, who is God, created all of the angels, including Lucifer. When Lucifer tried to take God's place as ruler over all things, he was cast from Heaven and became known as Satan. One day, Jesus will send Satan into the everlasting fire which God prepared for him and all his followers.

⑥ Satan left Jesus for a short time.

📖 Read Matthew 4:11.

LESSON 51: JESUS RESISTED SATAN'S TEMPTATIONS.

- **Satan knew he was defeated, so he left Jesus for a while.**

    Even though Satan left Jesus at this time, he came back many, many times and tried in every way he could to get Jesus to disobey God. He tempted Jesus with every temptation people have ever faced. But Jesus did not do anything Satan said to do. Jesus always did everything that pleased God His Father.

- **God sent angels to take care of Jesus.**

    Remember that Jesus had not eaten for forty days and forty nights. So after Satan had left Jesus, God sent some of His angels to provide all that Jesus needed.

? Questions

1. What was Satan's intention in tempting Jesus?

    Satan wanted Jesus to sin so that Jesus would not be able to be the Deliverer.

2. What was the reason Jesus didn't turn the stones into bread even though He was hungry?

    Jesus did not turn the stones into bread because His Father didn't tell Him to. Jesus would only do whatever His Father commanded Him to do.

3. What is more important than food?

    Knowing and believing what God says in the Bible is more important than food.

4. Does Satan know and use God's Word?

    Yes. Satan knows God's words, but he twists them in order to trick people.

5. What was the reason Satan could offer Jesus the position of ruler over all people in every part of the earth?

    When Adam rebelled against God and followed Satan, Satan took control of the human race.

6. Whose words did Jesus use to fight against Satan?

    Jesus used the words of God, written in the Bible.

LESSON 52: JESUS BEGAN HIS MINISTRY.

Scripture

Mark 1:14-28, 34-42

Lesson Outline

(1) John's work was finished. (Mark 1:14)

(2) Jesus began to teach. (Mark 1:14-15)

(3) Jesus chose men to assist Him in His work. (Mark 1:16-20)

(4) Jesus taught with authority. (Mark 1:21-22)

(5) Jesus cast out evil spirits. (Mark 1:23-28)

(6) Jesus healed many sick people and cast out demons. (Mark 1:34-39)

(7) Jesus healed a leper. (Mark 1:40-42)

(?) Review Questions from Lesson 51.

Lesson Outline Developed

(1) John's work was finished.

Read Mark 1:14.

- **John was a faithful messenger for God.**

    John faithfully taught God's message to prepare the people to trust in Jesus the Deliverer.

    Some of the people changed their minds about themselves and their sin. They knew that they needed a Savior to save them from the punishment for their sins, and they were waiting for the Deliverer to begin His work.

    Others, including the Pharisees, trusted in themselves. They thought that they were good enough for God, and they refused to repent.

- **King Herod had John killed.**

  Remember that John spoke strongly to the proud and arrogant. King Herod was proud and arrogant, and he did not like what John said to him. King Herod had John put in prison and later had him killed

- **John had finished his work.**

  John had faithfully done all the work God had given him to do. The time had come for Jesus to begin teaching.

  Jesus was about thirty years old when He began to teach.

② Jesus began to teach.

- **Jesus told the people that they needed to repent and believe God.**

  📖 Read Mark 1:14-15.

  Jesus commanded the people to change their attitude, to agree with God that they were helpless sinners, and to believe the good news that He had come to tell them.

- **We must believe God to be accepted by Him.**

  If we don't believe God, we cannot please God and be accepted by Him. We have already learned this.

  - Why did God accept Abel? Was it because Abel wasn't a sinner? No. It was because Abel believed what God said and trusted in Him.

  - Why did the Lord accept Enoch and take him to Heaven? It was because Enoch believed what God said.

  - Why did the Lord accept Noah and save him and his family from the flood in the big boat? It was because Noah believed God.

  - Why did the Lord accept Abraham and lead him to a country that the Lord promised to give him? It was because Abraham believed God.

  - Why did the Lord accept Moses and tell him what to do so the Israelites' firstborn children would not die? It was because Moses believed God.

  - Why did God protect the firstborn of the Israelites from death when the angel of death killed all the firstborn in Egypt? It was because they believed what God had told Moses and they put the blood on the doorposts and over the doors of their homes.

  - Why did God allow Joshua and Caleb to enter the promised land, when all the other Israelites in their generation died in the wilderness? It was because Joshua and Caleb believed that God would give the land of Canaan to the Israelites, even though there were giants in the land.

If you want to be accepted by the Lord, you must believe in God and trust His message that He is teaching you from the Bible.

- **Jesus told the people that God's rule on earth would begin soon.**

  Jesus told the people that they must repent and believe the good news that God's rule on earth was soon to begin. Satan had become the ruler of this world when Adam sinned against God. Because Adam followed Satan instead of obeying the true and living God, all of Adam's descendants have been born under the control of Satan. We were born into Satan's kingdom and under Satan's rule.

  Because God is loving, merciful and gracious to sinners, He sent Jesus, the Deliverer, into the world to overcome Satan and to deliver people from his control.

- **Jesus taught the people to agree with God and believe the Gospel.**

  When people believe God and trust in the Deliverer, they escape from Satan's control and come into oneness with God. Those who trust in the Deliverer are in God's kingdom and under His rule.

  This is also God's message to you today. You are under the control of Satan. God's good news is that, through believing God and trusting in the Deliverer, you can escape Satan's control and come into oneness with God.

③ Jesus chose men to assist Him in His work.

📖 Read Mark 1:16-20.

Jesus chose men to be His followers. He planned to teach them and send them out to tell others the message of God's coming rule on the earth.

④ Jesus taught with authority.

📖 Read Mark 1:21-22.

☞ **Teacher:** Show a picture of Jesus teaching in the synagogue.

- **Jesus taught the Jews in their synagogues.**

  The Jewish people gathered at meeting houses on the last day of the week to listen to God's Word. It was at the synagogues where the religious teachers would read and explain the writings of Moses and the prophets to the people.

  The Jews who lived in the country only went to the temple in Jerusalem for important feasts as God had instructed them through Moses. At other times they gathered in the synagogues.

- **Jesus taught differently than the scribes did.**

   The people who heard Jesus speak were surprised by the authoritative way in which Jesus explained the meaning of the words of God. This was very different from the way the teachers of the law taught.

   The religious leaders knew a lot about God's Word. Some of the religious leaders were scribes, the men who copied the words of God from the Scriptures. They were familiar with God's Word, but most of them did not really trust in God. Because they didn't know God, they did not understand God's Word clearly, so they could only tell the people what they thought the words meant.

   Jesus was not like the religious teachers. Jesus knew God, His Father, and He understood God's Word clearly. When Jesus taught, He told the people exactly what God was saying to them through the writings of Moses and the prophets.

(5) Jesus cast out evil spirits.

📖 Read Mark 1:23-28.

- **Satan's evil spirits hate people.**

   The evil spirits were the angels who rebelled against God and followed Satan as their leader. Sometimes the Bible calls them "demons." The evil spirits help Satan in opposing God.

   Evil spirits can indwell people who are the under Satan's rule.

- **The evil spirit recognized Jesus.**

   📖 Read Mark 1:24 again.

   Satan and the evil spirits know that Jesus is God, their Creator. They also know that He is holy. They know He is perfect and hates all sin.

   The evil spirit in this man knew that he and all demons will eventually be thrown into the Lake of Fire. The evil spirit knew that Jesus had the power to destroy him by having him thrown into the Lake of Fire right then.

- **Jesus commanded the evil spirit to be quiet.**

   Jesus did not want the evil spirits to tell people about Him. Jesus planned to tell the people God's truth and to show them His power by the miracles which He did. Jesus did not want the evil spirits to speak on His behalf.

- **Jesus commanded the evil spirit to leave the man.**

   The evil spirit obeyed Jesus and left the man.

⑥ Jesus healed many sick people and cast out demons.

📖 Read Mark 1:34-39.

- **Jesus was all-powerful.**

    Jesus had the power to heal sick people and to cast demons out of people. Because Jesus is God, all things are under His power. God is more powerful than anyone, any spirit or anything else in Heaven or on earth.

- **Jesus was compassionate.**

    Jesus felt compassion for the people who were sick and the people who were possessed by demons. He knew that all of the sad things in the world are because of sin and the rule of Satan over the world. Jesus feels compassion for all people who are under Satan's control.

- **Jesus has not changed.**

    He has compassion on you today, just as He had compassion on the people in the Bible times. He knows that Satan controls your life and that you cannot save yourselves from death. Jesus wants to deliver you from sin and Satan's power.

⑦ Jesus healed a leper.

📖 Read Mark 1:40-42.

- **The Jews were very afraid of leprosy.**

    Leprosy was considered to be highly contagious, and there was no known cure for this disease. A person with leprosy had a very difficult life because lepers were required to live apart from other people.

- **This leper realized that only Jesus could help him.**

    He could not heal himself. No ordinary man could help him. There was no medicine to heal him. Only Jesus could help him.

    The leper came to Jesus, asking for His mercy and His help.

- **The sickness of leprosy is like sin in your lives.**

    There is no way that you can rid yourselves of sin, and there is no way that you can escape from the punishment of sin. God hates sin, and He will punish sinners with separation forever in the Lake of Fire.

- **Only Jesus, the Deliverer, can help you.**

    That is why He came into the world. Continue to listen to God's message so you will understand what Jesus did to deliver you from Satan, sin and death.

- **Did Jesus heal the leper?**

    Yes, He did! Jesus reached out His hand to touch the leper, He spoke, and the sickness of leprosy was gone.

    Only Jesus could heal this leper. Jesus is God, and He had the power to heal.

(?) Questions

1. Why did the Pharisees and other religious leaders refuse to accept John's teaching and repent?

    The Pharisees and other leaders refused to accept John's teaching because they were proud and thought that they were good enough for God to accept them.

2. When Jesus began to teach, what did He tell the people that they must do?

    Jesus told them to change their attitude, agree with God that they were sinners, and believe the good news that He had come to tell them.

3. What is the only way a person can please God and be accepted by Him?

    In order to be accepted by God, we must believe God and trust in His message from the Bible.

4. What was the difference between the way Jesus taught and the way scribes taught?

    The scribes did not understand God's Word clearly, so they could only tell the people what they thought the words meant. Jesus understood God's Word clearly and explained exactly what God meant in His Word.

5. Who were the evil spirits?

    The evil spirits were the angels who rebelled against God and followed Satan as their leader.

6. What do the evil spirits do?

    They help Satan in opposing God. They hate people and can indwell people who are the children of Satan.

7. What did the evil spirits know about Jesus?

    The evil spirits knew that Jesus is God, their creator and their judge. They knew that, one day, He would throw them into the Lake of Fire to be punished forever.

8. Jesus healed many sick people and cast out demons. What does this tell us about Jesus?

    Jesus is all-powerful and compassionate.

LESSON 52: JESUS BEGAN HIS MINISTRY.

9. How does the sickness of leprosy remind you of the sin which controls your lives?

   Just as no ordinary person was able to cure leprosy, only God can deliver us from the control of sin.

CHAPTER 53: JESUS TAUGHT THAT PEOPLE MUST BE BORN AGAIN

Scripture

John 3:1-7, 9, 14-20

Lesson Outline

(1) Nicodemus came to Jesus. (John 3:1-2)

(2) Jesus told Nicodemus that he must be born again. (John 3:3)

(3) Jesus explained to Nicodemus what it meant to be born again. (John 3:4-7, 9)

(4) Jesus must be lifted up. (John 3:14-15)

(5) God sent His Son so people can be born again. (John 3:16)

(6) Jesus came to save people and to give them everlasting life. (John 3:17-20)

(?) Review Questions from Lesson 52.

Lesson Outline Developed

(1) Nicodemus came to Jesus.

Read John 3:1-2.

- **Nicodemus was a Pharisee.**

    The Pharisees were the religious leaders of the Jews. They thought they could please God and be accepted by Him by what they did. They did not think that they were sinners like other people.

    The Pharisees knew that Jesus had been performing miracles. Most of the Pharisees hated Jesus and said that He did His miracles by the power of Satan.

- **Nicodemus realized that Jesus had been sent by God.**

    Nicodemus knew that the great miracles which Jesus had done could only be accomplished by the power of God.

    Although Nicodemus was sure that Jesus had been sent by God, he came to Jesus at night, probably so that the other Jewish leaders would not see him.

    ☞ **Teacher:** Show a picture of Nicodemus being taught by Jesus.

② Jesus told Nicodemus that he must be born again.

📖 Read John 3:3.

- **The Jews, and especially the Pharisees, were very proud that they were the descendants of Abraham.**

    They thought that they were in God's family because they were Abraham's descendants. They did not realize that every person born into this world has been born under Satan's rule. All people are born in Satan's kingdom and are his children.

- **God created Adam and Eve in His own image.**

    God gave them a mind so they could know and understand Him. God gave them emotions so they could love Him. God also gave them a will so that they could choose to obey Him and do what He wanted them to do.

- **When Adam and Eve chose to sin, they died to God.**

    They were separated from Him. They were no longer in oneness with God. They were no longer His friends as they were when He created them.

- **The image of God in Adam and in Eve was marred.**

    I will give you an example which might help you to understand what I mean. This did not really happen. It is just an example.

A beautiful woman and her strong, handsome husband had a beautiful baby boy. Because he was so much like his father, everyone knew whose son he was. But he was very wayward and wouldn't obey his parents. One day, while drunk, he got into a fight and fell into a fire and was badly burned. His face, which had previously looked so much like his handsome father, was scarred so badly that it was no longer easy to recognize him as his father's son. Because of his own sin, the image of his father which he had when he was born was deeply marred.

After Adam and Eve sinned, they still had minds, but they were no longer able to know God and understand His words as they did when He created them. They still had emotions, but they could no longer love God as they could when He created them. They still had wills so they could make choices, but they were no longer able to obey God as they could when He created them. They were no longer able to please God. They were under the control of Satan. God's image, which was so evident in Adam and Eve when they were first created, had been marred by their sin.

All people born into the world since that time have been born in the image of Adam in whom God's image was marred by sin. We have all been born unable to know, understand, love and obey God. No person born into this world can please God. Every person in every place, regardless of nationality, color or language, has been born under Satan's authority.

You were born under the rule of Satan just as all people are. You were not born with a mind that could know and understand the ways of God. You cannot love God as God wants you to, and you are unable to please God.

- **Jesus taught that people must be born again in God's image.**

    Jesus told Nicodemus that the only way a person can escape Satan's rule and be able to know, love and obey God is to be born again. This means that we must be changed so we can know, understand, love and obey God as Adam and Eve could when God created them. We must be made new in God's image.

- **We were not born under Satan's authority because of what we personally had done.**

    Adam sinned and placed himself under Satan's authority, therefore, all of Adam's descendants have also been born under Satan's authority.

- **We cannot escape Satan's authority because of what we do.**

    Just as no person is born under Satan's rule because of something he did, so no one can escape from Satan's rule by something that he does. We cannot change ourselves so that we will be able to please God and live under His rule in the kingdom of God.

    When we were born into this world, we were born separated from God. We were dead to God. It is impossible for us to bring ourselves back into oneness with God.

- **Only God can bring people into oneness with Himself.**

    God is almighty, and nothing is impossible to Him. By His power, He causes people to be born again – born new into God's family.

③ Jesus explained to Nicodemus what it meant to be born again.

📖 Read John 3:4-5.

- **Nicodemus did not understand what it meant to be born again.**

    Nicodemus was very surprised when Jesus said that a person must be born again before he can come under the rule of God. Nicodemus thought that Jesus meant that a person had to be born a second time as a baby.

- **Jesus explained that people must be born by water and the Spirit.**

  The water that Jesus was talking about was not the water of baptism. Baptism cannot make us children of God. It cannot wash away our sin.

  The water that Jesus was talking about was the Word of God. The only way a person can come under God's rule is by hearing, understanding and believing the Word of God which is taught by God the Spirit.

  Teacher: As you prepare to teach, read Ephesians 5:26; John 13:10; 15:3; Psalm 119:9; 1 Peter 1:23-25; Titus 3:5, but do not read these verses to the people when you teach the lesson.

- **God the Spirit teaches all who will listen to Him.**

  God the Spirit teaches the truth through God's words which are written in the Bible. He teaches the only way to God.

  We have already learned that God the Spirit teaches people. In the days when Noah was building the big boat, God the Spirit was endeavoring to convince the people that they were sinners and that they should change their attitude, agree with God and trust in Him.

  God the Spirit is still doing that same work today. Every time I teach you the words of God and every time you think about the words of God, God the Spirit is teaching you the truth so that you, too, will agree with God, believe His Word and be born again.

- **To be born again, a person must believe the Word of God.**

  In order to enter the kingdom of God, a person must be born again. He will be born again by believing the Word of God and by being changed by God the Spirit.

  Only those who believe God's Word will be born again. When people are born again, God the Spirit changes them so they can know, love and obey God.

- **Each person is either under Satan's rule or under God's rule.**

  📖 Read John 3:6-7.

  God says that there are only two categories of people in the world.

  Do you think God categorizes people by whether they are black or white? No! Do you think God categorizes people by whether they are rich or poor? No!

  God categorizes people by whether they have been born once or born twice. Those who have been born only once are still in Satan's family and under Satan's rule. Those who have been born twice are in God's family and under God's rule.

- **What Jesus taught was new truth to Nicodemus.**

    Jesus told Nicodemus not to be surprised that he must be born again. But Nicodemus still could not understand how he could be born into God's family.

    📖 Read John 3:9.

④ Jesus must be lifted up.

- **Jesus reminded Nicodemus about the bronze serpent in the wilderness.**

    📖 Read John 3:14-15.

    Nicodemus knew about this event because, as one of the leading teachers of Israel, he knew the Scriptures. Nicodemus also knew about this event because the Israelites in the wilderness were his ancestors.

    We also know about this event because we have learned about it from the Bible. Let's review what happened.

☞ **Teacher:** Show the picture of the bronze snake on the pole which you used earlier.

- **The Israelites had sinned against God.**

    God punished them by sending poisonous snakes among them. Many of the Israelites died because they were bitten by the snakes. The Israelites could not escape the poisonous serpents sent by the Lord. The snakes were everywhere.

    Do you remember what the Israelites did when God sent the poisonous serpents? They changed their attitude toward God and acknowledged their sin.

- **When the Israelites repented, God provided the way so that those who were bitten by the snakes could be healed.**

    God told Moses to make a brass snake and put it on a pole. Through Moses, God instructed the Israelites to look at the brass snake on the pole when they were bitten. God promised to heal all who looked at the brass snake. God healed all of the Israelites who believed Him and looked at the brass snake as He instructed.

- **Our situation is like that of the Israelites in the wilderness.**

    Just as the Israelites in the wilderness died when they were bit by the poisonous snakes, all people die because of sin. When Adam sinned against God, Adam was separated from God. All of Adam's descendants are separated from God and die because they are sinners. The payment for sin is death.

Just as the Israelites could not save themselves from death when they were bitten by the poisonous snakes, we cannot save ourselves from death.

Just as God was the only One who could deliver the Israelites, God is the only One who can deliver us.

- **Everyone needs to be delivered from Satan, sin and death and be born again into God's family.**

Jesus said that there is only one way this could be accomplished. He said that He must be lifted up just as the snake was in the wilderness. Whoever trusts in Jesus, the Deliverer, will be born again. They will be born into God's family and come under God's rule. And they will be given eternal life by God.

5. God sent His Son so people can be born again.

📖 Read John 3:16.

- Whom does God love?

God loves every person in the world. The Bible says, "*For God so loved the world...*"

- What did God do because of His great love for people?

Because God doesn't want any person to go with Satan to everlasting destruction, God sent the Deliverer into the world. The Bible says, "*For God so loved the world that He gave His only begotten Son...*"

- Whom did God give to be the Deliverer?

God gave "*...His only begotten Son...*" Jesus was God's only Son. There is none other like Him.

- What does a sinner have to do to be delivered?

A sinner must believe. God said "*...that whoever believes in Him...*" When a person believes God's words and trusts in Jesus as his Deliverer, God gives a new life to that person. A person who believes is born again. That person is no longer under the rule of Satan but is under the rule of God. That person has become a child of God.

- Will a person who believes in the Deliverer go into everlasting punishment with Satan and his demons?

No! Jesus said that all who believe on Him "*...should not perish...*" Those who trust in the Deliverer, whom God sent, will not go to everlasting punishment with Satan and his demons.

- What will all who believe on Jesus as the Deliverer receive?

They will "*...have everlasting life.*"

CHAPTER 53: JESUS TAUGHT
THAT PEOPLE MUST BE
BORN AGAIN

⑥ Jesus came to save people and to give them everlasting life.

- **We do not have to wait until we die to know if we will be accepted or rejected by God.**

    📖 Read John 3:17-18.

    Those who agree with God and trust in the Deliverer are not condemned. Those who refuse the Deliverer are condemned and rejected by God right now. Only one Deliverer has been given by God for sinners, and that Deliverer is Jesus.

- **People love their sinful ways.**

    📖 Read John 3:19-20.

    People love their own sinful ways. That is why people do not agree with God's Word and trust in Him. They don't want to admit that they are wrong. They don't want God to change them. They try to keep away from God's truth so that their sinfulness will not be exposed.

Teacher: If individuals are prepared for the Gospel and want to be saved, then you will need to speak to them privately and teach them Lesson 69 which tells of the death, burial and resurrection of the Lord Jesus on their behalf. However, if the people are listening but not inquiring as to how salvation was accomplished on their behalf, do not jump ahead. Continue to teach chronologically.

❓ Questions

1. For what reason did Nicodemus believe that Jesus was sent by God?

    Nicodemus knew that the great miracles which Jesus had done could only be accomplished by the power of God.

2. What did the Pharisees think would make them acceptable to God?

    The Pharisees thought they could be accepted by God because of what they did. They also thought that they were in God's family because they were Abraham's descendants.

3. Under whose rule has everyone in this world been born?

    All people are born under Satan's rule.

4. Describe the condition of people who are under Satan's rule.

    People who are under Satan's rule are unable to know, understand, love and obey God. They are separated from God and are unable to please Him.

5. What did Jesus teach was the way to escape from Satan's rule and come under God's rule?

Building on Firm Foundations - Volume 2: Evangelism: Genesis to The Ascension

Jesus taught that the only way a person can escape Satan's rule and come under God's rule is to be born again into God's family.

6. How is a person born again?

   A person is born again by believing the Word of God and by being changed by God the Spirit.

7. What did Jesus mean when He said that we must be born of water?

   Jesus meant that we must be born again by hearing, understanding and believing God's Word.

8. Who causes us to be born into God's family by teaching us God's Word so that we can hear, understand and believe it?

   God the Spirit causes us to be born into God's family because He teaches the truth of God's Word to all who will listen to Him.

9. Into what two groups does God categorize people?

   God categorizes people by whether they have been born once or born twice.

10. In whose family are those who have been born only once?

    Those who have been born only once are still in Satan's family and under Satan's rule.

11. In whose family are those who have been born twice?

    Those who have been born twice are in God's family and under God's rule.

12. In what way is our situation like that of the Israelites in the wilderness when they were bit by the poisonous snakes?

    Just as the Israelites in the wilderness died when they were bit by the poisonous snakes, all people die because of sin. Just as the Israelites could not save themselves from death when they were bitten by the poisonous snakes, we cannot save ourselves from death. Just as God was the only One who could deliver the Israelites, God is the only One who can deliver us.

13. How does the brass serpent which Moses put on the pole remind us of Jesus the Deliverer?

    Just as the snake was put on a pole and lifted up, Jesus had to be lifted up. Just as those who looked at the snake on the pole were healed, whoever trusts in Jesus, the Deliverer, will be born again and saved from the power of Satan, sin and death.

14. For what purpose did God send Jesus to this world?

    God sent Jesus to deliver people from Satan, sin and death, and to give them everlasting life.

15. For what reason do many people refuse to agree with God's Word and trust in Him?

    People do not want to agree with God's Word and trust in Him because they love their sinful ways. They do not want God to change them.

LESSON 54: JESUS HAD POWER TO HEAL SICKNESS AND TO FORGIVE SINS.

Scripture

Mark 2:1-17

Lesson Outline

(1) Jesus forgave the paralyzed man's sins and healed him. (Mark 2:1-12)

(2) Jesus chose Levi to be a disciple. (Mark 2:13-14)

(3) Jesus came to call sinners. (Mark 2:15-17)

(?) Review Questions from Lesson 53.

Lesson Outline Developed

(1) Jesus forgave the paralyzed man's sins and healed him.

Read Mark 2:1-2.

- **Many people came to hear what Jesus was teaching.**

    Jesus taught them the Word of God.

    The message of God which Jesus taught to the people is the same message that we are teaching to you. God's message to sinners does not change. God wants you to listen carefully just as these people listened to Jesus.

    Read Mark 2:3-4.

- **The paralyzed man was helpless.**

    He couldn't do anything to heal himself. The doctors could not heal him. His friends couldn't make him better.

    When we think of the helplessness of this man, we are reminded of the helplessness of all people. No one is able to deliver himself from Satan's rule, the sin which controls his life and the punishment for his sin.

You cannot deliver yourselves. We cannot deliver you. Religion cannot deliver you. A religious leader cannot deliver you. Baptism cannot deliver you. Who can deliver you from sin, Satan and death? The same One who could help the paralyzed man is the One who can help you.

- **The paralyzed man's friends brought him to Jesus,.**

They knew that Jesus was the only One who could help their paralyzed friend. But, they could not get near to Jesus because so many people were crowded into the house where Jesus was. So they carried the paralyzed man up to the roof of the house.

The Jews built their houses with flat roofs. They made the roofs by laying beams across from wall to wall. They covered the beams with a mat of reeds or thorn bushes. They then put thick clay or earth over these mats. There was usually an outside stairway leading to the roof.

After this man's friends carried him up onto the roof of the house, they broke a hole through the roof and lowered him down on his sleeping mat right in front of Jesus.

☞ **Teacher:** Show a picture of the paralyzed man in the house with Jesus.

- **Jesus forgave the paralyzed man's sins.**

   📖 Read Mark 2:5.

   Jesus saw that these men believed in Him, and He forgave the man's sins.

   📖 Read Mark 2:6-7.

   These scribes were right when they reasoned in their hearts that only God can forgive sins. But they were wrong when they reasoned that Jesus had sinned by forgiving this man's sin. Because Jesus is God, He had the authority to forgive people their sins.

   These teachers of the law did not believe that Jesus was God the Son who had come down from Heaven to be the Deliverer. They thought that Jesus was just an ordinary man.

   Does a priest or any other man have the authority to forgive sins? No! Only God can forgive sins.

- **Jesus healed the paralyzed man.**

   📖 Read Mark 2:8-12.

   Even though the scribes had only been thinking that Jesus was a blasphemer, Jesus knew their thoughts. Jesus is God, and He knows everything.

   Jesus demonstrated His power as God by completely healing the paralyzed man.

LESSON 54: JESUS HAD POWER TO HEAL SICKNESS AND TO FORGIVE SINS.

The people who saw what Jesus did were amazed, and they praised God. They had never seen anything like that before.

② Jesus chose Levi to be a disciple.

📖 Read Mark 2:13-14.

We learned previously that Jesus chose men to be His followers and to assist Him in His work. We read today that Jesus chose a man named Levi to follow Him as one of His disciples.

- **When Jesus chose Levi to follow Him, Levi was a tax collector.**

Levi was working for the Romans, collecting taxes from his own people, the Jews. Because tax collectors worked for the Romans, the Jews usually hated and despised them. Furthermore, the tax collectors were usually greedy men who made the people pay more taxes than they were supposed to. They kept this extra money for themselves.

- **Levi repented.**

Levi changed his mind about himself, his sin and God's Word. He agreed with God. He trusted in Jesus as the Deliverer whom God had sent into the world.

Many years later, Levi wrote one of the books which is in the Bible. Levi was also known by the name, Matthew, and the book he wrote is the book of Matthew. The Holy Spirit told Matthew what he should write.

☞ **Teacher:** Show the students the book of Matthew in your Bible.

③ Jesus came to call sinners.

- **Jesus ate a meal at Levi's house.**

  📖 Read Mark 2:15-16.

  Who else was at this meal besides Levi, Jesus and His disciples? Other tax collectors and some other friends of Levi's were also there. Tax collectors were considered to be among the worst people in society.

- **The scribes and Pharisees questioned why Jesus ate with tax collectors and other sinners.**

  📖 Read Mark 2:16 again

  The scribes and Pharisees were proud. Because they fasted, prayed and did many other things to try to please God, they believed that they were far better than others. The scribes and Pharisees would never eat a meal with people who were known to be evil.

- **Jesus told the scribes and Pharisees that He came to call those who realize they are sinners.**

  📖 Read Mark 2:17.

  Just as people who have no sickness see no need to go to the doctor, so those who think that they are not sinners see no need for the Deliverer. Just as sick people need a doctor, so those who are sinners need the Deliverer.

  Jesus did not come to help people who think they are sinless or good enough for God to accept them. Those people are not going to repent and trust in Jesus because they think that they are already righteous.

  Jesus came to help people who are sinners. He came to tell sinners to change their minds about their sins and come to Him. Jesus came to call all those who would agree with God that they are helpless sinners and who would trust in Him as their Deliverer.

  Do you realize that you are a sinner, that you have broken God's laws, that you are condemned by God to go to everlasting punishment, and that only God's mercy can save you? If you do, then Jesus said that He came into the world to be your Deliverer.

❓ Questions

1. In what way is the paralyzed man's helplessness similar to the helplessness of all people?
   The paralyzed man couldn't heal himself, and people cannot deliver themselves from Satan's rule, the sin which controls their lives and the punishment for their sin.

2. Who was the only One who could help the paralyzed man?
   Jesus was the only One who could help the paralyzed man.

3. Why did Jesus have the authority to forgive the paralyzed man's sins?
   Jesus had the authority to forgive the man's sins because Jesus is God.

4. What did Jesus demonstrate when He healed the paralyzed man?
   Jesus demonstrated His power as God.

5. What was Levi's other name?
   Levi's other name was Matthew.

6. What was Levi's work when Jesus chose him to be His disciple?
   Levi was collecting taxes from the Jews for the Romans.

LESSON 54: JESUS HAD POWER TO HEAL SICKNESS AND TO FORGIVE SINS.

7. Whom did Jesus come to call and save?

   Jesus came to call and save all those who agree with God that they are sinners and admit that they can only be saved by the mercy of God.

8. Will those who trust in their own goodness be accepted by God?

   No. God will never accept anyone because of his own good works.

LESSON 55: JESUS FORETOLD HIS DEATH, BURIAL AND RESURRECTION.

Scripture

Matthew 12:38-41

Lesson Outline

(1) The Jews wanted a sign. (Matthew 12:38)

(2) Jesus said that the same kind of thing that happened to Jonah would happen to Him. (Matthew 12:39-40)

(3) The people of Nineveh had believed, but the Jews would not. (Matthew 12:41)

(?) Review Questions from Lesson 54.

Lesson Outline Developed

(1) The Jews wanted a sign.

📖 Read Matthew 12:38.

- **Jesus had done many wonderful miracles.**

    We have already learned about some of the miracles that Jesus did.

    - Jesus healed many sick people.
    - Jesus cast demons out of people.
    - Jesus healed the man with the terrible disease of leprosy.
    - Jesus healed the man who was paralyzed.

    The people were amazed when they saw Jesus do these miracles, but they were only interested in the miracles. They did not really believe that He was the Deliverer as He said.

- **These Jews were just like their ancestors.**

    Do you remember how the ancestors of the Jews acted when they were in the wilderness?

They believed God when they saw the great miracles which He did, but they soon forgot His miracles and complained against God. They did not believe He would do what He said.

The people who lived in Jesus' day were the same. They did not believe, even though they knew that Jesus did miracles.

- **The Jews asked for Jesus to give them a sign.**

People in every age would rather see miracles performed than simply believe God's Word.

If we say we will not believe God's Word until we see some evidence that what God says is true, we are saying that we think God is a liar. Without faith in what God has written in the Bible, it is impossible to please God.

2) Jesus said that the same kind of thing that happened to Jonah would happen to Him.

Read Matthew 12:39-40.

- **Jesus said that the people of His day were sinful and did not follow the ways of God.**

The people wanted Jesus to perform miracles to prove that He was God's Son and the promised Deliverer. They didn't believe what God had written in His Word about the Deliverer. They didn't accept what Jesus was teaching them.

Do you think they would have believed that Jesus was God even if they had seen Him perform more miracles? No! They had already seen Him perform miracles, and they did not believe so they would not believe even if they saw more miracles.

- **Jesus said that the only sign which would be given to them would be like what happened to Jonah.**

Just as Jonah was inside the big fish for three days and three nights, Jesus would die and be buried in the earth three days and three nights.

Just as Jonah was released by God from the belly of the big fish, Jesus would be released from death and brought out of the grave by God.

That Jesus would die and rise again would be the sign and proof that He was who He claimed to be – the Son of God, the Deliverer who God had promised to send into the world.

- **Jesus knew He would die and rise again.**

Jesus knew everything that would happen to Him because He is God. God knows everything.

LESSON 55: JESUS FORETOLD HIS DEATH, BURIAL AND RESURRECTION.

- **God can give life to the dead.**

    Jesus said that He would die and rise again. God the Father would raise Him from the dead. Only God can give life to the dead. God can do anything He wants to do.

③ The people of Nineveh had believed, but the Jews would not.

📖 Read Matthew 12:41.

- **The wicked people of Nineveh believed.**

    Think about the people of Nineveh.

    - They were not Israelites, the chosen people of God.
    - They had not received the teaching of God through Moses and all the prophets which the Jews had in the Scriptures.
    - They had not seen the great and wonderful things which God had done for the Israelites.

    The people of Nineveh did not know about God as the Israelites did. Nevertheless, when Jonah told them that God said to repent or He would punish them, the people of Nineveh repented. They believed God's message through Jonah.

- **The Jews who were Jesus' own fellow countrymen did not believe.**

    They were more wicked than the people in Nineveh because they would not believe even though they knew about God.

    - The Jews were the descendants of Abraham, Isaac and Jacob.
    - They had the Word of God written by Moses and the prophets.
    - God had sent John the Baptist to prepare them to hear and believe on the Deliverer. Although the majority of the Jews appeared to accept John's teachings for they were baptized by him, many did not believe in their hearts, and most of the religious leaders refused to accept God's message to them through John.
    - They saw Jesus, the Son of God, perform miracles. He healed the sick, cast out demons and taught the Word of God. Did the people believe when they saw the miracles that Jesus did and when they heard Him teach? No! The majority of the Jews and their leaders would not believe.

- **Jesus was much greater than Jonah.**

    Jonah was an ordinary man whom God had chosen to be His prophet, but Jesus was the Son of God, the Creator who had come down from Heaven and was born as a baby to be the Deliverer.

Because Jesus was greater than Jonah, the Jews should have listened to Him and responded to His message. But in spite of all God's warnings of coming judgment on those who refused to repent which were given through John and then through Jesus, the majority of the Jews would not agree with God, change their attitude and believe on Jesus as their Deliverer.

? Questions

1. What did the Jews ask Jesus to do to prove that He was God's Son and the promised Deliverer?

   They asked Him to give them a miraculous sign.

2. What sign did Jesus say would be given to the people in His time?

   Jesus said that the only sign which would be given to them would be like what happened to Jonah.

3. Jonah was three days and three nights in the belly of the fish and then was released by God. How was this similar to what would happen to Jesus?

   Jesus would die and be buried for three days and three nights and then God would release Him from death and bring Him out of the grave.

4. The people of Nineveh repented even though they had not seen great and mighty works done by God. Why did Jesus say that the people of His day were more wicked than the people of Nineveh?

   Jesus said this because the people of Jesus' day would not repent and believe even though they had the written Word of God, had heard John's teaching, and had seen the miracles and heard the teaching of Jesus, the Son of God.

LESSON 56: THE JEWISH LEADERS PLOTTED TO KILL JESUS BECAUSE HE HEALED A MAN ON THE SABBATH.

Scripture

Mark 3:1-19

Lesson Outline

(1) The Pharisees hoped they could catch Jesus doing wrong. (Mark 3:1-5)

(2) The Pharisees and the Herodians plotted Jesus' death. (Mark 3:6)

(3) Jesus taught the crowds and healed the sick. (Mark 3:7-10)

(4) The evil spirits knew Jesus. (Mark 3:11-12)

(5) Jesus chose the twelve apostles. (Mark 3:13-19)

(?) Review Questions from Lesson 55.

(1) Lesson Outline Developed

The Pharisees hoped they could catch Jesus doing wrong.

- **The Pharisees and the other Jewish leaders rejected the message of God.**

    They had refused to repent when John taught them God's message. They also refused to repent when they heard the teaching of Jesus, the Deliverer.

- **The Pharisees hated Jesus.**

    They hated Jesus because He claimed to be God's Son, the promised Deliverer. They also hated Him because Jesus told them that they were sinners and exposed their hypocrisy before the people. Furthermore, they were jealous of Jesus because crowds of people followed Him.

- **The Pharisees were constantly watching Jesus, hoping that He would do something that they considered to be wrong.**

    If Jesus did something they thought was wrong, the Jewish leaders would be able to arrest Him and condemn Him to death.

Do you think that Jesus ever disobeyed God's law? No! Jesus perfectly obeyed all the laws of God all the time.

So how would the Jewish leaders be able to catch Jesus doing something that they considered wrong? We learned previously that the religious leaders added their own rules to God's Law. They had added these rules to God's Word in an attempt to please God and be made acceptable to Him.

- **These Jewish leaders watched Jesus to see if He was following the rules which they had added to God's Word.**

One of the rules the religious leaders added was that it was wrong to heal on the Sabbath day. God's Law said that they were to keep the Sabbath day as a day of rest, but the Pharisees added that they were not allowed to heal because they considered that healing a person was working. Do you think that Jesus obeyed this rule that the Pharisees had added to God's Law? No! Jesus refused to follow this rule and the other rules which the leaders of the Jews had added to God's Word.

Let's read from God's Word to find out what the Pharisees planned and what Jesus did.

📖 Read Mark 3:1-5.

- **Jesus knew that the Jewish leaders wanted to accuse Him of breaking the law.**

Jesus is God, so He knew what the Jewish leaders were thinking.

- **Jesus was angry and grieved that the Jewish leaders had hardened their hearts.**

Jesus was angry with the Jewish leaders because He knew that the Jewish leaders had set their minds and hearts against the things which God wanted to teach them.

This is the same thing that the king of Egypt had done in Moses' time. When God sent Moses to tell Pharaoh to let the Israelites leave Egypt, Pharaoh set his mind and heart against God and was determined to do what he wanted to do. After sending devastating plagues on Pharaoh's country, God destroyed that wicked man and his army.

It is a very dangerous thing for people to set their minds against God and His message. God will eventually destroy all those who refuse to obey Him. No one who fights against God will win.

- **Jesus completely healed this man's hand.**

Only God could heal this man's hand. Jesus is God, and God is almighty.

What did Jesus do to heal this man's hand? Jesus gave a command, and the man's hand was healed.

We learned previously that when God created the world, He did it all just by speaking. He created all things by simply commanding them to come into existence. In the same way, Jesus commanded this man to stretch out his hand and it was healed instantly.

LESSON 56: THE JEWISH LEADERS PLOTTED TO KILL JESUS BECAUSE HE HEALED A MAN ON THE SABBATH.

② The Pharisees and the Herodians plotted Jesus' death.

- **The Pharisees saw that Jesus healed the man's hand.**

  Do you think that the Pharisees changed their minds and believed when they saw this great miracle? Let's read from the Bible to find out what happened next.

  📖 Read Mark 3:6.

- **The Pharisees joined with the Herodians to plot Jesus' death.**

  Instead of believing when they saw Jesus heal this man's hand, the Pharisees joined with the Herodians to plot against Jesus.

  The Herodians were the followers of King Herod. They did not want any other king. This King Herod was the son of the King Herod who tried to kill the Lord Jesus when He was a baby.

③ Jesus taught the crowds and healed the sick.

📖 Read Mark 3:7-10.

- **Great crowds of people came to Jesus.**

  Many people from nearby countries came to hear Jesus teach and to be healed of their sicknesses.

☞ **Teacher:** On the map, point to these countries, and point out the Sea of Galilee.

Jesus taught the people on the shore of the lake named the Sea of Galilee. Because there were so many people, Jesus told the disciples to have a boat ready in case the people accidentally pushed Him back into the water.

- **Jesus showed that He is God by the miracles that He did.**

  There has never been anyone like Jesus. He is greater than all. Even those who touched Him, hoping to be healed of their sicknesses, were healed immediately, regardless of the sicknesses that they had.

④ The evil spirits knew Jesus.

📖 Read Mark 3:11-12.

- **The evil spirits recognized that Jesus was God.**

  The Jewish leaders did not believe that Jesus was really the Son of God, but the evil spirits knew that He was the Son of God. They had known Him and served Him in Heaven before they followed Satan.

All the spirits know that Jesus is God and the only Deliverer. The spirits which your ancestors believed in and which you believe in know who Jesus is. However, they don't want you to believe that Jesus is the Deliverer because they don't want you to be delivered from their control. The spirits know that they never had the right to control you or your ancestors. They know that only God should be the ruler over every person.

- **Jesus commanded the evil spirits to be quiet.**

    Jesus did not want people to believe on Him because of what the spirits said. Jesus wanted the people to believe, through His teaching, that they were sinners and needed Him as their Savior.

    You too have heard teaching from the Bible, and God wants you to believe the things you have heard. God will not show you miracles to make you believe on Him. He expects you to believe because of what He has written in the Bible.

⑤ Jesus chose the twelve apostles.

📖 Read Mark 3:13-19.

- **Many people followed Jesus.**

    Jesus had many followers. They followed Him to learn the message of God. Jesus had chosen some of them to leave their work to be His apostles. We already learned that Jesus chose Levi, who was also named Matthew, to leave his work as a tax collector to be His disciple.

- **Jesus chose twelve men to become His apostles.**

    From all the people who followed Him, Jesus chose twelve men to help Him in His work of teaching, healing and casting out demons from people. Jesus planned to train these men to become His apostles.

👉 **Teacher:** Point to the words, "**The 12 Apostles**," on the chronological chart.

👉 **Teacher:** Show a picture of Jesus with the 12 apostles.

These twelve apostles whom Jesus chose were not highly educated, and they were not rich. Some of them were fishermen before they began to follow Jesus as His apostles.

- **One of the men whom Jesus chose was named Judas Iscariot.**

    Judas said that he agreed with God and believed on Jesus, but he spoke only with his lips. His mind and heart did not agree with God. He did not truly trust in Jesus to be his Deliverer from the power of Satan, sin and death.

    The other eleven apostles didn't know that Judas was not a true believer, but Jesus knew

LESSON 56: THE JEWISH LEADERS PLOTTED TO KILL JESUS BECAUSE HE HEALED A MAN ON THE SABBATH.

what he was really like. Jesus knew that Judas would eventually betray Him to His enemies.

We may be able to hide our true self from others, but we cannot hide our inner thoughts from God.

Lesson Developer: Give an illustration to show that people can only see the surface. For example:

> *What would you do if you had something valuable which you wanted to hide? You would probably bury it. After you buried it, you would smooth the ground and make it look as though it had never been dug up. People can only see the top of the ground. They cannot see what is hidden below.*
>
> *Can people see anger inside you? Sometimes you may smile when someone says something you do not like, but inside you are angry. The person looking at you cannot see the anger which you have hidden inside.*

Just saying with our lips that we agree with God and believe His message may fool other people, but God knows our real minds and hearts.

? Questions

1. For what reason did the Pharisees constantly watch Jesus?

   The Pharisees wanted to catch Him doing something they considered to be wrong so that they could have Him arrested and killed.

2. Why did the Pharisees hate Jesus so much?

   They hated Jesus because He claimed to be the Son of God and the promised Deliverer. They also hated Him because He told them that they were sinners and exposed their hypocrisy before the people. They were also jealous of Jesus that the crowds of people followed Him.

3. For what reason did the crowds of people come to Jesus?

   They came to hear Jesus teach and to be healed of their sicknesses.

4. Did the evil spirits recognize who Jesus was?

   Yes! The evil spirits recognized that Jesus was God.

5. Why did Jesus tell the evil spirits to be quiet and not tell the people who He was?

   Jesus did not want people to believe on Him because of what the evil spirits said.

6. Although many people followed Jesus, how many did He choose to be His apostles?
   Jesus chose twelve men to be His apostles.

7. Were these twelve men well-educated?
   No. The majority of them were not well-educated.

8. Who is the only One from whom nothing can be hidden?
   God is the only One from whom nothing can be hidden.

LESSON 57: JESUS TOLD THE PARABLE OF THE SOWER.

Scripture

Mark 4:1-20

Lesson Outline

(1) Jesus told the parable of the sower. (Mark 4:1-9)

(2) Jesus explained why He spoke in parables. (Mark 4:10-13)

(3) Jesus explained the parable of the sower. (Mark 4:14-20)

(?) Review Questions from Lesson 56.

Lesson Outline Developed

Teacher: If the people you are teaching are not familiar with the type of farming and sowing of seed that is described in this lesson, use pictures and simple explanations to make sure they understand how the farmer prepared the soil and sowed the seed.

(1) Jesus told the parable of the sower.

📖 Read Mark 4:1-9.

- **Multitudes came to hear Jesus teach.**

  Jesus sat in the boat out in the water, and the people listened from the seashore.

- **Jesus taught through a parable.**

  A parable in the Bible is a story about ordinary, earthly things which teaches something about God, His ways and our need of Him.

  👉 **Teacher:** Show a picture of the sower sowing seeds.

② Jesus explained why He spoke in parables.

📖 Read Mark 4:10-13.

- **Jesus spoke in parables because most of the people refused to believe His teaching.**

    Even though many people followed Jesus and listened to His teaching, Jesus knew that they did not really believe His words. Many people followed Jesus because of the great miracles He did, but few people believed His teaching or saw their need for Jesus to be their Deliverer from Satan, sin and death.

    Many people followed Jesus just to get material and physical help, but because they did not believe what He taught, Jesus spoke to them in parables. He knew that the people would not be able to understand the spiritual meanings of the parables. The people happily listened to the stories that Jesus told, but they were not interested in what the parable was teaching about God. They had chosen not to believe, so Jesus let them continue in their ignorance.

- **Jesus continued to teach those who believed His teaching.**

    Those who agreed with God that they were sinners and wanted Him to be their Deliverer understood that there was a greater meaning to the parables. Jesus continued to teach those who wanted to learn.

- **God teaches those who want to know the truth.**

    If you want to know the truth, God will continue to teach you. However, if you set your mind against the truth, God may allow you to continue to believe lies and to die in ignorance.

③ Jesus explained the parable of the sower.

📖 Read Mark 4:14.

- **Jesus explained about the seed and the sower.**

    Jesus said that people who teach the Word of God are like sowers of good seed. God's Word is like good seed because all of God's words are truth.

    God has always had men to tell His message to people so that they would know the truth. We have already learned about some of God's messengers: Noah, Moses, the prophets and John the Baptist. These teachers of God's Word were like sowers who planted good seed in the minds and hearts of people.

    The good seed which they planted was the Word of God.

- **Jesus explained about where the seed is planted.**

    The seed is planted in the hearts of those who listen to God's message. Jesus said that, just as there are different types of ground, so people have different types of minds and hearts.

LESSON 57: JESUS TOLD THE PARABLE OF THE SOWER.

There are many different reasons why the good seed, that is, God's Word, does not grow in people's hearts.

Listen carefully so you will know what type of ground your heart is like.

- **Jesus explained about the path.**

    📖 Read Mark 4:15.

Lesson Developer: Use an illustration about what happens to seeds that are dropped on a road or hard path. For example:

> *If you are eating a papaya on the way home from your garden and you scoop out the seeds and drop them on the jungle path, will they grow? No! Why won't they grow? They won't grow because the monkeys, birds, ants, or some other animal or insect will eat them.*

- **Jesus said that some people have minds and hearts which are like the hard path.**

    They don't really want to listen to God. They are determined to think their own thoughts. They are determined to follow the old ways passed on to them by their ancestors. They will not consider the message of God and allow God to teach them.

- **When people whose hearts are like a hard path hear God's words, they soon forget them.**

    The words of God do not take root and grow. Satan takes the truth away from people's minds when they are hard and unreceptive.

    Think about the people who lived in Noah's day. Before the flood, Noah told the people the truth, but they had hearts like hard ground. They would not receive God's warning that He was going to destroy the world with a flood. The good seed did not grow in their hearts because their hearts were hard. Satan snatched the truth away because he wanted them all to die.

- **Jesus explained about the shallow, rocky ground.**

    📖 Read Mark 4:16-17.

Lesson Developer: Use an illustration to describe how seeds planted in rocky ground do not grow well. For example:

> *When you prepare a rice field or a garden, sometimes you find that the soil on top looks good, but just below the surface, there is only rock. Do you plant on that ground? No! The seed would start to grow; but because the roots could not go deep, the plant would soon die.*

- **Jesus said that some people have minds and hearts like a thin layer of soil over rocks.**

    When they hear God's Word, they readily accept and claim to believe, but their faith in God's Word does not last long. On the surface, they appear to accept God's truth, but underneath, their hearts are hard and they do not really want God's Word.

- **People who have hearts that are like a thin layer of soil over rock will turn away from the truth of God's Word when persecution comes.**

    For example, if their relatives, friends, or other unbelievers ridicule them or threaten them, they will turn away from the truth. Or if the spirits begin to threaten or fight against them, they will turn away from the truth and follow the spirits again.

    Outwardly, these people seem like good soil, but underneath, their minds and hearts are hard like rock. The good seed of God's Word soon dies in their minds, and they turn back to their own ideas and the old ways which Satan gave to their ancestors.

- **Jesus explained about the ground overgrown with thorny bushes.**

    📖 Read Mark 4:18-19.

Lesson Developer: Use an illustration to describe plants that are choked by thorns or weeds. For example:

> 💡 *If you took your good seed and planted it at the side of your garden among many weeds and bushes, would your seed grow well? No. The weeds would choke out the good plants.*

- **Jesus said that some people have minds and hearts like ground that is covered with brambly, thorny bushes.**

    These people listen to God's Word and say that they believe, but they also listen to the ways of this world. They think that they can believe God's message, while filling their lives with the things of this world, such as making money and enjoying the pleasures of this world.

- **The ways of this world which they love crowd out God's truth which they have heard.**

    Satan uses these things to lure people away from God and the truth. These people are more interested in following pleasures and keeping their former friends than they are in accepting God's words into their hearts.

- **Jesus explained about the good ground.**

    📖 Read Mark 4:20.

LESSON 57: JESUS TOLD THE PARABLE OF THE SOWER.

Lesson Developer: Use an illustration to show the importance of planting seed in good soil. For example:

> *Will your seed grow well if the ground you have chosen for your garden is not good? No. You must have good soil for your plants to be strong and healthy. If you begin with good soil, then it is likely that you will have a good harvest.*

- **Jesus said that some people have minds and hearts like good ground.**

  Those who are like the good ground receive God's words in their minds and believe God's words in their hearts. They realize that they are sinners, under Satan's control, and going to everlasting punishment. These people turn from trusting in their own ideas, in the ways of the world and in Satan. They change their minds and attitudes and agree with God. They believe only in Jesus as their Savior.

- **Think about the type of ground that your heart is like.**

  Is God's Word taking root in your heart, or is it being taken away by Satan?

  Is God's truth able to grow in your heart, or are the old ways of your ancestors, the ways of the spirits, or the evil things of the world stopping God's Word from growing in your heart?

? Questions

1. What is a parable in the Bible?

   A parable in the Bible is a story about ordinary, earthly things which teaches something about God, His ways and our need of Him.

2. Why did Jesus begin to teach in parables?

   Because many of the people refused to believe the truth which He taught them, Jesus spoke to them in parables and left them in their ignorance.

3. After Jesus told the parable of the sower, who did He say the sower was like?

   The sower is like a person who teaches the Word of God.

4. After Jesus told the parable of the sower, what did He say the good seed was like?

   The good seed is like the Word of God.

5. Where is the Word of God planted?

    The Word of God is planted in the hearts of those who listen to God's message.

6. Which people are like the hard path?

    They are the people who don't really want to listen to God and who refuse to consider the message of God.

7. Who snatches the truth away from people's hearts when they are hard and unreceptive?

    Satan does.

8. Which people are like the shallow, rocky soil?

    They are the people who seem to readily accept God's Word but who soon turn away from the truth.

9. What would cause the people who seem to accept the truth to turn away from God's Word?

    They would turn away from God's Word when persecution comes, such as when their relatives or friends ridicule them or when they feel threatened by the spirits.

10. Which people are like the ground overgrown with thorny bushes?

    They are the people who listen to God's Word, say they believe but soon forget what they have heard because they are more interested in the things of this world.

11. What kinds of things does Satan use to lure people away from God and the truth?

    Satan lures people away from God by using the things of this world, such as making money and enjoying the pleasures of this world.

12. Which people are like the good ground?

    They are the people who agree with God that they are sinners, under Satan's control and going to everlasting punishment. They believe God's Word in their hearts and trust in Jesus as their own Deliverer.

LESSON 58: JESUS CALMED A STORM AND RELEASED A MAN FROM THE CONTROL OF DEMONS.

Scripture

Mark 4:35-41, Mark 5:1-20

Lesson Outline

(1) Jesus calmed a storm. (Mark 4:35-41)

(2) Jesus released a man from the control of demons. (Mark 5:1-20)

(?) Review Questions from Lesson 57.

Lesson Outline Developed

(1) Jesus calmed a storm.

📖 Read Mark 4:35-37.

- **Jesus decided that He and His disciples should go to the other side of the Sea of Galilee.**

    Jesus and His twelve disciples got into a boat and started for the other side.

- **After they were out on the water, a bad storm began.**

    The wind was howling, and great waves were tossing the little boat around. The storm was so bad that the waves were crashing over into the boat and it was filling up with water.

    Have you ever been out in a boat during a bad storm? How do you think the disciples felt? They were afraid.

    If you had been there with the disciples, what would you have done? Remember that Jesus was with them in the boat. Let's read what the disciples did.

    📖 Read Mark 4:38.

- **The disciples woke Jesus.**

    Jesus was asleep in the back of the boat. Even though Jesus was God, He was also a real man. He got tired and slept just as we do.

    The disciples couldn't understand how Jesus could sleep during this terrible storm. They knew that they needed His help, so they wakened Him.

    When they wakened Jesus, they asked Him, "Teacher, do You not care that we are perishing?" The disciples should not have asked Jesus if He cared what was happening to them. They should have known that Jesus cared whether they were safe or not. The disciples had seen Jesus' love and care because they had seen Him heal the sick and feed the hungry crowds.

    What do you think Jesus could do about the problem? We have already learned that Jesus had the power to heal the sick and to cast out demons. Do you think He could control the howling winds and the turbulent sea?

    Let's read what Jesus did.

    📖 Read Mark 4:39.

- **Jesus calmed the storm.**

    Think about what we have already learned:

    - Who created the water and the wind in the beginning?
    - Who told the water to move back so there would be dry land on the earth?
    - Who opened up the Red Sea so the Israelites were able to escape from the Egyptians?

    God did these things, and Jesus is God. All things, including all oceans and seas, are under His control because He is the maker of all things.

    Lesson Developer: Use an illustration to show that the one who makes something has control or authority over what he makes. For example:

    > The things you make are yours, and you can do what you want with them. A man who makes a spear can throw it wherever he wants to. A woman who makes a basket can put whatever she chooses into her basket.

- **The sea on which Jesus and His disciples were sailing rightfully belonged to Jesus.**

    He made all things in the beginning, including the water, the wind, the lightning and the clouds. The storm had to stop when Jesus commanded it to stop because He is the maker and rightful owner of all things.

LESSON 58: JESUS CALMED A STORM AND RELEASED A MAN FROM THE CONTROL OF DEMONS.

☞ **Teacher:** Show a picture of Jesus and His disciples in the boat before He calmed the storm.

📖 Read Mark 4:40-41.

- **Jesus asked the disciples why they were fearful and lacking in faith.**

    The disciples had seen Jesus heal many diseases and cast out demons so they knew that He was powerful. Yet, during this storm, they thought they were going to drown even though Jesus was there in the boat with them. The disciples had forgotten that God sees everything, at all times, whether good or bad. The disciples should have believed that, because Jesus was God, He knew all about their situation and cared for them. Even if they had not woken Him, He would not have allowed them to drown.

    When the disciples saw that Jesus could control the wind and the waves, they were amazed. They had never seen Him do anything like this before.

② Jesus released a man from the control of demons.

📖 Read Mark 5:1-5.

- **The demon-possessed man was helpless.**

    This man could not release himself from the power and control of the evil spirits. Others had tried to restrain him, but the demons in him were so strong that they even broke iron chains. There was no one who was able to help him. There was no hope for this man. Satan had him in his power, and no one could deliver him.

- **This man's condition reminds us of our spiritual condition at birth.**

    We may feel sorry for a person like this and think it is good that we are not like him. We need to remember, however, that every person born into this world is under Satan's control and is just as helpless and hopeless as this man was. We cannot help ourselves, and it is useless for us to hope that other people can deliver us from Satan. Satan doesn't make many people do the things that this man was made to do, but Satan holds all people under his control unless Jesus the Deliverer sets them free.

- **Satan and his demons want to destroy people.**

    Think about what the demons did to this man. They controlled his life. Because of them, he was living in caves which were used as graves. The demons made him cut his body with stones. Demons hate God and they hate people. Even when it seems that they treat people well, they are only waiting for an opportunity to destroy them.

- **Satan and his demons are deceivers.**

The spirits who controlled your ancestors and now control you act as though they are helping you, but they are only doing this to trick you so they can keep you under their power. They only have one purpose, and that is to eventually destroy every one of you so that you do not come to know God and the truth.

We will read on now to learn what happened when the demon-possessed man met Jesus after Jesus got out of the boat.

📖 Read Mark 5:6-7.

- **The demons called out because they recognized Jesus as God.**

This man was talking, but the demons were controlling what he said.

The demons knew that Jesus was their Creator, the Son of God. The demons feared that Jesus might punish them immediately by sending them to the everlasting fire.

God is the supreme ruler over Satan and all the spirits. He can do with them whatever He pleases. He will throw them all into the everlasting fire when the time comes which He has planned.

What do you think Jesus did when these demons called out from inside this man that they were living in?

- **Jesus commanded the demons to come out of this man.**

📖 Read Mark 5:8-10.

There were many demons in this man, and there are many, many evil spirits in the world. Satan is their master.

- **The demons knew that they could not stand against Jesus, their Creator.**

Jesus has all power over Satan and his demons. They know that they will eventually be brought under His authority. Yet, even though they know that they cannot win, they continually try to fight against God.

- **This should make you think about who has control** over you.

How foolish it is to serve spirits who are going to be thrown into the everlasting fire to be punished! How foolish it is to allow the spirits to continue to control you when only God who gave you life has the right to control you.

Listen carefully as we read what happened to the demons.

📖 Read Mark 5:11-13.

☞ **Teacher:** Show a picture of Jesus healing the demon-possessed man.

LESSON 58: JESUS CALMED A STORM AND RELEASED A MAN FROM THE CONTROL OF DEMONS.

- **Jesus gave the demons permission to go into the pigs.**

    When they entered the pigs, the pigs ran into the Sea of Galilee and drowned. The demons did not drown, however, because they do not have bodies as people or animals have.

    Jesus did not send these evil spirits into everlasting punishment at that time because it wasn't God's time to punish them for their rebellion and sin. Nevertheless, God does have a future time when Satan and all the evil spirits will be thrown into the Lake of Fire to be punished forever. No one can escape from God.

    We have already learned that at Jesus' command, the demons went out of the man and into the pigs. We will now read further to learn what happened when the pigs ran into the sea and were all drowned.

    📖 Read Mark 5:14-17.

- **The man who had been demon-possessed was set free.**

    This man was set free from the control of the evil spirits by the power of the Lord Jesus. He no longer had to do the things that the spirits told him to do. He was now under the authority of God.

    The people who came to see what had happened were afraid. Unlike the demons, the people didn't know Jesus was God the Deliverer, and so they were very afraid of Him and His power.

- **The people asked Jesus to leave their country.**

    These people were very foolish. Jesus, the Son of God and the Deliverer, had come to teach them, but they did not want Him to stay. They were more concerned about the loss of their pigs than they were about coming to know the truth and being liberated from the power of Satan, sin and death.

- **There are still people in the world today who refuse to listen to God's message.**

    They are more interested in the things of this world than in what will happen to them after death. They live only for the things of this life, but these things last for only a short time. We cannot take any of the things of this world with us when we die. The message of God in the Bible is much more important than the things of this world because God's words will teach us the way to receive everlasting life.

    The people living around the area where the pigs had drowned were so insistent that Jesus leave that He decided it was better if He did what they said. But, the man who had been demon possessed was not pleased. Listen to what he requested of Jesus.

    📖 Read Mark 5:18-20.

- **The man who was freed from the power of the demons had a purpose in life.**

    He told other people the message of what Jesus had done for Him.

    That is why we have come here – to tell you about Jesus and what He has done.

> **Teacher:** You may wish to give a short testimony at this point. See example below.
>
> Remember you have not yet told your hearers the Gospel (the death, burial and resurrection of the Lord Jesus). Therefore, if you give a testimony, do not include the Gospel except privately to those individuals who are prepared for the Gospel. Continue to build toward the full revelation of Christ's work on the cross by which He broke the power of Satan, sin and death and made it possible for believers to be reconciled to God.

> We were not controlled by spirits like this man was, but at one time, we were also under the control of Satan and were going to everlasting punishment. However, we heard the words of God and agreed with Him. We knew that we were sinners because we had disobeyed His laws. God taught us from the Bible that we could not make ourselves acceptable to God and that we could not escape God's punishment. Then we learned that God sent Jesus, His Son, to be the Savior of sinners. We trusted in Him.

? Questions

1. Why did Jesus get tired and hungry and experience all the other things people do?

    Jesus got tried and hungry because, although Jesus was God the Son, He was also a real man with a body like ours.

2. Who had the power to control the howling winds and the turbulent sea during the terrible storm?

    Jesus had the power to control the howling winds and the turbulent sea.

3. Why was Jesus able to command that the sea and wind to be quiet?

    Jesus could command the sea and the wind because Jesus is God and He created the wind and the sea.

4. Could the demon-possessed man deliver himself from the power of the demons, or could any other ordinary person deliver him?

    No! He was helpless.

5. Can you deliver yourself from the power of Satan and his demons or can any ordinary person deliver you?

    No! We are helpless.

LESSON 58: JESUS CALMED A STORM AND RELEASED A MAN FROM THE CONTROL OF DEMONS.

6. From this story, how can we tell that demons hate people?

   The demons tormented this man. They controlled his life and caused him to spend his life crying out, cutting himself with stones and living in caves where people were buried.

7. Who controls all the evil spirits who live here on earth?

   Satan controls all the evil spirits.

8. Who is greater than Satan and his demons?

   God is greater than Satan and his demons.

9. Did the demons drown in the sea?

   No. Demons are spirits. They cannot be drowned.

10. Who completely changed this man's life?

    Jesus, the Deliverer, changed this man's life.

11. Who is the only One who can deliver all people from the power of Satan, sin and death?

    Jesus is the only One who can deliver all people from the power of Satan, sin and death.

LESSON 59: JESUS FED FIVE THOUSAND PEOPLE.

Scripture

John 6:1-35

Lesson Outline

(1) Multitudes followed Jesus. (John 6:1-4)

(2) Jesus fed five thousand people. (John 6:5-15)

(3) Jesus walked on the water. (John 6:16-21)

(4) Jesus is the Bread of Life. (John 6:22-35)

(?) Review Questions from Lesson 58.

Lesson Outline Developed

(1) Multitudes followed Jesus.

📖 Read John 6:1-2.

- **The people followed Jesus for the wrong reason.**

    This multitude of people followed Jesus because they were looking for material benefits from Him. They did not follow Jesus because they recognized themselves as sinners who needed a Savior.

    Jesus did not come into the world to give people material benefits or earthly riches. God sent Jesus to be the Deliverer from Satan, sin and everlasting death. So if a person thinks he will receive earthly benefits or riches because he follows the teachings of the Bible, he is mistaken. God does not promise anyone better conditions if he follows the Bible.

    When Jesus saw the multitudes coming toward Him, it was close to the time when the Jews held an important yearly feast.

- **The Feast of the Passover would soon begin.**

    📖 Read John 6:3-4.

    At the Feast of the Passover, the Jews remembered the last night that their ancestors spent in Egypt. Do you remember what happened that night? God protected their firstborn from death because each family had killed a lamb and put the blood on the doorposts of the house as God had instructed. Every year, the Jewish people remembered that God had delivered His people by killing and eating a lamb. This feast was held in Jerusalem.

② Jesus fed five thousand people.

📖 Read John 6:5-7.

- **Jesus asked his disciples how they would feed the multitude.**

    Do you think Jesus asked this question because He didn't know what to do? No! Jesus knows everything. He knew what He would do to feed the people, but He asked Philip in order to give him the opportunity to express his thoughts.

    Philip should have trusted in Jesus to feed the people. Philip had seen all the miracles which Jesus had done so he should have known that it would be very easy for Jesus to feed all those people.

- **The disciples only found five loaves and two small fish to bring to Jesus.**

    📖 Read John 6:8-9.

    The disciples brought the boy with the five loaves and two fish to Jesus. Jesus took the loaves and fish and performed a miracle.

- **Jesus multiplied the loaves and fish.**

    📖 Read John 6:10-13.

    As Jesus broke the loaves and fish, they multiplied until there was more than enough for all the people.

Lesson Developer: Illustrate the truth that only God could multiply food. For example:

> 💡 *If you have insufficient rice for a meal, are you able to keep dividing it so that it will multiply to be enough to satisfy your family's needs? No!*

No one except God who is almighty could multiply food like that. Jesus was able to do this because He is almighty God.

LESSON 59: JESUS FED FIVE THOUSAND PEOPLE.

☞ **Teacher:** Show a picture of Jesus feeding the 5,000.

The people were so surprised and pleased with what Jesus had done that they decided on a plan.

- **The people wanted to make Jesus their king.**

    📖 Read John 6:14.

    After seeing this miracle, the people seemed ready to agree that Jesus was the Deliverer whom God had promised to send into the world. However, they still didn't realize that they needed Jesus to be their Savior from Satan's power, sin and death. They just wanted Jesus to heal their sicknesses, to give them food and to deliver them from the control of the Romans. They decided to force Jesus to be their king. But Jesus was not going to fit in with their plans.

- **Jesus would not allow them to make Him their king.**

    📖 Read John 6:15.

③ Jesus walked on the water.

📖 Read John 6:16-21.

- **Jesus demonstrated His power as creator of the sea.**

    Do you know of any other man who can walk on water? No! It is impossible for an ordinary man to walk on water. But Jesus was no ordinary man. He was God as well as man.

    No one else is like Jesus. We learned previously that He had told the wind and the sea to be calm. We learn today that Jesus walked on the Sea of Galilee. Jesus created all water so it wasn't difficult for Him to walk on it. Jesus can do anything He chooses to do.

④ Jesus is the Bread of Life.

- **The next day, the people looked for Jesus.**

    📖 Read John 6:22-26.

    Jesus knew the minds of these people. He knew the real reason why they were looking for Him.

    God knows every one of our thoughts. God knows why we are listening to His message. He knows if we don't believe His Word or if we agree with Him and realize our need for Him to be our Deliverer.

- **Jesus told the people to desire spiritual food.**

    📖 Read John 6:27.

    Jesus wasn't saying that it is wrong to work for food, but rather He was saying that it is not the most important thing. Food for the body only helps people while they live in this world. Jesus was talking about a different kind of food which is necessary even after we die. He was saying that they should greatly desire and constantly seek until they had obtained the everlasting, spiritual food which only Jesus could give them. This spiritual food is the truth which Jesus was teaching them.

- **We have learned from the Bible that life continues on even after our bodies die.**

    We will live forever in Heaven or in the place of everlasting punishment. Will a healthy body or riches help us if we go to the everlasting fire when we die? No! These things won't help us so it is extremely important that you listen to and believe the words of Jesus. He is God's greatest prophet because He came to explain to all people who God is and what He has done to deliver sinners.

- **Jesus told the people that they needed to believe.**

    📖 Read John 6:28-29.

    We have learned what it means to believe. Do you remember when the Israelites were in the wilderness and they had been bitten by the poisonous snakes? What did they have to do so they would not die? They had to look at the brass serpent put on the pole by Moses. By looking at the brass serpent, they showed that they believed God would save them. Believing God was the only way they could be saved from death.

Teacher: Acts 20:1-4 refers to Paul's visit to Corinth on his third missionary journey. It was during this time that he wrote his letter to Rome. Paul mentioned in Romans 15:20-29 that he intended to visit Spain after going to Rome. Don't read this portion from Romans to the people at this point because you will read it in a later lesson.

💡 When you ride in an airplane, what do you have to do to reach your destination? Nothing! You just sit there and trust the airplane and its pilot to take you where you want to go.

When you cross a deep river in a canoe, what do you trust in to keep you from sinking? You trust in your canoe.

We cannot do anything to please God or to make Him accept us. God requires us not to trust in anything we do or in anyone else, but to trust only in Jesus as our Deliverer.

The crowds saw how Jesus had already done many miracles, but they still were not satisfied.

LESSON 59: JESUS FED FIVE THOUSAND PEOPLE.

- **The people wanted more miracles.**

  📖 Read John 6:30-31.

  Instead of believing the truth that Jesus was teaching, the people asked for another sign. They were looking at the great miracles which Jesus did and were not really listening and understanding what He was teaching.

  The people reminded Jesus of the manna which their ancestors ate in the wilderness for forty years. They thought that Moses had given the manna to their ancestors. They said that if Jesus was really the Son of God, He should give them a sign as great as Moses had given.

- **Jesus explained that God gave them bread from Heaven.**

  📖 Read John 6:32-33.

  Jesus explained to the people that it was His Father, not Moses, who gave the manna to their ancestors.

  Then Jesus told them that, just as His Father had given the manna in the wilderness so the Israelites would not die physically, so God had given the true bread from Heaven so that the people in this world would not die spiritually. Jesus was speaking about Himself. Jesus is the bread which God gave so that whoever believes in Him would receive eternal life.

- **The people did not understand.**

  📖 Read John 6:34.

  The people were still thinking about food for their bodies. Jesus had fed them with bread and fish, so they wanted Him to keep giving them food.

  Do you remember that Nicodemus did not understand at first when Jesus said, "You must be born again"? Nicodemus thought that Jesus was saying that we have to be born as a baby again. These people, like Nicodemus, thought that Jesus was speaking about natural, earthly things.

- **Jesus explained that He was the bread of life.**

  📖 Read John 6:35.

  Just as God gave the Israelites manna from Heaven and water from the rock to save them from physical death in the wilderness, so God sent Jesus from Heaven into the world to be the only Deliverer of sinners. If a person refuses to eat food, then he will die physically. In the same way, all who refuse to trust in Jesus as their Deliverer will remain dead to God, separated from God, forever.

  Whoever trusts in Jesus as their Deliverer will not need to trust in the spirits or anyone or anything else. Just as your stomach feels full and satisfied after you have eaten a good meal, so all who trust only in Jesus as their Deliverer will be happy and satisfied in their hearts because they will know they are in oneness with God. Jesus fully satisfies those who depend on Him. He is the only One who sinners need to make them acceptable to God and to give them eternal life.

? Questions

1. Why did many of the people follow Jesus?

   They followed Jesus because they were looking for material benefits from Him.

2. What were the Jews remembering when they ate the Feast of the Passover?

   They were remembering the time when God protected the firstborn of the Israelites from death in Egypt because God saw the blood which they had placed on the doorposts of their houses.

3. How many loaves and how many fish did Jesus have when He started to feed the five thousand people?

   Jesus had five loaves and two small fish.

4. What happened to the loaves and fish as Jesus broke them?

   As Jesus broke the loaves and fish, they multiplied until there was more than enough to feed everyone who was there.

5. Why was Jesus able to do such a great miracle?

   Jesus could do this miracle because He is almighty God.

6. After seeing this great miracle, what did the people want to do?

   They wanted to make Jesus their king.

7. Why did Jesus refuse to let the people make Him their king?

   Jesus refused to let the people make Him their king because He knew that the people just wanted Him to be their king so He would heal their sicknesses, give them food and deliver them from the control of the Romans. Jesus knew that the people had not realized that they needed Him to be their Savior from the power of Satan, sin and death.

8. What is more important than physical food?

   Spiritual food which gives everlasting life is more important than physical food which only helps us while we live in this world.

9. Can we do any good works which will please God and make us acceptable to Him?

   No. We cannot do any good thing to please God or to make us acceptable to Him.

LESSON 59: JESUS FED FIVE THOUSAND PEOPLE.

10. What must we do to receive eternal life?

    We must put our trust in Jesus as our Deliverer.

11. Who gave manna to the Israelites in the wilderness?

    God gave them manna.

12. The manna that God gave to the Israelites in the wilderness came from Heaven. How does this remind us of Jesus?

    Jesus was given from Heaven by God.

13. The Israelites would have all died if God had not given them the manna. How does this remind us of Jesus?

    We would have all died and gone to everlasting punishment if God had not sent Jesus to be our Deliverer.

LESSON 60: THE WAY OF THE PHARISEES IS NOT GOD'S WAY.

Scripture

Mark 7:1-9, 14-23, Luke 18:9-14

Lesson Outline

(1) The Pharisees did not worship God in their hearts. (Mark 7:1-9, 14-23)

(2) Jesus told a parable about a tax collector and a proud Pharisee. (Luke 18:9-14)

(?) Review Questions from Lesson 59.

Lesson Outline Developed

(1) The Pharisees did not worship God in their hearts.

- **The Pharisees added their own rules to God's Word.**

    Read Mark 7:1-5.

    The Jewish leaders had made up many rules, adding their own rules to God's Word. They taught that a person must follow these rules in order to be accepted by God. The Pharisees disapproved of Jesus' disciples because they did not do many things which the Pharisees said were necessary for a person to be accepted by God.

    Teacher: Show a picture of the Pharisees in the temple.

    These Jewish leaders were very proud that they followed their own rules, but they were hypocrites. Although they did all the outward things, such as washing their hands, pots and tables before they ate, their hearts were evil. They cared what people thought of them, but they did not care that God saw their sinful hearts.

    Lesson Developer: Use an illustration to show that washing the outside of something does not clean the inside. For example:

> 💡 *If there are chicken droppings inside of your cooking pot, can you make the pot clean by washing the outside? No! Of course not!*

- **Jesus condemned the Pharisees.**

    📖 Read Mark 7:6-9.

    The prophet Isaiah wrote that the Jews said many good things about God with their lips, but in their hearts, they did not love God, and they did not believe and obey His Word.

    God did not accept the worship of the Jews who did not mean it in their hearts. God rejected the worship of all who did not agree with Him that they were sinners and trust in His promises regarding the Deliverer.

- **Even today, some people teach their own ideas instead of God's Word.**

    These people say they are following and worshiping God, but they are not. Instead of trusting God, they believe that God will accept them if they obey the rules that they have added to God's Word. These people are trying to come to God their own way instead of God's way. Keeping man-made rules will not make a person acceptable to God. It is very wrong to add to or take away anything from God's words.

- **Jesus taught that following outward rules will not make people acceptable to God.**

    📖 Read Mark 7:14-19.

    The scribes and Pharisees put great emphasis on not eating certain foods. They thought that God would accept them if they did not eat these foods.

    Jesus made it very clear that what we eat does not make us unacceptable to God. The sin in our hearts is what makes us unacceptable to God.

Lesson Developer: If the people among whom you are teaching think that conforming to another culture will make them acceptable to God, this would be an appropriate place to teach the fallacy of that way of thinking. For example: "The food which you eat is very different from the food which we eat. The clothes you wear are very different from the things we wear. Your culture is different from ours in many ways. But what we eat or wear are not the things which make us acceptable or unacceptable to God. Trying to eat or dress like us will not make you acceptable to God."

- **God sees the sin in our hearts.**

    📖 Read Mark 7:20-23.

    The wicked things that people do come from inside their hearts. Even if we do not actually do these wicked things, God sees the evil in our hearts and will not accept us.

LESSON 60: THE WAY OF THE PHARISEES IS NOT GOD'S WAY.

② Jesus told a parable about a tax collector and a proud Pharisee.

We are now going to read a parable which Jesus told to illustrate that God rejects the proud and unrepentant but has mercy on all who admit their sinfulness and trust in Him. Remember that a parable in the Bible is a story that teaches something about God and our need of Him. Jesus spoke this parable to those who were selfrighteous, people who thought that they could be accepted by God because of the things they did.

📖 Read Luke 18:9-14.

- **The Pharisee was proud.**

In the parable, the Pharisee went up to the temple to talk to God. He was a proud man, and he was trusting in his own goodness to be accepted by God. As he prayed, he listed things which he did that he thought would cause God to accept him.

This Pharisee was like Cain. Cain came to God in his own way, trusting in the things which he himself had grown from the ground. Just as God rejected Cain, God also rejected this proud Pharisee.

- **The tax collector was repentant.**

In the parable, the tax collector did not try to hide his sinfulness from God. He saw himself as God saw him. He agreed with God about his own sinfulness. He knew that if God did not send a Deliverer, he would go to the Lake of Fire to be punished forever by God. He trusted in the Lord as his Deliverer. God had mercy on him. God forgave him and accepted him.

This tax collector was like Abel. Abel agreed with God and trusted only in God to be his Deliverer.

- **Jesus taught that God gives mercy to those who realize that they need Him.**

📖 Read Luke 18:14 again.

The Pharisee would not admit that he was a guilty and helpless sinner who needed God's mercy, so his sins were not forgiven by God. God rejected him just as He had rejected unbelieving, rebellious Cain.

The tax collector had a different attitude. He believed God's Word and admitted that he was a helpless sinner who could only be saved from God's judgment by the mercy of God. This tax collector deserved to be separated from God forever, but because of God's love, mercy and grace, He accepted the tax collector just as He had accepted Abel who trusted in God's Word.

? Questions

1. Why did the Pharisees disapprove of Jesus' disciples?

   The Pharisees disapproved of Jesus' disciples because they did not follow all the rules which the Pharisees claimed were necessary to please God.

2. What did the prophet Isaiah write about people like the Pharisees?

   The prophet Isaiah wrote that they say good things about God with their lips, but in their hearts, they do not really believe God's Word, love God, or want to obey Him.

3. Is it right for anyone to add his own ideas and rules to the Bible?

   No. It is not right for anyone to add to or take anything away from what God has said in the Bible.

4. Does what we eat make us unacceptable to God?

   No! Jesus made it very clear that what we eat does not make us unacceptable to God.

5. What makes us unacceptable to God?

   The sin in our hearts makes us unacceptable to God.

6. People can only see the bad things that others do outwardly, but what does God see?

   God sees the bad things in our hearts.

7. What are some of the sinful things which God sees in every person's heart?

   God sees evil thoughts, sexual sin, murder, theft, covetousness, deceit, pride and foolishness.

   Teacher: Note the list of sins in Mark 7:21-22.

8. Why did God accept the tax collector?

   God accepted the tax collector because he agreed with God that he was a sinner and needed God's mercy.

9. Why did God refuse to accept the Pharisee?

   God would not accept the Pharisee because he was proud and thought that his own goodness would make him acceptable to God.

LESSON 61: JESUS IS THE CHRIST, THE SON OF GOD.

Scripture

Mark 8:27-31, Mark 9:2-8

Lesson Outline

(1) Jesus asked His disciples who people believed that He was. (Mark 8:27-30)

(2) Jesus foretold His death and resurrection. (Mark 8:31)

(3) Jesus was transfigured. (Mark 9:2-3)

(4) Jesus talked with Moses and Elijah. (Mark 9:4)

(5) God spoke about Jesus. (Mark 9:5-8)

(?) Review Questions from Lesson 60.

Lesson Outline Developed

(1) Jesus asked His disciples who people believed that He was.

Read Mark 8:27-28.

- **The people had different ideas about who Jesus was.**

    Some people thought that Jesus was John the Baptist. They thought John had come back to life after King Herod killed him.

    Some people thought that Jesus was Elijah come back to earth. Elijah was a prophet whom God had taken to Heaven without dying.

    Some people thought that Jesus was just another prophet.

    Even though Jesus had told the people that He was the Son of God and the promised Deliverer and even though He had shown them His power by the great miracles which

He did, the majority of the Jews still did not believe on Him.

It is very important for you to think about who you believe Jesus was. Do you think that Jesus was just a good man? Do you think that Jesus was just another prophet?

Did Jesus speak the truth? If He spoke the truth, then we must believe Him and trust what He said.

- **Jesus asked the disciples who they believed that He was.**

  📖 Read Mark 8:29.

  Jesus knew that His disciples would never be accepted by God His Father if they did not believe that He was God the Son and the Deliverer whom God had promised to send into the world.

  Peter believed that Jesus was the promised Deliverer.

  - He believed that Jesus was the One whom God had promised after Adam and Eve sinned.
  - He believed that Jesus was the One whom God had promised to send as the descendant of Abraham and David.
  - He believed that Jesus was the One whom God had promised through the prophets.

    Peter believed that Jesus was the Christ. We learned previously that Jesus was sent by God the Father to do three special things – to be God's prophet, to be God's high priest and to be God's king.

  - Jesus, the Christ, was God's great prophet. He was God's messenger to the whole world, and He only spoke the truth.
  - Jesus, the Christ, was the great high priest. He came from God to take away the sin of the world.
  - Jesus, the Christ, was the great king. He was sent by God to be the final ruler of the whole world.

- **Jesus wanted the people to listen to Him and to believe what He told them about Himself.**

  📖 Read Mark 8:30.

  Jesus didn't want people following Him just because the disciples said He was the Christ. Jesus wanted people to listen to His words and to believe His words in their hearts.

- **It is the same today.**

  God doesn't want you to say you believe in Jesus just because we believe in Him. You must believe in Jesus because of what the Word of God says. If you only follow us and do not believe the Word of God, you will not be accepted by God.

LESSON 61: JESUS IS THE CHRIST, THE SON OF GOD.

② Jesus foretold His death and resurrection.

📖 Read Mark 8:31.

- **Jesus knew that He must die.**

    Jesus knew that He would suffer. Jesus knew that Satan would use the Jewish leaders to kill Him because they did not believe that He was God's Son and the promised Deliverer. Jesus also knew that, although they would kill Him and He would be buried in the earth, He would come out of the grave after three days and three nights.

    We have already learned that Jesus had told the people that He would be in the ground for three days and three nights, just as Jonah had been in the belly of the big fish for three days and three nights. He also had told them that God would release Him from death and that He would come back to life, just as God had released Jonah from the belly of the big fish.

Lesson Developer: Ask questions to help the people think through the truth that people cannot anticipate what will happen to them in the future. For example:

> 💡 *Can you tell what is going to happen to you tomorrow? Are you going to get sick, or will you be healthy?*
>
> *What will happen to you when the new moon appears?*
>
> *Will you still be living after the next harvest?*

We cannot know our future, but Jesus knew His future. There isn't anything which Jesus didn't know.

Jesus knew His future because Jesus was not just a man like us. Jesus was God the Son who came into the world to be the Deliverer from Satan, sin and death.

- **Jesus knew that God's Word would be fulfilled.**

    Hundreds of years earlier, the prophets had foretold that Jesus would suffer many things, be rejected by the Jewish leaders, be killed, but be raised from the dead after three days. Jesus knew and believed what was written by the prophets about Him. He knew that He was the Deliverer whom God had promised, and Jesus believed that all that had been said about Him would come to pass.

    God's Word is always fulfilled. Everything happens just as God says it will. God never lies.

③ Jesus was transfigured.

📖 Read Mark 9:2-3.

- **Jesus looked like an ordinary man.**

    Jesus had a human body just as we do. When people looked at Him, they saw a man who looked like an ordinary man. But Jesus was not just an ordinary man, was He? Jesus was a real man, but He was also God. The things that Jesus did and said showed that He was different from ordinary men, but Jesus' human body usually hid the part of Jesus that was God.

    Teacher: As you prepare to teach, read Isaiah 53:1-2, but do not read these verses to the people when you teach the lesson.

- **The tabernacle reminds us of Jesus' body.**

    We have already learned about the tabernacle which God told Moses and the Israelites to build for Him when they were at Mt. Sinai in the wilderness. The outside of this building was covered with the skins of animals. When the people looked at it, they saw skins, but inside the inner room, underneath the skins, was the very bright light which showed that God was there.

    Jesus' human body looked like that of an ordinary man. However, Jesus was not just an ordinary man. Jesus was also the almighty God who created the heavens and the earth.

- **Jesus' deity showed through His human body.**

    This is the only time while Jesus was on earth when He showed that part of Him that was God through His human body.

    Matthew, who was one of Jesus' disciples, also wrote in the Bible about what happened there on the mountain. Matthew wrote that Jesus' face began to shine like the sun, and His clothes were white and shining like the light from the sun. His clothes were whiter than any other clothes have ever been.

    Teacher: As you prepare to teach, read Matthew 17:2, but do not read this verse to the people when you teach the lesson.

④ Jesus talked with Moses and Elijah.

📖 Read Mark 9:4.

- **Moses and Elijah had been in Heaven with God.**

    When Moses and Elijah were alive on the earth, they had believed God's Word and they

LESSON 61: JESUS IS THE CHRIST, THE SON OF GOD.

had trusted in God and the coming Deliverer. Therefore, when they left this world, they went to Heaven to be with God, instead of being separated from God in the place of everlasting fire. God accepted them because they agreed with Him that they were helpless sinners and trusted in Him to send the Deliverer.

- **Heaven is a real place.**

    Moses and Elijah had been in Heaven with God for hundreds of years. All of those who agree with God and trust in the Deliverer whom God sent will go to live with God in Heaven when they die.

    God allowed Moses and Elijah to come down from Heaven to earth to talk with Jesus.

☞ **Teacher:** Show a picture of Moses and Elijah with Jesus.

- **Moses and Elijah talked with Jesus about His death.**

    When Moses and Elijah were alive on the earth, they knew that the promised Deliverer had to be born and had to die.

    Luke, one of Jesus' followers, wrote in the Bible what happened there on the mountain. Luke wrote that Moses and Elijah talked to Jesus about His death which was to take place in Jerusalem.

Teacher: As you prepare to teach, read Luke 9:30-31, but do not read these verses to the people when you teach the lesson.

Even though these men left the world many years before Jesus was born, they knew that God's promises about the Deliverer would all happen exactly as God had promised. God never forgets His promises, even if they were made thousands of years ago.

⑤ God spoke about Jesus.

📖 Read Mark 9:5-8.

- **God the Father spoke with a voice out of the cloud.**

    God the Father told the disciples that Jesus was who He claimed to be, that is, the much-loved Son of God. God told the disciples that they must listen to and obey whatever Jesus said because Jesus was the Son of God.

    There has never been and there will never be anyone else like Jesus, the Son of God.

- **God speaks to us through the Bible.**

    God does not speak to us by a voice from Heaven now because all that He wants to say to us has been written in the Bible. God expects us to listen to His words and put our trust in them.

Jesus spoke the truth. His words were given to lead us to God and to eternal life.

ⓘ Questions

1. Did most of the people in Jesus' time believe that He was the Son of God and the promised Deliverer?

    No. The majority of the people did not believe on Jesus, even though He showed them by His miracles and by what He taught that He was the Son of God and the Deliverer.

2. Who did Peter believe Jesus to be?

    Peter believed that Jesus was the Christ, the promised Deliverer whom God had sent into the world.

3. Is it important that we believe that Jesus is the Deliverer whom God sent into the world?

    Yes. If we do not believe that Jesus is the Deliverer whom God sent into the world, then we will be separated from God and go to everlasting punishment.

4. What did Jesus tell His disciples was going to happen to Him?

    Jesus said that He would be rejected by the rulers of the Jews and be killed, but that He would rise from the dead after three days.

5. When people saw Jesus, did He look just like an ordinary man?

    Yes. Jesus looked like an ordinary man.

6. Even though Jesus looked like an ordinary man, what was different about Him?

    Jesus was God as well as man.

7. What showed through Jesus' body while He was on the mountain?

    That part of Jesus that was God showed through His human body.

8. Which two men came down from Heaven to talk with Jesus on the mountain?

    Moses and Elijah came down from Heaven to talk with Jesus.

9. What were Moses and Elijah talking about with Jesus there on the mountain?

    They were talking about Jesus' death.

10. Who spoke from the cloud on the mountain?

    God the Father spoke from the cloud on the mountain.

11. What did God the Father say to Peter and the others?

    God told them that Jesus was His much-loved Son and that they were to listen to and believe Him.

12. Where are the words of Jesus written?

    The words of Jesus which God wants us to know and trust are written in the Bible.

LESSON 62: JESUS IS THE ONLY DOORWAY TO ETERNAL LIFE.

Scripture

John 10:7-11, John 14:6

Lesson Outline

(1) Jesus is like the doorway into the sheepfold. (John 10:7-10)

(2) Jesus is the Good Shepherd. (John 10:11)

(3) Jesus is the way, the truth and the life. (John 14:6)

(?) Review Questions from Lesson 61.

Lesson Outline Developed

(1) **Jesus is like the doorway into the sheepfold.**

- **Many Jews were shepherds.**

    Many of the people whom we have learned about from the Bible, such as Abel, Abraham, Jacob, Joseph and Moses, were shepherds. When Jesus was alive here on earth, many Jews were still doing the work of shepherds. The people that Jesus taught knew about sheep and about the work that shepherds did.

    Much of the land of Israel was dry and barren, and sometimes it was hard for the shepherds to find grass for their sheep to eat. Often, the shepherds had to leave their homes and lead their sheep a long way in search of food for them. Many times, the shepherds would be so far from their homes at nightfall that they had to sleep out in the fields or in the mountains with their sheep.

    It was dangerous for a shepherd to leave his sheep out in the open at night because there were robbers who would try to steal the sheep and there were wild animals which could kill the sheep. So before the night came, the shepherd would find a place to put his sheep where they would be safe through the night. Sometimes, he would find a cave, but often he would make an enclosure with walls of thorn bushes and stones.

When night came, the shepherd would put his sheep into this safe place and then lie down at the entrance. Anyone who went into the sheepfold had to go past the shepherd. The shepherd was like the door into the sheepfold. There was only one door into the sheepfold, and that was where the shepherd was lying.

☞ **Teacher:** Show a picture of the shepherd lying in the doorway of the sheepfold.

- **Jesus said that He was like the door into the place of safety.**

    📖 Read John 10:7.

    When Jesus said that He was the door, He meant that He was the way into the place of safety, security and eternal life.

    Outside of the place of safety are Satan, his evil spirits, sin and death. They are like the robbers which stole sheep and the wild animals which killed sheep.

Teacher: As you prepare to teach, read 1 Peter 5:8 and Hebrews 2:14-15, but do not read these verses to the people when you teach the lesson.

As the wild animals destroyed sheep, Satan desires to destroy you. He held your ancestors under his control and he now controls you. Satan's purpose is to destroy you so you will be separated from God forever.

Just as a shepherd loved and cared for his sheep, the Lord Jesus loves and cares for all people. He wants to deliver us from Satan, sin and death.

There is only one door into the place of safety, security and life. Jesus is God, and He is the Deliverer. Jesus is the only door to eternal life. There is no other way.

- **Many people claimed to be the Jews' Deliverer.**

    📖 Read John 10:8.

    Before Jesus was born, other men had come to the Jews, claiming to be the Deliverer sent from God. Jesus said that these people were like the robbers who came at night to steal the sheep.

    Satan uses many tricks to make you think that the way he teaches is the right way.

    The ways of Satan and the spirits may seem right, but the end of all their ways is death. All who follow the ways of Satan will be separated from God forever in the fire where God will throw Satan.

LESSON 62: JESUS IS THE ONLY DOORWAY TO ETERNAL LIFE.

- **Jesus is the only door to eternal life.**

    📖 Read John 10:9.

    There was only one door into the sheepfold; likewise, Jesus is the only doorway into eternal life.

    Some people may say to you that what the Bible teaches is the right way for the missionary but that the way of your forefathers is the best way for you. That is not true. There are not many ways or many doors to acceptance and oneness with God. There are not many ways to eternal life.

    There is only one door to God and to eternal life. Jesus is that door. He came to be the Deliverer of all people, in every place, no matter what language they speak or how they live.

    We have already learned this. Think about the big boat that God had told Noah to build. God told Noah to build a big boat because God was going to punish the whole world. God commanded Noah to build only one boat and to put only one door to enter the boat. Only those who came through that one door into the boat were saved from God's judgment on the world because of sin.

    Noah believed God, and he entered by the door into the big boat. Because Noah trusted in God and His words, he entered by the door and was saved from the punishment of God.

    The way to enter the door to everlasting life is to agree with God and His Word and trust only in Jesus who is the Deliverer. Jesus is the doorway to God. There is no other way to God.

- **Jesus came to give us eternal life.**

    📖 Read John 10:10.

    Jesus said that He is not like Satan, the evil spirits, or the people who are controlled by them. What they teach will cause people to be separated from God forever. Jesus came into the world to give life forever with God to all who believe on Him. All who trust in Jesus as their Deliverer are called Jesus' sheep.

② Jesus is the Good Shepherd.

📖 Read John 10:11.

- **Jesus, the Good Shepherd, must die for His sheep.**

    Jesus said that He was like a shepherd who loved his sheep so much that he would die for them in order to save them from the robbers who would steal them or the wild animals who would kill them.

    Jesus knew that He would die. Jesus had already told His disciples that the leaders of the Jews would not believe that He was the Son of God and the Deliverer sent by God, and therefore, they would kill Him.

The prophet Isaiah said that the Deliverer would suffer and die for others. God did everything that He promised through His prophets.

 Tell them that God's words written by Isaiah were fulfilled. Then read Isaiah 53:4-5 and John 10:11 to them. Then point to the Prophetic Chart and write John 10:11 opposite Isaiah 53:4-5. (See example below.)

What God said about the Deliverer He would send		How God's Word Came True
Isaiah 53:4-5	Suffer for others	John 10:11

3) Jesus is the way, the truth and the life.

Read John 14:6.

Jesus is the way to God and everlasting life.

Jesus is the One who came to tell us everything that God wants to say to us. All that Jesus said is the truth. He cannot tell a lie.

Jesus is the Deliverer. He is the only One who can save us from everlasting death and give us everlasting life.

? Questions

1. When Jesus lived here on earth, how did a shepherd make himself like a doorway to the sheepfold?

   The shepherd would make himself like a doorway to the sheepfold by lying across the entrance to the enclosure where he had put his sheep to protect them at night.

2. Why did Jesus call Himself the door of the sheep?

   Jesus called Himself the door of the sheep because He is the door through whom we must enter into eternal life.

3. Of whom do the thieves and robbers who killed the sheep remind us?

   They remind us of Satan, the evil spirits, sin and death.

4. How does the one door into Noah's big boat remind us of Jesus?

   The one door into Noah's big boat reminds us of Jesus because, just as there was only one door into the big boat, Jesus is the only way to eternal life.

5. What did Jesus say He would do for His sheep?

   Jesus said that He would give His life for them.

6. What did Jesus come into the world to give to His sheep?

   Jesus came into the world to give everlasting life with God to all who believe on Him.

7. Who are called Jesus' sheep?

   Jesus' sheep are all those who have agreed with God that they are helpless sinners and have put their trust only in Jesus as their Deliverer.

LESSON 63: JESUS RAISED LAZARUS FROM THE DEAD.

Scripture

John 11:1-48

Lesson Outline

① Lazarus became sick and died. (John 11:1-16)

② Jesus planned to raise Lazarus from the dead. (John 11:17-27)

③ Jesus had compassion on the people. (John 11:28-38)

④ Jesus raised Lazarus from the dead. (John 11:39-48)

(?) Review Questions from Lesson 62.

Lesson Outline Developed

① Lazarus became sick and died.

📖 Read John 11:1-6.

Jesus knew what was going to happen to Lazarus even though Jesus was a long way from where Lazarus was. Jesus is God. He knows everything.

Jesus could have healed Lazarus without even going to where he was, or He could have gone immediately to where Lazarus was to heal him. Jesus, however, didn't heal Lazarus from far away, and Jesus didn't go immediately to where Lazarus was.

Jesus waited for two days before He left to go to Lazarus. Instead of healing Lazarus, Jesus allowed him to die because Jesus knew that this situation was going to be another opportunity for Him to show His mighty power as the Son of God.

- **Jesus loved Lazarus and his sisters.**

  Because Jesus did not heal Lazarus, it may seem as though Jesus didn't love Martha, Mary and Lazarus, but that is not so. He loved them and was concerned about them. Jesus truly loves every person and wants everyone to trust in Him as his Deliverer.

- **Jesus told his disciples that it was time to go to Lazarus.**

    📖 Read John 11:7-16.

    The disciples thought that it was unwise for Jesus to return to Judea where His enemies were. They thought His enemies would try to kill Him.

    Jesus wanted His disciples to know that He was not afraid of being caught and killed so He explained to them that He was not like a man stumbling around in the dark, not knowing where He was going. He said He was like a man who could clearly see where he was going because he was walking in the sunlight. Jesus knew that His enemies could not kill Him because God's time for Him to die had not yet come.

    The disciples still misunderstood Jesus. The disciples thought that Jesus was going to allow the Jewish leaders to kill Him so He could die also and thus be with Lazarus.

② Jesus planned to raise Lazarus from the dead.

- **Jesus went to see the sisters of Lazarus.**

    📖 Read John 11:17-22.

    Martha believed that Jesus had the power to heal her brother. She also believed that

    God the Father would do whatever Jesus asked Him to do.

- **All people will be brought back to life to be judged by God.**

    📖 Read John 11:23-24.

    Jesus meant for Martha to understand that He intended to bring her brother back to life right away.

    Martha thought that Jesus was referring to the time at the end of the world when all people will be brought back to life again. Through His prophets, God had taught the Jews that all people will be made alive again.

    Because of sin, people die and are separated from their bodies. However, God will bring all people back to life and those who have refused to trust in the Deliverer will stand before God to be judged.

    Teacher: As you prepare to teach, read Revelation 20:11-15, but do not read these verses to the people when you teach the lesson.

    God can do this because He is powerful. He gave life to each person and He will give life to the dead.

    All you have ever done is remembered by God. Even though you die, God will bring you back to life again, and He will judge you for all of your sins. The only way to escape the punishment for your sins is through Jesus, the Deliverer.

LESSON 63: JESUS RAISED LAZARUS FROM THE DEAD.

- **Jesus had the power to give life to Lazarus.**

  📖 Read this phrase from John 11:25, *"Jesus said to her, "I am the resurrection and the life."*

  Jesus wanted Martha to understand that Lazarus did not have to remain dead until the day when God will judge all people. Jesus gave life to all people, and He has the power to give life even to those who have died.

  No other person can give life to the dead. Satan cannot give life to those who are dead. The spirits cannot give life to dead people. Only God can give life to the dead, for He is the almighty Creator who gave life to everyone and everything.

- **Those who believe in Jesus will never die.**

  📖 Read John 11:25-26.

  Jesus explained that, although those who trust in Him as their Deliverer die physically, their souls and spirits will live forever with God. They will never be separated from God to be punished for their sins. When they die, their souls and spirits leave their bodies, and they go to live with God in Heaven.

- **Martha believed Jesus.**

  📖 Read John 11:27.

  Martha was not like the majority of the people. They only followed Jesus because they wanted healing or food for their bodies. They were not interested in knowing Him as their Savior from sin and everlasting punishment.

  Martha believed and trusted in Jesus as the promised Deliverer who had come from God.

③ Jesus had compassion on the people.

📖 Read John 11:28-38.

- **Jesus wept.**

  The people were crying because they were so sad that Lazarus had died. Although Jesus knew that He was going to bring Lazarus back to life again, He also wept. Jesus wept because He was sad to see the problems which sin and death have caused all people.

- **God feels compassion for all people.**

  God feels sorry for all people because there is sin in the world. Because there is sin, there is sickness and death. Sin and death came into the world because of Adam's disobedience to God. All people are now sinners, and we die because we are all the descendants of Adam.

  Does God care when you are sick or when your people die? Yes, God does care. God loves you, and He wants you to believe His words and trust in Jesus as your Deliverer. God wants you to be with Him forever. Because God doesn't want any of you to go to the place of everlasting separation and punishment, He sent Jesus into the world to be your Deliverer. Continue to listen very carefully so you will know what Jesus did so your sins can be forgiven and you can be accepted by God and be in oneness with Him.

④ Jesus raised Lazarus from the dead.

📖 Read John 11:39-44.

☞ **Teacher:** Show a picture of Lazarus coming out of the tomb.

- **Jesus is almighty.**

   Jesus is God. There has never been anyone like Him. Nothing is impossible to Him.

   Jesus raised Lazarus from the dead to demonstrate the power of God. In the beginning, He, with God the Father and God the Spirit, created all things. They created all things just by speaking. Now Jesus stood at the entrance to the tomb and spoke. He commanded Lazarus to come back to life, and Lazarus came back to life. Whatever Jesus says always happens.

- **When they saw Jesus' great power, some believed, and others refused to believe.**

   📖 Read John 11:45-48.

   Many of the Jews believed on the Lord Jesus because they saw His power when He raised Lazarus from the dead. However, most of the religious leaders refused to believe on Jesus even though they saw His great power. The priests and the Pharisees were only interested in retaining their position and keeping their wealth. They were afraid that the people might make Jesus their king. If this happened, the Romans who controlled the Jews and their land would be angry. They would blame the Jewish leaders and replace them with Roman leaders. Because the scribes, priests and Pharisees wanted to keep their place of authority, they planned to kill Jesus.

   Satan was leading these men. Satan does not want anyone to believe on Jesus and be saved from Satan's power.

   Are you going to be like the Jewish leaders and follow Satan? Or are you going to believe God and trust in Jesus?

LESSON 63: JESUS RAISED LAZARUS FROM THE DEAD.

? Questions

1. Who has the power to give life, even to a person who is dead?

   God has the power to give life, even if a person is dead.

2. Will all people be raised from the dead?

   Yes. All people, whether they believe God's words or not, will one day be raised from the dead.

3. Why didn't Lazarus have to wait until the end of the world to be raised?

   Lazarus didn't have to wait until the end of the world to be raised because Jesus who was God was able to give life to the dead.

4. Did Jesus know before He got to Bethany that Lazarus had died?

   Yes. Jesus is God, and He knows everything.

5. Why did Jesus raise Lazarus back to life?

   He raised Lazarus from the dead to demonstrate the power of God.

6. What did Jesus mean when He said that those who believe in Him will never die?

   Jesus meant that although they die physically, they will never be separated from God to be punished for their sins in the everlasting fire.

7. Why did Jesus cry?

   Jesus cried because He was sad to see the problems which sin and death have caused all people.

8. What was the reaction of the people when they saw Jesus demonstrate His mighty power by raising Lazarus from the dead?

   Some of the people believed, and some refused to believe.

9. Why were the priests and Pharisees unhappy to see Jesus performing these great miracles?

   They were afraid the people might make Jesus king and that the Romans would blame them and remove them from their position of power and wealth.

10. What did the priests and Pharisees plan to do?

    They planned to kill Jesus.

11. Who was leading the priests and Pharisees to plan to kill Jesus?

    Satan was leading them.

LESSON 64: JESUS TAUGHT THAT WE NEED TO BE HUMBLE AND ADMIT OUR GUILT.

Scripture

Mark 10:13-24

Lesson Outline

(1) Jesus loved the children. (Mark 10:13-16)

(2) Jesus taught a rich young man. (Mark 10:17-24)

(?) Review Questions from Lesson 63.

Lesson Outline Developed

(1) **Jesus loved the children.**

   📖 Read Mark 10:13-16.

- **Jesus wanted the children to come to Him.**

   ☞ **Teacher:** Show a picture of Jesus with little children.

   The disciples thought that Jesus would not want to take the time to show love and care for little children, but Jesus told the disciples to let the children come to Him.

   Jesus loves children. Children can believe His Word and trust in Him just as adults can.

   It is important that you children listen carefully so you, too, can understand and believe God's Word. You, too, are sinners and are under the power of Satan and death. The only way you can be rescued is by putting your trust in Jesus as your Deliverer.

- **People must trust God in the same way that a child trusts his parents.**

   Those who are unwilling to come to God and trust in Him like a little child will not enter Heaven.

> **Lesson Developer:** Describe how a little child trusts and depends on his parents. For example:

> 💡 When you pick up your little baby, he rests in your arms. He is not afraid that you might drop him. He trusts you to hold him securely and to take care of him.
>
> When you tell your little child something, he believes you. Little children do not usually try to reason or work things out for themselves. They simply believe what their parents tell them

Jesus said that we must accept what God tells us in the Bible just as if we were little children. Many people will go to everlasting punishment because they will not trust God and His Word, just as a little child trusts his parents. If you refuse to accept God's Word like a little child, you will never be delivered from the control of Satan, sin and death.

② Jesus taught a rich young man.

📖 Read Mark 10:17.

- **The rich young man asked Jesus what he could do to inherit eternal life.**

👉 **Teacher:** Show a picture of the rich young man.

This young man thought that he could please God and gain entrance to God's kingdom by his own goodness and by obeying God's laws. He thought that he could do good things to merit eternal life.

This young man was just like Cain. Cain thought that he could obtain God's favor by bringing to God the things which he had grown. Did God accept Cain because of the things which he brought to God? No! God rejected Cain because he came his own way and not the way God had said.

📖 Read Mark 10:18-20.

- **Only God is good.**

This young man did not understand that no man had ever been good enough to please God. He didn't realize that God is the only One who is good. He thought that he was good, and he thought that Jesus was just another good man like himself. Even though he did not realize that Jesus was God, he called Jesus "good."

When Jesus answered him, He wasn't denying that He Himself was good or that He was God. Jesus answered this way because He wanted the young man to realize that no ordinary man is good. If this young man believed that Jesus was good, then he should also

LESSON 64: JESUS TAUGHT THAT WE NEED TO BE HUMBLE AND ADMIT OUR GUILT.

conclude that Jesus was God, for the only One who is good is God.

- **No person can perfectly obey God's Law.**

    This young man did not realize that he could never perfectly obey God's commandments because he was born a sinner and was under Satan's control. God's Word says that there is not one person on earth who is good and therefore able to please God. No one, except Jesus, has perfectly obeyed God's laws.

    Teacher: As you prepare to teach, read Romans 3:9-20, but do not read these verses to the people when you teach the lesson.

    This man thought he had kept God's commandments because he had obeyed them outwardly. However, even if he did obey the commandments of God outwardly, he had not obeyed them fully and always in his heart.

    Jesus had already taught the people that, in God's sight, thoughts and intentions are as important as actions. For example:

    - If a man looks at a woman and desires her, he has committed adultery.
    - If a person hates another person in his heart, he has committed murder.
    - If a person would like to take something which belongs to someone else, he has stolen.
    - If a child outwardly obeys his parents but is angry in his heart or obeys grudgingly, he has sinned before God.

    God does not judge a person according to his outward acts alone. God also judges a person according to his inner thoughts and desires.

- **All people have failed to reach God's standard of goodness.**

    God did not give His commandments to Israel because He thought that they could obey them. Rather, God gave His Ten Commandments to prove to them and to all people that all have sinned and come short of God's standard of goodness.

    Lesson Developer: Illustrate what it means to come short of a standard. For example:

    > *Some boys were sent out with their blowguns into the jungle to shoot birds for their families' meal. Each of the boys tried to shoot a bird. Some of them tried very hard, but they missed by just a little bit every time. Some of them were careless and did not try very hard, and they missed by a great distance. Neither those who really tried nor those who were careless returned with birds for their families' meal. Each one failed.*

This is how it is with God's laws. Even those who try very hard are not able to obey God's laws perfectly as God demands. We have all failed to reach God's standard of goodness and perfection.

- **You can never merit God's favor by your own efforts.**

    You may think that you are a good person and that you do not deserve to go to the everlasting fire. Nevertheless, you, too, have failed to do what God requires. It is impossible for you to please God because, as a descendant of Adam, you are a sinner and separated from God. God looks at your heart, and He says that it is wicked just like everyone else's heart.

- **Jesus loved this young man.**

    📖 Read Mark 10:21.

    Even though this young man was proud and did not see himself as a sinner as God saw him, Jesus still loved him.

    God loves you even though you are a sinner. He does not want you to be separated from Him forever.

- **Jesus wanted this rich young man to realize that he had broken God's commandments.**

    Jesus wanted to show the young man that he was a sinner because he had not obeyed God's commandments perfectly as he thought he had. Therefore, Jesus told this young man to sell his possessions and give the proceeds to the poor and to leave his home and follow Jesus.

    Jesus knew that the young man loved his riches more than he loved his fellowman. By telling the young man to sell his possessions and give the proceeds to the poor, Jesus was trying to show him that he had not obeyed God's law perfectly because he had not loved others as much as he loved himself.

    Teacher: As you prepare to teach, read Mark 12:30-31, but do not read these verses to the people when you teach the lesson.

    By telling the young man that he should leave his home and follow Jesus, Jesus was trying to show him that the only way he could fully please God was for him to love God with all his heart, with all his soul, with all his mind and with all his strength. Jesus was endeavoring to teach this young man that he was not good – he was a sinner. He loved his wealth more than his fellowman or God.

    Because this young man had broken God's laws, he was a condemned sinner in the sight of God. Jesus wanted him to realize that he could not be accepted by God by the things he did. He was already dead to God and rejected by Him.

- **Every person has broken the commandments of God.**

LESSON 64: JESUS TAUGHT THAT WE NEED TO BE HUMBLE AND ADMIT OUR GUILT.

None of us has given God the highest place in our thoughts or given Him praise and thanks for everything as God commanded. Likewise, none of us has loved others as God commanded.

The payment for breaking God's commandments is death – separation from God in the place of punishment. God will not overlook the payment for sin. He will never forgive us unless the full payment for sin has been made.

Is there any way that our sin can be paid for so that we can be saved from the everlasting fire? Yes, there is! Continue to listen carefully, and it will become very clear to you what Jesus came to do so that you might be delivered from everlasting punishment.

- **This young man made his choice.**

    Read Mark 10:22-24.

This young man went away sad because, although he wanted eternal life, he did not want to admit that he was a sinner. He did not want to admit that he loved his money more than he loved God or other people, and he didn't want to change.

Maybe you are like this young man and think that the most important thing is to get the riches of this world. When you die, however, you will not be able to take any of your riches with you.

The rich and the poor are the same in the sight of God. God does not look at how many riches a man has. Our material possessions are not important to God, but whether we are willing to listen to His words and believe them is very important to God.

Previously, we read from God's Book how Jesus had fed five thousand men with five loaves and two small fish. Following this, the people came looking for Jesus, hoping to get some more food. Jesus reminded them that believing in Him was the most important thing.

Read John 6:27-29.

? Questions

1. Did Jesus care about children?

    Yes. Jesus loves all children.

2. Do children need to be rescued from the power of Satan, sin and death?

    Yes. Children need to be rescued from the power of Satan, sin and death just as adults do.

3. What did Jesus mean when He said that we must become as little children if we are to enter His kingdom?

Jesus meant that we must trust in Jesus, the Deliverer, just as a little child trusts his parents.

4. What did the rich young man think he could do to please God and inherit eternal life?

   This young man thought that he could please God and inherit eternal life by his own goodness and obedience to God's laws.

5. What did Jesus want the young man to understand when He said, "Why do you call Me good? No one is good but One, that is, God"?

   Jesus wanted him to understand that no ordinary man is good because all have disobeyed God's laws. He also wanted him to understand that God is the only One who is good.

6. Was Jesus saying that He is not good and that He is not God when He said to the rich young man, "Why do you call Me good? No one is good but One, that is, God"?

   No. Jesus is God and is therefore good like God the Father and God the Spirit.

7. Does God judge a person based only on his outward actions?

   No. God also judges a person according to his inner thoughts and desires.

8. If a person tries really hard to obey God's Law, will God accept him?

   No. Trying hard is not good enough for God. God will only accept those who reach His standard of goodness.

9. Why is it impossible for a person to obey God's Law perfectly?

   It is impossible for a person to obey God's Law perfectly because all people are born as sinners and are under Satan's control.

10. What did Jesus tell the rich young man to do?

    Jesus told him to sell his possessions and give the proceeds to the poor and to leave his home and follow Jesus.

11. By telling the young man to sell his possessions and give the proceeds to the poor and to come and follow Jesus, what did Jesus want this young man to understand?

    Jesus wanted him to understand that he was a sinner for he had not obeyed God's commandments perfectly as he thought he had.

12. Why did this young man go away sad?

    The young man was sad because, although he wanted eternal life, he did not want to admit that he was a sinner. He did not want to admit that he loved his money more than he loved God or other people.

13. Our material possessions are not important to God; what is?

    Whether we are willing to listen to His words and believe them is very important to God.

LESSON 65: IT IS FOOLISH TO TRUST IN RICHES.

Scripture

Luke 12:15-21, Luke 16:19-31

Lesson Outline

(1) Jesus told a parable to teach that it is foolish to live only for the things of this life. (Luke 12:15-21)

(2) Jesus told a true story about a rich man and a poor man. (Luke 16:19-31)

(?) Review Questions from Lesson 64.

Lesson Outline Developed

(1) Jesus told a parable to teach that it is foolish to live only for the things of this life.

- **Many people live only for the things of this life.**

  Many people desire the things of this world more than anything else. They are jealous of what other people have, and they think that they would be happy and satisfied if they were rich.

  Listen carefully to what Jesus said about living only for the things in this life.

  📖 Read Luke 12:15

  Jesus wanted people to know that money and things we own do not guarantee us a happy and contented life and what we own has no influence on where we will go when we die. Jesus told a parable to illustrate that it is foolish to think that lots of wealth brings happiness and security.

- **Jesus told a parable about a rich man.**

  📖 Read Luke 12:16.

  Do you remember what a parable in the Bible is? It is a story about ordinary, earthly things which teaches us something about God and our relationship with Him.

Jesus told this parable because He wanted the people to realize that our relationship with God is far more important than the riches of this world. Even if a man had all the riches in the world, it wouldn't be of any benefit to him when he dies and goes to everlasting punishment. Believing God and having everlasting life is of far more value than earthly riches.

- **The rich man planned to enjoy his riches for many years.**

    📖 Read Luke 12:16-19.

☞ **Teacher:** Show a picture of the rich man.

This rich man thought that he had all that he needed. He thought that he had nothing to worry about because he was rich. He thought that he could ignore God and live his life the way he wanted.

This man did not take into account that God is the One who gives life and the One who takes life. Although he did not acknowledge God's authority in his life, God had not forgotten him. The rich man made plans to enjoy his riches for many years, but God had a different plan for him.

- **God planned that the rich man would die that very night.**

    📖 Read Luke 12:20.

When God decides that it is the time for a person to die, he will die. No one can do anything to keep that person from dying. Satan and the spirits cannot hinder God from doing whatever He pleases.

God called this rich man a fool because he lived only for the riches of this world and did not acknowledge God's authority or think about what would happen when he died.

- **Every person who lives for the riches of this earth is like the man in the parable.**

    📖 Read Luke 12:21.

God said that the person who lives only for the things of this world and is uninterested in what God says to him is a fool just like the rich man Jesus told about in this parable. This man had lots of wealth in this world, but he had no spiritual wealth.

He foolishly put his trust in his riches and ignored God and the spiritual wealth that God wanted him to have

The things that God does for those who trust in Him are far better than the riches of this world. Those who trust in Jesus will have their sins forgiven, and they will be delivered from sin, Satan and death.

The things of this world only last for a short time, and we never know when we may have to leave them, but the things that God does for those who trust in Him will last forever.

LESSON 65: IT IS FOOLISH TO TRUST IN RICHES.

Are you like the man in the parable? If you put all your time and effort into living for the things of this life, then you are foolish just like the man in the parable. God is warning you to be wise and to invest your time and energy into learning about Him and trusting Him. Don't be foolish!

② Jesus told a true story about a rich man and a poor man.

We are now going to read a true story which Jesus told at another time. This story is about a rich man and a poor man. It was not a parable like the previous one we read. This really happened. At one time, the rich man and the poor man actually lived on this earth.

The poor man's name was Lazarus just like the man whom Jesus raised from the dead, but they were not the same person. The Lazarus whom Jesus raised from the dead was not a poor beggar like this poor man we are going to read about in this next story.

Let's read the first part of this story.

📖 Read Luke 16:19-21.

- **One man was rich; the other was a beggar.**

Of these two men, who do you think was the fortunate one?

Do you think the rich man was fortunate? He had enough money so that he could dress well and eat good food. He seemed to have everything that he needed, didn't he?

Or, do you think that Lazarus was the fortunate one? Lazarus was a beggar. He had to depend on other people to give him what he needed to live. He was sick and he did not have enough food to eat.

Of these two men, it seems as if the rich man was better off, but we have not yet read the end of the story. Listen to what Jesus said happened to these two men.

📖 Read Luke 16:22-23.

- **Both men died.**

Where did Lazarus go when he died? Jesus said that when Lazarus died, he went to the same place where Abraham was. Abraham had died hundreds of years before Lazarus had, and he was still living with God. This was a place of happiness and acceptance with God.

- **The men went to different places after they died.**

Where did the rich man go when he died? Did he go where Lazarus went? No. Jesus said that when the rich man died, his body was buried and his spirit went to the place of torment.

How did Jesus know where Lazarus and the rich man went after they died? He is God, and so He knows where every person is, even after he has died.

- **The rich man's wealth did not keep him from dying.**

  When God decides that it is the time for a person to die, he will die. It doesn't matter if he is rich or poor.

  The rich man's wealth did not help him after he died. Even though he was a wealthy man, he still went into the place of punishment. The things of this world are of no benefit to us after we die, and they cannot save us from the punishment of God for our sins.

- **The rich man is still in Hell, and Lazarus is in Heaven.**

  Even though thousands of years have gone by since these men died, the man who was rich is still in the place of punishment, and Lazarus is still with God.

Teacher: We will not teach the difference between Hades and the Lake of Fire at this time. Although Hades is not the final destination of the unsaved, those who are there have already entered into everlasting suffering. After the Great White Throne judgment, those who occupy Hades will be cast into the Lake of Fire which was prepared for Satan and his demons. As you prepare to teach, read Revelation 20:10, 12-15, but do not read these verses to the people when you teach the lesson.

You need to think about this: When you die, you will either go to be with God in Heaven or to the place of punishment. You will be with God in Heaven forever, or you will be in the place of fire and punishment forever.

Lesson Developer: Describe the people's incorrect beliefs regarding what happens to the spirit when a person dies. For example:

> *Your ancestors believed that when a person dies, his spirit wanders around on this earth. They also believed that their dead relatives could talk with them. They believed the spirits could come back to the houses where they once lived. These are lies of Satan. The voices you hear and the messages which you think are from the spirits of your dead relatives are really from Satan and his evil spirits.*

The spirits and souls of the dead do not stay in this world. As soon as a person dies, his spirit and soul are immediately in Heaven or in the place of punishment.

Satan tries to trick people about what happens when a person dies. Satan is a liar and a deceiver. He lied to Adam and Eve, and he is still doing the same to you. Don't believe what Satan says and what his evil spirits tell you. Don't believe what people say. Only God can tell us the truth, and He tells us the truth in the Bible.

LESSON 65: IT IS FOOLISH TO TRUST IN RICHES.

- **The man who had been rich cried out for mercy.**

  📖 Read Luke 16:24.

  There is great suffering in the place of punishment.

  ☞ **Teacher:** Show a picture of the rich man in the place of fire and Lazarus with Abraham.

  All who refuse to believe what God says in His Word will go to this place of terrible torment. God is not merely threatening about the punishment of sin. God hates sin. All sin must be paid for in full.

- **Abraham answered the man who had been rich.**

  📖 Read Luke 16:25.

  Think about this. Did Lazarus go to the place of happiness and acceptance with God because he was poor on this earth? Did the rich man go to the place of punishment because he was wealthy? No! God does not reject the rich and accept the poor. That is not what made the difference between the two men.

- **The rich man went to the place of everlasting punishment because he did not agree with God that he was a sinner.**

  He did not trust in God and His promises to send the Deliverer to rescue him from the power of Satan, sin and death. The rich man didn't take time to think of God or to believe His Word. He lived his life on this earth to enjoy his riches. He lived for himself and did not care about God or other people.

- **Lazarus agreed with God that he was a sinner.**

  Lazarus had a different attitude than the rich man did. Lazarus trusted in God and His promises to send the Deliverer, just as Abraham did when he was alive.

- **There is no escape from the place of everlasting punishment.**

  📖 Read Luke 16:26.

  Once a person dies and goes to the place of punishment, there is no way he can be delivered. There is no way of escape. He will be there forever.

  If you refuse to listen to God's Word and you die while you are still unacceptable to God, then you will go to the place of punishment. You will never be able to leave that place. Some people teach that those who go to the place of punishment will have another chance to be freed and go to the place of God, but that is not what God's Word teaches. That is Satan's lie.

Lesson Developer: If the people you are working with believe in purgatory, you may need to teach more extensively on the fact that when a person dies, he goes either to Hell or Heaven and that those who go to Hell will never be able to leave that place of punishment.

- **The man who had been rich wanted Lazarus to go to earth to warn his brothers.**

    📖 Read Luke 16:27-28.

    Even though he was in terrible suffering, this man still remembered his brothers and his relatives. People in the place of punishment still remember this world. They remember what they did when they were alive, and they remember the relatives and friends that they have left behind.

    Think about this: Why did this man want Abraham to send Lazarus back to the home of his brothers?

If the people you are teaching believe that the dead need items from this life, mention specific items and teach that Satan has lied to them about the dead needing those things. For example:

> 💡 *Did the man who had been rich want Lazarus to ask his brothers for blankets? Did this man want Lazarus to ask the brothers for food? Did he want Lazarus to ask them for the blood of animals? No! Those things cannot be used by people who have died. Satan and his evil spirits have made you believe that you need to offer these things because your dead relatives need them, but Satan is lying to you.*

Jesus said that the man in Hell wanted Abraham to send Lazarus back to earth to warn his relatives so they wouldn't also go to the same terrible place of punishment where he was.

- **Lazarus was not needed to warn those still living.**

    Lazarus was not sent back to this world to warn the relatives of the man in Hell because God had already provided sufficient warning.

    Let's read what Abraham said to the man who had been rich.

    📖 Read Luke 16:29.

- **God's message in the Bible is sufficient warning.**

    Abraham told this man that his brothers should believe the writings of Moses and all the prophets in God's Word, the Bible.

    No one needs to go to this place of fire and punishment. If we listen to God's Word, He will teach us the way to everlasting life through the Lord Jesus.

LESSON 65: IT IS FOOLISH TO TRUST IN RICHES.

📖 Read Luke 16:30-31.

- **God's message in the Bible is more important than miracles.**

    If people refuse to believe God's written Word, they will not believe even if God did send someone back from the dead to warn them. We learned in a previous lesson that even though the leaders of the Jews saw Jesus raise Lazarus from the dead, they still would not believe.

    How important it is to listen to and believe God's Word! Continue to listen to God's Word so that you can learn the way to everlasting life with God.

❓ Questions

1. What is much more important than being rich in this world?

    Believing God and having everlasting life is much more important than having earthly riches.

2. Who decides when it is time for a person to die?

    God decides when it is time for a person to die.

3. Why did God call the rich man in the parable a fool?

    God called this rich man a fool because he lived only for the riches of this world and did not consider what would happen to him after he died.

4. What are the things that God does for those who trust in Him which are far better than the riches of this world?

    Those who trust in Jesus will have their sins forgiven, and they will be delivered from sin, Satan and death.

5. Is the story of the rich man and Lazarus a parable?

    No. This story really happened.

6. Where do people go when they die?

    When people die, they either go to Heaven or to the place of punishment

7. Where did the beggar, Lazarus, go when he died?

    His spirit and soul went to be with God.

8. Where did the rich man go when he died?

The rich man's body was buried and his spirit and soul went to the place of fire and everlasting punishment.

9. Why did Lazarus go to be with God and the rich man go to place of everlasting punishment?

   Lazarus agreed with God that he was a sinner and trusted in God and His promises to send the Deliverer so he went to be with God. The rich man did not agree with God that he was a sinner and he did not trust in God and His promises to send the Deliverer so he went to the place of everlasting punishment.

10. Will anyone ever be released from the place of punishment?

    No. There is no escape from the place of everlasting punishment.

11. What did the man who had been rich ask Abraham to do to ease his torment?

    He asked Abraham to send Lazarus with a drop of water to cool his tongue.

12. What did the man who had been rich ask Abraham to do to for his brothers on earth?

    He asked Abraham to send Lazarus back to earth to warn his brothers so they wouldn't go to the place of punishment also.

13. What did Abraham tell the man who had been rich that his brothers should do?

    Abraham said that they should believe the writings of Moses and the prophets in God's Word.

14. How can we learn the way to God and to everlasting life?

    We can learn the way to God and to everlasting life through God's Word, the Bible.

LESSON 66: JESUS HEALED BLIND BARTIMAEUS AND RODE INTO JERUSALEM.

Scripture

Mark 10:45-52, Mark 11:1-10

Lesson Outline

(1) Jesus is the Deliverer. (Mark 10:45)

(2) Jesus healed blind Bartimaeus. (Mark 10:46-52)

(3) The people welcomed Jesus as He rode into Jerusalem. (Mark 11:1-10)

(?) Review Questions from Lesson 65.

Lesson Outline Developed

(1) Jesus is the Deliverer.

📖 Read Mark 10:45.

- **Jesus did not come into the world so that people could work for Him.**

    Jesus does not ask people to give Him anything or to do anything for Him. He is God. God doesn't need anything.

    Jesus does not ask people to work in order to earn their way into Heaven. We've already learned that no person is good enough to earn his way into Heaven because each person is a sinner.

- **Jesus came to do the work for us.**

    Jesus came into this world to be our Deliverer. The only way that He could be our Deliverer was for Him to give His life for us.

(2) Jesus healed blind Bartimaeus.

- **Bartimaeus was blind, and he was helpless to heal himself.**

Read Mark 10:46.

Bartimaeus could not do anything to give himself sight.

Think about this: Can a blind man see simply because he chooses to see? Can a crippled man walk and jump simply because he chooses to do so? No! That is impossible!

Just as Bartimaeus was blind and helpless to heal himself, so all people in this world have been born blind and helpless. We may not be blind or helpless physically, however, we all were born blind to the truth and helpless to know the truth.

When Adam followed Satan, Adam became blind to the truth and the way to God. His mind, which could previously understand God, became unable to understand God and the truth. The Bible says that all of Adam's descendants were born with minds that are blind. We are born unable to know the truth. We are born helpless and incapable of finding the way to God.

- **Bartimaeus believed that Jesus could heal him.**

   Read Mark 10:47.

  Bartimaeus knew that he could not help himself and that Jesus was the only person who could heal him. Bartimaeus had heard about the great miracles which Jesus had done, so when he heard that Jesus was passing by on the road to Jericho, he called out, asking Jesus to help him.

  Bartimaeus asked Jesus to have mercy on him. He knew that he did not deserve to be healed. He knew that he could not repay Jesus for healing him. He knew that, if Jesus healed him, it would have to be a free gift from Jesus.

  Just as Bartimaeus could only be given sight by God's mercy, so all people can only be shown the truth by God's mercy. We all were born sinners, blinded to the truth and the way to God. Only Jesus, the Deliverer who came from God, can help us. The only way we can be saved from the power of Satan, sin and death is by the free gift of God through Jesus, the Deliverer.

- **Bartimaeus called out to Jesus.**

  Bartimaeus addressed him as "Jesus, Son of David." Bartimaeus believed that Jesus was the descendant whom God had promised to King David. Do you remember what God had promised to David? He had promised that the Deliverer would be one of David's descendants and that the Deliverer would rule as king forever. Bartimaeus believed that Jesus was the promised Deliverer.

  Even though God made these promises to David many years earlier, God had not forgotten or changed His mind. Sometimes we make promises, but after time passes, we forget or wish we had not promised what we did. God does not forget or change His mind as time passes. Time does not change for Him. There is no day or night to God.

LESSON 66: JESUS HEALED BLIND BARTIMAEUS AND RODE INTO JERUSALEM.

There are no weeks, months or years to Him. Everything that happened when David was alive is just as real to God today as it was at the time when it happened.

Time has no effect on God. God is the same today as He was when David was living on the earth.

- **The people thought that Jesus would not be interested in Bartimaeus.**

  📖 Read Mark 10:48.

  Many of the people told Bartimaeus to be quiet. They didn't think that Jesus would be interested in a blind, poor man like him. Was that true? Was Jesus only interested in the rich, the well-educated and the healthy? No! That is not true.

  📖 Read Mark 10:49.

  Every person is important to God. It makes no difference to Him whether we are rich or poor, tall or short, educated or uneducated, healthy or sick, or what color our skin is. He loves every person and wants everyone to believe and trust in Him.

- **Jesus gave sight to Bartimaeus.**

  📖 Read Mark 10:50-52.

☞ **Teacher:** Show a picture of Jesus healing blind Bartimaeus.

Jesus had the power to give sight to Bartimaeus because Jesus is God. God created every person's eyes. Only God can give blind people their sight. God is almighty.

③ The people welcomed Jesus as He rode into Jerusalem.

Jesus and His disciples were walking to Jerusalem when Jesus healed Bartimaeus. After Jesus healed Bartimaeus, they continued walking until they came to a little town named Bethany. Lazarus, whom Jesus had raised from the dead, lived in Bethany.

- **Jesus sent His disciples to get a colt for Him to ride.**

  📖 Read Mark 11:1-7.

  Jesus sat on the colt and rode into Jerusalem. Through one of the prophets, God had said that the Deliverer would ride into Jerusalem on a colt.

Teacher: As you prepare to teach, read Zechariah 9:9. We did not list this prophecy on the prophetic chart, so do not read the prophecy from Zechariah to the people.

- **The crowds welcomed Jesus.**

    📖 Read Mark 11:8-10.

> 👉 **Teacher:** Show a picture of Jesus riding the colt into Jerusalem.

The people praised Jesus, saying that He was the One whom the prophets had promised that God would send to be their king. The people desired a king because they wanted to be delivered from the Romans who ruled their country. Therefore, on this day, they welcomed Jesus, wanting Him to be their king.

Sadly, however, the majority of these people did not trust in Jesus to deliver them from Satan's power, their sins and God's punishment.

❓ Questions

1. Does Jesus ask people to work for Him so they can earn their way to heaven?

    No! Jesus does not ask people to work for Him to earn their way to heaven.

2. What work did Jesus come to earth to do?

    Jesus came to earth to give His life to be our Deliverer.

3. Why did Bartimaeus address Jesus as "the Son of David"?

    Bartimaeus believed that Jesus was King David's descendant whom God had promised would be the Deliverer and King.

4. Did Jesus care for Bartimaeus even though he was poor and blind?

    Yes. It made no difference to Jesus that Bartimaeus was poor and blind. Jesus loved all people.

5. How does the blindness and helplessness of Bartimaeus remind us of the condition of all the descendants of Adam?

    Just as Bartimaeus was blind and helpless physically, so all Adam's descendants have been born with minds which are blinded to the truth and are unable to find the way to God.

6. Who was the only One who could give Bartimaeus his sight?

    God is the only One who could give sight to Bartimaeus.

7. Who is the only One who can give us understanding of the truth?

    God is the only One who can give us understanding of the truth.

LESSON 66: JESUS HEALED BLIND BARTIMAEUS AND RODE INTO JERUSALEM.

8. When Jesus rode into Jerusalem on the colt, the people welcomed Him. What did they say about Him?

   The people said that Jesus was the One whom the prophets had promised that God would send to be their king.

9. In what way did the people want Jesus to deliver them?

   The people wanted Jesus to be their king and to deliver them from the Romans who ruled their country.

10. Did these people trust in Jesus to deliver them from Satan's power, their sins and God's punishment?

    No. Most of them did not trust in Jesus to deliver them from the power of Satan, sin and death.

LESSON 67: JESUS AND HIS DISCIPLES CELEBRATED THE PASSOVER.

Scripture

Mark 14:1-2, 10-26

Lesson Outline

(1) The Jewish leaders and Judas conspired against Jesus. (Mark 14:1-2, 10-11)

(2) Jesus sent the disciples to prepare for the Passover Feast. (Mark 14:12-16)

(3) Jesus knew that Judas would betray Him. (Mark 14:17-21)

(4) Jesus used bread and wine to remind His disciples of His fast-approaching death. (Mark 14:22-26)

(?) Review Questions from Lesson 66.

Lesson Outline Developed

(1) The Jewish leaders and Judas conspired against Jesus.

- **The Jewish leaders planned to have Jesus killed.**

  Read Mark 14:1-2.

  The Jewish leaders were determined to have Jesus killed. Satan was guiding these men. Satan thought that, if he could get the Jewish leaders to have Jesus killed, he would hinder God's plan. Satan knew that the Deliverer was sent to destroy him and deliver sinners from his control.

  These leaders wanted to have Jesus killed, but they were afraid of the people. Jesus was very popular because of the great miracles which He had done, so the leaders thought that if they arrested Him, the people might turn on them and kill them.

  Teacher: As you prepare to teach, read Luke 20:19; 22:2, but do not read these verses to the people when you teach the lesson.

- **Judas planned to betray Jesus.**

    📖 Read Mark 14:10.

    Judas was one of the twelve men whom Jesus had chosen to be His closest companions, but Judas did not trust in Jesus as the Deliverer. Judas was not concerned about his own sinfulness before God. He followed Jesus for his own personal gain. When it seemed that he wasn't going to receive any personal benefits from following Jesus, he was willing to sell Jesus to His enemies.

    What God said in His Word came true. God said that a friend of Jesus would sell Him to His enemies. Judas had been a close companion of Jesus for three years.

★ Tell them that God's words written by David were fulfilled. Then read Psalm 41:9 and Mark 14:10 to them. Then point to the Prophetic Chart and write Mark 14:10 opposite Psalm 41:9. (See example below.)

What God said about the Deliverer He would send		How God's Word Came True
Psalm 41:9	Betrayed by a friend	Mark 14:10

Satan was guiding Judas to sell Jesus. Satan hates Jesus because He is God and speaks the truth.

Judas went to the enemies of Jesus and told them that he was willing to betray Jesus for money.

- **The Jewish leaders agreed to pay Judas money for betraying Jesus.**

    📖 Read Mark 14:11.

    Matthew wrote in his book that the Jewish leaders promised to pay Judas thirty pieces of silver. This was what God's prophet Zechariah said would happen to the promised Deliverer.

★ Tell them that God's words written by Zechariah were fulfilled. Then read Zechariah 11:12-13 and Matthew 26:14-15

What God said about the Deliverer He would send		How God's Word Came True
Zechariah 11:12-13	Sold for 30 pieces of silver	Matthew 26:14-15

LESSON 67: JESUS AND HIS DISCIPLES CELEBRATED THE PASSOVER.

② Jesus sent the disciples to prepare for the Passover Feast.

- **It was time for the Passover Feast.**

    📖 Read Mark 14:12.

    Every year, the Jews had a feast to remember that God had saved their ancestors from the plague of the death of the firstborn and delivered them from slavery in Egypt.

    Do you remember what God did to save the Israelites from the plague of the firstborn? God had given the Israelites instructions to kill a lamb and put the blood of the lamb over the door and on the doorposts of their houses. When God saw the blood on the doorposts of their houses, He did not allow the plague to enter and kill their firstborn.

    God had told the Israelites that they were to celebrate this event each year with a feast.

    Jesus' disciples asked Him where they were to go to prepare for this important celebration.

- **Jesus told the disciples where to prepare for the feast.**

    📖 Read Mark 14:13-15.

    Jesus said that the disciples would meet a man carrying a water jar. This was an unusual thing to see because the work of getting and carrying water was usually left to women, but Jesus said it would be so. Jesus was God and God knows even the smallest and most insignificant things. God even knows when one little sparrow falls to the ground and dies.

    Do you think that the man carrying the water jar was really there just as Jesus had said? Yes!

    📖 Read Mark 14:16.

☞ **Teacher:** Show a picture of Jesus and His disciples celebrating the Passover Feast.

③ Jesus knew that Judas would betray Him.

📖 Read Mark 14:17-20.

Jesus knew what Judas had planned.

Jesus knew that Judas was going to betray Him. Jesus is God and He knows everything.

- **Jesus said that the man who would betray him was dipping pieces of bread with him into the same dish.**

    When the Jews ate together, they broke pieces of bread from the loaves on the table and dipped the pieces of bread into a large bowl of broth in the center of the table. This broth was usually made from mashed fruit.

Judas was sharing this meal with Jesus just as a good companion would, when all along he was planning to sell Jesus to His enemies. Jesus was the host at this Passover meal. It was a very evil thing for Judas to eat with Jesus and then betray Him to His enemies. In that culture, a person should never eat at a person's table and then injure that person in any way.

Jesus told the disciples that the one who would betray him was dipping into the same dish as Jesus because He wanted Judas to realize what an evil thing he was planning to do. Jesus loved Judas, even though Judas had an evil plan. Jesus was giving Judas an opportunity to repent.

- **Judas would be punished for betraying the Deliverer.**

    Read Mark 14:21.

    Jesus often referred to Himself as "the Son of Man," for although He was the Son of God, He was also a real man.

    We have learned previously that Jesus came to earth to die so that He could deliver us from sin, Satan and death. Jesus knew that He had to die, just as God had foretold through the prophets.

    Even though Jesus had to die, God did not make Judas betray Jesus. Judas was still responsible for betraying Jesus. Judas would be punished forever for his terrible deed.

4) Jesus used bread and wine to remind His disciples of His fast-approaching death.

- **Jesus used bread to remind His disciples of His body.**

    Read Mark 14:22.

    Jesus took some bread and broke it. He explained that, just as He had broken the bread, so His body would soon be broken by wicked men.

- **Jesus used wine to remind His disciples of His blood.**

    Read Mark 14:23-24.

    After breaking the bread, Jesus picked up a cup of wine. He explained that the wine which was poured out for them to drink was an illustration of His blood which would flow out of His body when He died.

    Jesus said that that His blood would flow out for others. When Jesus died, He would be giving His life instead of us having to be punished forever.

    Read Mark 14:25-26.

LESSON 67: JESUS AND HIS DISCIPLES CELEBRATED THE PASSOVER.

Teacher: Although through these words, you are virtually giving the Gospel, do not teach further details regarding the Gospel story to the whole group. If there are individuals who inquire and are prepared for the Gospel, then, of course, you may share the Gospel story privately with these individuals.

(?) Questions

1. Why didn't the priests and Jewish leaders arrest and kill Jesus immediately?

   They knew that Jesus was very popular, and they thought that if they arrested Him, the people might turn on them and kill them.

2. Which disciple planned to betray Jesus?

   Judas planned to betray Jesus.

3. Had Judas ever realized his sinfulness, repented and trusted in Jesus as His Deliverer?

   No. Judas was not concerned about his own sinfulness before God, and He did not repent and trust in Jesus.

4. According to what the prophet wrote, for how much money would the Deliverer be sold?

   The prophet had written that the Deliverer would be sold for thirty pieces of silver.

5. For how much money was Jesus sold?

   Jesus was sold for thirty pieces of silver.

6. How did Jesus know what Judas planned to do?

   Jesus knows everything because He is God.

7. According to what the prophet wrote, who would betray the Deliverer?

   The prophet had written that a friend and close companion would betray the Deliverer.

8. Of what was the bread to remind the disciples?

   The bread was to remind the disciples of Jesus' body which would be broken by His enemies.

9. Of what was the wine to remind the disciples?

   The wine was to remind the disciples of Jesus' blood.

10. For whom did Jesus say His blood would flow out?

    Jesus said that His blood would flow out for other people.

LESSON 68: JESUS WAS ARRESTED BY HIS ENEMIES.

Scripture

Mark 14:32-65, Mark 15:1-20

Lesson Outline

(1) Jesus prayed in the Garden of Gethsemane. (Mark 14:32-42)

(2) Jesus was betrayed and arrested. (Mark 14:43-52)

(3) Jesus was tried by the Jewish leaders. (Mark 14:53-65)

(4) Jesus was tried by Pilate. (Mark 15:1-19)

(5) Jesus was taken to be crucified. (Mark 15:20)

(?) Review Questions from Lesson 67.

Lesson Outline Developed

(1) Jesus prayed in the Garden of Gethsemane.

Read Mark 14:32-36.

Teacher: Show a picture of Jesus praying in the Garden of Gethsemane.

- **Jesus knew He would suffer greatly to be our Deliverer.**

    Jesus was God, so He knew what was going to happen to Him. He knew that He would endure suffering that was more terrible than anyone had ever endured.

    Even though Jesus was God, He was also a real man, so it was very hard for Him to face the terrible things He knew He would suffer.

    Yet, even though Jesus knew that the suffering would be very great, He was willing to go through it so that He could fulfill God's plan and be our Deliverer.

- **Jesus knew that the time had come for Him to be betrayed.**

  📖 Read Mark 14:37-42.

2 Jesus was betrayed and arrested.

- **Judas betrayed Jesus.**

  📖 Read Mark 14:43-47.

☞ **Teacher:** Show a picture of Jesus being betrayed and arrested.

They probably didn't realize it, but Judas and all the men who came to arrest Jesus were being guided by Satan.

All those who oppose or ignore God's Word and refuse to trust Jesus as the Deliverer sent from God today are also being led by Satan.

Satan was leading Jesus' enemies, but Jesus is greater than Satan. He is God. It would not have been difficult for Him to escape from His enemies. He could have killed them all just by speaking. Instead, He allowed them to take Him as a prisoner.

- **Jesus knew that the Scriptures had to be fulfilled.**

  📖 Read Mark 14:48-49.

Jesus knew that everything which had been foretold about Him by the prophets would happen just as God had said. The disciples, however, were not thinking about the Scriptures being fulfilled. They were filled with fear because they thought that they, too, were going to be taken as prisoners.

- **The disciples fled.**

  📖 Read Mark 14:50-52.

The disciples ran away and left Jesus, just as He had predicted they would. The disciples were afraid, disappointed and confused. They believed that Jesus was the Deliverer sent from God, but they couldn't understand how He could be the Deliverer if He was going to be killed by His enemies.

How could Jesus' death deliver them from Satan, sin and death? The answer to this question will become clear as you hear the remainder of the story.

3 Jesus was tried by the Jewish leaders.

- **Those who arrested Jesus brought him to the religious leaders.**

  📖 Read Mark 14:53-54.

LESSON 68: JESUS WAS ARRESTED BY HIS ENEMIES.

- **The religious leaders couldn't find any lawful reason to condemn Jesus.**

  📖 Read Mark 14:55-56.

  Jesus hadn't done anything wrong; therefore, the religious leaders could not find any lawful reason to put Him to death.

  These religious leaders hated Jesus, not because He had done anything wrong, but because they loved their own sinful ways and did not want to obey God's words which Jesus had told them.

- **False witnesses told lies about Jesus.**

  📖 Read Mark 14:57-59.

  God guided David to write that false witnesses would tell lies about the Deliverer.

★ Tell them that God's words written by David were fulfilled. Then read Psalm 27:12 and Mark 14:56-57 to them. Then point to the Prophetic Chart and write Mark 14:56-57 opposite Psalm 27:12. (See example below.)

What God said about the Deliverer He would send		**How God's Word Came True**
Psalm 27:12	Accused by false witnesses	Mark 14:56-57

- **Jesus did not defend Himself against the lies of the false witnesses.**

  📖 Read Mark 14:60-62.

  When the false witnesses told lies about Him, Jesus was quiet and wouldn't answer. Jesus was trusting in God, His Father, to do what He had planned for Him. Jesus knew that all that would happen to Him was according to His Father's plan in order that we could be delivered from the power of Satan, sin and death.

- **Jesus did answer when the high priest asked Him if He really was the Christ.**

  Jesus answered very plainly that He was the Christ, the promised Deliverer and the Son of God.

  When Jesus was born through Mary, He came to be the Deliverer. When Jesus comes to this world the next time, He will come as the almighty Son of God to judge all people. Everyone will see Him sitting beside His Father, and it will be obvious to all that He is equal to God His Father. But it was not obvious to the religious leaders. They did not believe what Jesus said. They just saw an ordinary man who was claiming to be equal with God so they thought He had blasphemed God.

- **The religious leaders condemned Jesus because He said He was equal to God.**

  📖 Read Mark 14:63-64.

When the Jews wanted to show that they were very angry or distressed, it was their custom to rip their clothes. The high priest was very angry because, by His answer, Jesus had said that He was equal to God.

To these religious leaders, Jesus had committed blasphemy. If a person ridicules God, says evil things about Him or claims to be like God or greater than God, he has committed a sin called blasphemy. Death was the punishment for this sin under the Jewish law. These religious leaders believed that Jesus was just a man who claimed to be equal to God. Therefore, they condemned Him to death.

- **The Jews spit on Jesus and hit Him.**

    Read Mark 14:65.

God had guided the prophet Isaiah to write that the Deliverer would be hit and spit upon. Everything that the prophets wrote about the Deliverer happened.

★ Tell them that God's words written by Isaiah were fulfilled. Then read Isaiah 50:6 and Mark 14:65 to them. Then point to the Prophetic Chart and write Mark 14:65 opposite Isaiah 50:6. (See example below.)

What God said about the Deliverer He would send		How God's Word Came True
Isaiah 50:6	Smitten and spat upon	Mark 14:65

(4) Jesus was tried by Pilate.

- **The religious leaders brought Jesus to Pilate.**

    Read Mark 15:1.

☞ **Teacher:** Show a picture of Jesus before Pilate.

The Romans controlled the Jews' land, and they would not allow the Jews to kill anyone unless they gave permission. So the religious leaders took Jesus to Pilate to persuade him to condemn Jesus to death. The king of the Romans, Caesar, had appointed Pilate to be the governor of Judea and Samaria.

☞ **Teacher:** Point to Judea and Samaria on the map.

- **Pilate asked Jesus if He was the King of the Jews.**

    Read Mark 15:2.

LESSON 68: JESUS WAS ARRESTED BY HIS ENEMIES.

Jesus really was the King of the Jews, wasn't He? He was a descendant of David the king and should have been King over the Jews.

- **Jesus did not respond to the lies and false accusations.**

    📖 Read Mark 15:3-5.

    The prophet Isaiah had written that the Deliverer would be silent when He was falsely accused. God's Word is always fulfilled in every detail.

- **Pilate asked the Jews which man they wanted him to release, whether Barabbas or Jesus.**

    📖 Read Mark 15:6-11.

    The Roman governor had a custom that he would release one prisoner at the time of the Feast of the Passover. He would release whichever prisoner the Jews asked for.

    Pilate knew that Jesus had not done anything wrong and that the Jews' leaders only wanted to put Jesus to death because they were jealous of His popularity. Pilate offered to release Jesus, hoping that the Jews would choose to let Jesus go free rather than Barabbas, who was a murderer.

    But the religious leaders urged their followers to ask that Pilate release Barabbas instead of Jesus.

- **The Jewish leaders and their followers wanted Jesus to be crucified.**

    📖 Read Mark 15:12-14.

★ Tell them that God's words written by Isaiah were fulfilled. Then read Isaiah 53:7 and Mark 15:3-5 to them. Then point to the Prophetic Chart and write Mark 15:3-5 opposite Isaiah 53:7. (See example below.)

What God said about the Deliverer He would send		**How God's Word Came True**
Isaiah 53:7	Silent when accused	Mark 15:3-5

Crucifixion was a terrible form of punishment which the Romans used for the very worst of criminals. When a person was crucified, he was nailed by his hands and feet to a cross until he died.

It may seem strange to you that the crowd of Jews that had gathered should want Jesus to die in such a terrible way. But they agreed with their leaders that He was not the Son of God. They, too, disliked Jesus because He said they were sinners and that they needed to be delivered from their sins. They didn't care about their sin. They wanted a Deliverer to save them from the Romans.

- **The majority of the Jews hated Jesus, and they rejected Him.**

  God had said through the prophet Isaiah that most Jews would despise the Deliverer and that they would reject Him. God had said through King David that the great majority of Jews would hate the Deliverer even though there was no legitimate reason for them to do so.

  Everything that God said through His prophets about the Deliverer was fulfilled through what happened to Jesus.

  ★ Tell them that God's words written by Isaiah and by David were fulfilled. Then read Isaiah 53:3, Psalm 69:4 and Mark 15:9-14 to them. Then point to the Prophetic Chart and write Mark 15:9-14 opposite Isaiah 53:3. Then write Mark 15:10 opposite Psalm 69:4. (See example below.)

What God said about the Deliverer He would send		How God's Word Came True
Isaiah 53:3	Rejected by the Jews	Mark 15:9-14
Psalm 69:4	Hated without a cause	Mark 15:10

- **Jesus was whipped and mocked.**

  📖 Read Mark 15:15.

  When a prisoner was beaten like this, a whip of many lashes was used. Pieces of sharp metal and bone were tied onto the lashes so they would cut the back of the prisoner when he was beaten.

  📖 Read Mark 15:16-19.

  👉 **Teacher:** Show a picture of the soldiers mocking Jesus.

  The soldiers mocked Jesus by dressing Him in a purple robe. Purple was the color which kings wore during that time.

  The soldiers also mocked Jesus by placing a crown of thorns on His head. Kings at that time wore crowns of gold on their heads. The crown that the soldiers put on Jesus was made from twigs which had large sharp thorns. When Adam and Eve sinned, God cursed the earth and said that thorns would grow. Jesus came to suffer and die to deliver us from God's curse. God allowed Jesus' enemies to place these thorns on Jesus' head as a sign that He was going to deliver those who believe on Him from God's curse by dying for the sins of the world.

  The soldiers also mocked Jesus by kneeling in front of Him. This is how respect and honor were shown to kings at that time.

LESSON 68: JESUS WAS ARRESTED BY HIS ENEMIES.

5) Jesus was taken to be crucified.

📖 Read Mark 15:20.

Would Jesus really be crucified, or would God save Him from this terrible death? Be sure to come to our next lesson to find out what happened next.

❓ Questions

1. Why was it hard for Jesus who was God to face the terrible suffering He would endure to be our Deliverer?

   It was hard for Jesus to face, for although He was God, He was also a real man, and He knew that the suffering which He would endure was more terrible than any man had ever endured.

2. Who was leading Judas to betray Jesus and the Jewish leaders to have Jesus arrested?

   Satan was leading them.

3. What people are being guided by Satan today?

   All who refuse to believe God's Word, agree with Him and trust in Jesus as the Deliverer are being guided by Satan.

4. Did Jesus deserve to be put to death?

   No! Jesus had done nothing to deserve death.

5. What did Jesus answer when false witnesses lied about Him?

   He did not answer or try to defend Himself against the lies of the false witnesses.

6. What did Jesus answer when the high priest asked Him if He was the Christ?

   Jesus answered plainly that He was the Christ and that, one day in the future, He will come as the almighty Son of God to judge all people.

7. Why did the religious leaders condemn Jesus to death?

   The religious leaders condemned Jesus to death because He said He was equal to God.

8. What were some of the prophecies about the Deliverer that were fulfilled when Jesus was tried before the Jewish religious leaders and before Pilate?

   False witnesses would tell lies about the Deliverer.

   The Deliverer would be hit and spit upon.

The Deliverer would be silent when He was falsely accused.

The Jews would hate the Deliverer even though there was no reason and they would reject Him.

9. What things did the soldiers do to mock Jesus as King of the Jews?

    The soldiers mocked Jesus by dressing Him in a purple robe, by placing a crown of thorns on His head, and by kneeling in front of Him.

10. Of what does the crown of thorns remind us?

    It reminds us of the curse which God put on the earth because of Adam's sin and the fact that Jesus was going to deliver those who believe on Him from God's curse by dying for the sins of the world.

LESSON 69: JESUS WAS CRUCIFIED, BURIED, AND RAISED FROM THE DEAD.

Scripture

Mark 15:20-47, Mark 16:1-8

Lesson Outline

(1) Jesus was crucified. (Mark 15:20-32)

(2) Jesus paid for sin by death. (Mark 15:33-37)

(3) The curtain in the temple was ripped. (Mark 15:38)

(4) People witnessed Jesus' death. (Mark 15:39-41)

(5) Jesus was buried. (Mark 15:42-47)

(6) Jesus rose again. (Mark 16:1-8)

(?) Review Questions from Lesson 68.

Lesson Outline Developed

Teacher: This lesson on the Gospel is longer than the usual lesson. The reason it has not been divided into two lessons is because the Gospel includes the death, burial and resurrection of the Lord Jesus Christ (1 Corinthians 15:1-4). It is important that you teach the resurrection as an integral part of the Gospel. Your hearers must know that Christ died for their sins and was buried but that God raised Him from the dead. Their faith must be in a living Savior if they are to be saved (Romans 10:9).

(1) Jesus was crucified.

We have come now to a very important part of the story of the Bible. Do you agree with God that you are a sinner and that, unless someone delivers you, you will go to the everlasting fire? If you want to be delivered, then you need to listen very carefully in order to understand what Jesus did for you so that you can be fully accepted by God and never go to everlasting punishment.

- **The soldiers took Jesus to the hill of Golgotha to be crucified.**

    📖 Read Mark 15:20-22.

    The hill to which they led Jesus to crucify Him was just outside the walls of Jerusalem.

- **They offered Jesus a drink, but He did not drink it.**

    📖 Read Mark 15:23.

    This drink was prepared by women of Jerusalem as an act of mercy to help dull the pain of those who were being crucified. Myrrh was a sap from a small tree.

- **Jesus' hands and feet were pierced.**

    📖 Read Mark 15:24.

    The soldiers hammered nails through Jesus' hands and feet, attaching Jesus to a wooden cross.

    Many, many years before, God had guided King David to write that the Deliverer's hands and feet would be pierced.

★ Tell them that God's words written by David were fulfilled. Then read Psalm 22:16 and Mark 15:24 to them. Then point to the Prophetic Chart and write Mark 15:24 opposite Psalm 22:16. (See example below.)

What God said about the Deliverer He would send		How God's Word Came True
Psalm 22:16	His hands and feet pierced	Mark 15:24

- **Jesus was lifted up.**

Teacher: As you prepare to teach, read John 3:14-15, but do not read these verses to the people when you teach the lesson.

After the soldiers hammered the nails through Jesus' hands and feet into the wooden cross, they stood the cross in an upright position.

We learned previously that Jesus had told Nicodemus that, as Moses lifted up the serpent in the wilderness on a pole, even so Jesus, the Deliverer, had to be lifted up so that sinners could be saved from punishment. Jesus was nailed to the cross and lifted up just as He said He would be. Later, we will read about two other men who were also crucified at the same time that Jesus was.

☞ **Teacher:** Show a picture of the crucifixion.

LESSON 69: JESUS WAS CRUCIFIED, BURIED, AND RAISED FROM THE DEAD.

- **The soldiers gambled for Jesus' clothing.**

   Many years before, God had guided King David to write that the Deliverer's clothes would become the prize in a gambling game.

★ Tell them that God's words written by David were fulfilled. Then read Psalm 22:18 and Mark 15:24 to them. Then point to the Prophetic Chart and write Mark 15:24 opposite Psalm 22:18. (See example below.)

What God said about the Deliverer He would send		How God's Word Came True
Psalm 22:18	His clothing gambled for	Mark 15:24

- **Pilate ordered that a nameplate be placed above Jesus' head.**

   📖 Read Mark 15:25-26.

   John, one of Jesus' apostles, wrote that it was Pilate the governor who commanded that this nameplate was to be put on the cross above the head of Jesus.

Teacher: As you prepare to teach, read John 19:19-22, but do not read these verses to the people when you teach the lesson.

Pilate did not believe that Jesus was the King of the Jews. Pilate probably ordered that this nameplate be placed above Jesus' head to mock the Jews and their desire to be liberated from the control of the Romans and to have their own king.

The Jews did not want Pilate to put this nameplate above Jesus' head because they did not accept Jesus as their king.

- **Two robbers were crucified at the same time as Jesus was crucified.**

   📖 Read Mark 15:27-28.

   The Romans were punishing these two robbers because of the evil things they had done, but Jesus was different. He had done nothing wrong. God had guided the Prophet Isaiah to write that the Deliverer would die in the company of evil men.

★ Tell them that God's words written by Isaiah were fulfilled. Then read Isaiah 53:12 and Mark 15:27 to them. Then point to the Prophetic Chart and write Mark 15:27 opposite Isaiah 53:12. (See example below.)

What God said about the Deliverer He would send		How God's Word Came True
Isaiah 53:12	Die with the wicked	Mark 15:27

- **Jesus was mocked and insulted while He was on the cross.**

    📖 Read Mark 15:29-32.

    We learned previously that Jesus said that if they destroyed the temple, He would build it again in three days. When Jesus said this, He was referring to His body. Even though they crucified Him, He planned to rise up again three days later. The Jews didn't understand that Jesus meant His body. They thought that He was talking about the great stone temple in Jerusalem.

    God had guided King David to write that the Deliverer's enemies would mock Him and laugh at His sufferings. God knew exactly what was going to happen to His Son long before He came into the world.

★ Tell them that God's words written by David were fulfilled. Then read Psalm 22:6-8 and Mark 15:29-32 to them. Then point to the Prophetic Chart and write Mark 15:29-32 opposite Psalm 22:6-8. (See example below.)

What God said about the Deliverer He would send		How God's Word Came True
Psalm 22:6-8	Mocked and insulted	Mark 15:29-32

② Jesus paid for sin by death.

We have now reached the most important part of the story. We have already learned from God's Word that God sent Jesus into this world to be the Deliverer of sinners. We will now learn exactly what Jesus did so that we could be delivered forever from Satan, sin and death. Listen carefully so you will understand what Jesus did for you so you can be saved from the Lake of Fire.

- **Sin must be paid for.**

    God could never forgive us for our sin and accept us unless the punishment for our sin was completely paid.

    What is the punishment for sin? The punishment for sin is death. This doesn't just mean physical death; it also means separation from God in the place of everlasting punishment.

    The only way Jesus could deliver us was to take our place before God and be punished for our sins by being separated from God.

- **Jesus was sinless.**

    Jesus did not have any of His own sins for which He must die. Jesus was perfect.

    We learned previously that, when John baptized Jesus, God the Father spoke from Heaven and said that Jesus was His well-beloved Son with whom He was fully pleased. Jesus was the only one who did everything that pleased God. Jesus did not have any sin before God.

LESSON 69: JESUS WAS CRUCIFIED, BURIED, AND RAISED FROM THE DEAD.

Because Jesus was sinless, He was able to offer Himself to God as the sacrifice for our sins.

God always required that, whenever a person offered a sacrifice to God for sin, the animal had to be without fault. It must not be sick or have any broken parts on its body.

We learned previously the story of Isaac when he was tied to the altar. When Abraham was just about to kill him, God stopped Abraham. Abraham looked up and saw a ram caught in a bush. God had put the ram there to be a substitute for Isaac. Which part of the ram was caught in the bush? Yes, the ram was caught by its horns. Why did God make sure that the ram was caught by its horns? God secured the ram in the bush by its horns so it would be a perfect sacrifice. If it had been caught by any other part of its body, it would have injured itself by struggling to get free. If the ram had been injured, it would not have been acceptable as a substitute for Isaac. God would only accept a healthy, strong animal as a sacrifice.

Because God is perfect, any offering made to Him had to be without fault.

Was Jesus without fault before God? Yes! Jesus was without fault; therefore, He was able to offer Himself to God in our place. Just as the ram died in place of Isaac, so Jesus came into the world to die in our place.

- **Jesus was separated from God for our sins.**

Listen carefully to what happened to Jesus when He was hanging on the cross.

Remember, He was dying to deliver us from sin, death and Satan.

📖 Read Mark 15:33.

Even though it was the middle of the day [from noon till 3 p.m.], the light of the sun was blotted out and there was darkness for three hours. The darkness showed that God had turned His back on Jesus. God turned away from Jesus and left His beloved Son, Jesus, completely alone.

📖 Read Mark 15:34.

- **God turned away from Jesus.**

Throughout Jesus' life, God the Father was always with Him, but now God turned away from Him. This was the first time that God the Father and God the Son had ever been separated.

Why did God turn His back on Jesus? Had Jesus done anything wrong? No! Jesus had always obeyed God. Jesus had never done anything wrong. Why then do you think God turned away from Jesus? It was because God was punishing Jesus for your sins, for my sins and for the sins of the whole world.

- **Sin must be paid for by separation from God.**

We learned this previously when we learned about Adam. God had told Adam that, if he ate fruit from the tree of the knowledge of good and evil, he would die. This meant that Adam's body would die, and that he would be separated from God forever in the place of terrible punishment which God prepared for Satan and his evil spirits. The payment for sin is death – separation from God.

📖 Read Mark 15:34 again, then read Mark 15:35-36.

The people around the cross misunderstood what Jesus had said. They thought that Jesus wanted Elijah the prophet to rescue him. But they were wrong. If Jesus had wanted to be delivered, He could have saved Himself and destroyed His enemies. Jesus was not calling out to Elijah. Jesus was calling out to God who had turned away from Jesus because Jesus was taking the responsibility for our sin.

While Jesus was on the cross, He was separated from God in order to pay the punishment for our sins. Jesus suffered the complete punishment for our sins. Because of Jesus' death for us, God will freely forgive and accept as His children all those who agree with God and trust only in Jesus.

- **Jesus gave His blood, His life.**

When Jesus was nailed to the cross, His blood flowed out of His body just as the blood of the animals flowed out of their bodies when the Jews offered them to God.

God had said from the beginning that, whenever anyone came to Him, trusting in His promises to send the Deliverer, he must bring an animal. The animal must be killed, and its blood must be allowed to flow out. God said that they must do this because God knew that one day His Son, the Deliverer, would give His blood to pay for the sins of the world.

Let's think about some of the sacrifices that we have learned about.

- Cain brought an offering to God, but it did not have any blood. God would not accept Cain or his offering.
- Abel also brought an offering to God. He brought a lamb. He killed the lamb and allowed its blood to flow out. God accepted Abel and his offering.
- When the Israelites were in Egypt and the angel of death was going to kill all the firstborn children, God instructed each Israelite family to select a lamb that was without fault. Do you remember what they had to do with it? Could they just tie the living lamb at their door? No! The lamb had to die so that its blood could be put on the doorposts and over the doors of their homes. This was the only way the firstborn children could be saved from death.
- When the Israelites were in the wilderness, God told them to build a tabernacle in the middle of their camp where He would live. God evidenced His presence in the inner room of the tabernacle by a very bright light above the mercy seat. Do you remember what the high priest had to do every year? Once each year, the high priest had to bring the blood of an animal and sprinkle it on the mercy seat.

LESSON 69: JESUS WAS CRUCIFIED, BURIED, AND RAISED FROM THE DEAD.

- After King Solomon built the temple to replace the tabernacle, the sacrifices continued at the temple. Once each year, the high priest brought the blood of an animal and sprinkled it on the mercy seat which was in the inner room of the temple. This was still being done year by year in the temple in Jerusalem when Jesus was here on earth as a man.

The blood sacrifices of animals reminded the offerers that the payment for sin is death, but the blood of animals could never pay for sin. Sin was paid for when Jesus came and offered His blood to God. Jesus is the Deliverer! He gave His blood and His life as a sacrifice to God to pay for the sins of the world.

- **Jesus did all that was necessary to deliver us from Satan, sin and death.**

  📖 Read Mark 15:37.

  Mark wrote that Jesus cried out with a loud voice, and then Jesus' spirit and soul left His body. Mark doesn't tell us what Jesus said with a loud voice. However, John also wrote about what happened to Jesus on the cross, and he wrote exactly what Jesus said. He said, "It is finished."

Teacher: As you prepare to teach, read John 19:30, but do not read this verse to the people when you teach the lesson.

What do you think was finished? Did Jesus mean that His life was finished and that His enemies had won? No, because Jesus had said that He would rise again after three days. What then was finished? The work that Jesus came into the world to do was completely finished. Jesus came into the world to deliver sinners from Satan, sin and death. Jesus finished this work by being separated from God and by giving His blood and His life as the full payment for our sins.

Because Jesus paid to God all that was necessary for our sins, God forgives the sins of all who agree with God and trust in Jesus and His death for them, and God gives them the gift of everlasting life. There is no longer any need for anyone to be separated from God.

In the garden in Eden, God promised that He would send a Deliverer, and God kept His promise. Jesus finished the work which His Father had given Him to do for us.

③ The curtain in the temple was ripped.

📖 Read Mark 15:38.

- **The curtain in the temple showed that people were shut out of God's presence.**

  We first learned about the curtain when we learned about the tabernacle. The thick curtain was hung in front of the inner room in the tabernacle. This inner room was a special room, set apart to be God's dwelling place among the Israelites.

Later, when the temple was built to replace the tabernacle, a thick, long curtain was hung in front of the inner room in the temple.

Teacher: The veil in the temple was a handbreadth in thickness and was sixty feet long and thirty wide.

God had told the Jews to put this curtain in front of the inner room so they would never forget that they were shut out of God's presence because of sin. Behind this curtain shone the very bright light to show that God was there living with them. Only the high priest was allowed to go into the inner room where God showed His presence by the bright light. But, the high priest could only go into the room once a year and he had to bring the blood of an animal and sprinkle it on the mercy seat as an offering for sin.

When Jesus cried out, "It is finished" and died, the curtain in the temple was ripped from the top down to the bottom. Who do you think ripped this curtain from the top down to the bottom? It wasn't a man who tore it. God ripped the curtain!

- **God was satisfied with Jesus' payment for sin.**

    God ripped the curtain to show that He was fully satisfied with the payment that Jesus made to Him for sinners. Sinners would no longer be shut out from God if they admitted their sinfulness and trusted only in Jesus as their Deliverer.

- **God no longer required animal sacrifices to be made to Him.**

    Ever since Adam sinned in the Garden of Eden, God required that those who came to Him had to bring the blood of animals as a sacrifice. Even though the blood of animals could never pay for sin, God forgave the sins of those who trusted in Him and who brought the blood sacrifices. God forgave their sins because God knew that His own Son would come and give His blood as a complete payment for all sin.

    When Jesus died, God ripped the curtain in the temple to show everyone that He was completely satisfied and that there was no more need to offer the blood of animals. The way back to God was open because Jesus gave His blood as the complete payment for sin.

    God has promised that all who agree with Him and trust only in Jesus and His payment for their sins will be fully accepted by God, and they will never go to the everlasting punishment in the Lake of Fire.

④ People witnessed Jesus' death.

Read Mark 15:39-41.

A centurion was a soldier who was in charge of one hundred soldiers. When Jesus died, the centurion recognized that Jesus really was the Son of God.

The women that Mark wrote about were women who trusted in God's Word and had accepted that Jesus was the promised Deliverer.

LESSON 69: JESUS WAS CRUCIFIED, BURIED, AND RAISED FROM THE DEAD.

⑤ Jesus was buried.

📖 Read Mark 15:42-46.

Joseph of Arimathea was a rich man. Jesus was buried in the burial cave which belonged to Joseph.

God had guided the Prophet Isaiah to write that the Deliverer would be buried in a rich man's tomb.

★ Tell them that God's words written by Isaiah were fulfilled. Then read Isaiah 53:9 and Mark 15:43-46 to them. Then point to the Prophetic Chart and write Mark 15:43-46 opposite Isaiah 53:9. (See example below.)

What God said about the Deliverer He would send		How God's Word Came True
Isaiah 53:9	Buried with the rich	Mark 15:43-46

⑥ Jesus rose again.

- **The women came to the tomb.**

    📖 Read Mark 16:1.

    After Jesus had been buried for three days and three nights, some of the women who had believed in Jesus and had been present when Jesus had died went to the burial cave.

    It was the Jews' custom to put fragrant spices on the bodies of the dead before they were buried. Because Jesus had been hurriedly buried before the Sabbath, they hadn't had time to put the spices on His body. So these women came early on Sunday morning to anoint the body of Jesus. They expected to find the body of Jesus still in the cave. But what a shock they received!

- **The stone was rolled away.**

    📖 Read Mark 16:2-4

    Just before the women arrived at the tomb, there had been a great earthquake. God had sent His angel to roll the great stone away from the entrance to the grave where the body of Jesus had been buried.

Teacher: As you prepare to teach, read Matthew 28:1-4, but do not read these verses to the people when you teach the lesson.

📖 Read Mark 16:5.

☞ **Teacher:** Show a picture of the empty tomb.

Who do you think this young man was? He was an angel of God.

Now listen to what this angel said to the women.

📖 Read Mark 16:6.

- **Jesus said He would rise again, and He did!**

    Jesus had told His followers many times before He died that He would rise on the third day. They should have been waiting for Him and expecting Him to rise from the dead. We don't know why they didn't expect Him to rise again. Perhaps they didn't understand or remember what He had said, or perhaps they just didn't believe that it was possible that He would come out of the grave alive. However, regardless of how impossible it may seem, God always does what He promises.

    How did Jesus know that He would rise again? Jesus is God who came down to earth and became a man to deliver us from Satan, sin and death. Because He is God, He knew before He left Heaven that He must give His life to deliver us from Satan, sin and death, and He also knew that He would rise again and that He would never die again.

★ Tell them that God's words written by David were fulfilled. Then read Psalm 16:10 and Mark 16:6 to them. Then point to the Prophetic Chart and write Mark 16:6 opposite Psalm 16:10. (See example below.)

What God said about the Deliverer He would send		How God's Word Came True
Psalm 16:10	Rise again	Mark 16:6

The angel told the frightened women to go and tell the disciples of Jesus that He had risen from the dead. The women fled from the tomb, trembling and afraid, and as they ran, they didn't stop to tell anyone what had happened at the tomb.

📖 Read Mark 16:7-8.

- **The resurrection shows that Jesus is the Son of God and the Deliverer.**

    The Jewish leaders crucified Jesus because He claimed to be the Son of God and the Deliverer. God raised Jesus from the dead so that everyone would know that Jesus was who He claimed to be. Jesus truly was the Son of God and the Deliverer promised by God.

Teacher: As you prepare to teach, read Romans 1:4; 10:9, but do not read these verses to the people when you teach the lesson.

LESSON 69: JESUS WAS CRUCIFIED, BURIED, AND RAISED FROM THE DEAD.

- **The resurrection shows that God was satisfied with Jesus' payment for our sin.**

    We know that God was fully satisfied with the payment which Jesus gave for our sins because God ripped the curtain in the temple from the top to the bottom. By ripping the curtain, God was showing that the way back to Him was now open, for the complete payment for sin had been made by Jesus' blood.

    In addition, the fact that God raised Jesus from the dead assures us that God was completely satisfied with the payment of our sins which Jesus made with His blood. God would not have raised Jesus if God had not been fully satisfied with the payment which Jesus had made.

Lesson Developer: Illustrate that a person who is under a judge's sentence must pay his complete sentence. For example:

> 💡 If a judge sentences a man to a certain amount of time in prison, that man must stay in prison until he is released. If he breaks out of prison, then the police will recapture him and put him back. But if the man stays in prison and finishes the time of punishment which was stipulated by the judge, then he has no need to be afraid when he is released. The police may see him after he has been released, but they will not arrest him and put him back in prison. He has been released because he has paid the full punishment for his crime.

The complete price for our sins had to be paid if we were to be accepted by God. Jesus took our place before God, the Judge, and God punished Jesus instead of us. It was just as if Jesus went into prison to take the punishment for our sins.

We know that Jesus paid the full price for our sins and that God the Judge is completely satisfied because God released Jesus from death and raised Him back to life. If God, the Judge, had not been satisfied, He would not have released Jesus from death.

Teacher: As you prepare to teach, read Romans 4:25, but do not read this verse to the people when you teach the lesson.

If you are to be delivered from Satan, sin and everlasting separation from God, then you must trust only in the Lord Jesus, believing that He gave His blood as the full payment for your sins and rose again from the dead to give you eternal life.

Building on Firm Foundations - Volume 2: Evangelism: Genesis to The Ascension

? Questions

1. Where was Jesus crucified?

   Jesus was crucified on a hill outside of Jerusalem.

2. What did King David write would happen to the hands and feet of the promised Deliverer?

   King David had written that the Deliverer's hands and feet would be pierced.

3. God required that a sacrifice to Him be without fault. Was Jesus without fault before God?

   Yes. Because Jesus was sinless, He was able to offer Himself to God as the sacrifice for our sins.

4. For what reason was God the Father and Jesus separated from each other while Jesus hung on the cross?

   Jesus was taking the punishment for sin by being separated from God.

5. What did Jesus mean when He called out, "It is finished"?

   Jesus meant that He had completed the work given to Him by His Father which was to pay the punishment for sinners to be delivered from the power of Satan, sin and death.

6. What did Jesus do to pay the punishment for sinners?

   Jesus died on the cross as our substitute, shedding His own blood to pay for our sins.

7. When Jesus called out "It is finished" and died, what happened to the curtain in the temple?

   God ripped the curtain in the temple from top to bottom.

8. What was God showing by ripping the curtain in the temple from top to bottom?

   God ripped the curtain to show that He was fully satisfied with the payment which Jesus made to Him for sinners and that there was no more need to offer the blood of animals.

9. How long had Jesus been buried when the women went to the burial cave?

   Jesus had been buried for three days and three nights.

10. What did the women find had happened to the stone in front of the cave where Jesus was buried?

    The stone had been rolled away from the door of the cave.

11. What had happened just prior to the arrival of the women at the burial cave?

    There had been a great earthquake, and God had sent an angel to roll away the stone from the door.

12. What did the women see when they entered the burial cave?

LESSON 69: JESUS WAS CRUCIFIED, BURIED, AND RAISED FROM THE DEAD.

The women saw that the body of Jesus was gone, and they saw an angel of God.

13. What did the angel of God tell the women?

    The angel told them that Jesus had risen from the dead.

14. What does the resurrection of Jesus show us?

    The resurrection shows us that Jesus was the Son of God and the Deliverer just as He claimed to be. The resurrection also shows us that God was fully satisfied with the payment which Jesus made for our sins.

15. How can we be forgiven by God and receive the gift of everlasting life which Jesus bought for us with His blood?

    We can be forgiven and receive the gift of everlasting life by agreeing with God that we are helpless sinners and trusting only in Jesus who died to pay for our sins and rose from the dead to give us eternal life.

LESSON 70: JESUS APPEARED TO HIS DISCIPLES AND RETURNED TO HEAVEN.

Scripture

Mark 16:9-15, Acts 1:9-11

Lesson Outline

(1) Jesus appeared to some of His followers. (Mark 16:9-14)

(2) Jesus gave a final command to His disciples. (Mark 16:15)

(3) We must believe the Word of God.

(4) Jesus ascended into Heaven. (Acts 1:9)

(5) Jesus will come again. (Acts 1:10-11)

(?) Review Questions from Lesson 69.

Lesson Outline Developed

(1) Jesus appeared to some of His followers.

📖 Read Mark 16:9-13.

- **The disciples did not understand that Jesus had risen from the dead.**

  Even though Mary and these other followers of Jesus saw Him and talked with Him, the disciples would not believe them when they told their experience and said that Jesus was really alive.

- **Jesus reproached His disciples for their unbelief.**

  📖 Read Mark 16:14.

  Jesus showed Himself later to His eleven apostles. Jesus was displeased with them because they did not believe Mary Magdalene and the other two followers when they told them that they had seen Jesus alive from the dead.

- **Jesus proved to His disciples that He was alive.**

    After His resurrection, Jesus spent 40 days with His disciples. During this time He showed Himself to them many times, and He convinced them that He was alive by many infallible proofs.

    Teacher: As you prepare to teach, read Acts 1:1-3; Luke 24:36-43, but do not read these verses to the people when you teach the lesson.

② Jesus gave a final command to His disciples.

📖 Read Mark 16:15.

This was Jesus' command to His apostles, and it is also His command to all those who believe in Him and accept His payment for them. The Gospel is the good news that Jesus died for the sins of all people, He was buried and He rose again.

God wants all people to know that they can be delivered from Satan, sin and death. God doesn't want anyone to go to the place which He prepared for Satan and his evil spirits.

📖 Read John 3:16.

This is why we have taught you the Bible. We want you to understand and believe this good news so you will be accepted by God. If you believe in Jesus, you will not perish and go to the everlasting fire, but instead, you will receive everlasting life and go to be with God forever.

③ We must believe the Word of God.

- **We believe the Gospel.**

    Teacher: Give a testimony about believing the Gospel. The testimony can either be personal, or on behalf of all Christians who are present. For example:

    > 🕯 We have not seen Jesus, but we believe that Jesus came into the world. We believe that He died for our sins and rose again on the third day. We know this and believe it because God has recorded it in His Book, the Bible. We have agreed with God that we are helpless sinners, and we have trusted in Jesus. His payment for us by His death is the only thing that we trust in for our acceptance before God

- **It is important that you believe this message which God has written in His Word.**

    If you believe God's Word and put your trust in the Lord Jesus Christ, you will receive eternal life. But if you refuse to believe what God has said, you will remain separated from God and go to everlasting punishment.

LESSON 70: JESUS APPEARED TO HIS DISCIPLES AND RETURNED TO HEAVEN.

We learned previously the story that Jesus told about the rich man and Lazarus. Both men died. God accepted Lazarus, but God sent the man who was rich into the everlasting fire. The man who was rich was in terrible suffering, and he asked Abraham to send Lazarus back to earth to warn his brothers so that they would not go to everlasting punishment. What did Abraham tell the man who was rich? Abraham told him that his brothers had the writings of God's prophets and that they were responsible to believe God's message in the Bible.

That is also what God expects of you. Although you haven't seen Jesus, you have heard God's message from the Bible.

God says that you must believe this good news that Jesus is the Deliverer and that He died for your sins. This is how you, too, can know that your sins are forgiven by God and that God will accept you. If you agree with what God has written in His Word and trust only in Jesus and His payment for your sins, then God will forgive all your sin, and He will accept you and give to you the gift of everlasting life.

④ Jesus ascended into Heaven.

After Jesus commanded His disciples to take this good news to every person, He left them and returned to His Father in Heaven.

☞ **Teacher:** Show a picture of Jesus ascending in the clouds.

📖 Read Acts 1:9.

Many years earlier, God guided King David to write that the Deliverer would ascend into Heaven. God always keeps His Word.

⑤ Jesus will come again.

- **As the disciples watched Jesus leave, two men appeared.**

    📖 Read Acts 1:10-11.

    The two men in white were two of God's angels.

- **The angels said that Jesus will come back.**

    The first time that Jesus came to the earth, His work was to deliver sinners from Satan, sin and death. He completed that work when He died on the cross and rose again. God now commands everyone to agree with God that they are helpless sinners and to trust only in the payment which Jesus has made for them.

★ Tell them that God's words written by David were fulfilled. Then read Psalm 68:18 and Acts 1:9 to them. Then point to the Prophetic Chart and write Acts 1:9 opposite Psalm 68:18. (See example below.)

What God said about the Deliverer He would send	How God's Word Came True
Psalm 68:18 Go back to Heaven	Acts 1:9

The next time that Jesus comes to earth, He will come as the almighty Judge of the whole earth. When Jesus was tried by the Jewish leaders, He told them that He would come again and that He would be recognized as the almighty Son of God and the judge of all people.

Teacher: As you prepare to teach, read Mark 14:61-62; Acts 17:30-31, but do not read these verses to the people when you teach the lesson.

When Jesus comes again as the almighty Judge, all those who have not agreed with God and trusted in Jesus and His payment for them will be thrown, along with Satan and all his demons, into the everlasting fire.

Teacher: As you prepare to teach, read Revelation 20:10-15, but do not read these verses to the people when you teach the lesson.

? Questions

1. What did Mary Magdalene and two other followers tell the other disciples?
   They told them that they had seen Jesus, for He had risen from the dead and had appeared to them.

2. Did the disciples believe Mary Magdalene and the other followers who had seen Jesus?
   No. The disciples did not believe that Jesus had risen from the dead.

3. What was Jesus' last command to His disciples?
   He told them to go into all the world and tell the Gospel to all people.

4. What is the Gospel?
   The Gospel is the good news that Jesus died for our sins, was buried and rose again.

5. Will Jesus ever return to this earth?
   Yes. Jesus will return to the earth.

LESSON 70: JESUS APPEARED TO HIS DISCIPLES AND RETURNED TO HEAVEN.

6. When Jesus comes back to this world again, what will He do?

   The next time Jesus comes back to this earth, He will judge those who have refused to trust in Him as their Deliverer, and He will throw them, along with Satan and all his demons, into the everlasting fire to be punished forever.

ADDITIONAL LESSONS TO PRESENT THE GOSPEL

Even though you have now presented the last Phase 1 lesson, some of your hearers may not have put their trust in Christ as their Savior. Some may not understand sufficiently the work of Christ on their behalf to trust in Him alone for salvation. Others may understand but are still unwilling to declare their faith in the Lord Jesus. This chapter addresses what you should do in these situations.

> (?) Review the Gospel from Lesson 69.

The first thing you should do is to review Lesson 69, reemphasizing the death, burial and resurrection of the Lord Jesus. In prayerful dependence on the Holy Spirit, press home the sinfulness and condemnation of those you are teaching, and stress the impossibility of salvation apart from faith in the Lord Jesus Christ.

As you review the Gospel, make certain that each of your hearers clearly understands Christ's redemptive work on his behalf. Do all that you can to clearly communicate the pure Gospel, not only publicly, but also privately and individually to those who are yet unsaved. As you meet individually with those who have attended the teaching but are yet unsaved, try to determine what it is that is hindering them from trusting only in Christ as their own personal Savior and do all that you can to remove all barriers to faith through the presentation of the completed work of Christ for their salvation.

> (?) Review the Gospel from he Old Testament.

You may also present the Gospel topically by reviewing stories and redemptive analogies from the Old Testament.

When you taught the Old Testament lessons, you presented the redemptive types uninterrupted by their fulfillment through the life, death, burial and resurrection of Christ. Now, however, as you review these stories to present the Gospel, show clearly that the Lord Jesus fulfilled every detail as the Deliverer of sinners.

Do for your hearers what the Lord Jesus did for two dejected, disillusioned disciples as He walked with them on the road to Emmaus. Beginning in Genesis and continuing through the Pentateuch and all the writings of the prophets, the Lord Jesus Christ taught those two men the correct interpretation of the Scriptures which pointed forward to His life, death, burial, resurrection and ascension (Luke 24:25-27).

> Sample lesson showing how to present the Gospel from an Old Testament lesson.

All the redemptive types given in the Old Testament present some aspect of the suitability of Christ to be the perfect Savior and the complete salvation He procured for sinners. However, none is clearer than the picture presented through the story of the Passover Lamb. When writing to the Corinthians, Paul said, *"Christ, our Passover, was sacrificed for us"* (1 Corinthians 5:7).

The following lesson shows how to present the Gospel from the story of the Passover. This lesson is based on Lesson 31, "God killed the firstborn of the Egyptians, but He saved the firstborn of the Israelites."

This lesson demonstrates how to use Phase 1 Old Testament lessons to teach the Gospel. By comparing the following lesson with its original presentation in Phase 1, you will see what changes will need to be made to present the Gospel from other Old Testament lessons. "Gospel Presentation Notes" draw your attention to the types of changes you will need to make.

LESSON 31: GOD KILLED THE FIRSTBORN OF THE EGYPTIANS, BUT HE SAVED THE FIRSTBORN OF THE ISRAELITES.

Scripture

Exodus 12:1-7, 12-14, 28-30

Lesson Outline

(1) The Lord planned to send one last plague on the Egyptians.

(2) God told Moses how the Israelites must prepare for the final plague. (Exodus 12:1-7)

(3) God promised the Israelites that He would protect their firstborn if they believed and obeyed Him. (Exodus 12:12-14)

(4) The Israelites believed God and obeyed Him. (Exodus 12:28)

(5) None of the Israelites' firstborn died. (Exodus 12:29-30)

Gospel Presentation Note: It is unnecessary to read every passage or include every point from the original lesson. When presenting the Gospel from the Phase 1 lessons, read only those verses necessary to present the need of the sinner and God's provision through Christ.

Lesson Outline Developed

Gospel Presentation Note: It is unnecessary and could distract our hearers' attention from the Gospel if we were to review every doctrinal theme covered in the original lessons. For example, in the first point of Lesson 31, we emphasized that God knows everything before it happens and that He always has His plan worked out so that He wins, no matter what people say or do. But in this adapted lesson, we want to help our students realize that they need to repent and believe the Gospel. Therefore, we need to change the focus of the lesson to emphasize God's punishment of unrepentant Pharaoh. By changing the focus, we have provided an opportunity to remind our hearers that God has not changed and therefore He will also punish them unless they repent and put their faith in the Lord Jesus Christ as their Savior.

As you adapt other lessons to present the Gospel, your focus should only be on themes that emphasize (1) man's sinfulness and helplessness to save himself, (2) God's judgment on the unrepentant but (3) His merciful provision of salvation for all who put their faith in the Lord Jesus Christ who took the full punishment for sin on the cross.

Building on Firm Foundations
- Volume 2: Evangelism:
Genesis to The Ascension

① The Lord planned to send one last plague on the Egyptians.

Today, we are going to review the story from the time when the Israelites were slaves in Egypt and Moses had been sent by God to Pharaoh, the king of Egypt, to demand that he release all God's people, the Israelites.

Because Pharaoh had refused to obey the Lord and let the Israelites go free, the Lord had sent nine terrible plagues on the rebellious Egyptians. In spite of these judgments, the king continued to refuse to obey the Lord.

Therefore, the Lord planned to send one last terrible judgment on the Egyptians. The Lord told Moses that, following this judgment, the king would release Israel.

Gospel Presentation Note: When you review a lesson from the Old Testament as a basis for presenting the Gospel, choose those points from the lesson which set the scene and remind the people of the circumstances surrounding the story. Point to the Chronological Chart to help put the story in its correct historical and chronological position and use the appropriate pictures.

- **The Lord has not changed.**

    He is still exactly the same today as He was in the time of Moses. The Lord will punish all those who refuse to obey His voice.

    Think about this: Pharaoh refused to obey the command of the Lord to release the Israelites, so the Lord punished him. Has God changed? Will He not also punish all those who refuse to obey His command?

    What do you think will happen to all who refuse to obey God's command to repent and believe on the Lord Jesus Christ as their Deliverer? Will those who refuse to obey God's command escape His punishment on sin? No! All who ignore God's command will be punished forever by God.

Gospel Presentation Note: Use questions to get the people to think through their need of salvation and their need to respond to the truth of the Gospel.

You have all heard how God sent the Lord Jesus into the world to die for you. Because the Lord Jesus died, God now offers you forgiveness of all your sins and oneness with Him. If you reject God's offer of mercy, then there is no other hope for you. When you die, you will be separated from God forever. You will be banished from the presence of God to the place that God has prepared for Satan and his angels.

ADDITIONAL LESSONS TO PRESENT THE GOSPEL

Gospel Presentation Note: When you taught the Phase 1 lessons originally, you did not speak of God's gift of mercy through the Lord Jesus Christ. You didn't even use the name of the Deliverer. As you review points from Phase 1 lessons to apply the Gospel, use Jesus' name when you speak of the Deliverer, and emphasize that there is no hope apart from God's gift of mercy through the Lord Jesus Christ.

② God told Moses how the Israelites must prepare for the final plague.

- **God did not allow His people to be punished with the Egyptians.**

    God told Moses what the Israelites must do to escape this final and most terrible plague of all.

    Because the Israelites were also sinners, their firstborn children and cattle would also have suffered through this last terrible judgment along with the Egyptians. If God in His mercy and grace had not shown them what to do, the firstborn children of the Israelites would also have died.

    Are you any better than the Israelites? Are we teachers any better than the Israelites? No! Just as the Israelites were sinners and deserved to be punished by God, so all of us have broken God's commandments and deserve His punishment.

    Gospel Presentation Note: Emphasize that all people are sinners and condemned before God.

    Why did God send the Lord Jesus to die for us all? Was it because we deserve it? No! It is only because of His love, mercy and grace.

    God saved the Israelites from this terrible judgment because He is loving, merciful, and gracious, and because He remembered His promises to Abraham, Isaac and Jacob.

    This is what the Lord told Moses the Israelites must do in order to save their firstborn children from death.

- **They must choose a lamb without blemish.**

    📖 Read Exodus 12:1-5.

    The head of each home had to choose a lamb or goat. The lamb or goat had to be without blemish.

    What do you think would have happened if an Israelite had said, "I'm not going to choose one of my good lambs. I have a sick one. I'll take the sick one and kill it"? Would God have accepted the blood of a sick lamb? No! God would only accept a lamb without blemish.

Do you remember the ram that God provided to die instead of Isaac? The ram was caught by its horns in a bush. Why was it caught by the horns? The ram was caught by its horns in the bush so that it could not injure itself by struggling to get free. If it had become imperfect through cuts and bruises as it tried to free itself, it would not have been an acceptable offering to God. Because God is perfect, He will only accept what is perfect. God would only accept a healthy, strong animal as a sacrifice. He would never accept an animal that was sick or hurt.

- **The lamb without blemish was a picture of the Lord Jesus.**

   God's chosen Lamb, the Lord Jesus Christ, was without sin. He was born the son of a virgin so that He would not inherit Adam's sin as all other people have. In addition, the Lord Jesus was perfect throughout His life in everything that He thought, said and did. He obeyed all God's commandments.

   Because He was perfect, the Lord Jesus was God's chosen Lamb to die for us. This is why, when John the Baptist saw the Lord Jesus walking toward him, he said, "Behold! The Lamb of God who takes away the sin of the world!"

- **They must kill the lamb; the lamb had to die.**

   Read Exodus 12:6.

   The Israelites were to keep the lamb until the fourteenth day of the month. They were to kill the lamb in the evening of that day.

   What do you think would have happened if an Israelite had said, "I do not want to kill this good lamb. I will just tie it up at the door. God will see this perfect, living lamb, and He will not kill my child by the plague"?

   Would God have accepted a lamb whose blood had not been shed? No! Even though the lamb chosen by the Israelites was perfect, it still must die. The perfect living lamb could not save the firstborn of the Israelites. The lamb's blood, which gave it life, must be allowed to flow out. The lamb had to die, and the blood had to be shed so that the firstborn could live. This was to remind the Israelites that the punishment for sin is death.

- **Christ had to die so that we could be saved.**

   Although the Lord Jesus was sinless and fully pleasing to God, His perfect life could not save us. The Lord Jesus had to die so that we could be delivered from sin, Satan and everlasting separation from God.

   The judgment of God on all sin is separation from Him. God is a loving God and wants all people to be saved, but He will not deliver anyone unless the full payment is made for his sins.

ADDITIONAL LESSONS TO PRESENT THE GOSPEL

Gospel Presentation Note: Emphasize that the Lord Jesus had to die to pay the punishment for our sins.

Because God loved the world, He gave the Lord Jesus to take the full punishment for our sins by dying on the cross. The Lord Jesus' life was given for us when He was separated from God on the cross.

What did the Lord Jesus cry out when He was separated from God for our sins? He cried, "My God, My God, why have You forsaken me?" Why was the Lord Jesus forsaken by God? It was for us. He died for our sins. His blood flowed out, and He died so that we could be forgiven and fully accepted by God as His children.

Just as the lambs chosen by the Israelites had to die to save the Israelites' firstborn children, so the Lord Jesus had to die. His blood had to flow out to pay for our sins.

But was that all that was necessary? Once the Israelites had killed their perfect lamb, could they then go to bed feeling safe and quite sure that their firstborn would not die? No! There was something else that must be done if the firstborn was to be saved.

- **They must place the blood on the doorposts and above the doors of their homes.**

  📖 Read Exodus 12:7.

  God told the Israelites that, when they killed the lamb, they were to catch the blood in a basin. Then they were to take a branch from a particular bush and dip it into the blood. With this branch, they were to put some of the blood on the sides and tops of the door frames on the outside of each of their houses. If their firstborn was to be saved from God's judgment, they must apply the blood of the lamb as God commanded. Even if they killed the lamb, their firstborn would still die if they failed to brush the blood on their houses as God had commanded them.

  What does this teach us about ourselves?

- **We must put our faith in the blood of Christ.**

  Merely knowing that we are sinners and that the Lord Jesus died for our sins will not save us from God's terrible judgment. Merely saying with our lips that we are sinners will not save us.

  We must repent before God. We must agree with God's verdict about us. We must agree with God that we are sinners deserving only separation from Him, and we must trust personally in the Lord Jesus and His death as the payment for our sins to God. We must believe that what the Lord Jesus did on the cross was for us individually, and we must trust only in Him for the forgiveness of our sins.

Gospel Presentation Note: Emphasize that each person must trust in the Lord Jesus and in His blood as the payment for their salvation. When explaining to people how to appropriate the Gospel, beware that you don't use unscriptural terminology such as, "Give your life to Christ," "Give your heart to the Lord," or "Ask Jesus into your heart."

③ God promised the Israelites that He would protect their firstborn if they believed and obeyed Him.

- **God made a promise to the Israelites.**

    📖 Read Exodus 12:12-14.

    God promised the Israelites that, when He saw the blood on the doorposts of their houses, He would not allow the plague to enter and kill their firstborn. Did God pass over the Israelites' homes which had the blood on the outside as God had told them? Yes. He did.

- **God has also given promises to us which He has written in His Word.**

    Listen carefully to these promises of God.

    📖 Read John 3:14-18.

Gospel Presentation Note: When you taught this lesson originally, you did not jump forward to read New Testament Scriptures. When teaching this lesson to apply the Gospel, you may now read any appropriate verses that you have already used during the Phase 1 teaching.

Can we trust God's promises to give eternal life to all those who put their trust in the Lord Jesus as their Deliverer? Yes, we can.

Did God ever promise anything that He did not do? No! God kept all of His promises in the past. He kept all His promises to send the Lord Jesus to be the Deliverer of sinners.

Would God have given the Lord Jesus to die for us if He will not now keep His promise to give everlasting life to all true believers?

④ The Israelites believed God and obeyed Him.

- **The Israelites believed what God had told them, and they obeyed Him.**

    📖 Read Exodus 12:28.

- **Are you going to believe what**

    God has told you about the Deliverer? Many of you have already agreed with God and trusted in the Lord Jesus and His death for you, but what about those of you who have not?

ADDITIONAL LESSONS TO PRESENT THE GOSPEL

Gospel Presentation Note: Be careful when you ask direct questions like these lest you force people to give mere verbal assent to the Gospel. An individual's public claim to faith should also be affirmed by a private testimony so you can ascertain more clearly whether the person understands his sinfulness and helplessness and whether he is trusting in Christ and His death alone as absolutely sufficient for the sinner's acceptance by God.

⑤ None of the Israelites' firstborn died.

- **The Lord did not kill the firstborn children of the Israelites.**

    📖 Read Exodus 12:29-30.

Gospel Presentation Note: Adapt the points from the original lesson to focus on Gospel themes. For example, the original outline point here was, "All the Egyptians' firstborn died." Because you are adapting this lesson to apply the Gospel, you should emphasize instead that none of the Israelites' firstborn died because the Israelites believed God.

The Lord passed through Egypt just as He said He would, and the firstborn died in every Egyptian home. But what happened when the Lord saw the blood on the Israelites' homes? He did not kill the Israelites' firstborn by the plague. Not one of the firstborn children of the Israelites died. Why not? Was it because of their own goodness? No! The firstborn of the Israelites did not die because the Israelites had believed God and had put the blood of the perfect lambs on their houses in obedience to the Lord.

God always does what He says. He said He would destroy the firstborn in the Egyptian homes, and He did. He said He would pass over every house where He saw the blood, and He did. The Lord can be trusted to do everything He says He will do.

- **All who trust in Christ as their Savior have eternal life.**

    No sinner who trusts in the death of the Lord Jesus needs to be afraid of the judgment of God. God will keep His promise. He will not send believers to the place of everlasting fire because the Lord Jesus took all the punishment for their sin. All true believers have everlasting life. They are the children of God, and they will one day go to live with God in Heaven.

Gospel Presentation Note: When you adapt a lesson to present the Gospel, do not ask the original questions found at the close of the lesson. It is not our purpose to have the hearers' attention centered on the historical details of the story. Any closing questions should be about the Gospel and the need for the sinner to appropriate the Gospel. The aim is to see each person leave the meeting thinking only of his own personal need and of what Christ has done for him.

Present the Gospel using Old Testament lessons

After presenting the Gospel by teaching the adaptation of Lesson 31, some of those who have heard Phase 1 teaching may still not have put their faith in Christ for salvation. Should this be the case, adapt other Old Testament lessons to continue emphasizing the Gospel.

On the following pages, you will find the lessons which I recommend you adapt and use to further present the Gospel. I suggest you review these Old Testament lessons in chronological order so you don't confuse the people's understanding of their historical sequence.

For each lesson, I have selected outline points from the original lesson which I recommend you include in your adapted lesson. As you teach, use the original script for these selected points, adding emphasis and application to clearly present the Gospel.

Note that because you will only be teaching selected points, the point numbers for the adapted lesson may not line up with point numbers in the original lesson. Nevertheless, it should be a simple matter for you to find the point in the original lesson that corresponds with the point listed for the adapted lesson. Be sure to use the original script of each point as the basis for your adaptation.

Remember, when teaching these lessons with the purpose of applying the Gospel, it is unnecessary to review every point from the original lesson. Focus your teaching on the themes pertaining specifically to the Gospel.

LESSON 16: GOD REJECTED CAIN AND HIS OFFERING, BUT HE ACCEPTED ABEL AND HIS OFFERING.

① Cain and Abel both were born outside of the garden in Eden. (Genesis 4:2)

Application: We were all born sinners, separated from God.

② Cain and Abel both came to offer sacrifices to God. (Genesis 4:3-4)

Application: There is no offering that we can make to God that will pay for our sins.

③ God accepted Abel's offering. (Genesis 4:4)

Emphasis: The blood of the lamb that Abel offered did not pay for his sins. God accepted Abel because he believed God and trusted Him to send a Deliverer.

Application: The blood of the lamb that Abel offered pointed forward to the blood of Jesus, the only payment that God will accept for our sins. (John 1:29)

④ God rejected Cain's offering. (Genesis 4:5)

Application: God will not accept our good works as the payment for our sins. The only payment for sin is death. Jesus died and was buried. God raised Him from the dead as proof that all our sins have been paid for in full.

⑤ Cain refused to listen to God. (Genesis 4:6-8)

Application: All who refuse to accept what Christ has done for them will be separated from God forever in the eternal fire.

LESSON 18-19: GOD SAID HE WOULD PUNISH THE WORLD, BUT HE PROMISED TO SAVE NOAH AND ALL WHO ENTERED THE BOAT.

[Note that I selected suitable points from Lesson 18 and Lesson 19 to form one adapted lesson for the presentation of the Gospel.]

① God's Spirit was striving with the people through Noah's preaching. (Genesis 6:3)

Application: God's Spirit is striving with those of you who have heard the Gospel but have not yet trusted only in the Lord Jesus and His death.

② God decided to destroy the people on the earth. (Genesis 6:6-7)

Application: God says that all who refuse to repent and trust only in the Lord Jesus will be punished with Satan in the everlasting fire.

③ God was gracious to Noah. (Genesis 6:8-10)

Application: God has been gracious to us by providing us with a Savior.

④ God told Noah what was going to happen and what he must do. (Genesis 6:13-21)

Application: Just as God warned Noah of the coming flood, God has warned us of the coming judgment if we die without trusting in Christ.

⑤ Noah obeyed God. (Genesis 6:22)

Application: Are you going to obey God by repenting and believing the Gospel?

⑥ God told Noah to bring his family, the animals and the birds into the boat. (Genesis 7:1-5)

Application: Just as Noah and his family hid in the big boat and were saved from God's judgment, all who put their faith in Christ will be delivered from the judgment they deserve because of their sins.

⑦ They all entered by one door. (Genesis 7:6-16)

Application: The Lord Jesus is the only way to oneness with God (John 14:6; 10:7, 9).

ADDITIONAL LESSONS TO PRESENT THE GOSPEL

⑧ God shut them in. (Genesis 7:16)

Application: All who put their trust in the Lord Jesus are safe forever from the judgment of God. (John 3:16)

⑨ God destroyed all those outside the boat. (Genesis 7:17, 21-23)

Application: All those who refuse to put their faith in the Lord Jesus will go to everlasting punishment.

LESSON 24: GOD GAVE ISAAC AND DELIVERED ISAAC FROM DEATH.

① **God fulfilled His promise to give Abraham and Sarah a son. (Genesis 21:1-3)**

② **God commanded Abraham to sacrifice Isaac. (Genesis 22:1-2)**

③ **Abraham believed God. (Genesis 22:3-5)**

④ **Abraham and Isaac went to make the sacrifice to God. (Genesis 22:6-10)**

⑤ **God provided a ram to take Isaac's place. (Genesis 22:11-13)**

Emphasis: The ram was caught in the bush by its horns so it would be a suitable sacrifice. (Genesis 22:13)

Application: The Lord Jesus was a suitable sacrifice to pay for our sins because He was without sin.

Emphasis: Abraham took Isaac off the altar and put the ram on the altar instead of Isaac.

Application: God gave His Son to take our place. He died instead of us.

⑥ **Abraham trusted God to send the Deliverer. (Genesis 22:14-19)**

Application: The Deliverer that Abraham was waiting for has come. (John 8:56) The Lord Jesus died and was buried and rose again as the perfect sacrifice for our sins. Believe on the Lord Jesus Christ as the perfect sacrifice for your sins and you will be saved.

LESSON 33: GOD GAVE FOOD AND WATER TO THE ISRAELITES.

① **The Israelites complained. (Exodus 16:1-3)**

② **God provided food for them. (Exodus 16:11-16, 35)**

   Application: God provided the Lord Jesus. He is the Bread of Life. (John 10:22-35. See Lesson 60, point 4.)

③ **The Israelites complained again. (Exodus 17:1-4)**

④ **God provided water for them. (Exodus 17:5-6)**

   Application: Just as Moses struck the rock and God gave water from the rock so the Israelites would not die, so God punished Christ for us so that through Him we could receive eternal life. (Isaiah 53:4-6) (Teacher: As you prepare to teach, read 1 Corinthians 10:1-3, but do not read these verses to the people when you teach the lesson.)

⑤ **God provided what the Israelites needed because He is merciful.**

   Emphasis: God provided water for all the Israelites, but they were individually responsible to drink. If they refused, they would die.

   Application: God in His mercy has provided Christ for all, but each person is responsible to put his faith in Christ. If we refuse to believe in Christ, we will be separated from God forever.

LESSON 37: GOD TOLD THE ISRAELITES TO BUILD THE TABERNACLE.

(1) God commanded Moses to have the Israelites build the Tabernacle. (Exodus 25:1-8)

(2) The Tabernacle had to be built exactly as God commanded Moses. (Exodus 25:9)

Emphasis: God gave the Tabernacle so the Israelites' sin could be forgiven and they could be in oneness with Him.

Application: God provided the Lord Jesus so our sins could be forgiven and we could be in oneness with Him.

(3) The Tabernacle was to have two rooms.

(4) The ark and the mercy seat were to be built and put in the Most Holy Place. (Exodus 25:10-11, 17-22)

(5) A curtain was to hang between the Holy Place and the Most Holy Place. (Exodus 26:31-33)

(6) The brazen altar was to be set up inside the courtyard. (Exodus 27:1-2; Leviticus 1:1-5)

Application: Just as the animals died for the sins of the offerer at the altar, so Christ offered Himself once for all as the perfect sacrifice for our sins. (Teacher: As you prepare to teach, read Hebrews 9:27-28, but do not read these verses to the people when you teach the lesson.)

(7) God chose Aaron and his sons to serve Him as priests. (Exodus 28:1; Leviticus 16:2-3, 15)

Application: God chose the Lord Jesus to be our Deliverer. Only the Lord Jesus could satisfy God for our sins.

LESSON 40: THE LORD GAVE THE ISRAELITES WATER FROM THE ROCK. HE HEALED THOSE WHO LOOKED AT THE BRONZE SNAKE.

(1) **The Israelites murmured again. (Numbers 21:4-5)**

(2) **God sent poisonous serpents. (Numbers 21:6-7)**

Application: Because of sin, all people were born under the power of Satan, sin and death.

(3) **God healed those who looked at the snake on the pole. (Numbers 21:8-9)**

Application: God gave His Son to be lifted up on the cross so He could die for our sins. All who believe on the Lord Jesus Christ have eternal life (John 3:14-16; see Lesson 54.)

Present the Gospel using New Testament lessons

After reviewing Old Testament lessons, New Testament lessons may also be adapted in the same way. On the following pages, you will find the New Testament lessons which I recommend you adapt to present the Gospel, using selected outline points from the original lesson. Remember to use the original script for these selected points, adding the emphasis and application listed to clearly present the Gospel.

I had recommended that you review Old Testament lessons in chronological order so you don't confuse the people's understanding of their historical sequence. However, when reviewing New Testament lessons, the chronological order is not of great significance. So you may choose not to follow the order that you previously taught them in Phase 1. Because some of the adapted lessons are short, you may decide to teach two lessons in one meeting.

LESSON 53: JESUS TAUGHT THAT PEOPLE MUST BE BORN AGAIN.

(1) Nicodemus came to Jesus. (John 3:1-2)

(2) Jesus told Nicodemus that he must be born again. (John 3:3)

Application: What Jesus said to Nicodemus is applicable to all people. Unless you are born again you cannot come under God's rule and will never enter Heaven.

(3) Jesus explained to Nicodemus what it meant to be born again. (John 3:4-7, 9)

(4) Jesus must be lifted up. (John 3:14-15)

Emphasis: Jesus was lifted up on the cross to die for our sins. He was buried and rose again the third day.

(5) God sent His Son so people can be born again. (John 3:16)

(6) Jesus came to save people and to give them everlasting life. (John 3:17-20)

LESSON 59: JESUS FED FIVE THOUSAND PEOPLE.

(1) Multitudes followed Jesus. (John 6:1-4)

Emphasis: Just read the Scriptures.

(2) Jesus fed five thousand people. (John 6:5-15)

Emphasis: Just read the Scriptures.

(3) Jesus walked on the water. (John 6:16-21)

Emphasis: Just read the Scriptures.

(4) Jesus is the Bread of Life. (John 6:22-35)

Emphasis: God has given the Lord Jesus to die so He can be spiritual food for us. If we refused to eat food, our bodies would die. If we refuse to put our faith in the Lord Jesus Christ, the only spiritual food, we will experience eternal death – separation from God forever.

LESSON 62: JESUS IS THE ONLY DOORWAY TO ETERNAL LIFE.

(1) Jesus is like the doorway into the sheepfold. (John 10:7-10)

Application: We can only be delivered from Satan, sin and death if we enter Christ, the one door into eternal life.

(2) Jesus is the Good Shepherd. (John 10:11)

Emphasis: The Lord Jesus died, was buried and rose again so our sins could be forgiven and we could have eternal life.

(3) Jesus is the way, the truth and the life. (John 14:6)

Emphasis: Christ is the only way to eternal life.

Emphasis: Christ is the truth. All others who claim that they are the way to eternal life are liars.

Emphasis: Christ is the life. We can only receive eternal life through Him.

Application: We must believe on the Lord Jesus Christ as the way, the truth, the life.

Suiting your teaching to their response

After completing Phase 1, it is encouraging and stimulating if there is a genuine, enthusiastic, and strong numerical response to the Gospel. This gives great incentive to begin teaching the Word of God to the new believers in order to see them begin to function as a New Testament church.

However, the effect on the missionary is very different when, after months of hard labor, none repent and believe the Gospel. If this is your situation, I suggest that you, in prayerful dependence on the Lord who alone is capable of bringing people to repentance and faith, review lessons from the Old and New Testaments as laid out in this chapter.

Having reviewed some or all of the lessons I have suggested, you will then be faced with a decision as to how you should proceed in your teaching program. If all those you are teaching have clearly responded to the Gospel, then do not hesitate to move on into Phase 2. On the other hand, if some have not yet responded to the Gospel but still want to be taught, you will need the Lord's wisdom in how to proceed. You may decide to continue reviewing the Gospel with the whole group, but it is vitally important that you do not treat or teach a mixed group, saved and unsaved, as though they are a church. It is important not to wait too long before you begin teaching those who have trusted in Christ for their salvation the things which they should know as God's children. But for their sakes and for those yet unsaved, this teaching should not be given while the believers are meeting in a combined gathering with the unsaved. The scriptural and practical reasons for this are given in the next volume of this series. If you decide to begin teaching the believers, it is vitally important you read and follow the guidelines given in the introduction to Phase 2.

But what if after all your teaching, there is no response at all? In that case you will probably be asking yourself, "What should I do now? How will I go about teaching these people now?"

You may begin looking for other ways and methods of teaching the people. Should you be tempted to think this way, ask yourself why you decided to teach the Scriptures chronologically. Was it because you were convinced that you were following Scriptural principles, or did you just think of it as yet another teaching outline which might work?

If you taught (as I trust you did) on the basis of conviction and faith, believing that the chronological approach is the most simple and clearest way to present God's Word, then lack of results should not cause you to look for another teaching method. Truth still remains truth even if people reject it. Remember that people may clearly understand and come under the conviction of the Holy Spirit but deliberately refuse what they have been taught (Acts 7:51-54).

If the teaching of God's Word, as given in Phase 1, won't "work," then what will? It is God's Word you have taught, and He has promised to bless and use it in the convicting and saving of souls. If it did not "work," then what is the use of trying something else?

Therefore, if you have completed the overview of the Old Testament and the life of Christ, and there isn't any apparent conviction of the Holy Spirit, I would encourage you to carefully and prayerfully reread Volume 1, Part 2, Chapter 13, "Little or No Response." That chapter gives suggestions to guide you as you decide what form your future teaching should take.

Other missionaries in your situation found that they needed to make adjustments to their teaching techniques, but even then, the truth only dawned on their hearers after the complete chronological outline was taught two, and in some cases, three times.

Taking your responsibility for those who have believed

If the people have responded to the Gospel, putting their trust in Christ, congratulations on the birth of your spiritual children! Your parenting work has just begun!

In his letter to the Galatian believers, Paul expressed his heart-felt agony for them in these words, "*My little children, for whom I labor in birth again until Christ is formed in you*" (Galatians 4:19). Paul used the analogy of a mother giving birth to express his deep emotional agony that he had experienced before the Galatian believers were converted and was experiencing once again as he prayed and wrote to see them delivered from the false teachings of the Judaizers who had come to Galatia preaching another Gospel.

Why was Paul so concerned? Hadn't he faithfully discharged his responsibility when he had clearly presented the Gospel to the Galatians and when he had seen that they had put their faith in Christ for their salvation? Indeed not! Is a mother's and father's responsibility complete at the birth of their healthy child? Certainly not! With the birth of their child, they automatically are propelled into another work and another role. They are now parents of a child who is rightfully dependent on them for all his needs. So it is with you. God by His Spirit has used you to bring people to faith in Christ. Therefore, God now holds you responsible for the spiritual life and growth of those who have been born again through your ministry. You, more than anyone else in the world, are responsible to make sure that these new believers are taught the Word of God so they will grow in their knowledge and faith and be protected from all who would lead them astray.

In similar words as those he wrote to the Galatians, Paul wrote to the Corinthians, "*I do not write these things to shame you, but as my beloved children I warn you. For though you might have ten thousand instructors in Christ, yet you do not have many fathers; for in Christ Jesus I have begotten you through the gospel*" (1 Corinthians 4:14-15).

Paul had once been Saul, the persecutor of Christ and His Church. After Paul had been transformed by a face-to-face encounter with the resurrected and glorified Lord Jesus from Heaven, the Lord Jesus had personally instructed Paul as His child in the Arabian desert. It was during this time that the Lord probably charged Paul with the same words as He had His other apostles just prior to His ascension.

Matthew tells us that *"Jesus came and spoke to them, saying, 'All authority has been given to Me in heaven and on earth. Go therefore and make disciples of all the nations, baptizing them in the name of the Father and of the Son and of the Holy Spirit, teaching them to observe all things that I have commanded you; and lo, I am with you always, even to the end of the age'"* (Matthew 28:18-20). Not only were they responsible to preach the Gospel, but they were to teach converts so they in turn would become evangelists and Bible teachers.

Because new believers are like newborn babies who need food, it is important that you begin soon to teach them the things which God wants them to know as His children. 533

Furthermore, if there isn't a local church which follows the Word of God, then you are responsible to teach and guide or have someone else take up the work of instructing and leading the new believers so they can meet and function scripturally as an assembly of Jesus Christ.

How will you form them into a New Testament church? What and how should you teach them so they will grow in their knowledge of Christ and be able to live for the glory of God and the blessing of others?

These questions are answered in the next volume of *Building on Firm Foundations. Volume 3, Teaching New Believers: Genesis to the Ascension*, covers the transition from evangelism to the beginning of the local church. Phase 2 lessons are provided so you will be able to guide the emerging church and teach the new believers the security of their position in Christ.

APPENDIX

Scripture Portions to be used with Phase 1 Lessons

Lesson 1	No specific Scriptures
Lesson 2	Genesis 1:1
Lesson 3	Genesis 1:1
Lesson 4	Genesis 1:2-13
Lesson 5	Genesis 1:14-25
Lesson 6	Genesis 1:26-31 Genesis 2:7
Lesson 7	Genesis 2:1-8
Lesson 8	Genesis 2:9, 16-17
Lesson 9	Genesis 2:18-25
Lesson 10	No specific Scriptures
Lesson 11	Genesis 1 Genesis 2
Lesson 12	Genesis 3:1-6
Lesson 13	Genesis 3:7-8

Lesson 14	Genesis 3:9-20
Lesson 15	Genesis 3:21-24
Lesson 16	Genesis 4:1-16
Lesson 17	Genesis 4:16-26 Genesis 5:3-5, 22-32
Lesson 18	Genesis 6:1-3, 5-22
Lesson 19	Genesis 7:1-17, 21-23 Genesis 8:1-4, 14-22 Genesis 9:1-19
Lesson 20	Genesis 11:1-9
Lesson 21	Genesis 11:27-32 Genesis 12:1-5
Lesson 22	Genesis 13:5-17 Genesis 15:5-6, 12-16 Genesis 17:1-5, 15-17
Lesson 23	Genesis 18:20-21 Genesis 19:1-17, 24-26
Lesson 24	Genesis 21:1-3 Genesis 22:1-19

Lesson 25	Genesis 24:67 Genesis 25:20-34 Genesis 27:41-44 Genesis 28:10-15 Genesis 29:1 Genesis 31:13 Genesis 32:28	Lesson 36	Exodus 20:12-17
Lesson 26	Genesis 37:1-35 Genesis 39:1-23	Lesson 37	Exodus 24:12-18 Exodus 25:1-11, 17-22 Exodus 26:31-33 Exodus 27:1-2, 9 Exodus 28:1 Leviticus 1:1-5 Leviticus 16:2-3, 15
Lesson 27	Genesis 41:1-8, 14-16, 25-49 Genesis 42:1-20 Genesis 43:1-5, 11-17 Genesis 45:1-11, 25-28 Genesis 46:5-7	Lesson 38	Exodus 32:1-20 Exodus 34:1-2 Exodus 39:42-43 Exodus 40:17, 34-35
Lesson 28	Exodus 1:1-22 Exodus 2:1-22	Lesson 39	Exodus 40:36-38 Numbers 13:1-3, 17-21, 23-33 Numbers 14:1-10, 26-32
Lesson 29	Exodus 2:23-25 Exodus 3:1-20 Exodus 4:1-20	Lesson 40	Numbers 20:1-12, 23-25, 28 Numbers 21:4-9
Lesson 30	Exodus 4:27-31 Exodus 5:1-2 Exodus 6:1-8 Exodus 7:4-5, 20-21 Exodus 8:5-6, 16-17, 24 Exodus 9:3, 6-7, 10, 23-26 Exodus 10:13-15, 21-23, 28-29	Lesson 41	Numbers 27:18-23 Deuteronomy 34:1-5, 9 Joshua 1:1-2 Joshua 11:23 Joshua 23:14-16 Judges 2:7-19 1 Samuel 8:1-7 1 Samuel 11:14-15
Lesson 31	Exodus 11:1, 4-7 Exodus 12:1-7, 12-14, 22-23, 28-33, 46, 51	Lesson 42	1 Samuel 13:13-14 1 Samuel 16:1-5, 11-13 2 Samuel 5:1-4 2 Samuel 7:1-3, 12-17 1 Chronicles 22:5-6 1 Chronicles 29:26-28 2 Chronicles 2:1 2 Chronicles 5:1
Lesson 32	Exodus 13:21-22 Exodus 14:1-31		
Lesson 33	Exodus 16:1-3, 11-16, 35 Exodus 17:1-6		
Lesson 34	Exodus 19:1-25		
Lesson 35	Exodus 20:1-11		

APPENDIX

Lesson 43	Jonah 1 Jonah 2:1, 10 Jonah 3:1-5, 10 Psalm 139:1-18 Isaiah 10:5-6 Jeremiah 20:5	Lesson 54	Mark 2:1-17
		Lesson 55	Matthew 12:38-41
		Lesson 56	Mark 3:1-19
Lesson 44	Psalm 16:10 Psalm 22:6-8, 16, 18 Psalm 27:12 Psalm 41:9 Psalm 68:18 Psalm 69:4 Isaiah 7:14 Isaiah 9:7 Isaiah 11:2 Isaiah 50:6 Isaiah 53:3-5, 7, 9, 12 Jeremiah 6:13-14 Hosea 11:1 Micah 5:2 Zechariah 11:12-13	Lesson 57	Mark 4:1-20
		Lesson 58	Mark 4:35-41 Mark 5:1-20
		Lesson 59	John 6:1-35
		Lesson 60	Mark 7:1-9, 14-23 Luke 18:9-14
		Lesson 61	Mark 8:27-31 Mark 9:2-8
		Lesson 62	John 10:7-11 John 14:6
		Lesson 63	John 11:1-48
		Lesson 64	Mark 10:13-24
		Lesson 65	Luke 12:15-21 Luke 16:19-31
		Lesson 66	Mark 10:45-52 Mark 11:1-10
Lesson 45	2 Kings 17:1-8 2 Kings 25:1-12	Lesson 67	Mark 14:1-2, 10-26 Matthew 26:14-15
Lesson 46	Luke 1:5-17, 24-38		
Lesson 47	Luke 1:57, 67-79	Lesson 68	Mark 14:32-65 Mark 15:1-20
Lesson 48	Matthew 1:1-2, 18-25		
Lesson 49	Matthew 2 Luke 2:40-52	Lesson 69	Mark 15:20-47 Mark 16:1-8
Lesson 50	Matthew 3:1-17 John 1:29-34	Lesson 70	Mark 16:9-15 Acts 1:9-11
Lesson 51	Matthew 4:1-11		
Lesson 52	Mark 1:14-28, 34-42		
Lesson 53	John 3:1-7, 9, 14-20		

Phase 1 Scripture Portions Organized by Book

Genesis	1:1-31
	2:1-9, 16-25
	3:1-24
	4:1-16
	5:3-5, 22-32
	6:1-3, 5-22
	7:1-17, 21-23
	8:1-4, 14-22
	9:1-19
	11:1-9, 27-32
	12:1-5
	13:5-17
	15:5-6, 12-16
	17:1-5, 15-17
	18:20-21
	19:1-17, 24-26
	21:1-3
	22:1-19
	24:67
	25:20-34
	27:41-44
	28:10-15
	29:1
	31:13
	32:28
	37:1-35
	39:1-23
	41:1-8, 14-16, 25-49
	42:1-20
	43:1-5, 11-17
	45:1-11, 25-28
	46:5-7

Exodus	1:1-22
	2:1-22
	2:23-25
	3:1-20
	4:1-20, 27-31
	5:1-2
	6:1-8
	7:4-5, 20-21
	8:5-6, 16-17, 24
	9:3, 6-7, 10, 23-26
	10:13-15, 21-23, 28-29
	11:1, 4-7
	12:1-7, 12-14, 22-23, 28-33, 46, 51
	13:21-22
	14:1-31
	16:1-3, 11-16, 35
	17:1-6
	19:1-25
	20:1-17
	24:12-18
	25:1-11, 17-22
	26:31-33
	27:1-2, 9
	28:1
	32:1-20
	34:1-2
	39:42-43
	40:17, 34-38
Leviticus	1:1-5
	16:2-3, 15

Numbers	13:1-3, 17-21, 23-33 14:1-10, 26-32 20:1-12, 23-25, 28 21:4-9 27:18-23
Deuteronomy	34:1-5, 9
Joshua	1:1-2 11:23 23:14-16
Judges	2:7-19
1 Samuel	8:1-7 11:14-15 13:13-14 16:1-5, 11-13
2 Samuel	5:1-4 7:1-3, 12-17
2 Kings	17:1-8 25:1-12
1 Chronicles	22:5-6 29:26-28
2 Chronicles	2:1 5:1
Psalm	16:10 22:6-8, 16, 18 27:12 41:9 68:18 69:4 139:1-18
Isaiah	7:14 9:7 10:5-6 11:2 50:6 53:3-5, 7, 9, 12
Jeremiah	6:13-14 20:5
Jonah	1 2:1, 10 3:1-5, 10
Hosea	11:1
Micah	5:2
Zechariah	11:12-13
Luke	1:5-17, 24-38, 1:57, 67-79 2:40-52 12:15-21 16:19-31 18:9-14
Matthew	1:1-2, 18-25 2 3:1-17 4:1-11 12:38-41 26:14-15
Mark	1:14-28, 34-42 2:1-17 3:1-19 4:1-20, 4:35-41 5:1-20 7:1-9, 14-23 8:27-31 9:2-8 10:13-24 10:45-52 11:1-10 14:1-2, 10-26, 32-65 15:1-47 16:1-15
John	1:29-34 3:1-7, 9, 14-20 6:1-35 10:7-11 11:1-48 14:6
Acts	1:9-11

www.ingramcontent.com/pod-product-compliance
Lightning Source LLC
Chambersburg PA
CBHW060416010526
44118CB00017B/2245